ActiveMQ in Action

ActiveMQ in Action

BRUCE SNYDER
DEJAN BOSANAC
ROB DAVIES

MANNING

Greenwich
(74° w. long.)

Manning Publications Co.   Development editor: Jeff Bleiel
    180 Broad St.   Copyeditor: Benjamin Berg
    Suite 1323   Proofreader: Katie Tennant
    Stamford, CT 06901   Typesetter: Dottie Marsico
                                   Cover designer: Marija Tudor

ISBN 978-1-933988-94-8
Printed in the United States of America
1 2 3 4 5 6 7 8 9 10 – MAL – 16 15 14 13 12 11

brief contents

v

contents

14 *Administering and monitoring ActiveMQ 331*

preface

To this day, enterprise message queuing is a concept that is not well understood by most software developers. Commercial message-oriented middleware (MOM) did not help to encourage adoption of the process; most of the MOMs on the market were closed source, were costly to buy and support, and required trained system administrators for proper installation. ActiveMQ was developed to provide an open source alternative: its central theme is to put the power in the hands of developers. To date, the ActiveMQ project has been successful in this endeavor by creating a MOM that is easy to install, administer, and utilize, while providing a large number of unique features.

Today, six or seven years after ActiveMQ was originally created, it's surprising how far and widely it is being used. ActiveMQ is a crucial component in many applications. Used by small businesses and very large enterprises alike, ActiveMQ is deployed throughout a wide variety of industries around the world including manufacturing, government, retail, healthcare, finance, military, telecom, and many more. The versatility of not only ActiveMQ but also event-based systems has appealed to a very large audience of users and that appeal continues to grow.

In writing a book about ActiveMQ, our intent was to provide a comprehensive guide for its features and how to use them. Although ActiveMQ implements the JMS specification, which has not moved in many years, ActiveMQ provides many features beyond this spec and it has not stopped innovating. As is always the case, authoring a book about software is a game of chase; as the software evolves, so must the book that is still being written. We did our best to keep this book up to date with ActiveMQ 5.4.1.

We hope that, by reading this book, you will come to appreciate not only ActiveMQ but the concepts surrounding event-based systems. After all, some of the largest systems in the world are designed using events and message queuing.

acknowledgments

The authors would collectively like to thank the following individuals:

Jeff Bleiel, our development editor, for his work liaising with Manning—without Jeff's input, the book would not be what it is today; Gary Tully for his tireless technical reviews of the entire book; the Manning staff for their arduous work on the book; Filip Hanik for his assistance with Tomcat; Jan Bartel and Greg Wilkins for their assistance with Jetty; David Jencks and Kevan Miller for their assistance with Geronimo; and Jaikiran Pai for his assistance with JBoss.

We would also like to thank the following reviewers, who read the manuscript at different stages of its development, for their invaluable feedback: Jeff Davis, Deepak Vohra, Robert Hanson, Davide Piazza, David Strong, Tijs Rademakers, Prasad A. Chodavarapu, John Merryman, Jeroen Benckhuijsen, Pratik Patel, Scott Dawson, Jason Kolter, Rod Biresch, and Roberto Rojas.

Finally, thanks to the many readers of Manning's Early Access Program (MEAP) for their comments and input on early drafts of the manuscript posted in the Author Online forum.

BRUCE SNYDER

I would like to thank my incredible wife Janene for her patience and understanding during another book project, and my girls Bailey and Jade for reminding me what really matters in life.

DEJAN BOSANAC

I would like to thank my lovely wife for supporting me through yet another book project.

ROB DAVIES

I would like to thank my wife Karen for editing and proofreading my chapters; my children Chris, Connor, and Michael for keeping the zombies at bay; and my dog Rex for forcing me to go on walks in the snow and the rain.

about this book

ActiveMQ in Action is for software architects, developers, and integrators interested in enterprise message queuing in general and ActiveMQ in particular. This book is designed to serve as part introduction and part reference for both beginners and experienced application developers. It begins with an introduction to ActiveMQ and a high-level overview of JMS, followed by a progressively deeper dive into ActiveMQ as the book advances.

The concepts discussed throughout this book assume that the reader possesses enough knowledge of Java EE to design and develop applications. Though such knowledge is not a strict requirement, it will make it easier to grasp many of the concepts touched upon throughout the chapters. Chapter 9 even discusses using ActiveMQ with languages other than Java, including C++, C#, JavaScript, Perl, PHP, Python, and Ruby.

Roadmap

This book is divided into four parts:

Part 1 provides an introduction to ActiveMQ, a high-level overview of JMS, and a brief discussion of the examples used throughout the book. Chapter 1 introduces ActiveMQ at a high level and discusses why and when to use ActiveMQ. It also demonstrates how to download and install ActiveMQ and how to run the examples that come with *ActiveMQ in Action*.

Chapter 2 introduces enterprise messaging, message-oriented middleware (MOM) and the JMS specification.

Chapter 3 introduces the examples to be used throughout *ActiveMQ in Action*.

Part 2 focuses on the three standard components in ActiveMQ including connectivity into the message broker, message persistence, and message broker security.

Chapter 4 covers all the connectivity options for ActiveMQ. It discusses ActiveMQ URIs and all the transport connectors for both client-to-broker and broker-to-broker communications including TCP, NIO, STOMP, failover, SSL, HTTP/S, and much more.

Chapter 5 discusses message persistence in ActiveMQ; how messages are stored for queues and topics, the four styles of message stores available, and message caching.

Chapter 6 introduces and elaborates on security in ActiveMQ. It covers authentication, authorization, and certificate-based security, as well as how to create a custom security plug-in.

The theme of part 3 is using ActiveMQ to build applications using technologies such as the Spring Framework, leading open source application servers, and numerous applications beyond just Java.

Chapter 7 deals with creating Java applications using ActiveMQ. It shows some options for embedding ActiveMQ in Java applications, developing a request/reply application, and writing JMS clients using Spring.

Chapter 8 is all about integrating ActiveMQ with some popular open source application servers including Tomcat, Jetty, Geronimo, and JBoss. It also discusses the client-side JNDI support provided by ActiveMQ.

Chapter 9 discusses messaging with ActiveMQ using languages other than Java including C++, C#, JavaScript, Perl, PHP, Python, and Ruby.

Part 4 discusses advanced features in ActiveMQ such as high availability, scalability, many advanced broker and client features, performance tuning, and administration of ActiveMQ.

Chapter 10 discusses concepts around deploying ActiveMQ for production systems. Topics in this chapter are focused on high availability and scalability.

Chapter 11 presents advanced features provided by ActiveMQ such as wildcards and composite destinations, advisory messages, virtual topics, some info about ActiveMQ plug-ins, and an introduction to message routing with Apache Camel.

Chapter 12 covers advanced ActiveMQ client features including exclusive consumers, message groups, ActiveMQ streams and large objects, the failover transport, and message scheduling.

Chapter 13 deals with ActiveMQ performance tuning. It presents some general tuning techniques covering such topics as persistent versus nonpersistent messages, transactions, embedded brokers, tuning the wire level protocol, tuning the TCP transport, and some optimizations for message producers and message consumers.

Chapter 14 finishes up by discussing the administration and monitoring of ActiveMQ. It shows how to configure ActiveMQ for JMX monitoring and demonstrates this using JConsole. It also discusses and demonstrates the use of advisory messages for monitoring ActiveMQ. There is also coverage of command-line tools, the command agent, use of XMPP, JConsole, and the web console. The discussion then moves on to broker- and client-level logging.

CODE CONVENTIONS AND DOWNLOADS

This book contains many code examples in many different programming languages, all of which are presented using a `fixed-width font like this` to set it apart from the regular text. Many code listings are annotated to point out important items, and the listings are discussed by the surrounding text.

The full source code that is presented in the book is freely available for download from the publisher's website at http://manning.com/ActiveMQinAction.

AUTHORS' NOTE

This book was authored using DocBook XML and was processed using the Docbkx Tools Maven plug-in on Mac OS X. Other items that became part of the book-writing process include MacBook Pros, Google Docs, GMail, Foonz (until it shut down), Free-ConferenceCall.com, barking dogs during conference calls, company acquisitions, lots and lots of music, loud construction next door, sleepless nights, too much work on airplanes, and plain old exhaustion.

Author Online

Purchase of *ActiveMQ in Action* includes free access to a private web forum run by Manning Publications where you can make comments about the book, ask technical questions, and receive help from the authors and from other users. To access the forum and subscribe to it, point your web browser to www.manning.com/ActiveMQinAction. This page provides information on how to get on the forum once you are registered, what kind of help is available, and the rules of conduct on the forum.

Manning's commitment to our readers is to provide a venue where a meaningful dialog between individual readers and between readers and the authors can take place. It is not a commitment to any specific amount of participation on the part of the authors, whose contribution to the book's forum remains voluntary (and unpaid). We suggest you try asking them some challenging questions lest their interest stray!

The Author Online forum and the archives of previous discussions will be accessible from the publisher's website as long as the book is in print.

About the cover illustration

The figure on the cover of *ActiveMQ in Action* is taken from a French travel book, *Encyclopédie Des Voyages* by J. G. De Saint-Sauveur, published in 1796. Travel for pleasure was a relatively new phenomenon at the time and travel guides such as this one were popular, introducing both the tourist as well as the armchair traveler to the inhabitants of other regions of France and abroad.

The diversity of the drawings in the *Encyclopédie Des Voyages* speaks vividly of the uniqueness and individuality of the world's towns and provinces just 200 years ago. This was a time when the dress codes of two regions separated by a few dozen miles identified people uniquely as belonging to one or the other. The travel guide brings to life a sense of isolation and distance of that period and of every other historic period except our own hyperkinetic present.

Dress codes have changed since then and the diversity by region, so rich at the time, has faded away. It is now often hard to tell the inhabitant of one continent from another. Perhaps, trying to view it optimistically, we have traded a cultural and visual diversity for a more varied personal life, or a more varied and interesting intellectual and technical life.

We at Manning celebrate the inventiveness, the initiative, and the fun of the computer business with book covers based on the rich diversity of regional life two centuries ago brought back to life by the pictures from this travel guide.

Part 1

An introduction to messaging and ActiveMQ

Apache ActiveMQ is a message broker for remote communication between systems using the JMS (Java Message Service) specification. Although ActiveMQ is written in Java, APIs for many languages other than Java are provided, including C/C++, .NET, Perl, PHP, Python, Ruby, and many more. This book provides the information you need to understand, configure, and use ActiveMQ successfully to meet the requirements of many business applications.

In part 1, you'll be introduced to ActiveMQ briefly to get you up and running. We'll discuss the concepts surrounding message-oriented middleware and JMS so that you have an adequate background on how enterprise messaging came to be what it is today. We'll also introduce the examples for the book, including their use cases and how to run each example. We'll use these examples throughout the book, so it's important to understand them before they're applied through the chapters. The chapters in part 1 provide a good base set of knowledge that prepares you for the rest of the book.

Introduction to Apache ActiveMQ

Enterprise messaging software has been in existence since the late 1980s. Not only is messaging a style of communication between applications, it's also a style of integration. Therefore, messaging fulfills the need for both notification as well as interoperation among applications. But open source solutions have only emerged in the last 10 years. Apache ActiveMQ is one such solution, providing the ability for applications to communicate in an asynchronous, loosely coupled manner. This chapter will introduce you to ActiveMQ.

ActiveMQ is an open source, Java Message Service (JMS) 1.1–compliant, message-oriented middleware (MOM) from the Apache Software Foundation that provides high availability, performance, scalability, reliability, and security for enterprise messaging. ActiveMQ is licensed using the Apache License, one of the most liberal and business-friendly Open Source Initiative (OSI)–approved licenses available. Because of the Apache License, anyone can use or modify ActiveMQ without any repercussions for the redistribution of changes. This is a critical point for businesses who use ActiveMQ in a strategic manner. As described later in chapter 2, the job of a MOM is to mediate events and messages among distributed applications, guaranteeing that they reach their intended recipients. So it's vital that a MOM be highly available, performant, and scalable.

The goal of ActiveMQ is to provide standards-based, message-oriented application integration across as many languages and platforms as possible. ActiveMQ implements the JMS spec and offers dozens of additional features and value on top of this spec. These additional features will be introduced and discussed in detail throughout this book.

Your first steps with ActiveMQ are important to your success in using it for your own work. To the novice user, ActiveMQ may appear to be daunting, and yet to the seasoned hacker, it might be easier to understand. This chapter will walk you through the task of becoming familiar with ActiveMQ in a simple manner. You'll not only gain a high-level understanding of the ActiveMQ feature set, but you'll also be taken through a discussion of why and where to use ActiveMQ in your application development. Then you'll be prepared enough to install and begin using ActiveMQ.

1.1   *ActiveMQ features*

ActiveMQ provides an abundance of features created through hundreds of man-years of effort. The chapters in this book break down ActiveMQ into sets of features to focus on describing many of them. The following is a high-level list of some of the features that will be discussed throughout this book:

- *JMS compliance*—A good starting point for understanding the features in ActiveMQ is that ActiveMQ is an implementation of the JMS 1.1 spec. As discussed later in this chapter, the JMS spec provides important benefits and guarantees, including synchronous or asynchronous message delivery, once-and-only-once message delivery, message durability for subscribers, and much more. Adhering to the JMS spec for such features means that no matter what JMS provider is used, the same base set of features will be made available.

- *Connectivity*—ActiveMQ provides a wide range of connectivity options, including support for protocols such as HTTP/S, IP multicast, SSL, STOMP, TCP, UDP, XMPP, and more. Support for such a wide range of protocols equates to more flexibility. Many existing systems utilize a particular protocol and don't have the option to change, so a messaging platform that supports many protocols lowers the barrier to adoption. Though connectivity is important, the ability to closely integrate with other containers is also important. Chapter 4 addresses both the transport connectors and the network connectors in ActiveMQ.

- *Pluggable persistence and security*—ActiveMQ provides multiple flavors of persistence and you can choose between them. Also, security in ActiveMQ can be completely customized for the type of authentication and authorization that's best for your needs. For example, ActiveMQ offers its own style of ultra-fast message persistence via KahaDB, but also supports standard JDBC-accessible databases. ActiveMQ also supports its own simple style of authentication and authorization using properties files as well as standard JAAS login modules. These two topics are discussed in chapters 5 and 6.

- *Building messaging applications with Java*—The most common route with ActiveMQ is with Java applications for sending and receiving messages. This task entails use of the JMS spec APIs with ActiveMQ and is covered in chapter 7.

- *Integration with application servers*—It's common to integrate ActiveMQ with a Java application server. Chapter 8 provides examples of integrating with some of the most popular application servers, including Apache Tomcat, Jetty, Apache Geronimo, and JBoss.

- *Client APIs*—ActiveMQ provides client APIs for many languages besides just Java, including C/C++, .NET, Perl, PHP, Python, Ruby, and more. This opens the door to opportunities where ActiveMQ can be utilized outside of the Java world. Many other languages also have access to all of the features and benefits provided by ActiveMQ through these various client APIs. Of course, the ActiveMQ broker still runs in a Java VM, but the clients can be written using any of the supported languages. Client connectivity to ActiveMQ is covered in chapter 9.

- *Broker clustering*—Many ActiveMQ brokers can work together as a federated network of brokers for scalability purposes. This is known as a *network of brokers* and can support many different topologies. This topic is covered in chapter 10.

- *Many advanced broker features and client options*—ActiveMQ provides many sophisticated features for both the broker and the clients connecting to the broker. ActiveMQ also supports the use of Apache Camel within the broker's XML configuration file. These features are discussed in chapters 11 and 12.

- *Dramatically simplified administration*—ActiveMQ is designed with developers in mind. As such, it doesn't require a dedicated administrator because it provides easy-to-use yet powerful administration features. There are many ways to monitor different aspects of ActiveMQ, including via JMX using tools such as JConsole or the ActiveMQ web console, by processing the ActiveMQ advisory messages, by using command-line scripts, and even by monitoring various types of logging. This is all covered in chapter 14.

This is just a taste of the features offered by ActiveMQ. As you can see, these topics will be addressed through the rest of the chapters of the book. For demonstration purposes, a couple of simple examples will be carried throughout and these examples will be introduced in chapter 3. But before we take a look at the examples, and given the fact that you've been presented with numerous different features, we're sure you have some questions about why you might use ActiveMQ.

1.2   *Using ActiveMQ: why and when?*

Back around 2003, a group of open source developers got together to form Apache Geronimo. In doing so, they discovered that there was no good message broker available that utilized a BSD-style license. Geronimo needed a JMS implementation for reasons of Java EE compatibility, so a few of the developers starting discussing the possibilities. Possessing vast experience with commercial MOMs and even having built a few MOMs themselves previously, these developers set out to create the next great open source message broker. Additional inspiration for ActiveMQ came from the fact that most of the MOMs in the market were commercial, closed source, and were costly to buy and support. The commercial MOMs were popular with businesses, but some businesses couldn't afford the steep costs required. This further increased the motivation to build an open source alternative. There was clearly a market available for an open source MOM using an Apache License. What evolved over time is Apache ActiveMQ.

ActiveMQ was meant to be used as the JMS spec intended, for remote communications between distributed applications. To better understand what this means, the best thing to do is look at a few of the ideas behind distributed application design, specifically communications.

1.2.1   *Loose coupling and ActiveMQ*

ActiveMQ provides the benefits of loose coupling for application architecture. Loose coupling is commonly introduced into an architecture to mitigate the classic tight coupling of Remote Procedure Calls (RPC). Such a loosely coupled design is considered to be asynchronous, where the calls from either application have no bearing on one another; there's no interdependence or timing requirements. The applications can rely upon ActiveMQ's ability to guarantee message delivery. Because of this, it's often said that applications sending messages just fire-and-forget—they send the message to ActiveMQ and aren't concerned with how or when the message is delivered. In the same manner, the consuming applications have no concern with where the messages originated or how they were sent to ActiveMQ. This is an especially powerful benefit in heterogeneous environments, allowing clients to be written using different languages and even possibly different wire protocols. ActiveMQ acts as the middleman, allowing heterogeneous integration and interaction in an asynchronous manner. More on this in the next section.

When considering distributed application design, coupling is important. *Coupling* refers to the interdependence of two or more applications or systems. An easy way to think about coupling is to consider the effect of changes to any application in the system: the implications across the other applications in the architecture as features are added. Do changes to one application force changes to other applications involved? If the answer is yes, then those applications are tightly coupled. But if one application can be changed without affecting other applications, then those applications are more loosely coupled. The overall lesson here is that tightly coupled applications are

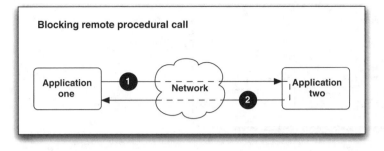

Figure 1.1 Two tightly coupled applications using remote procedure calls to communicate

more difficult to maintain compared to loosely coupled applications. Said another way, loosely coupled applications can easily deal with unforeseen changes.

Technologies such as those discussed in chapter 2 (COM, CORBA, DCE, and EJB) using RPC are considered to be tightly coupled. Using RPC, when one application calls another application, the caller is blocked until the callee returns control to the caller. The diagram in figure 1.1 depicts this concept.

The caller (application one) in figure 1.1 is blocked until the callee (application two) returns control. Many system architectures use RPC and are successful. But there are numerous disadvantages to such a tightly coupled design: most notable is the higher amount of maintenance required, since even small changes ripple throughout the system architecture. Correct timing between the two applications is a necessity. Both applications must be available at the same time for the request from application one to reach application two ❶, and for the response to travel from application two to application one ❷. Such timing requirements can be cumbersome, causing the application to be fragile. Compare such a tightly coupled design with a design where two applications are completely unaware of one another such as that depicted in figure 1.2.

Application one in figure 1.2 sends a message to the MOM in a one-way fashion. Then, possibly sometime later, application two receives a message from the MOM, in a one-way fashion. Neither application has any knowledge that the other even exists, and there's no timing between the two applications. This one-way style of interaction results in much lower maintenance because changes in one application have little to no effect on the other application. For these reasons, loosely coupled applications offer big advantages over tightly coupled architectures when considering distributed application design. This is where ActiveMQ enters the picture.

Consider the changes necessary when an application must move to a new location. This can happen when new hardware is introduced or the application needs to be moved. With a tightly coupled system design, such movement is difficult because all segments of the application must experience an outage. With an application designed using loose coupling, different segments of the system can be moved independent of one another. Consider a scenario where there are multiple instances of application A and multiple instances of application B, where each instance resides on a different machine. ActiveMQ is installed on still another machine independent of either

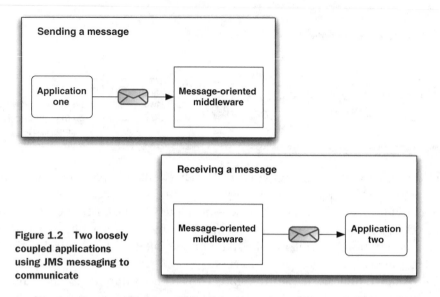

Figure 1.2   Two loosely
coupled applications
using JMS messaging to
communicate

application A or application B. In this scenario, any one of the application A or application B instances can be moved around without affecting one another. In fact, multiple instances of ActiveMQ could be used in what's known as a *network of brokers* configuration. This would allow the ActiveMQ instances to be moved around without affecting either application A or application B. This means that any segment of this architecture can be taken down for maintenance at any time without taking down the entire system. More details about this are available in chapter 10.

So ActiveMQ provides an incredible amount of flexibility in application architecture, allowing the concepts surrounding loose coupling to become a reality. ActiveMQ also supports the request/reply paradigm of messaging if a completely asynchronous style of messaging isn't possible for a given use case. But when should ActiveMQ be used to introduce these benefits?

1.2.2   *When to use ActiveMQ*

There are many occasions where ActiveMQ and asynchronous messaging can have a meaningful impact on a system architecture. Here are just a few example scenarios:

- *Heterogeneous application integration*—The ActiveMQ broker is written using the Java language, so naturally a Java client API is provided. But ActiveMQ also provides clients for C/C++, .NET, Perl, PHP, Python, Ruby, and a few other languages. This is a huge advantage when considering how you might integrate applications written in different languages on different platforms. In cases such as this, the various client APIs make it possible to send and receive messages via ActiveMQ no matter what language is used. In addition to the cross-language capabilities provided by ActiveMQ, the ability to integrate such applications without the use of RPC is definitely a big benefit because messaging truly helps to decouple the applications.

- *As a replacement for RPC*—Applications using RPC-style synchronous calls are widespread. Consider that the vast majority of client-server applications use RPC including ATMs, most web applications, credit card systems, point-of-sale systems, and more. Even though many of these systems are successful, conversion to the use of asynchronous messaging can bring about benefits without giving up the guarantee of a response. Systems that rely upon synchronous requests typically have a limited ability to scale because eventually requests will begin to back up, thereby slowing the whole system. Instead of experiencing this type of a slowdown, using asynchronous messaging, additional message receivers can be easily added so that messages are consumed concurrently and therefore handled faster. This, of course, assumes that your applications can be decoupled.

- *To loosen the coupling between applications*—As already discussed, tightly coupled architectures can be problematic for many reasons, especially if they're distributed. Loosely coupled architectures, on the other hand, exhibit fewer dependencies, making them better at handling unforeseen changes. Not only will a change to one component in the system not ripple across the entire system, but component interaction is also dramatically simplified. Instead of using a synchronous scheme for component interaction (where one method calls another and the caller waits for a response from the callee), components utilize asynchronous communications (where they simply send a message without waiting for a response—also known as *fire-and-forget*). Such loose coupling throughout a system can lead to what's known as an *event-driven architecture* (EDA).

- *As the backbone of an event-driven architecture*—The decoupled, asynchronous style of architecture described in the previous point allows the broker itself to scale much further and handle considerably more clients via tuning, additional memory allocation, and so on (known as *vertical scalability*) instead of only relying upon the ability of the number of broker nodes to be increased to handle many more clients (known as *horizontal scalability*). Consider an incredibly high-traffic e-commerce site such as Amazon. When a user makes a purchase on Amazon, there are quite a few separate stages through which that order must travel including order placement, invoice creation, payment processing, order fulfillment, shipping, and more. But when a user actually places an order, the user is immediately taken to a page stating, "Thanks for your order." Not only that, but without delay, the user also receives an email stating that the order was received. The order placement process that's employed by Amazon is a good example of the first stage in a much larger set of asynchronous processes. Each stage of the order is handled discretely by a separate service. When the user places the order, there's a synchronous call to submit the order, but the entire order process doesn't take place behind a synchronous call via the web browser. Instead, the order is accepted and acknowledged immediately. The rest of the steps in the process are handled asynchronously. If a problem occurs that prevents the process from proceeding, the user is notified via email. Such asynchronous processes are what afford massive scalability and high availability.

- *To improve application scalability*—Many applications utilize an event-driven architecture in order to provide massive scalability including such domains as e-commerce, government, manufacturing, and online gaming, just to name a few. By separating an application along lines in the business domain using asynchronous messaging, many other possibilities begin to emerge. Consider the ability to design an application using a service for a specific task. This is the backbone of service-oriented architecture (SOA). Each service fulfills a discrete function and only that function. Then applications are built through the composition of these services, and the communication among services is achieved using asynchronous messaging and eventual consistency. This style of application design makes it possible to introduce such concepts as *complex event processing* (CEP). Using CEP, the interactions among the components in a system are tracked for further analysis. Such possibilities are truly endless when you consider that asynchronous messaging is simply adding a level of indirection between components in a system.

Now that you've been offered some examples of where to use ActiveMQ, it's time to install ActiveMQ and begin using it.

1.3   *Getting started with ActiveMQ*

Getting started with ActiveMQ isn't difficult. You simply need to start up the broker and make sure that it's capable of accepting connections and sending messages. ActiveMQ comes with some simple examples that will help you with this task, but first we need to install Java and download ActiveMQ.

In this section, you'll download and install the Java SE, download and install ActiveMQ, examine the ActiveMQ directory, and start up ActiveMQ for the first time.

1.3.1   *Downloading and installing the Java SE*

ActiveMQ requires a minimum of the Sun Java SE 1.5, though 1.6 is preferred. This must be installed prior to attempting this section. If you don't have the Sun J2SE installed and you're using Linux, Solaris, or Windows, download and install it from the following URL: http://www.oracle.com/technetwork/java/javase/downloads/index.html.

If you're using Mac OS X, you should already have Java installed. But just in case you don't, you can grab it from the following URL: http://developer.apple.com/java/download/.

Once you have the Java SE installed, you'll need to test that it is set up correctly. To do this, open a terminal or command line and enter the command shown in the following listing.

Listing 1.1 Check the Java version

```
[~]$ java version "1.6.0_20"
Java(TM) SE Runtime Environment (build 1.6.0_20-b02-279-10M3065)
Java HotSpot(TM) 64-Bit Server VM (build 16.3-b01-279, mixed mode)
```

Your output may be slightly different depending on the operating system you're using, but the important part is that there's output from the Java SE. The command tells us two things: that the J2SE is installed correctly and that Java version 1.6 is being used. If you don't see similar output, then you'll need to rectify this situation before moving on to the next section.

Downloading and Installing Ant

Ant will be used to build and run the examples that ship with ActiveMQ. Ant is available from the Apache Ant website at the following URL: http://ant.apache.org/bindownload.cgi.

Click on the link to the appropriate archive for your operating system (the tarballs are for Linux and Unix; the zip is for Windows). Please follow the instructions for intalling Ant at this URL: http://ant.apache.org/manual/install.html. Make sure to set up the $ANT_HOME environment variable and to put $ANT_HOME/bin in the $PATH environment variable. Once Ant is properly installed, you should be able to run the following command from a terminal to see the Ant version:

```
$ ant -version
Apache Ant version 1.8.1 compiled on April 30 2010
```

You may be using a slightly different version of Ant, but that shouldn't matter. Once Ant outputs its version as shown above, you know that both the Java SE and Ant have been installed properly.

1.3.2 Downloading ActiveMQ

ActiveMQ is available from the Apache ActiveMQ website at the following URL: http://activemq.apache.org/download.html.

Click on the link to the 5.4.1 release and you'll find both tarball and zip formats available (the tarball is for Linux and Unix; the zip is for Windows). Once you've downloaded one of the archives, expand it and you're ready to move along. Once you get to this point, you should have the Java SE all set up and working correctly, and you're ready to take a peek at the ActiveMQ directory.

1.3.3 Examining the ActiveMQ directory

From the command line, move into the apache-activemq-5.4.1 directory and enter the command shown here.

Listing 1.2 List the contents of the ActiveMQ directory

```
[apache-activemq-5.4.1]$ ls -1
LICENSE
NOTICE
```

```
README.txt
WebConsole-README.txt
activemq-all-5.4.1.jar
bin
conf
data
docs
example
lib
user-guide.html
webapps
```

The contents of the directory are fairly straightforward:

- *LICENSE*—A file required by the Apache Software Foundation (ASF) for legal purposes; contains the licenses of all libraries used by ActiveMQ.
- *NOTICE*—Another ASF-required file for legal purposes; it contains copyright information of all libraries used by ActiveMQ.
- *README.txt*—A file containing some URLs to documentation to get new users started with ActiveMQ.
- *WebConsole-README.txt*—Contains information about using the ActiveMQ web console.
- *activemq-all-5.4.1.jar*—A jar file that contains all of ActiveMQ; it's placed here for convenience if you need to grab it and use it.
- *bin*—The bin directory contains binary/executable files for ActiveMQ; the startup scripts live in this directory.
- *conf*—The conf directory holds all the configuration information for ActiveMQ.
- *data*—The data directory is where the log files and message persistence data is stored.
- *docs*—Contains a simple index.html file referring to the ActiveMQ website.
- *example*—The ActiveMQ examples; these are what we'll use shortly to test out ActiveMQ quickly.
- *lib*—The lib directory holds all the libraries needed by ActiveMQ.
- *user-guide.html*—A brief guide to starting up ActiveMQ and running the examples.
- *webapps*—The webapps directory holds the ActiveMQ web console and some other web-related demos.

The next task is to start up ActiveMQ and verify it using the examples.

1.3.4   *Starting up ActiveMQ*

After downloading and expanding the archive, ActiveMQ is ready for use. The binary distribution provides a basic configuration to get you started easily and that's what we'll use in the examples. So start up ActiveMQ now as shown next.

Listing 1.3 Start up ActiveMQ

```
$ ./bin/activemq console
INFO: Using default configuration
(you can configure options in one of these file: /etc/default/activemq
/Users/bsnyder/.activemqrc)
INFO: Invoke the following command to create a configuration file
./bin/activemq setup [ /etc/default/activemq | /Users/bsnyder/.activemqrc ]
INFO: Using java '/System/Library/Frameworks/JavaVM.framework/Home/bin/java'
INFO: Starting in foreground, this is just for debugging purposes
(stop process by pressing CTRL+C)
Java Runtime: Apple Inc. 1.6.0_20
/System/Library/Frameworks/JavaVM.framework/Versions/1.6.0/Home
Heap sizes: current=258880k free=253105k max=258880k
JVM args: -Xms256M -Xmx256M
-Dorg.apache.activemq.UseDedicatedTaskRunner=true
-Djava.util.logging.config.file=logging.properties
-Dcom.sun.management.jmxremote
-Dactivemq.classpath=/Users/bsnyder/amq/apache-activemq-5.4.1/conf;
-Dactivemq.home=/Users/bsnyder/amq/apache-activemq-5.4.1
-Dactivemq.base=/Users/bsnyder/amq/apache-activemq-5.4.1
ACTIVEMQ_HOME: /Users/bsnyder/amq/apache-activemq-5.4.1
ACTIVEMQ_BASE: /Users/bsnyder/amq/apache-activemq-5.4.1
Loading message broker from: xbean:activemq.xml
WARN | destroyApplicationContextOnStop parameter is deprecated,
please use shutdown hooks instead
INFO | PListStore:/Users/bsnyder/amq/apache-activemq-5.4.1/data/localhost/
tmp_storage started INFO | Using Persistence Adapter:
KahaDBPersistenceAdapter[/Users/bsnyder/amq/apache-activemq-5.4.1/data/
    kahadb]
INFO | KahaDB is version 2
INFO | Recovering from the journal ...
INFO | Recovery replayed 1 operations from the journal in 0.029 seconds.
INFO | ActiveMQ 5.4.1 JMS Message Broker (localhost) is starting
...
INFO | ActiveMQ Console at http://0.0.0.0:8161/admin
INFO | Initializing Spring root WebApplicationContext
INFO | Connector vm://localhost Started
INFO | Camel Console at http://0.0.0.0:8161/camel
INFO | ActiveMQ Web Demos at http://0.0.0.0:8161/demo
INFO | RESTful file access application at http://0.0.0.0:8161/fileserver
INFO | Started SelectChannelConnector@0.0.0.0:8161
```

NOTE The examples in the listings in this book were developed on Mac OS X, a Unix operating system. For readers who are using Windows, simply do not use the 'console' argument from any of the examples. To run the example command shown in Listing 1.3 above on Windows, use the following command from the command prompt:

```
C:\apache-activemq-5.4.1>bin\activemq
```

Please note that the command used to start up ActiveMQ on Windows should not contain the 'console' argument. This applies to all the example listings in the book.

This command starts up the ActiveMQ broker and some of its connectors to expose it to clients via a few protocols, namely, TCP, SSL, STOMP, and XMPP. Just be aware that ActiveMQ has started and is available to clients via TCP on port 61616. This is all configurable and will be discussed later in chapter 4. For now, the preceding output tells you that ActiveMQ is up and running and ready for use. Now it's ready to begin handling some messages. The best way to begin sending and receiving messages is by using some of the examples that come with ActiveMQ. The next section walks you through this in a step-by-step manner.

1.4   *Running your first examples with ActiveMQ*

The previous section walked you through starting up ActiveMQ in one terminal. For verification of this, you should open two more terminals to run the ActiveMQ examples. In the second terminal, move into the example directory and look at its contents as shown in the following listing.

> **Listing 1.4   List the contents of the ActiveMQ example directory**

```
[apache-activemq-5.4.1]$ cd ./example/
bsnyder@mongoose [example]$ ls -1
build.xml
conf
perfharness
ruby
src
transactions
```

The example directory contains a few different items. Here's a quick description of each item in that directory:

- *build.xml*—An Ant build configuration for use with the Java examples.
- *conf*—The conf directory holds configuration information for use with the Java examples.
- *perfharness*—The perfharness directory contains a script for running the IBM JMS performance harness against ActiveMQ.
- *ruby*—The ruby directory contains some examples of using ActiveMQ with Ruby and the STOMP connector.
- *src*—The src directory is where the Java examples live; this directory is used by the build.xml.
- *transactions*—The transactions directory holds an ActiveMQ implementation of the TransactedExample from Sun's JMS Tutorial.

Using the second terminal, start up a JMS consumer as shown here.

> **Listing 1.5   Start up the ActiveMQ consumer example**

```
[example]$ ant consumer
Buildfile: build.xml

init:
```

```
compile:

consumer:
     [echo] Running consumer against server at $url =
tcp://localhost:61616 for subject $subject = TEST.FOO
     [java] Connecting to URL: tcp://localhost:61616
     [java] Consuming queue: TEST.FOO
     [java] Using a non-durable subscription
     [java] Running 1 parallel threads
     [java] [Thread-2] We are about to wait until we consume:
2000 message(s) then we will shutdown
```

The command compiles the Java examples and starts up a simple JMS consumer. As you can see from the output, this consumer is

- Connecting to the broker using the TCP protocol (tcp://localhost:61616)
- Watching a queue named TEST.FOO
- Using nondurable subscription
- Waiting to receive 2000 messages before shutting down

Basically, the JMS consumer is connected to ActiveMQ and waiting for messages. Now you can send some messages to the TEST.FOO destination.

In the third terminal, move into the example directory and start up a JMS producer as shown below. This will immediately begin to send messages.

Listing 1.6 Start up the ActiveMQ producer example

```
[example]$  ant producer
Buildfile: build.xml

init:

compile:

producer:
     [echo] Running producer against server at $url =
tcp://localhost:61616 for subject $subject = TEST.FOO
     [java] Connecting to URL: tcp://localhost:61616
     [java] Publishing a Message with size 1000 to queue: TEST.FOO
     [java] Using non-persistent messages
     [java] Sleeping between publish 0 ms
     [java] Running 1 parallel threads
     [java] [Thread-2] Sending message: 'Message: 0 sent at: Thu Oct 14
21:24:07 MDT 2010  ...'
     [java] [Thread-2] Sending message: 'Message: 1 sent at: Thu Oct 14
21:24:07 MDT 2010  ...'
     [java] [Thread-2] Sending message: 'Message: 2 sent at: Thu Oct 14
21:24:07 MDT 2010  ...'
```

Although the output has been truncated for readability, the command starts up a simple JMS producer and you can see from the output that it

- Connects to the broker using the TCP connector (tcp://localhost:61616)
- Publishes messages to a queue named TEST.FOO
- Uses nonpersistent messages
- Doesn't sleep between publishing messages

Once the JMS producer is connected, it then sends 2,000 messages and shuts down. This is the number of messages the consumer is waiting to consume before it shuts down. So as the messages are being sent by the producer in terminal three, flip back to terminal two and watch the JMS consumer as it consumes those messages. Here's the output you'll see in terminal two:

```
    [java] [Thread-2] Received: 'Message: 0 sent at: Thu Oct 14 21:23:56
MDT 2010  ...' (length 1000)
    [java] [Thread-2] Received: 'Message: 1 sent at: Thu Oct 14 21:23:56
MDT 2010  ...' (length 1000)
    [java] [Thread-2] Received: 'Message: 2 sent at: Thu Oct 14 21:23:56
MDT 2010  ...' (length 1000)
...
    [java] [Thread-2] Received: 'Message: 1999 sent at: Thu Oct 14 21:23:56
MDT 2010  ...' (length 1000)
```

Again, the output has been truncated for brevity but this doesn't change the fact that the consumer received 2,000 messages and shut itself down. At this time, both the consumer and the producer should be shut down, but the ActiveMQ broker is still running in the first terminal. Take a look at the first terminal again and you'll see that ActiveMQ appears to not have budged at all. This is because the default logging configuration doesn't output anything beyond what's absolutely necessary. If you'd like to tweak the logging configuration to output more information as messages are sent and received, you can do so. Logging will be covered further in chapter 14.

So what did you learn here? Through the use of the Java examples that come with ActiveMQ, it has been proven that the broker is up and running and can mediate messages. This doesn't seem like much but it's an important first step. If you were able to successfully run the Java examples, then you know that you have no networking problems on the machine you're using and you know that ActiveMQ is behaving properly. If you were unable to successfully run the Java examples, then you'll need to troubleshoot the situation. If you need some help, heading over to the ActiveMQ mailing lists is the best way to find help. These examples are just to get you started but can be used to test many scenarios. Throughout the rest of the book, some different examples surrounding a couple of common use cases will be used to demonstrate ActiveMQ and its features. These examples are explained further in chapter 3.

1.5   Summary

ActiveMQ is a versatile, easy-to-use messaging middleware. You learned about some of the ActiveMQ features that will be covered throughout this book and about some scenarios where ActiveMQ can be applied. The scenarios introduced in this chapter are real-world use cases that are deployed in businesses throughout the world. The JMS spec was designed for use in business applications with these scenarios in mind. For those who aren't familiar with the JMS spec, or even those who'd like a refresher on the topic, the next chapter covers enterprise messaging and provides an overview of JMS. If you're already fluent in these two topics, you can skip ahead to chapter 3 to explore the examples for the book.

Understanding message-oriented middleware and JMS

This chapter covers

- Enterprise messaging and message-oriented middleware
- Understanding the Java Message Service (JMS)
- Using the JMS APIs for sending and receiving messages
- An example of a message-driven bean

To help you better understand the ideas behind ActiveMQ, it's important to have some background and history on enterprise messaging in general. After discussing enterprise messaging, you'll be prepared for a brief introduction to JMS followed by some small examples of its use. The purpose of this chapter is to briefly review enterprise messaging and the JMS specification. If you're already familiar with these topics, you can skip ahead to the next chapter.

At one time or another, every software developer needs to communicate between applications or transfer data from one system to another. Not only are there various solutions to this sort of problem, but depending on your constraints and requirements, deciding how to go about such a task can be a big decision. Business requirements often place restrictions on items that directly impact such a decision including performance, scalability, reliability, and more. There are numerous applications that we use every day that impose such requirements including ATMs, airline reservation systems, credit card systems, point-of-sale systems, and telecommunications, to name a few. Where would we be without most of these applications in our daily lives?

For a moment, think about how these types of services have made your life easier. These applications and others like them are made possible because of their reliable and secure nature. Behind the scenes of these applications, just about all of them are composed of many applications, usually distributed, communicating by passing events or messages back and forth. Even the most sophisticated financial trading systems are integrated in this manner, operating completely through the sending and receipt of business information among all the necessary systems using messaging.

Many products provide messaging for various purposes. Necessity is the mother of invention, and this is how messaging middleware was born. A form of software became necessary for communication and data transfer capabilities that could more easily manage the disparity among data formats, operating systems, protocols, and even programming languages. Additionally, capabilities such as sophisticated message routing and transformation began to emerge as part of or in conjunction with these solutions. Such systems came to be known as *message-oriented middleware* (MOM).

ActiveMQ is a MOM product that provides asynchronous messaging for such business systems. By providing a MOM that utilizes the JMS spec, ActiveMQ facilitates application architectures that support such reliability and scalability.

2.1   *Introduction to enterprise messaging*

Most systems like those mentioned previously were built using mainframe computers and many still use them today. So how can these applications work in such a reliable manner? To answer this and other questions, let's briefly explore some of the history behind such solutions and how enterprise messaging was born.

Starting in the 1960s, large organizations invested in mainframes for critical applications to facilitate functions such as data processing, financial processing, statistical analysis, and much more. Mainframes provided appreciable benefits including high availability, redundancy, reliability and scalability, upgradability without service interruption, and many other critical features required by business. Although these systems were extremely powerful, access to such systems was restricted, as input options were few. Also, interconnectivity among systems hadn't yet been invented, meaning that parallel processing wasn't yet possible.

Figure 2.1 shows a diagram demonstrating how terminals connect to a mainframe. In the 1970s, users began to access mainframes through terminals, which dramatically expanded the use of these systems by allowing thousands of concurrent users. It was during this period that computer networks were invented and connectivity among mainframes themselves now became possible. By the 1980s, not only were graphical terminals available, but PCs were also invented and terminal emulation software quickly became common. Interconnectivity became even more important because applications needing access to the mainframe were being developed to run on PCs and workstations. Figure 2.2 shows these various types of connectivity to the mainframe. Note how this expanded connectivity introduced additional platforms and protocols, posing a new set of problems to be addressed.

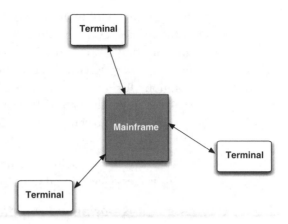

Figure 2.1   Standalone terminals connecting to a mainframe using a single protocol

Connecting a source system and a target system wasn't easy since each data format, each piece of hardware, and each protocol required a different type of adapter. As the list of adapters grew, so did the versions of each, causing them to become difficult to maintain. Soon the effort required to maintain the adapters outweighed that of the systems themselves. This is where enterprise messaging entered the picture.

The purpose of enterprise messaging was to transfer data among disparate systems by sending messages from one system to another. There have been numerous technologies for various forms of messaging through the years, including the following list:

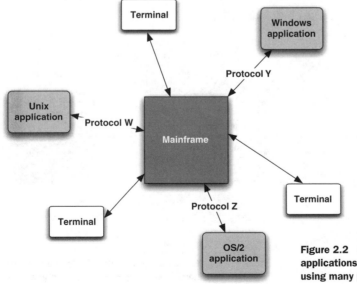

Figure 2.2   Standalone terminals and applications connecting to a mainframe using many protocols.

- Solutions for remote procedure calls (RPC) such as COM, CORBA, DCE, and EJB
- Solutions for event notification, inter-process communication, and message queuing that are baked into operating systems such as FIFO buffers, message queues, pipes, signals, sockets, and others
- Solutions for a category of middleware that provides asynchronous, reliable message queuing such as IBM WebSphere MQ, SonicMQ, TIBCO Rendezvous, and Apache ActiveMQ, commonly used for Enterprise Application Integration (EAI) purposes

The last category of messaging middleware products is what we'll discuss here. So what exactly is message-oriented middleware?

2.2   *What's message-oriented middleware?*

Message-oriented middleware (MOM) is best described as a category of software for communication in an asynchronous, loosely-coupled, reliable, scalable, and secure manner among distributed applications or systems. MOMs were an important concept in the distributed computing world. They allowed application-to-application communication using APIs provided by each vendor, and began to deal with many issues in the distributed system space.

The overall idea behind a MOM is that it acts as a message mediator between message senders and message receivers. This mediation provides a whole new level of loose coupling. Figure 2.3 demonstrates how a MOM is used to mediate connectivity and messaging not only between each application and the mainframe but also from application to application.

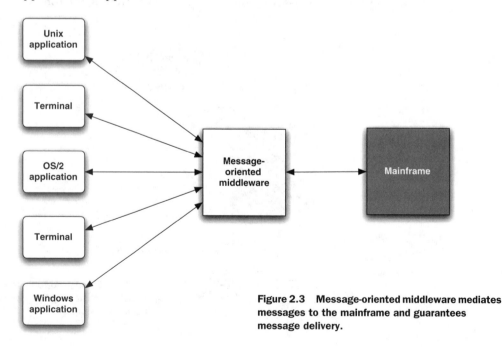

Figure 2.3   **Message-oriented middleware mediates messages to the mainframe and guarantees message delivery.**

At a high level, messages are a unit of business information that's sent from one application to another via the MOM. Applications send and receive messages via the MOM using what are known as *destinations*. Messages are addressed to and delivered to receivers that connect or subscribe to the destinations. This is the mechanism that allows for loose coupling between senders and receivers, as there's no requirement for each to be connected to the MOM at the same time for sending and receiving messages. Senders know nothing about receivers and receivers know nothing about senders. This is known as *asynchronous messaging*.

MOMs added welcome additional features to enterprise messaging that weren't previously possible when systems were tightly coupled—features such as message persistence, robust communication over slow or unreliable connections, complex message routing, message transformation, and much more. Message persistence helps to mitigate slow or unreliable connections made by senders and receivers; or in a situation where a receiver simply fails, it won't affect the state of the sender. Complex message routing opens up a huge number of possibilities, including delivering a single message to many receivers, message routing based on properties or the content of a message, and so forth. Message transformation allows two applications that don't handle the same message format to now communicate via a custom message format that's transformed on the fly.

Additionally, many MOMs on the market today provide support for a diverse set of protocols for connectivity. Some commonly supported protocols include HTTP/S, multicast, SSL, TCP/IP, UDP, and more. Some vendors even provide support for multiple languages, further lowering the barrier to using MOMs in a wide variety of environments. ActiveMQ provides exactly these types of features and more.

Furthermore, it's typical for a MOM to provide an API for sending and receiving messages and otherwise interacting with the MOM. For years, all MOM vendors provided their own proprietary APIs for whatever languages they chose. That is, until the Java Message Service (JMS) came along.

2.3 *What's the Java Message Service?*

The Java Message Service (JMS) moved beyond vender-centric MOM APIs to provide an API for enterprise messaging. JMS aims to provide a standardized API to send and receive messages using the Java programming language in a vendor-neutral manner. The JMS API minimizes the amount of enterprise messaging knowledge a Java programmer is required to possess in order to develop complex messaging applications, while still maintaining a certain amount of portability across JMS provider implementations.

JMS isn't itself a MOM. It's an API that abstracts the interaction between messaging clients and MOMs in the same manner that JDBC abstracts communication with relational databases. Figure 2.4 shows at a high level how JMS provides an API used by messaging clients to interact with MOM-specific JMS providers, which handle interaction with the vendor-specific MOM. The JMS API lowers the barrier to creating enterprise messaging applications. It also eases the portability to other JMS providers.

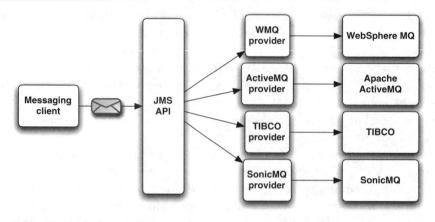

Figure 2.4   JMS allows a single client to easily connect to many JMS providers.

Originally created by Sun in conjunction with a group of companies from the enterprise messaging industry, the first version of the JMS spec was released in 1998. The latest release was in 2002 and offered some necessary improvements. The JMS 1.1 release unified the two sets of APIs for working with the two messaging domains, so working with both messaging domains now only requires a single common API. This was a dramatic change that improved the APIs. Backward compatibility with the old APIs is still supported.

In standardizing the API, JMS formally defined many concepts and artifacts from the world of messaging:

- *JMS client*—An application is written using 100% pure Java to send and receive messages.
- *Non-JMS client*—An application is written using the JMS provider's native client API to send and receive messages instead of JMS.
- *JMS producer*—A client application that creates and sends JMS messages.
- *JMS consumer*—A client application that receives and processes JMS messages.
- *JMS provider*—The implementation of the JMS interfaces, which is ideally written in 100% pure Java.
- *JMS message*—The most fundamental concept of JMS; sent and received by JMS clients.
- *JMS domains*—The two styles of messaging that include point-to-point and publish/subscribe.
- *Administered objects*—Preconfigured JMS objects that contain provider-specific configuration data for use by clients. These objects are typically accessible by clients via JNDI.
- *Connection factory*—Clients use a connection factory to create connections to the JMS provider.
- *Destination*—An object to which messages are addressed and sent and from which messages are received.

Besides these concepts, others are also important. The next few sections will dive deeper into these concepts and focus on describing these building blocks of JMS.

2.4 The JMS specification

As mentioned in the previous section, the JMS spec defines two types of clients—JMS clients and non-JMS clients. The differences are worth a brief discussion, so let's address them.

2.4.1 JMS clients

JMS clients utilize the JMS API for interacting with the JMS provider. Similar in concept to using the JDBC API to access data in relational databases, JMS clients use the JMS API for standardized access to the messaging service. Many JMS providers (including ActiveMQ) include features beyond those required by JMS. It's worth noting that a 100% pure JMS client would only use the JMS APIs and would avoid using such additional features. But the choice to use a particular JMS provider is often driven by the additional features offered. If a JMS client uses such additional features, this client may not be portable to another JMS provider without a refactoring effort.

JMS clients utilize the `MessageProducer` and `MessageConsumer` interfaces in some way. It's the responsibility of the JMS provider to furnish an implementation of each of these interfaces. A JMS client that sends messages is known as a *producer* and a JMS client that receives messages is known as a *consumer*. It's possible for a JMS client to handle both the sending and receiving of messages.

JMS PRODUCERS

JMS clients use the JMS `MessageProducer` class for sending messages to a destination. The default destination for a given producer is set when the producer is created using the `Session.createProducer()` method. But this can be overridden for individual messages by using the `MessageProducer.send()` method. The `MessageProducer` interface is shown here.

Listing 2.1 The `MessageProducer` interface

```
public interface MessageProducer {
    void setDisableMessageID(boolean value) throws JMSException;

    boolean getDisableMessageID() throws JMSException;

    void setDisableMessageTimestamp(boolean value) throws JMSException;

    boolean getDisableMessageTimestamp() throws JMSException;

    void setDeliveryMode(int deliveryMode) throws JMSException;

    int getDeliveryMode() throws JMSException;

    void setPriority(int defaultPriority) throws JMSException;

    int getPriority() throws JMSException;

    void setTimeToLive(long timeToLive) throws JMSException;

    long getTimeToLive() throws JMSException;
```

```
        Destination getDestination() throws JMSException;

        void close() throws JMSException;

        void send(Message message) throws JMSException;

        void send(Message message, int deliveryMode, int priority,
                long timeToLive)
            throws JMSException;

        void send(Destination destination, Message message)
            throws JMSException;

        void send(
            Destination destination,
            Message message,
            int deliveryMode,
            int priority,
            long timeToLive)
            throws JMSException;
    }
```

The MessageProducer provides methods not only for sending messages but also for
setting various message headers including the JMSDeliveryMode, the JMSPriority, the
JMSExpiration (via the get/setTimeToLive() method), as well as a utility send()
method for setting all three of these at once. These message headers are discussed in
section 2.4.5.

JMS CONSUMERS

JMS clients use the JMS MessageConsumer class for consuming messages from a destination. The MessageConsumer can consume messages either synchronously by using
one of the receive() methods or asynchronously by providing a MessageListener
implementation to the consumer. The MessageListener.onMessage() method is
invoked as messages arrive on the destination. The MessageConsumer interface is
shown next.

Listing 2.2   The JMS MessageConsumer interface

```
public interface MessageConsumer {
    String getMessageSelector() throws JMSException;

    MessageListener getMessageListener() throws JMSException;

    void setMessageListener(MessageListener listener) throws JMSException;

    Message receive() throws JMSException;

    Message receive(long timeout) throws JMSException;

    Message receiveNoWait() throws JMSException;

    void close() throws JMSException;
}
```

There's no method for setting the destination on the MessageConsumer. Instead the
destination is set when the consumer is created using the Session.createConsumer()
method.

2.4.2 Non-JMS clients

As noted earlier, a non-JMS client uses a JMS provider's native client API instead of the JMS API. This is an important distinction because native client APIs might offer some different features than the JMS API. Such non-JMS APIs could consist of utilizing the CORBA IIOP protocol or some other native protocol beyond Java RMI. Messaging providers that predate the JMS spec commonly have a native client API, but many JMS providers also provide a non-JMS client API.

2.4.3 The JMS provider

The JMS provider is the vendor-specific MOM that implements the JMS API. Such an implementation provides access to the MOM via the standardized JMS API (remember the analogy to JDBC).

2.4.4 The JMS message

The JMS message is the most important concept in the JMS specification. Every concept in the JMS spec is built around handling a JMS message because it's how business data and events are transmitted. A JMS message allows anything to be sent as part of the message, including text and binary data as well as information in the headers. As depicted in figure 2.5, JMS messages contain two parts, including headers and a payload. The headers provide metadata about the message used by both clients and JMS providers. The payload is the actual body of the message and can hold both textual and binary data via the various message types.

The JMS message is designed to be easy to understand and flexible. All the complexity of the JMS message resides in the headers.

2.4.5 JMS message internals

As mentioned previously, the complexity of a JMS message lies in the details provided by the headers. There are actually two types of headers, which are basically the same logical concept but differ semantically. Whereas a standard list of *headers* and methods to work with them are provided by the JMS spec, *properties* are designed to facilitate custom headers based on primitive Java types. Both are referred to generically as headers.

JMS MESSAGE HEADERS

As shown in figure 2.5, JMS messages support a standard lists of headers and the JMS API provides methods for working with them. Many of the headers are automatically assigned. The following list describes each of these headers, and how they are assigned to the message.

Figure 2.5 A graphical representation of a JMS message

Headers set automatically by the client's `send()` method:

- *JMSDestination*—The destination to which the message is being sent. This is valuable for clients who consume messages from more than one destination.
- *JMSDeliveryMode*—JMS supports two types of delivery modes for messages: persistent and nonpersistent. The default delivery mode is persistent. Each delivery mode incurs its own overhead and implies a particular level of reliability.
  - * *Persistent*—Advises the JMS provider to persist the message so it's not lost if the provider fails. A JMS provider must deliver a persistent message *once and only once*. In other words, if the JMS provider fails, the message won't be lost and won't be delivered more than once. Persistent messages incur more overhead due to the need to store the message, and value reliability over performance.
  - * *Nonpersistent*—Instructs the JMS provider not to persist the message. A JMS provider must deliver a nonpersistent message *at most once*. In other words, if the JMS provider fails, the message may be lost, but it won't be delivered twice. Nonpersistent messages incur less overhead and value performance over reliability.

  The delivery mode is set on the producer and is applied to all messages sent from that producer. But the delivery mode can be overridden for individual messages.
- *JMSExpiration*—The time that a message will expire. This header is used to prevent delivery of a message after it has expired. The expiration value for messages can be set using either the `MessageProducer.setTimeToLive()` method to set the time-to-live globally for all messages sent from that producer, or using one of the `MessageProducer.send()` methods to set the time-to-live locally for each message that is sent. Calling any of these methods sets the default length of time in milliseconds that a message should be considered usable, although the `MessageProducer.send()` methods take precedence.

  The JMSExpiration message header is calculated by adding the time-to-live to the current time in GMT. By default the time-to-live is zero, meaning that the message won't expire. If a time-to-live isn't specified, the default value is used and the message won't expire. If the time-to-live is explicitly specified as zero, then the same is true and the message will not expire.

  This header can be valuable for time-sensitive messages. But be aware that JMS providers shouldn't deliver messages that have expired, and JMS clients should be written so as to not process messages that have expired.
- *JMSMessageID*—A string that uniquely identifies a message that's assigned by the JMS provider and must begin with *ID*. The message ID can be used for message processing or for historical purposes in a message storage mechanism. Because message IDs can cause the JMS provider to incur some overhead, the producer can advise the JMS provider that the JMS application doesn't depend on the value of this header via the `MessageProducer.setDisableMessageID()` method. If the JMS provider accepts this advice, the message ID must be set to null. Be aware that a JMS provider may ignore this call and assign a message ID anyway.

- *JMSPriority*—Used to assign a level of importance to a message. This header is also set on the message producer. Once the priority is set on a producer, it applies to all messages sent from that producer. The priority can be overridden for individual messages. JMS defines 10 levels of message priority, ranging from 0 (the lowest) to 9 (the highest):

  * *Priorities 0–4*—These priorities are finer granularities of the *normal* priority.
  * *Priorities 5–9*—These priorities are finer granularities of *expedited* priority.

  JMS providers aren't required to implement message ordering, although most do. They should simply attempt to deliver higher-priority messages before lower-priority messages.

- *JMSTimestamp*—This header denotes the time the message was sent by the producer to the JMS provider. The value of this header uses the standard Java millis time value. Similar to the JMSMessageID header, the producer may advise the JMS provider that the JMSTimestamp header isn't needed via the `Message-Producer.setDisableMessageTimestamp()` method. If the JMS provider accepts this advice, it must set the JMSTimestamp to zero.

Header set optionally by the client:

- *JMSCorrelationID*—Used to associate the current message with a previous message. This header is commonly used to associate a response message with a request message. The value of the JMSCorrelationID can be one of the following:

  * A provider-specific message ID
  * An application-specific String
  * A provider-native byte[] value

  The provider-specific message ID will begin with the ID: prefix, whereas the application-specific String must not start with the ID: prefix. If a JMS provider supports the concept of a native correlation ID, a JMS client may need to assign a specific JMSCorrelationID value to match that expected by non-JMS clients, but this isn't a requirement.

- *JMSReplyTo*—Used to specify a destination where a reply should be sent. This header is commonly used for request/reply style of messaging. Messages sent with this header populated typically expect a response, but it's actually optional. The client must make the decision to respond or not.

- *JMSType*—Used to semantically identify the message type. This header is used by few vendors and has nothing to do with the payload Java type of the message.

Headers set optionally by the JMS provider:

- *JMSRedelivered*—Used to indicate the liklihood that a message was previously delivered but not acknowledged. This can happen if a consumer fails to acknowledge delivery, or if the JMS provider hasn't been notified of delivery such as an exception being thrown that prevents the acknowledgement from reaching the provider.

JMS MESSAGE PROPERTIES

Properties are simply additional headers that can be specified on a message. JMS provides the ability to set custom headers using generic methods. Methods are provided for working with many primitive Java types for header values including Boolean, byte, short, int, long, float, double, and also the String object type. Examples of these methods can be seen in the next listing, taken from the Message interface.

Listing 2.3   The JMS Message interface

```
public interface Message {
...
    boolean getBooleanProperty(String name) throws JMSException;
    byte getByteProperty(String name) throws JMSException;
    short getShortProperty(String name) throws JMSException;
    int getIntProperty(String name) throws JMSException;
    long getLongProperty(String name) throws JMSException;
    float getFloatProperty(String name) throws JMSException;
    double getDoubleProperty(String name) throws JMSException;
    String getStringProperty(String name) throws JMSException;
    Object getObjectProperty(String name) throws JMSException;
...
    Enumeration getPropertyNames() throws JMSException;
    boolean propertyExists(String name) throws JMSException;
...
    void setBooleanProperty(String name, boolean value) throws JMSException;
    void setByteProperty(String name, byte value) throws JMSException;
    void setShortProperty(String name, short value) throws JMSException;
    void setIntProperty(String name, int value) throws JMSException;
    void setLongProperty(String name, long value) throws JMSException;
    void setFloatProperty(String name, float value) throws JMSException;
    void setDoubleProperty(String name, double value) throws JMSException;
    void setStringProperty(String name, String value) throws JMSException;
    void setObjectProperty(String name, Object value) throws JMSException;
....
}
```

Also note the two convenience methods for working with generic properties on a message—the getPropertyNames() method and the propertyExists() method. The getPropertyNames() method returns an Enumeration of all the properties on a given message to easily iterate through all of them. The propertyExists() method is for testing whether a given property exists on a message. Note that the JMS-specific headers aren't considered generic properties and aren't included in the Enumeration returned by the getPropertyNames() method.

There are three types of properties: custom properties, JMS defined properties, and provider-specific properties.

CUSTOM PROPERTIES

Custom properties are arbitrary and are defined by a JMS application. Developers of JMS applications can freely define any properties using any Java types necessary, by using the generic methods shown in the previous section (getBooleanProperty()/setBooleanProperty(), getStringProperty()/setStringProperty(), and so on).

JMS-DEFINED PROPERTIES

The JMS spec reserves the *JMSX* property name prefix for JMS-defined properties, and support for these properties is optional:

- *JMSXAppID*—Identifies the application sending the message
- *JMSXConsumerTXID*—The transaction identifier for the transaction within which this message was consumed
- *JMSXDeliveryCount*—The number of message delivery attempts
- *JMSXGroupID*—The message group of which this message is a part
- *JMSXGroupSeq*—The sequence number of this message within the group
- *JMSXProducerTXID*—The transaction identifier for the transaction within which this message was produced
- *JMSXRcvTimestamp*—The time the JMS provider delivered the message to the consumer
- *JMSXState*—Used to define a provider-specific state
- *JMSXUserID*—Identifies the user sending the message

The only recommendation provided by the spec for use of these properties is for the JMSXGroupID and JMSXGroupSeq properties, and that these properties should be used by clients when grouping messages and/or grouping messages in a particular order.

PROVIDER-SPECIFIC PROPERTIES

The JMS spec reserves the JMS_<vendor-name> property name prefix for provider-specific properties. Each provider defines its own value for the <vendor-name> place-holder. These are most typically used for provider-specific non-JMS clients and shouldn't be used for JMS-to-JMS messaging.

Now that JMS headers and properties on messages have been discussed, for what exactly are they used? Headers and properties are important when it comes to filtering the messages received by a client subscribed to a destination.

2.4.6 Message selectors

There are times when a JMS client is subscribed to a given destination, but it may want to filter the types of messages it receives. This is exactly where headers and properties can be used. For example, if a consumer registered to receive messages from a queue is only interested in messages about a particular stock symbol, this is easy as long as each message contains a property that identifies the stock symbol of interest. The JMS client can utilize JMS message selectors to tell the JMS provider that it only wants to receive messages containing a particular value in a particular property.

Message selectors allow a JMS client to specify which messages it wants to receive from a destination based on values in message headers. Selectors are conditional expressions defined using a subset of SQL92. Using *Boolean logic*, message selectors use message headers and properties as criteria for *simple Boolean evaluation*. Messages not matching these expressions aren't delivered to the client. Message selectors can't reference a message payload, only the message headers and properties.

Selectors use conditional expressions for selectors that are passed as String arguments using some of the creation methods in the `javax.jms.Session` object. The syntax of these expressions uses various identifiers, literals, and operators taken directly from the SQL92 syntax and are defined in table 2.1.

Table 2.1 JMS selector syntax

Item	Values
Literals	Booleans TRUE/FALSE; numbers such as 5, -10, +34; numbers with decimal or scientific notation such as 43.3E7, +10.5239
Identifiers	A header or property field
Operators	AND, OR, LIKE, BETWEEN, =, <>, <, >, <=, =>, +, -, *, /, IS NULL, IS NOT NULL

The items shown in table 2.1 are used to create queries against message headers and properties. Consider the message defined in the next listing. This message defines two properties that will be used for filtering messages in the example that follows.

Listing 2.4 A JMS message with custom properties

```
public void sendStockMessage(Session session,
                             MessageProducer producer,
                             Destination destination,
                             String payload,
                             String symbol,
                             double price)
       throws JMSException {

    TextMessage textMessage = session.createTextMessage();
    textMessage.setText(payload);
    textMessage.setStringProperty("SYMBOL", symbol);
    textMessage.setDoubleProperty("PRICE", price);
    producer.send(destination, textMessage);
}
```
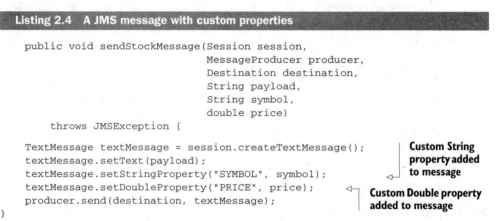

Custom String property added to message

Custom Double property added to message

Now let's look at some examples of filtering messages via message selectors using the preceding message.

Listing 2.5 Filter messages using the SYMBOL header

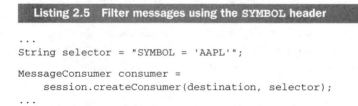

```
...
String selector = "SYMBOL = 'AAPL'";

MessageConsumer consumer =
    session.createConsumer(destination, selector);
...
```

Listing 2.5 defines a selector to match messages for Apple, Inc. This consumer receives only messages matching the query defined in the selector.

Listing 2.6 Filter messages using both the SYMBOL and PRICE headers

```
...
String selector = "SYMBOL = 'AAPL' AND PRICE > "
    + getPreviousPrice();

MessageConsumer consumer =
    session.createConsumer(destination, selector);
...
```

This example specifies a selector to match messages for Apple, Inc. whose price is greater than the previous price. This selector will show stock messages whose price is increasing. But what if you want to take into account the timeliness of stock messages in addition to the price and symbol? Consider the next example.

Listing 2.7 Filter messages using headers

```
...
String selector = "SYMBOL IN ('AAPL', 'CSCO') AND PRICE > "
        + getPreviousPrice() + " AND PE_RATIO < "
        + getCurrentAcceptedPriceToEarningsRatioThreshold();

MessageConsumer consumer =
    session.createConsumer(destination, selector);
...
```

The last example of message selectors in listing 2.7 defines a more complex selector to match messages for Apple, Inc., and Cisco Systems, Inc., whose price is increasing and whose price-to-earnings ratio is less than the currently accepted threshold.

These examples should be enough for you to begin using message selectors. But if you want more in-depth information, see the Javadoc for the JMS Message type.

MESSAGE BODY

JMS defines six Java types for the message body, also known as the *payload*. Through the use of these objects, data and information can be sent via the message payload.

- *Message*—The base message type. Used to send a message with no payload, only headers and properties. Typically used for simple event notification.
- *TextMessage*—A message whose payload is a String. Commonly used to send simple textual and XML data.
- *MapMessage*—Uses a set of name/value pairs as its payload. The names are of type String and the values are a Java primitive type.
- *BytesMessage*—Used to contain an array of uninterpreted bytes as the payload.
- *StreamMessage*—A message with a payload containing a stream of primitive Java types that's filled and read sequentially.
- *ObjectMessage*—Used to hold a serializable Java object as its payload. Usually used for complex Java objects. Also supports Java collections.

2.4.7   JMS domains

As noted earlier, the creation of JMS was a group effort, and the group contained vendors of messaging implementations. It was the influence of existing messaging implementations that resulted in JMS identifying two styles of messaging (or *domains* as they're referred to in the spec)—*point-to-point* and *publish/subscribe*. Most MOMs already supported both of these messaging styles, so it only made sense that the JMS API support both. Let's examine each of these messaging styles to better understand them.

THE POINT-TO-POINT DOMAIN

The point-to-point (PTP) messaging domain uses destinations known as *queues*. Through the use of queues, messages are sent and received either synchronously or asynchronously. Each message received on the queue is delivered once and only once to a single consumer. This is similar to a person-to-person email sent through a mail server. Consumers receive messages from the queue either synchronously using the `MessageConsumer.receive()` method or asynchronously by registering a `MessageListener` implementation using the `MessageConsumer.setMessage-Listener()` method. The queue stores all messages until they're delivered or until they expire.

Multiple consumers can be registered on a single queue as shown in figure 2.6, but only one consumer will receive a given message and then it's up to that consumer to acknowledge the message. Note that the message in figure 2.6 is sent from a single producer and is delivered to a single consumer, not all consumers. As mentioned earlier, the JMS provider guarantees the delivery of a message once and only once to the next available registered consumer. In this regard, the JMS provider is distributing the messages in a sort of round-robin style across all the registered consumers.

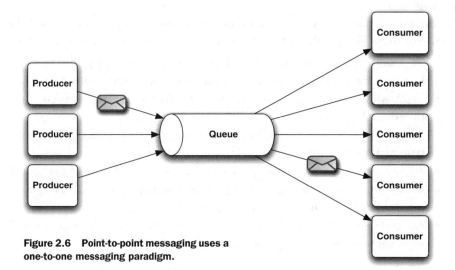

Figure 2.6   Point-to-point messaging uses a one-to-one messaging paradigm.

THE PUBLISH/SUBSCRIBE DOMAIN

The publish/subscribe (pub/sub) messaging domain uses destinations known as *topics*. Publishers send messages to the topic and subscribers register to receive messages from the topic. Any messages sent to the topic are automatically delivered to all subscribers. This messaging domain is similar to subscribing to a mailing list where all subscribers will receive all messages sent to the mailing list in a one-to-many paradigm. The pub/sub domain is depicted in figure 2.7.

Much the same as PTP messaging in the previous section, subscribers register to receive messages from the topic either synchronously using the `Message-Consumer.receive()` method or asynchronously by registering a `MessageListener` implementation using the `MessageConsumer.setMessageListener()` method. Topics don't hold messages unless explicitly instructed to do so. This can be achieved via the use of a *durable subscription*. Using a durable subscription, when a subscriber disconnects from the JMS provider, it's the responsibility of the JMS provider to store messages for the subscriber. Upon reconnecting, the durable subscriber will receive all unexpired messages from the JMS provider. Durable subscriptions allow for subscriber disconnection without missing any messages.

DISTINGUISHING MESSAGE DURABILITY FROM MESSAGE PERSISTENCE

Two points within JMS that are often confused are message durability and message persistence. Though they're similar, there are some semantic differences between them and each has its specific purpose. Message durability can only be achieved with the pub/sub domain. When clients connect to a topic, they can do so using a durable or a nondurable subscription. Consider the differences between the two:

- *Durable subscription*—A durable subscription is *infinite*. It's registered with the topic subscription to tell the JMS provider to preserve the subscription state in the event that the subscriber disconnects. If a durable subscriber disconnects,

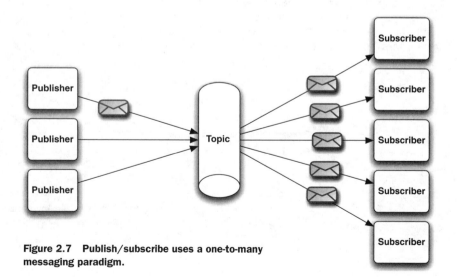

Figure 2.7   Publish/subscribe uses a one-to-many messaging paradigm.

the JMS provider will hold all messages until that subscriber connects again or until the subscriber explicitly unsubscribes from the topic.

- *Nondurable subscription*—A nondurable subscription is *finite*. It's registered with the topic subscription to tell the JMS provider to not preserve the subscription state in the event that the subscriber disconnects. If a subscriber disconnects, the JMS provider won't hold any messages during the disconnection period.

Message persistence is independent of the message domain. Message persistence is a quality of service property used to indicate the JMS application's ability to handle missing messages in the event of a JMS provider failure. As discussed previously, this quality of service is specified on the message producer's setDeliveryMode method using one of the JMSDeliveryMode class's PERSISTENT or NON-PERSISTENT properties as an argument.

Request/reply messaging in JMS applications

Although the JMS spec doesn't define request/reply messaging as a formal messaging domain, it does provide some message headers and a couple of convenience classes for handling basic request/reply messaging. Request/reply messaging is an asynchronous back-and-forth conversational pattern utilizing either the PTP domain or the pub/sub domain through a combination of the JMSReplyTo and JMSCorrelationID message headers and temporary destinations. The JMSReplyTo specifies the destination where a reply should be sent, and the JMSCorrelationID in the reply message specifies the JMSMessageID of the request message. These headers are used to link the reply message(s) to the original request message. Temporary destinations are those that are created only for the duration of a connection and can only be consumed from by the connection that created them. These restrictions make temporary destinations useful for request/reply.

The convenience classes for handling basic request/reply are the QueueRequestor and the TopicRequestor. These classes provide a request() method that sends a request message and waits for a reply message through the creation of a temporary destination where only one reply per request is expected. These classes are useful only for this most basic form of request/reply, as shown in figure 2.8—one reply per request.

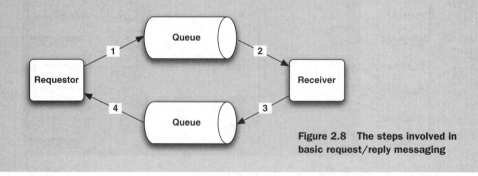

Figure 2.8   The steps involved in basic request/reply messaging

(continued)
Figure 2.8 depicts the basic request/reply style of messaging between two end-points. This is commonly achieved using the JMSReplyTo message header and a temporary queue where the reply message is sent by the receiver and consumed by the requestor. As stated previously, the `QueueRequestor` and the `TopicRequestor` can handle basic request/reply but aren't designed to handle more complex cases of request/reply, such as a single request and multiple replies from many receivers. Such a sophisticated use case requires you to develop a custom JMS application.

2.4.8　Administered objects

Administered objects contain provider-specific JMS configuration information and are supposed to be created by a JMS administrator; hence, the name. Administered objects are used by JMS clients. They're used to hide provider-specific details from the clients and to abstract the JMS provider's administration tasks. It's common to look up administered objects via JNDI, but not required. This is most common when the JMS provider is hosted in a Java EE container. The JMS spec defines two types of administered objects: `ConnectionFactory` and `Destination`.

CONNECTIONFACTORY

JMS clients use the `ConnectionFactory` object to create connections to a JMS provider. Connections typically represent an open TCP socket between a client and the JMS provider, so the overhead for a connection is large. It's a good idea to use an implementation that pools connections if possible. A connection to a JMS provider is similar to a JDBC connection to a relational database, in that it's used by clients to interact with the database. JMS connections are used by JMS clients to create `javax.jms.Session` objects that represent an interaction with the JMS provider.

DESTINATION

The `Destination` object encapsulates the provider-specific address to which messages are sent and from which messages are consumed. Although destinations are created using the `Session` object, their lifetime matches the connection from which the session was created.

Temporary destinations are unique to the connection that was used to create them. They'll only live as long as the connection that created them and only the connection that created them can create consumers for them. As mentioned previously, temporary destinations are commonly used for request/reply messaging.

2.5　Using the JMS APIs to create JMS applications

JMS applications can be as simple or as complex as necessary to suit the business requirements. Just as with other APIs such as JDBC, JNDI, EJBs, and so on, it's common to abstract the use of JMS APIs so as to not intermingle the JMS code with the business logic. This concept won't be demonstrated here, as this is a much lengthier exercise involving patterns and full application infrastructure. Here the simplest example will be demonstrated to show a minimalist use of the JMS APIs.

2.5.1   *A simple JMS application*

A JMS application is written using the Java programming language and composed of many parts for handling different aspects of working with JMS. These parts were identified earlier in the chapter via the list of JMS artifacts in section 2.3. A simple JMS application will utilize the following steps:

  1 Acquire a JMS connection factory
  2 Create a JMS connection using the connection factory
  3 Start the JMS connection
  4 Create a JMS session from the connection
  5 Acquire a JMS destination
  6 Create a JMS producer, OR
       a Create a JMS producer
       b Create a JMS message and address it to a destination
  7 Create a JMS consumer
       a Create a JMS consumer
       b Optionally register a JMS message listener
  8 Send or receive JMS message(s)
  9 Close all JMS resources (connection, session, producer, consumer, and so forth)

These steps are meant to be abstract in order to demonstrate the overall simplicity of working with JMS. Using a minimal amount of code, the following listing demonstrates the steps for creating a JMS producer to send a message.

Listing 2.8   Sending a JMS message

```
public class MyMessageProducer {
...
  ConnectionFactory connectionFactory;
  Connection connection;
  Session session;
  Destination destination;
  MessageProducer producer;
  Message message;
  boolean useTransaction = false;
  try {
    Context ctx = new InitialContext();
    connectionFactory =
        (ConnectionFactory) ctx.lookup("ConnectionFactoryName");
    connection = connectionFactory.createConnection();
    connection.start();
    session = connection.createSession(useTransaction,
        Session.AUTO_ACKNOWLEDGE);
    destination = session.createQueue("TEST.QUEUE");
    producer = session.createProducer(destination);
    message = session.createTextMessage("this is a test");
    producer.send(message);
  } catch (JMSException jmsEx) {
```

```
...
  } finally {
    producer.close();
    session.close();
    connection.close();
  }
}
```

In listing 2.8, first an initial context is created. Most typically, the context is fetched from a provider using a JNDI path. This one is for demonstration purposes only. Using the initial context, a JMS connection factory is acquired using the unique name to identify it. Using the connection factory, a JMS connection is created and started. This is a requirement so that the JMS client begins to communicate with the broker. Using the JMS connection, a JMS session is created and the example uses auto-acknowledgement of messages. A JMS queue is then created via the JMS session object. Next, a JMS message producer is created using the session and the destination. Then a simple text message is created via the session and sent via the message producer. The last action taken in this example is to close all the objects that were being used.

The example in listing 2.8 demonstrates the simplest steps to create a JMS producer and send a message to a destination. Note that there's no concern whether a JMS consumer is on the other end waiting for the message. This mediation of messages between producers and consumers is what MOMs provide and is a big benefit when creating JMS applications. There was no special consideration to achieve this result either. The JMS APIs make this task simple. Now that the message has been sent to the destination, a consumer can receive the message. The following listing demonstrates the steps for creating a JMS consumer and receiving the message.

Listing 2.9　Receiving a JMS message synchronously

```
public class MySyncMessageConsumer {
...
  ConnectionFactory connectionFactory;
  Connection connection;
  Session session;
  Destination destination;
  MessageConsumer consumer;
  Message message;
  boolean useTransaction = false;
  try {
    Context ctx = new InitialContext();
    connectionFactory =
        (ConnectionFactory) ctx.lookup("ConnectionFactoryName");
    connection = connectionFactory.createConnection();
    connection.start();
    session = connection.createSession(useTransaction,
        Session.AUTO_ACKNOWLEDGE);
    destination = session.createQueue("TEST.QUEUE");
    consumer = session.createConsumer(destination);
    message = (TextMessage) consumer.receive(1000);
    System.out.println("Received message: " + message);
```

```
    } catch (JMSException jmsEx) {
...
  } finally {
    producer.close();
    session.close();
    connection.close();
  }
}
```

The example in listing 2.9 is similar to listing 2.8 because both need the same setup up until the creation of the JMS message consumer. After that step, the consumer is used to receive the message that was sent to the destination in the previous example and the message is printed out. The last action is to close all the objects that were being used. Again, note that no timing consideration was needed to make sure that the producer is there sending a message. All mediation and temporary storage of the message is the job of the JMS provider implementation. Listing 2.9 demonstrates the synchronous consumption of messages. This means that the JMS consumer sends a request to the JMS provider to receive a message and waits for a response for the given amount of time. The consumer must poll for messages over and over again in a loop. Consuming messages using synchronous polling of a destination isn't the only flavor of message consumption in JMS.

The JMS API also provides the ability to asynchronously receive messages. The JMS provider will push messages to the consumer. A simple example of asynchronous message consumption follows.

Listing 2.10 Receiving a JMS message asynchronously

```
public class MyAsyncMessageConsumer implements MessageListener {
...
  ConnectionFactory connectionFactory;
  Connection connection;
  Session session;
  Destination destination;
  MessageProducer producer;
  Message message;
  boolean useTransaction = false;
  try {
    Context ctx = new InitialContext();
    connectionFactory =
        (ConnectionFactory) ctx.lookup("ConnectionFactoryName");
    connection = connectionFactory.createConnection();
    connection.start();
    session = connection.createSession(useTransaction,
        Session.AUTO_ACKNOWLEDGE);
    destination = session.createQueue("TEST.QUEUE");
    consumer = session.createConsumer(destination);
    consumer.setMessageListener(this);
  } catch (JMSException jmsEx) {
...
  } finally {
    producer.close();
```

```
    session.close();
    connection.close();
  }
  public void onMessage(Message message) {
    if (message instanceof TextMessage) {
      System.out.println("Received message: " + message);
    }
  }
}
```

The difference between listings 2.9 and 2.10 is the implementation of the onMessage method from the MessageListener interface and the registration of the implementation with the JMS provider. Asynchronously receiving messages as shown in listing 2.10 is extremely powerful. It means that the consumer no longer needs to manually poll for messages repeatedly. Instead, the MessageListener implementation is registered with the JMS provider to act as a sort of callback where the message will be delivered automatically to the onMessage method in an asynchronous manner.

A note on multithreading in JMS applications

The JMS spec specifically defines concurrency for various objects in the JMS API and requires that only a few objects support concurrent access. The ConnectionFactory, Connection, and Destination objects are required to support concurrent access, whereas the Session, MessageProducer, and MessageConsumer objects don't support concurrent access. The point is that the Session, MessageProducer, and MessageConsumer objects shouldn't be shared across threads in a Java application.

There's one additional aspect to the JMS APIs for consuming messages. It involves asynchronous message consumption but concerns the EJB API known as message-driven beans.

2.5.2   *Message-driven beans*

Message-driven beans (MDBs) were born out of the EJB 2.0 spec. The motivation was to allow simple JMS integration into EJBs, making asynchronous message consumption by EJBs almost as easy as using the standard JMS APIs. Through the use of a JMS MessageListener interface, the EJB automatically receives messages from the JMS provider in a push style. An example of a simple MDB is shown here.

Listing 2.11   A simple message-driven bean example

```
import javax.ejb.EJBException;
import javax.ejb.MessageDrivenBean;
import javax.ejb.MessageDrivenContext;
import javax.jms.Message;
import javax.jms.MessageListener;

public class MyMessageProcessor
    implements MessageDrivenBean, MessageListener {
```

```
public void onMessage(Message message) {
    TextMessage textMessage = null;

    try {
        if (message instanceof TextMessage) {
            textMessage = (TextMessage) message;
            System.out.println("Received message: " + msg.getText());
            processMessage(textMessage);
        } else {
            System.out.println("Incorrect message type: " +
                message.getClass().getName());
        }
    } catch (JMSException jmsEx) {
        jmsEx.printStackTrace();
    }
}

public void ejbRemove() throws EJBException {
    // This method is called by the EJB container
}

public void setMessageDrivenContext(MessageDrivenContext ctx)
    throws EJBException {
    // This method is called by the EJB container
}

private void processMessage(TextMessage textMessage) {
    // Do some important processing of the message here
}
}
```

Note that the MyMessageProcessor class in listing 2.11 implements both the Message-DrivenBean interface and the MessageListener interface. The MessageDrivenBean interface requires an implementation of the setMessageDrivenContext() method and the ejbRemove() method. Each of these methods is invoked by the EJB container for the purposes of creation and destruction of the MDB. The MessageListener interface contains only a single method named onMessage(). The onMessage() method is invoked automatically by the JMS provider when a message arrives in a destination on which the MDB is registered.

In addition to allowing the EJB container to manage all necessary resources including Java EE resources (such as JDBC, JMS, and JCA connections), security, transactions, and even JMS message acknowledgement, one of the biggest advantages of MDBs is that they can process messages concurrently. Not only do typical JMS clients need to manually manage their own resources and environment, but they're usually built for processing messages serially—one at a time (unless they're specifically built with concurrency in mind). Instead of processing messages one at a time, MDBs can process multiple messages at the same time because the EJB container can create as many instances of the MDBs as are allowed by the EJB's deployment descriptor. Such configuration is typically specific to the Java EE container. If you're using a Java EE container for this, consult the documentation for the container on how this is configured in the EJB deployment descriptor.

A disadvantage of MDBs is their requirement of a full Java EE container. Just about every EJB container available today can support MDBs only if the entire Java EE container is used. MDBs are extremely useful when using a full Java EE container, but there's an alternative that doesn't require the full Java EE container. Using the Spring Framework's JMS APIs makes developing message-driven POJOs (MDPs) easy. These are Plain Old Java Objects (POJOs) that act as if they're message driven. This style of development has become popular in the Java development community because it avoids the overhead of using a full Java EE container. Such development with the Spring Framework will be discussed in further detail in chapter 7.

> **Not every EJB container requires a full Java EE container—try OpenEJB**
>
> At the time of this writing, nearly all EJB containers on the market require a full Java EE container to support MDBs. The exception to this rule is Apache OpenEJB (http://openejb.apache.org/). OpenEJB supports MDBs from the EJB 1.1 spec, the EJB 2 spec, and the EJB 3 spec in OpenEJB's embedded mode as well as in its standalone mode. OpenEJB can be embedded inside of Apache Geronimo (http://geronimo.apache.org/), Apache Tomcat (http://tomcat.apache.org/), or your own Java application and will still provide support for MDBs.

2.6 Summary

The impact of enterprise messaging on the business world has been significant. Enterprise messaging and the concepts surrounding it have influenced the development of many additional technologies and concepts. Without enterprise messaging, developers wouldn't have an option beyond synchronous calls for application development, and the concept of decoupling an application design wouldn't exist in nearly the same form. SOA, CEP, and many other higher-level concepts built on top of enterprise messaging wouldn't have come about. Furthermore, the JMS spec wouldn't exist today without enterprise messaging.

The JMS spec has had a tremendous effect on the Java world, making messaging a first-class citizen and making it available to all Java developers. This was an important step in allowing Java to join the business of mission-critical applications, because it provides a standardized manner to utilize messaging. The examples provided in this chapter are admittedly short and simple in order to get your feet wet with JMS. As you move though the rest of the book, richer examples will be discussed and made available for download.

Now that you have a basic understanding of JMS and what it provides, the next step is to review the samples for the book. Chapter 3 provides an introduction to the sample applications that will be used throughout the rest of the book.

The ActiveMQ
in Action *examples*

This chapter covers

- Introduction to the use case for each of the book examples
- Use of Maven for compiling and running the examples
- How to use the example applications with ActiveMQ

ActiveMQ provides all the features from the JMS specification and adds many more powerful features on top of that. This is depicted in figure 3.1 and these features will be discussed through the rest of the book. In order to best demonstrate these features, two new examples have been created that are modeled after real business domains. Compared to the example that's part of the ActiveMQ distribution, these examples lend themselves to demonstrating the features in ActiveMQ in a more complete and easy manner.

One of the examples is based on a stock portfolio and the other is based on a job queue. These two examples are more extensive than the examples that come with ActiveMQ. The use case for each of these examples is introduced briefly, followed by a deeper discussion of how to use them. You can refer back to this chapter at any time throughout the book if you need a refresher on the examples.

The stock portfolio demonstrates the publish/subscribe messaging domain. Publishers broadcast stock price messages to many interested subscribers. Messages are published to a JMS destination called a *topic* and clients with active subscriptions receive messages. Using this model, the broker delivers messages to each subscriber without the need to poll for messages. Every active subscriber receives its own copy of each message published to the topic. Publishers are decoupled from subscribers via the topic. Unless durable subscriptions are used, subscribers must be active in order to

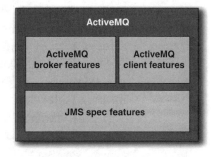

Figure 3.1 ActiveMQ implements all the features from the JMS specification, as well as many additional features.

receive messages sent by publishers to the topic. A copy of each message on a given destination is delivered to all topic subscribers using the pub/sub domain.

The job queue demonstrates the point-to-point (PTP) messaging domain. Message producers send job messages to a JMS queue, from which message consumers receive the job messages for processing. There's no timing requirement for the producers and consumers to be online at the same time with the point-to-point domain. The queue holds messages until consumers are available to receive them. As consumers are available, messages are delivered to all consumers, but no two consumers receive the same message. Messages on a given destination are delivered to queue consumers in a round-robin fashion using the PTP domain.

Not only is each example focused on a different messaging domain, but each is also focused on a separate use case. Additionally, although the diagrams depicted later in this chapter for each example look nearly the same at first glance, the important difference between the two lies in the two messaging domains. The stock portfolio example uses topics for pub/sub messaging, whereas the job queue example uses queues for point-to-point messaging. The source for these examples is readily available and can be downloaded from the Manning website via the following URL: http://manning.com/snyder/activemq-in-action-examples-src.zip.

In this chapter, first we'll download Maven and install it in order to compile and run the examples. After this is complete, we'll review each example and demonstrate how each one should behave. After the completion of these exercises, you'll be familiar enough with the examples to recognize them throughout the book and see how they're used to demonstrate the features in ActiveMQ.

3.1 *Downloading Maven and compiling the examples*

Here are the steps to download and install Maven:

1 Download Maven from the Apache Software Foundation: http://maven. apache.org/.

Maven is provided in both tarball and zip format, depending on your operating system.

2   Expand the downloaded archive to a permanent location on your computer.

3   Create an environment variable named M2_HOME that points to the Maven directory.

4   On Unix, add the $M2_HOME/bin directory to the PATH environment variable (on Windows, add the %M2_HOME%\bin directory to the %PATH% environment variable).

5   Verify the Maven installation by running the following command from the command line:

```
$ mvn -version
Apache Maven 2.2.1 (r801777; 2009-08-06 13:16:01-0600)
Java version: 1.5.0_19
Java home: /System/Library/Frameworks/JavaVM.framework/Versions/1.5.0/
Home
Default locale: en_US, platform encoding: MacRoman
OS name: "mac os x" version: "10.6.2" arch: "i386" Family: "unix"
```

You should see similar output which indicates that Maven is properly installed. If you don't see similar output, you'll need to rectify this before proceeding. See the Maven installation instructions for more information: http://maven.apache.org/download.html#Installation.

YOU NEED AN INTERNET CONNECTION   To use the examples in this book, you'll need a broadband connection to the Internet. This is so that Maven can download the necessary dependencies for the examples.

If you've successfully installed Maven, the examples need to be unzipped and compiled. After expanding the zip file containing the example source code, you'll be ready to compile the examples. To do so, move into the amq-in-action-example-src directory and run the command shown next. For the convenience of recognizing the actual command apart from the rest of the output, the command itself is listed in bold.

Listing 3.1   Compile the examples

```
[amq-in-action-example-src] $ mvn clean install
[INFO] Scanning for projects...
[INFO] ----------------------------------------------------------------
-----
[INFO] Building ActiveMQ in Action Examples
[INFO]    task-segment: [clean, install]
[INFO] ----------------------------------------------------------------
-----
Downloading: http://localhost:8081/nexus/content/groups/public/org/apache/
maven/plugins/maven-clean-plugin/2.2/maven-clean-plugin-2.2.pom
3K downloaded  (maven-clean-plugin-2.2.pom)
...
[INFO] [install:install {execution: default-install}]
[INFO] Installing /private/tmp/amq-in-action-example-src/target/
activemq-in-action-examples.jar to /Users/bsnyder/.m2/repository/org/
apache/activemq/book/activemq-in-action-examples/1.0-SNAPSHOT/
```

```
activemq-in-action-examples-1.0-SNAPSHOT.jar
[INFO] Installing /private/tmp/amq-in-action-example-src/target/
activemq-in-action-examples-src.zip to /Users/bsnyder/.m2/repository/org/
apache/activemq/book/activemq-in-action-examples/1.0-SNAPSHOT/
activemq-in-action-examples-1.0-SNAPSHOT-src.zip
[INFO] -----------------------------------------------------------------
-----
[INFO] BUILD SUCCESSFUL
[INFO] -----------------------------------------------------------------
-----
[INFO] Total time: 57 seconds
[INFO] Finished at: Fri Dec 04 22:35:57 MST 2009
[INFO] Final Memory: 24M/44M
[INFO] -----------------------------------------------------------------
-----
```

Much of the output from the compilation of the examples has been elided for brevity. Suffice it to say that this output represents a successful compilation. As long as you see the BUILD SUCCESSFUL message, you're ready to move on to the next section. If, on the other hand, you see the BUILD FAILURE message, you'll need to troubleshoot and correct the situation before proceeding.

3.2   *Use case one: the stock portfolio example*

As mentioned earlier in the chapter, the first use case revolves around a stock portfolio use case for demonstrating publish/subscribe messaging. This example is simple and utilizes a Publisher class for sending stock price messages to a topic, as well as a Consumer class for registering a Listener class to consume messages from topics in an asynchronous manner. These three classes embody the functionality of generating ever-changing stock prices that are published to topics on which the consumer is subscribed.

In this example, stock prices are published to an arbitrary number of topics. The number of topics is based on the number of arguments sent to the Publisher and the Consumer on the command line. Each class will dynamically send and receive to/from the topics (an example is provided next). Take a look at figures 3.2 and 3.3 to see at a high level what the examples seek to achieve.

For the sake of this demonstration, two topics will be used. The Publisher class uses a single JMS MessageProducer to send 1,000 fictitious stock price messages in blocks of 10, randomly distributed across the topics named in the command-line argument. After it sends 1,000 messages, it shuts down. The Consumer class creates one JMS MessageConsumer per topic and registers a JMS MessageListener for each topic. Because this example demonstrates publish/subscribe, the Consumers must be online to consume messages being sent by the Publisher, because durable consumers aren't used in the basic stock portfolio example. The next step is to actually run the example so that you can see them in action.

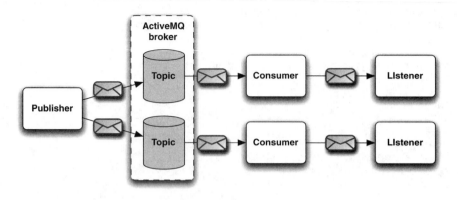

Figure 3.2   The stock portfolio example uses topics to deliver every message to every consumer on a destination.

3.2.1   Running the stock portfolio example

There are three basic steps to running this example:

1 Start up ActiveMQ
2 Run the Consumer class
3 Run the Publisher class

These steps appear to be simple, and they are. The only item of note is that the Con-sumer should be started before the Publisher, in order to receive all messages that are published. This is because this example demonstrates pub/sub messaging and topics won't hold messages unless the consumer makes a durable subscription, and we're not using durable subscriptions here. So let's get started with the stock portfolio example.

The first task is to open a terminal or command line and execute ActiveMQ. This only requires a single command as demonstrated in the following listing.

Listing 3.2   Start up ActiveMQ

```
[apache-activemq-5.4.1] $ ./bin/activemq console
INFO: Using default configuration
(you can configure options in one of these file:
/etc/default/activemq /Users/bsnyder/.activemqrc)

INFO: Invoke the following command to create a configuration file
./bin/activemq setup [/etc/default/activemq | /Users/bsnyder/.activemqrc]

INFO: Using java
'/System/Library/Frameworks/JavaVM.framework/Home/bin/java'
INFO: Starting in foreground, this is just for debugging purposes
(stop process by pressing CTRL+C)
Java Runtime: Apple Inc. 1.6.0_20
/System/Library/Frameworks/JavaVM.framework/Versions/1.6.0/Home
  Heap sizes: current=258880k  free=253105k  max=258880k
    JVM args: -Xms256M -Xmx256M
```

```
-Dorg.apache.activemq.UseDedicatedTaskRunner=true
-Djava.util.logging.config.file=logging.properties
-Dcom.sun.management.jmxremote
-Dactivemq.classpath=/Users/bsnyder/amq/apache-activemq-5.4.1/conf;
-Dactivemq.home=/Users/bsnyder/amq/apache-activemq-5.4.1
-Dactivemq.base=/Users/bsnyder/amq/apache-activemq-5.4.1
ACTIVEMQ_HOME: /Users/bsnyder/amq/apache-activemq-5.4.1
ACTIVEMQ_BASE: /Users/bsnyder/amq/apache-activemq-5.4.1
Loading message broker from: xbean:activemq.xml
...
INFO | Started SelectChannelConnector@0.0.0.0:8161
```

The next task is to open a second terminal or command line to execute the `Consumer` class. The `Consumer` is executed using the maven-exec-plugin (http://mng.bz/bf7g) by passing it some system properties as arguments using the `exec.args` property. An example of running the `Consumer` is shown next.

> **Listing 3.3 Run the stock portfolio consumer**

```
[amq-in-action-example-src] $ mvn exec:java \ -
    Dexec.mainClass=org.apache.activemq.book.ch3.portfolio.Consumer \ -
    Dexec.args="CSCO ORCL"
[INFO] Scanning for projects...
[INFO] Searching repository for plugin with prefix: 'exec'.
[INFO] org.apache.maven.plugins: checking for updates from central
[INFO] org.codehaus.mojo: checking for updates from central
[INFO] artifact org.codehaus.mojo:exec-maven-plugin: checking for
updates from central
[INFO] snapshot org.codehaus.mojo:exec-maven-plugin:1.1.2-SNAPSHOT:
checking for updates from public-snapshots
[INFO] snapshot org.codehaus.mojo:exec-maven-plugin:1.1.2-SNAPSHOT:
checking for updates from central
Downloading:
http://localhost:8081/nexus/content/groups/public/org/codehaus/mojo/
exec-maven-plugin/1.1.2-SNAPSHOT/
exec-maven-plugin-1.1.2-20091120.114446-3.pom
4K downloaded  (exec-maven-plugin-1.1.2-20091120.114446-3.pom)
Downloading:
http://localhost:8081/nexus/content/groups/public/org/codehaus/mojo/
mojo-parent/22/mojo-parent-22.pom
18K downloaded  (mojo-parent-22.pom)
Downloading:
http://localhost:8081/nexus/content/groups/public-snapshots/org/codehaus/
mojo/exec-maven-plugin/1.1.2-SNAPSHOT/
exec-maven-plugin-1.1.2-20091120.114446-3.jar
36K downloaded  (exec-maven-plugin-1.1.2-20091120.114446-3.jar)
[INFO] -----------------------------------------------------------------
-----
[INFO] Building ActiveMQ in Action Examples
[INFO]    task-segment: [exec:java]
[INFO] -----------------------------------------------------------------
-----
[INFO] Preparing exec:java
[INFO] No goals needed for project - skipping
```

```
[WARNING] POM for 'woodstox:wstx-asl:pom:3.2.7:compile' is invalid.

Its dependencies (if any) will NOT be available to the current build.
Downloading:
http://localhost:8081/nexus/content/groups/public/org/apache/commons/
commons-exec/1.0.1/commons-exec-1.0.1.pom
7K downloaded  (commons-exec-1.0.1.pom)
Downloading:
http://localhost:8081/nexus/content/groups/public/org/apache/commons/
commons-exec/1.0.1/commons-exec-1.0.1.jar
48K downloaded  (commons-exec-1.0.1.jar)
[INFO] [exec:java {execution: default-cli}]
```

You can see in listing 3.3 that Maven downloads the necessary artifacts it needs to run the examples. Once this has completed, the `Publisher` can start up and begin publishing stock prices to the two topics named on the command line, *CSCO* and *ORCL*. These two topic names were picked at random and can be replaced with any Strings you desire. The important part is that the same arguments be used for both the `Consumer` and the `Publisher` (the `Publisher` is shown next) via the system property `exec.args`.

> **BUILD ERRORS WHEN RUNNING THE CONSUMER**   If you receive a BUILD ERROR while attempting to run the consumer class, you'll need to compile the source code before running it. To compile all the source, run the following command:
>
> `$ mvn clean install`
>
> This command will compile and package the source so that it's ready to be run. After this command completes, you can go back and run the command consumer using the command shown earlier.

Note that the output just seems to stop as the `Consumer` hangs there. This behavior is correct because it's waiting for messages to arrive in the topics to be consumed. When the `Publisher` begins sending messages, the `Consumer` will begin to consume them.

Why are all the artifacts being downloaded from the localhost in the output shown?

As long as Maven was set up correctly in section 3.1, then Maven will download all the necessary artifacts it needs to run the examples. You can see it downloading artifacts in the first portion of the output. Note that all the artifacts are being downloaded from the localhost instead of from a remote Maven repository. This is because the example is being run with Maven, which is configured to use a Maven repository manager named *Nexus* on the local computer. Nexus provides many benefits, one of which is a proxy to remote Maven repositories with a local cache of all downloaded artifacts. After Maven downloads artifacts the first time via Nexus, they're held in a local cache. During successive builds, Nexus provides the artifacts from the local cache instead of checking a remote repository, and this speeds up the build time quite dramatically. For more information about Nexus and to discover more about its features, see: http://nexus.sonatype.org/.

The next task is to open a third terminal or command line to execute the Publisher class. Note that the same arguments are used in exec.args that were used for executing the Consumer class earlier, because the maven-exec-plugin is used to execute the Publisher class as well. An example of running Publisher is shown here.

Listing 3.4 Running the stock portfolio publisher

```
[amq-in-action-example-src] $ mvn exec:java \
    -Dexec.mainClass=org.apache.activemq.book.ch3.portfolio.Publisher \
    -Dexec.args="CSCO ORCL"
[INFO] Scanning for projects...
[INFO] Searching repository for plugin with prefix: 'exec'.
[INFO] -------------------------------------------------------------
-----
[INFO] Building ActiveMQ in Action Examples
[INFO]     task-segment: [exec:java]
[INFO] -------------------------------------------------------------
-----
[INFO] Preparing exec:java
[INFO] No goals needed for project - skipping
[WARNING] POM for 'woodstox:wstx-asl:pom:3.2.7:compile' is invalid.

Its dependencies (if any) will NOT be available to the current build.
[INFO] [exec:java {execution: default-cli}]
Sending: {offer=62.6861410176471, price=62.62351750014696, up=true,
stock=ORCL} on destination: topic://STOCKS.ORCL
Sending: {offer=55.508573596887715, price=55.45312047641131, up=true,
stock=CSCO} on destination: topic://STOCKS.CSCO
Sending: {offer=62.527946513790205, price=62.46548103275745, up=false,
stock=ORCL} on destination: topic://STOCKS.ORCL
Sending: {offer=55.78778713074073, price=55.73205507566507, up=true,
stock=CSCO} on destination: topic://STOCKS.CSCO
Sending: {offer=55.593918646251986, price=55.53838026598601, up=false,
stock=CSCO} on destination: topic://STOCKS.CSCO
Sending: {offer=55.83360390719586, price=55.777826081114746, up=true,
stock=CSCO} on destination: topic://STOCKS.CSCO
Sending: {offer=55.99233608275527, price=55.93639968307221, up=true,
stock=CSCO} on destination: topic://STOCKS.CSCO
Sending: {offer=62.006501598331475, price=61.94455704129019, up=false,
stock=ORCL} on destination: topic://STOCKS.ORCL
Sending: {offer=55.53698948617822, price=55.48150797820003, up=false,
stock=CSCO} on destination: topic://STOCKS.CSCO
Sending: {offer=61.43866500377897, price=61.377287716062916, up=false,
stock=ORCL} on destination: topic://STOCKS.ORCL
Published '10' of '10' price messages
Sending: {offer=55.466945358331216, price=55.41153382450671, up=false,
stock=CSCO} on destination: topic://STOCKS.CSCO
Sending: {offer=61.27694222131968, price=61.215726494824864, up=false,
stock=ORCL} on destination: topic://STOCKS.ORCL
...
Published '10' of '30' price messages
...
```

When executing the `Publisher` class, Maven already has all the necessary dependencies from the earlier execution of the `Consumer` class, so nothing should be downloaded. The lower portion of the output shows the stock price messages being sent to the two topics in blocks of 10. The example output is truncated for space, so just know that the `Publisher` will run until it sends a total of 1,000 messages.

After running the `Publisher`, if you switch back to the second terminal where the `Consumer` was started, you should see that it's now consuming messages from the topics:

```
...
[INFO] [exec:java {execution: default-cli}]
ORCL    62.62    62.69    up
CSCO    55.45    55.51    up
ORCL    62.47    62.53    down
CSCO    55.73    55.79    up
CSCO    55.94    55.99    up
CSCO    55.41    55.47    down
ORCL    61.22    61.28    down
ORCL    61.42    61.48    up
...
```

The preceding output comes from the `Listener` class that's registered by the `Consumer` on the two topics named ORCL and CSCO. This output shows the consumption of the stock price messages from the same two topics to which the `Publisher` is sending messages. Once the `Publisher` reaches 1,000 messages sent, it'll shut down. But the `Consumer` will continue to run and just hang there waiting for more messages to arrive on those two topics. You can press CTRL-C in the second terminal to shut down the `Consumer` at this point.

Now that you've seen how ActiveMQ works well in a pub/sub messaging scenario, the following section will explore how it works in point-to-point messaging.

3.3   *Use case two: the job queue example*

The second use case focuses on job queues to illustrate point-to-point messaging. This example uses a `Producer` class to send job messages to a job queue and a `Consumer` class for registering a `Listener` class to consume messages from queues in an asynchronous manner. These three classes provide the functionality necessary to show how JMS point-to-point messaging should work. The classes in this example are extremely similar to those used in the stock portfolio example. The difference between the two examples is the JMS messaging domain that each uses.

The `Producer` class in this example sends messages to the JOBS.suspend and JOBS.delete queues and the `Consumer` class consumes. Figure 3.3 contains a high-level diagram of the job queue example's functionality.

The `Producer` class uses a single JMS `MessageProducer` to send 1,000 job messages in blocks of 10 randomly across the two queues. After sending 1,000 messages total, it'll shut down. The `Consumer` class uses one JMS `MessageConsumer` per queue and registers a JMS `MessageListener` on each queue to utilize the message and output its contents.

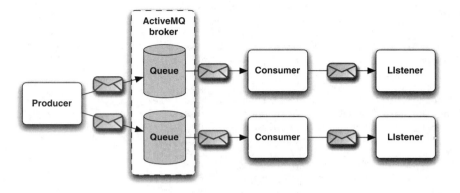

Figure 3.3 The job queue example uses queues to deliver one message to each consumer on a destination in a round-robin fashion.

3.3.1 *Running the job queue example*

The steps for executing the job queues example are nearly identical to the previous example:

1 Start up ActiveMQ
2 Run the Producer class
3 Run the Consumer class

Again, these steps are simple, but there's one exception to note. When using PTP messaging, queues will hold messages until they're consumed or the messages expire. So the Producer can be started before the Consumer and the Consumer won't miss any messages.

Just as in the stock portfolio example, the first task is to start up ActiveMQ. You'll be spared the output from this task, as it's the same as shown in section1.6 and none of the default configuration has been changed.

Next, open a second terminal or command line to execute the Producer as shown here.

Listing 3.5   Running the job queue publisher

```
[amq-in-action-example-src] $ mvn exec:java \
    -Dexec.mainClass=org.apache.activemq.book.ch3.jobs.Publisher
[INFO] Scanning for projects...
[INFO] Searching repository for plugin with prefix: 'exec'.
[INFO] ------------------------------------------------------------------
-----
[INFO] Building ActiveMQ in Action Examples
[INFO]     task-segment: [exec:java]
[INFO] ------------------------------------------------------------------
-----
[INFO] Preparing exec:java
[INFO] No goals needed for project - skipping
[WARNING] POM for 'woodstox:wstx-asl:pom:3.2.7:compile' is invalid.
```

```
Its dependencies (if any) will NOT be available to the current build.
[INFO] [exec:java {execution: default-cli}]
Sending: id: 1000000 on queue: queue://JOBS.delete
Sending: id: 1000001 on queue: queue://JOBS.delete
Sending: id: 1000002 on queue: queue://JOBS.delete
Sending: id: 1000003 on queue: queue://JOBS.delete
Sending: id: 1000004 on queue: queue://JOBS.delete
Sending: id: 1000005 on queue: queue://JOBS.delete
Sending: id: 1000006 on queue: queue://JOBS.delete
Sending: id: 1000007 on queue: queue://JOBS.delete
Sending: id: 1000008 on queue: queue://JOBS.delete
Sending: id: 1000009 on queue: queue://JOBS.delete
Published '10' of '10' job messages
Sending: id: 1000010 on queue: queue://JOBS.delete
Sending: id: 1000011 on queue: queue://JOBS.suspend
...
Published '10' of '30' job messages
...
```

Note that no arguments are necessary to execute the Producer in listing 3.5. The
Publisher class contains two queues to which it publishes named *delete* and *suspend*;
hence, the use of those words in the output. The Producer will continue until it sends
a total of 1,000 messages to the two queues and then it'll shut down.

The third task is to open another terminal or command line and execute the Consumer to consume the messages from the two queues. This command is shown next.

Listing 3.6   Running the job queue consumer

```
[amq-in-action-example-src] $ mvn exec:java \
    -Dexec.mainClass=org.apache.activemq.book.ch3.jobs.Consumer
[INFO] Scanning for projects...
[INFO] Searching repository for plugin with prefix: 'exec'.
[INFO] ------------------------------------------------------------
-----
[INFO] Building ActiveMQ in Action Examples
[INFO]    task-segment: [exec:java]
[INFO] ------------------------------------------------------------
-----
[INFO] Preparing exec:java
[INFO] No goals needed for project - skipping
[WARNING] POM for 'woodstox:wstx-asl:pom:3.2.7:compile' is invalid.

Its dependencies (if any) will NOT be available to the current build.
[INFO] [exec:java {execution: default-cli}]
suspend id:1000003
suspend id:1000010
suspend id:1000012
suspend id:1000013
suspend id:1000015
suspend id:1000022
suspend id:1000025
suspend id:1000027
delete id:1000000
delete id:1000001
```

```
delete id:1000002
delete id:1000004
delete id:1000005
...
```

The Consumer will run fast at first, consuming all the messages already on the queues. When it catches up to where the Producer is in sending the 1,000 messages, the Consumer slows down and keeps up with the Publisher until it completes. When all the messages have been sent and the Producer shuts itself down, you'll need to press CTRL-C in the third terminal where the Consumer is running to shut it down.

This concludes the job queue example. Now you've seen how well ActiveMQ works in a point-to-point messaging scenario.

3.4   *Summary*

This brief introduction to the book examples is meant to be just that—quick and focused. The jobs and portfolio use cases are common in the business world, but they're only two use cases of many available for using messaging. Although these two use cases are meant to demonstrate the two JMS messaging domains at a high level, that doesn't mean that they can't do more. Using the features available in ActiveMQ, these two examples will be changed and adapted as the book progresses. So you'll see much more of these examples throughout the chapters, just with slight variations.

Part 1 of the book took you through an introduction to ActiveMQ, where you gained a quick high-level understanding of ActiveMQ. Then the focus shifted to understanding message-oriented middleware and the JMS spec. Although these topics aren't strictly about only ActiveMQ, each is important when it comes to understanding ActiveMQ. You also walked through the examples that will be used throughout the rest of the book. The subjects in this first part of the book are meant to be a warm-up for diving deeper into ActiveMQ. In part 2, you'll learn about configuring various aspects of ActiveMQ for connectivity, message persistence, and security.

Part 2

Configuring standard ActiveMQ components

Out of the box, so to speak, using ActiveMQ is straightforward: start it up, send some messages, receive some messages. What you don't see in such a use case are the details behind ActiveMQ. Understanding these details and how to customize the configuration is a requirement for more advanced situations. Although ActiveMQ provides a vast set of configuration options, understanding a core set of these options is necessary for the most basic of broker configurations.

Part 2 dives into the critical configuration options in ActiveMQ, including connectivity into the broker, message persistence, and security. These three main topics are the first points of configuration that you'll encounter with ActiveMQ so it's important that you understand them first.

Connecting to ActiveMQ

This chapter covers

- A description and demonstration of ActiveMQ connector URIs
- How to connect your clients to ActiveMQ using transport connectors
- How to create a cluster of ActiveMQ message brokers using network connectors

The main role of a JMS broker such as ActiveMQ is to provide a communication infrastructure for client applications. For that reason, ActiveMQ provides *connectors*, a connectivity mechanism that provides client-to-broker communications (using transport connectors) as well as broker-to-broker communications (using network connectors). ActiveMQ allows client applications to connect using a variety of protocols, but also allows other brokers to create communication channels and to build complex networks of ActiveMQ brokers.

We start this chapter by explaining *connector URIs*, which are used to address the broker. After that, we'll dig into *transport connectors* and explain what protocols clients can use to connect to the ActiveMQ broker.

NOTE   We use the terms *connector* and *protocol* interchangeably. Protocols are general-purpose concepts and connectors are ActiveMQ-specific mechanisms, but every ActiveMQ connector, as you'll see, implements a specific protocol and is named after it. It should be clear from the context whether we're talking about a protocol in general or a specific ActiveMQ connector.

We'll first explain how to configure transport connectors and demonstrate it by adapting the stock portfolio example for use over different connectors, so we can demonstrate them later on. Then we'll be ready to move on to specific connectors. The various transport connectors that allow you to connect to ActiveMQ will be discussed including TCP, SSL, and HTTP. Next, embedded brokers using the VM protocol will be introduced.

Finally some basic concepts of ActiveMQ clustering using *network connectors* will be covered. We'll demonstrate how you can create static networks of brokers using the *static* protocol and how clients can reliably connect to the network of brokers using the *failover* protocol. Dynamic networks using such protocols as *multicast* and *discovery* will also be covered. This section will only introduce basic concepts and protocols used for networks of brokers, whereas more information on them can be found in chapter 10.

4.1   *Understanding connector URIs*

Before discussing the details of connectors and their role in the overall ActiveMQ architecture, it's important to understand *connector URIs*. *Uniform resource identifiers* (URIs), as a concept, aren't new, and you've probably used them over and over again without realizing it. URIs were first introduced for addressing resources on the World Wide Web. The specification (http://mng.bz/8iPP) defines the URI as "a compact string of characters for identifying an abstract or physical resource." Because of the simplicity and flexibility of the URI concept, they found their place in numerous internet services. Web URLs and email addresses we use every day are just some common examples of URIs in practice.

Without going too deep into discussing URIs, let's briefly summarize the URI structure. This will serve as an ideal introduction to URI usage in ActiveMQ in regard to connectors.

Basically, every URI has the following string format:

```
<scheme>:<scheme-specific-part>
```

Consider the following URI:

```
mailto:users@activemq.apache.org
```

Note that the `mailto` scheme is used, followed by an email address to uniquely identify both the service we're going to use and the particular resource within that service.

The most common form of URIs are hierarchical URIs, which take the following form:

```
<scheme>://<authority><path><?query>
```

This kind of URI is used by web browsers to identify websites. It's a type of URI known as a *URL* (Uniform Resource Locator). Below is an example:

```
http://www.nabble.com/forum/NewTopic.jtp?forum=2356
```

This URL uses the `http` scheme and contains both `path` and `query` elements which are used to specify additional parameters.

Because of their flexibility and simplicity, URIs are used in ActiveMQ to address specific brokers through different types of connectors. If we go back to the examples discussed in chapter 3, you can see that the following URI was used to create a connection to the broker:

```
tcp://localhost:61616
```

This is a typical hierarchical URI used in ActiveMQ, which translates to *"create a TCP connection to the localhost on port 61616."*

ActiveMQ connectors using this kind of simple hierarchical URI pattern are sometimes referred to as *low-level connectors* and are used to implement basic network communication protocols. Connector URIs use the scheme part to identify the underlying network protocol, the path element to identify a network resource (usually host and port), and the query element to specify additional configuration parameters for the connector. The anatomy of a URI is shown in figure 4.1. This URI extends the previous example by also telling the broker to log all commands sent over this connector (the trace=true part). This is just one example of an option that's available on the TCP transport.

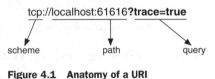

Figure 4.1 Anatomy of a URI

The failover transport in ActiveMQ supports automatic reconnection as well as the ability to connect to another broker just in case the broker to which a client is currently connected becomes unavailable. As will be discussed in chapter 10, ActiveMQ makes this easy to use and configure through the use of *composite* URIs. These composite URIs are used to configure such automatic reconnection. In figure 4.2, you can see an example of a typical composite URI.

Note that the scheme part or the URI now identifies the protocol being used (the static protocol will be described later in this chapter) and the scheme-specific part contains one or more low-level URIs that will be used to create a connection. Of course, every low-level URI and the larger composite URI can contain the query part providing specific configuration options for the particular connector.

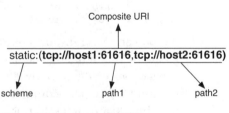

Figure 4.2 A composite URI

> **NOTE** Since composite URIs tend to be complex, users are often tempted to insert white spaces to make them more readable. Such white space is not allowed, since the URI specification (and its standard Java implementation) doesn't allow it. This is a common ActiveMQ configuration mistake, so be careful not to put white space in your URIs.

Now that you have some familiarity with ActiveMQ URI basics, let's move on to discuss various connectors supported by ActiveMQ. In the rest of this chapter, we'll discuss transport connectors and network connectors and how to configure them.

4.2   *Transport connectors*

In order to exchange messages, producers and consumers (clients) need to connect to the broker. This client-to-broker communication is performed through *transport connectors*. ActiveMQ provides an impressive list of protocols clients can use to exchange messages. The requirements of ActiveMQ users in terms of connectivity are diverse. Some users focus on performance, others on security, and so on. ActiveMQ tries to cover all these aspects and provide a connector for every use case.

In this section you'll learn how transport connectors are configured in the ActiveMQ configuration files and adapt the stock portfolio example to demonstrate various connectors. In the following sections, we'll go through protocols available for connecting to the broker over the network, as well as introduce the concept of the *embedded broker* and *Virtual Machine Protocol* used for communicating with brokers inside your application (a topic that will be continued in chapter 7).

4.2.1   *Configuring transport connectors*

From the broker's perspective, the transport connector is a mechanism used to accept and listen to connections from clients. If you take a look at the ActiveMQ demo configuration file (`conf/activemq-demo.xml`), you'll see the configuration snippet for transport connectors similar to the following example:

```
<transportConnectors>
  <transportConnector name="openwire" uri="tcp://localhost:61616"
    discoveryUri="multicast://default"/>
  <transportConnector name="ssl"      uri="ssl://localhost:61617"/>
  <transportConnector name="stomp"    uri="stomp://localhost:61613"/>
  <transportConnector name="xmpp"     uri="xmpp://localhost:61222"/>
</transportConnectors>
```

As you can see, transport connectors are defined within the `<transportConnectors>` element. You define particular connectors with the appropriate nested `<transportConnector>` element. ActiveMQ simultaneously supports many protocols listening on different ports. The configuration for a connector must uniquely define the name and the URI attributes. In this case, the URI defines the network protocol and optional parameters through which ActiveMQ will be exposed for connectivity. The `discoveryUri` attribute as shown on the OpenWire connector is optional and will be discussed further in section 4.3.1.

The preceding snippet defines four transport connectors. Upon starting up ActiveMQ using such a configuration file, you'll see the following log in the console as these connectors start up:

```
INFO  TransportServerThreadSupport  - Listening for connections at:
  tcp://localhost:61616
```

```
INFO  TransportConnector              - Connector openwire Started
INFO  TransportServerThreadSupport    - Listening for connections at:
  ssl://localhost:61617
INFO  TransportConnector              - Connector ssl Started
INFO  TransportServerThreadSupport    - Listening for connections at:
  stomp://localhost:61613
INFO  TransportConnector              - Connector stomp Started
INFO  TransportServerThreadSupport    - Listening for connections at:
  xmpp://localhost:61222
INFO  TransportConnector              - Connector xmpp Started
```

From the client's perspective, the transport connector URI is used to create a connection to the broker in order to send and receive messages. Sending and receiving messages will be discussed in detail in chapter 7, but the following code snippet should be enough to demonstrate the usage of the transport connector URIs in Java applications:

```
ActiveMQConnectionFactory factory =
  new ActiveMQConnectionFactory("tcp://localhost:61616");
Connection connection = factory.createConnection();
connection.start();
Session session =
  connection.createSession(false, Session.AUTO_ACKNOWLEDGE);
```

Note in the preceding example that the transport connector URIs defined in ActiveMQ configuration are used by the client application to create a connection to the broker. In this case, the URI for the TCP transport is used and is shown in bold text.

> **NOTE** The important thing to know is that we can use the query part of the URI to configure connection parameters both on the server and client sides. Usually most of the parameters apply both for client and server sides of the connection, but some of them are specific to one or the other, so be sure you check the protocol reference before using the particular query parameter.

With this basic understanding of configuring transport connectors, it's important to become aware of and understand the available transport connectors in ActiveMQ. But before we start explaining particular connectors, we must first adapt our stock portfolio example so it can be used with different transport connectors.

4.2.2 *Adapting the stock portfolio example*

Chapter 3 introduced a stock portfolio example that uses ActiveMQ to publish and consume stock exchange data. There, we used the fixed standard connector URI since we wanted to make those introductory examples as simple as possible. In this chapter, we'll explain all protocols and demonstrate them by running the stock portfolio example using each of them. For that reason, we need to modify the stock portfolio example so it will work using any of the protocols.

Listing 4.1 is a modified version of the `main()` method from the stock portfolio publisher.

Listing 4.1   Modifying stock portfolio publisher to support various connector URIs

```
public static void main(String[] args) throws JMSException {
  if (args.length == 0) {
   System.err.println("Please define a connection URI!");
   return;
  }

  Publisher publisher = new Publisher(args[0]);                ⟵ Define
                                                                 connection URI
  String[] topics = new String[args.length - 1];                ⟵ Create
  System.arraycopy(args, 1, topics, 0, args.length - 1);    ⟵    array for
      while (total < 1000) {                                      topic
          for (int i = 0; i < count; i++) {            Extract    names
              publisher.sendMessage(topics);         topics from
          }                                          arguments
          total += count;
          System.out.println(
              "Published '" + count + "' of '"
            + total + "' price messages"
          );
          try {
            Thread.sleep(1000);
          } catch (InterruptedException x) {
          }
      }
     publisher.close();
 }
```

The preceding code ensures that the connector URI is passed as the first argument and extracts topic names from the rest of the arguments passed to the application. Now the stock portfolio publisher can be run with the following command:

```
$ mvn exec:java -Dexec.mainClass=org.apache.activemq.book.ch4.Publisher \
-Dexec.args="tcp://localhost:61616 CSCO ORCL"

...

Sending: {price=65.713356601409, stock=JAVA, offer=65.779069958011,
up=true}
  on destination: topic://STOCKS.JAVA
Sending: {price=66.071605671946, stock=JAVA, offer=66.137677277617,
up=true}
  on destination: topic://STOCKS.JAVA
Sending: {price=65.929035001620, stock=JAVA, offer=65.994964036622,
up=false}
  on destination: topic://STOCKS.JAVA

...
```

Note that one more argument has been added to the publisher: the URL to be used to connect to the appropriate broker.

The same principle can be used to modify the stock portfolio consumer. In the following listing, you'll find the stock portfolio consumer's `main()` method modified to accept the connection URI as a first parameter.

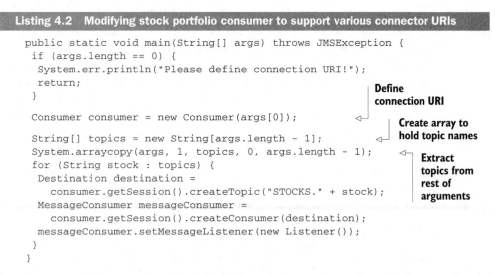

Listing 4.2   Modifying stock portfolio consumer to support various connector URIs

```
public static void main(String[] args) throws JMSException {
  if (args.length == 0) {
   System.err.println("Please define connection URI!");
   return;
  }

  Consumer consumer = new Consumer(args[0]);

  String[] topics = new String[args.length - 1];
  System.arraycopy(args, 1, topics, 0, args.length - 1);
  for (String stock : topics) {
   Destination destination =
     consumer.getSession().createTopic("STOCKS." + stock);
   MessageConsumer messageConsumer =
     consumer.getSession().createConsumer(destination);
   messageConsumer.setMessageListener(new Listener());
  }
 }
}
```

- **Define connection URI**
- **Create array to hold topic names**
- **Extract topics from rest of arguments**

In order to achieve the same functionality as in the chapter 3 example, you should run the consumer with an extra URI argument. The following example shows how to do this:

```
$ mvn exec:java -Dexec.mainClass=org.apache.activemq.book.ch4.Consumer \
-Dexec.args="tcp://localhost:61616 CSCO ORCL"

...

ORCL 65.71 65.78 up
ORCL 66.07 66.14 up
ORCL 65.93 65.99 down
CSCO 23.30 23.33 up

...
```

Note that the message flow between the producer and the consumer is the same as in the original example. With these changes, the examples are now ready to be run using a variety of supported protocols. Let's now dig into the particular transport connectors. In the following section we'll see what options you have if you want to connect to the broker over the network.

4.3   Connecting to ActiveMQ over the network

The most common usage scenario is to run ActiveMQ as a standalone Java application. This implies that clients (producer and consumer applications) will use some of the network protocols to access the broker's destinations. In this section, we'll describe available network protocols you can use to achieve client-to-broker communication.

We'll start with default *TCP connector*, which is most widely used and provides optimal performance. Next we'll dig into the *NIO connector*, which also uses TCP network protocol underneath, but additionally provides a bit better scalability than TCP connector since it uses the NIO Java API. The UDP network protocol is often used on the internet, so *UDP connector* is next on our list. UDP protocol introduces some performance advantages, sacrificing reliability compared to the TCP protocol. The same applies to appropriate ActiveMQ connectors, so a UDP connector can offer some performance advantages over the TCP connector, but it's still not often used because of the unreliability it introduces (as explained in more detail later). The SSL connector can be used to establish a secure connection to the broker, and finally we'll show you how to communicate with the broker using HTTP. Of course, in every section we'll discuss the pros and cons of every protocol. Therefore, you may want to consider reading just the subsections that interest you at the moment and then move along to other chapters. Table 4.1 contains a summarization of the connectors with a brief description.

Now, let's start with the default TCP protocol.

Table 4.1 Summary of network protocols used for client-broker communication

Protocol	Description
TCP	Default network protocol for most use cases.
NIO	Consider NIO protocol if you need to provide better scalability for connections from producers and consumers to the broker.
UDP	Consider UDP protocol when you need to deal with the firewall between clients and the broker.
SSL	Consider SSL when you want to secure communication between clients and the broker.
HTTP(S)	Consider HTTP(S) when you need to deal with the firewall between clients and the broker.
VM	Although not a network protocol per se, consider VM protocol when your broker and clients communicate with a broker that is embedded in the same Java Virtual Machine (JVM).

4.3.1 *Transmission Control Protocol (TCP)*

Transmission Control Protocol (TCP) is today probably as important to humans as electricity. As one of the fundamental internet protocols, we use it for almost all of our online communication. It's used as an underlying network protocol for a wide range of internet services such as email and the web, for example.

Hopefully you are already familiar with the basics of TCP, but let's start our discussion of TCP by quoting from the specification, RFC 793 (http://mng.bz/Bns2):

> *The Transmission Control Protocol (TCP) is intended for use as a highly reliable host-to-host protocol between hosts in packet-switched computer communication networks, and in interconnected systems of such networks.*

Since the broker and client applications are network hosts trying to communicate in a reliable manner, it's easy to see why TCP is an ideal network protocol for a JMS implementation. So it shouldn't come as a surprise that the *TCP transport connector* is the most frequently used ActiveMQ connector.

Before exchanging messages over the network, we need to serialize them to a suitable form. Messages must be serialized in and out of a byte sequence to be sent over the wire using what's known as a *wire protocol*. The default wire protocol used in ActiveMQ is called *OpenWire*. The protocol specification can be found on the ActiveMQ website (http://mng.bz/u2eT). The OpenWire protocol isn't specific to the TCP network transport and can be used with other network protocols. Its main purpose is to be efficient and allow fast exchange of messages over the network. Furthermore, a standardized and open protocol such as OpenWire allows native ActiveMQ clients to be developed for various programming environments. This topic and a description of other wire level protocols available for ActiveMQ are covered in chapter 9.

As we've seen in previous sections, a default broker configuration starts the TCP transport listening for client connections on port 61616. The TCP connector URI uses the following syntax:

```
tcp://hostname:port?key=value&key=value
```

Please note that the bold portion of the URI denotes the required part. Any key/value pairs to the right of the question mark are optional and separated by an ampersand.

We won't discuss all transport options for appropriate protocols in this section or the sections that follow. This kind of material is best presented via the online reference pages. An up-to-date reference for the TCP connector can be found on the ActiveMQ website (http://mng.bz/ngU2).

The following configuration snippet provides an example of using the TCP connector in the ActiveMQ configuration file:

```
<transportConnectors>
    <transportConnector name="tcp"
      uri="tcp://localhost:61616?trace=true"/>
</transportConnectors>
```

Note that the `trace` option has been added to the transport connector URI. This option instructs the broker to log all commands sent over this connector and can be helpful for debugging purposes. We have it here as an example of a transport tuning feature using a transport option. For more information on using the `trace` option for debugging, see chapter 14.

IMPORTANT After changing the configuration file, ActiveMQ must be restarted for the changes to take effect.

The previous section outlined the use of this protocol in the client applications to connect to the broker. Just for reference, the following example shows how to run the consumer using the TCP transport connector:

```
$ mvn exec:java -Dexec.mainClass=org.apache.activemq.book.ch4.Consumer \
-Dexec.args="tcp://localhost:61616 CSCO ORCL"

...
```

```
ORCL 65.71 65.78 up
ORCL 66.07 66.14 up
ORCL 65.93 65.99 down
CSCO 23.30 23.33 up

...
```

Some of the benefits of the TCP transport connector include the following:

- *Efficiency*—Since this connector uses the OpenWire protocol to convert messages to a stream of bytes (and back), it's very efficient in terms of network usage and performance.
- *Availability*—TCP is one of the most widespread network protocols and has been supported in Java from the early days, so it's almost certainly supported on your platform of choice.
- *Reliability*—The TCP protocol ensures that messages won't be lost on the network (due to glitches, for example).

Now let's explore some alternatives to the TCP transport connector.

4.3.2   *New I/O API protocol (NIO)*

The *New I/O (NIO) API* was introduced in Java SE 1.4 to supplement the existing (standard) I/O API used in Java until then. Despite the prefix *new* in its name, NIO was never meant to be a replacement for the traditional Java I/O API. Its purpose was to provide an alternative approach to network programming and access to some low-level I/O operations of modern operating systems. The most prominent features of NIO are selectors and nonblocking I/O programming, allowing developers to use the same resources to handle more network clients and generally heavier loads on their servers.

From a client perspective, the *NIO transport connector* is practically the same as the standard TCP connector, in terms of its use of TCP as the underlying network protocol and OpenWire as the message serialization protocol. The only difference is under the covers with the implementation of the transport, where the NIO transport connector is implemented using the NIO API. This makes the NIO transport connector more suitable in situations where

- *You have a large number of clients you want to connect to the broker*—Generally, the number of clients that can connect to the broker is limited by the number of threads supported by the operating system. Since the NIO connector implementation starts fewer threads per client than the TCP connector, you should consider using NIO in case TCP doesn't meet your needs.
- *You have a heavy network traffic to the broker*—Again, the NIO connector generally offers better performance than the TCP connector (in terms of using less resources on the broker side), so you can consider using it when you find that the TCP connector doesn't meet your needs.

At this point it's important to note that performance tuning of ActiveMQ isn't just related to choosing the right connector. Many other aspects of ActiveMQ can be tuned, including the use of a network of brokers topology (see chapter 10) and setting various options for brokers, producers, and consumers (see chapter 13).

The URI syntax for the NIO connector is practically the same as that of the TCP connector URI syntax. The only difference is the use of the nio scheme instead of tcp, as shown:

nio://hostname:port?key=value

Now take a look at the configuration snippet. The NIO part is in bold.

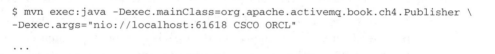

Listing 4.3   Configuring the NIO transport connector

```
<transportConnectors>
   <transportConnector
           name="tcp"
           uri="tcp://localhost:61616?trace=true" />               tcp connector
                                                                    listens on
                                                                    port 61616
   <transportConnector
          name="nio"
          uri="nio:localhost:61618?trace=true" />                  nio connector
                                                                    listens on port 61618
</transportConnectors>
```

Now run the stock portfolio example, but this time you'll connect the publisher and consumer using different transport connectors. As figure 4.3 shows, the publisher will send messages using the NIO transport connector, whereas the consumer will receive those messages using the TCP transport connector.

To achieve this, the stock portfolio publisher should be run using the following command:

```
$ mvn exec:java -Dexec.mainClass=org.apache.activemq.book.ch4.Publisher \
-Dexec.args="nio://localhost:61618 CSCO ORCL"

...

Sending: {price=65.713356601409, stock=JAVA, offer=65.779069958011, up=true}
  on destination: topic://STOCKS.JAVA
Sending: {price=66.071605671946, stock=JAVA, offer=66.137677277617, up=true}
```

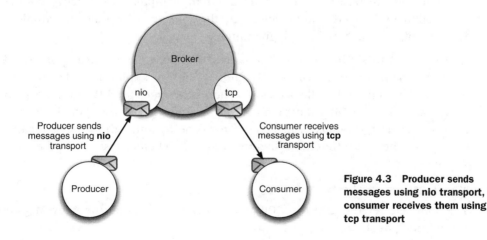

Figure 4.3   Producer sends messages using nio transport, consumer receives them using tcp transport

```
  on destination: topic://STOCKS.JAVA
Sending: {price=65.929035001620, stock=JAVA, offer=65.994964036622, up=false}

  on destination: topic://STOCKS.JAVA

. . .
```

Note that the `nio` scheme is used in the connection URI to specify the NIO connector.

The consumer should use the TCP connector as shown below:

```
$ mvn exec:java -Dexec.mainClass=org.apache.activemq.book.ch4.Consumer \
-Dexec.args="tcp://localhost:61616 CSCO ORCL"

. . .

ORCL 65.71 65.78 up
ORCL 66.07 66.14 up
ORCL 65.93 65.99 down
CSCO 23.30 23.33 up

. . .
```

After both the consumer and producer are started, you'll notice that messages are exchanged between applications as expected. The fact that they are using different connectors to communicate with the broker plays no role in this exchange.

4.3.3   *User Datagram Protocol (UDP)*

User Datagram Protocol (UDP) along with TCP make up the core of internet protocols. The purpose of these two protocols is identical—to send and receive data packets (datagrams) over the network. But there are two main differences between them:

- *TCP is a stream-oriented protocol,* which means that the order of data packets is guaranteed. There's no chance for data packets to be duplicated or arrive out of order. UDP, on the other hand, doesn't guarantee packet ordering, so a receiver can expect data packets to be duplicated or arrive out of order.
- *TCP also guarantees reliability of packet delivery,* meaning that packets won't be lost during the transport. This is ensured by maintaining an active connection between the sender and receiver. On the contrary, UDP is a connectionless protocol, so it can't make such guarantees.

As a result of these differences, TCP is used in applications that require reliability (such as email), whereas UDP usually finds it place in applications that require fast data transfers and can handle occasional packet loss (such as VoIP or online gaming).

You can use the UDP protocol to connect to ActiveMQ by using the UDP transport connector. The URI syntax of this connector is pretty much the same as for the TCP connector. The only difference is the use of the `udp` scheme, as shown in the following snippet:

udp://hostname:port?key=value

The complete reference of the UDP protocol can be found at the ActiveMQ website (http://mng.bz/1i4g).

Comparing the TCP and UDP transports

When considering the TCP and the UDP transports, questions arise that compare these two protocols. When should you use the UDP transport instead of the TCP transport? There are basically two such situations where the UDP transport offers an advantage:

- The broker is located behind a firewall that you don't control and you can access it only over UDP ports.
- You're using time-sensitive messages and you want to eliminate network transport delay as much as possible.

But there are also a couple of pitfalls regarding the UDP connector:

- Since UDP is unreliable, you can end up losing some of the messages, so your application should know how to deal with this situation.
- Network packets transmitted between clients and brokers aren't just messages, but can also contain so-called *control commands*. If some of these control commands are lost due to UDP unreliability, the JMS connection could be endangered.

Now let's configure ActiveMQ to use both TCP and UDP transports on different ports. Here's an example of such a configuration; the UDP part is in bold:

```
<transportConnectors>
   <transportConnector
           name="tcp"
           uri="tcp://localhost:61616?trace=true"/>
   <transportConnector
        name="udp"
        uri="udp://localhost:61618?trace=true" />
</transportConnectors>
```

Note that there are two separate transport connectors on different ports.

To run a stock portfolio publisher using the UDP protocol, use the following command:

```
$ mvn exec:java -Dexec.mainClass=org.apache.activemq.book.ch4.Publisher \
-Dexec.args="udp://localhost:61618 CSCO ORCL"

...

Sending: {price=65.713356601409, stock=JAVA, offer=65.779069958011, up=true}
  on destination: topic://STOCKS.JAVA
Sending: {price=66.071605671946, stock=JAVA, offer=66.137677277617, up=true}
  on destination: topic://STOCKS.JAVA
Sending: {price=65.929035001620, stock=JAVA, offer=65.994964036622, up=false}
  on destination: topic://STOCKS.JAVA

...
```

The consumer can be run using the TCP protocol with the following command:

```
$ mvn exec:java -Dexec.mainClass=org.apache.activemq.book.ch4.Consumer \
-Dexec.args="tcp://localhost:61616 CSCO ORCL"
```

```
. . .
ORCL 65.71 65.78 up
ORCL 66.07 66.14 up
ORCL 65.93 65.99 down
CSCO 23.30 23.33 up

. . .
```

As expected, the behavior of the overall system is the same as it was in the original example when only the TCP transport connector was used. This is due to the fact that the reliability of a local network is typically very good and there is generally no packet loss.

4.3.4   *Secure Sockets Layer Protocol (SSL)*

Imagine yourself in a situation where you need to expose the broker over an unsecured network and you need data privacy. The same requirement emerged when the web outgrew its academic roots and was considered for corporate usage. Sending plain data over TCP became unacceptable, and a solution had to be found. The solution for secure data transfers was the *Secure Sockets Layer* (SSL), a protocol designed to transmit encrypted data over the TCP network protocol. It uses a pair of keys (one private and one public) to ensure a secure communication channel. ActiveMQ provides the *SSL transport connector*, which adds an SSL layer over the TCP communication channel, providing encrypted communication between brokers and clients. As always with SSL, keys and certificates are involved in configuring it, so this section is longer, as we'll dig into this configuration in detail.

The URI syntax for this protocol is

ssl://hostname:port?key=value

Since the SSL transport is based on the TCP transport, configuration options are the same. More information for using the SSL connector is available on the ActiveMQ website (http://mng.bz/s8I2).

ActiveMQ uses the *Java Secure Socket Extension* (JSSE) to implement its SSL functionality. Since its detailed description is out of the scope of this book, please refer to the online information for JSSE (http://mng.bz/7TYe) before proceeding to the rest of this section.

To configure the ActiveMQ broker to use the SSL transport, the first thing to do is configure the ActiveMQ SSL transport.

Change the <transportConnectors> element in the ${ACTIVEMQ_HOME}/conf/activemq.xml file as shown:

```
<transportConnectors>
  <transportConnector name="ssl" uri="ssl://localhost:61617?trace=true" />
</transportConnectors>
```

But the SSL transport needs a few more items in order to work properly. Such required items include SSL certificates for successful SSL communication. Basically, JSSE defines two types of files for storing keys and certificates. The first are so-called *keystores,* which hold your own private certificates with their corresponding private keys. Trusted certificates of other entities (applications) are stored in *truststores.* To actually get the SSL transport working properly, the additional required items are discussed in detail in the next two sections.

A note about the default keystores and truststores in ActiveMQ

The default keystores and truststores that are distributed with ActiveMQ are located in the ${ACTIVEMQ_HOME}/conf/directory. In that directory, you'll find a keystore containing a default broker certificate (broker.ks) as well as a truststore used by the broker to hold trusted client certificates (broker.ts). By default, ActiveMQ will use broker.ks and broker.ts for the SSL transport connector. Please note that *the default keystore and truststore are for demonstration purposes only and shouldn't be used for the production deployment of ActiveMQ.* For production use, it's highly recommended that you create your own keystore and truststore.

For more information on configuring SSL, see chapter 6.

Now that you understand all the necessary elements needed for successful SSL communication, it's time to connect to the secured transport. First, you'll connect to the broker that's secured with its default certificate. Next, you'll walk through the procedure for creating your own certificates and running a broker and clients with them.

USING SSL

First a small experiment to see what happens when you try to connect to a broker using SSL and without providing any other SSL-related parameters. Connecting the stock portfolio consumer by changing the transport to use SSL without creating the proper stores will cause errors. Here's an example of simply changing the transport:

```
$ mvn exec:java -Dexec.mainClass=org.apache.activemq.book.ch4.Consumer \
-Dexec.args="ssl://localhost:61617 CSCO ORCL"
```

Without creating and denoting the proper keystore and truststore, you can expect to see the following exceptions:

```
WARNING: Async exception with no exception listener:
  javax.net.ssl.SSLHandshakeException:
sun.security.validator.ValidatorException: PKIX path building failed:
  sun.security.provider.certpath.SunCertPathBuilderException:
unable to find valid certification path to requested target
javax.net.ssl.SSLHandshakeException:
  sun.security.validator.ValidatorException:
PKIX path building failed:
  sun.security.provider.certpath.SunCertPathBuilderException:
unable to find valid certification path to requested target
```

Also, in the broker's log you'll see the following error:

```
ERROR TransportConnector
  - Could not accept connection : Received fatal alert: certificate_unknown
```

These errors mean that the SSL connection couldn't be established. This is a generic error all clients will receive when trying to connect to the untrusted broker (without the proper keystore and truststore).

When using JSSE, you must provide some SSL parameters using the appropriate system properties. In order to successfully connect to the broker via SSL, we must provide the keystore, the keystore password, and the truststore to be used. This is accomplished using the following system properties:

- javax.net.ssl.keyStore—Defines which keystore the client should use
- javax.net.ssl.keyStorePassword—Defines an appropriate password for the keystore
- javax.net.ssl.trustStore—Defines an appropriate truststore the client should use

Now take a look at the following example of starting the stock portfolio publisher using the default client certificate stores distributed with ActiveMQ:

```
$ mvn \
 -Djavax.net.ssl.keyStore=${ACTIVEMQ_HOME}/conf/client.ks \
 -Djavax.net.ssl.keyStorePassword=password \
 -Djavax.net.ssl.trustStore=${ACTIVEMQ_HOME}/conf/client.ts \
 exec:java -Dexec.mainClass=org.apache.activemq.book.ch4.Publisher \
 -Dexec.args="ssl://localhost:61617 CSCO ORCL"

...

Sending: {price=65.713356601409, stock=JAVA, offer=65.779069958011, up=true}
  on destination: topic://STOCKS.JAVA
Sending: {price=66.071605671946, stock=JAVA, offer=66.137677277617, up=true}
  on destination: topic://STOCKS.JAVA
Sending: {price=65.929035001620, stock=JAVA, offer=65.994964036622, up=false}
  on destination: topic://STOCKS.JAVA

...
```

Note the use of the JSSE system properties in bold. These properties provide the necessary keystore, keystore password, and truststore. After providing these necessary SSL-related parameters, the publisher will connect successfully to the broker as intended without error. Of course, if the client isn't located on the same computer as your broker, you'll need to copy these files and adapt the paths appropriately.

Similarly, the consumer can be run using the following command:

```
$ mvn \
 -Djavax.net.ssl.keyStore=${ACTIVEMQ_HOME}/conf/client.ks \
 -Djavax.net.ssl.keyStorePassword=password \
 -Djavax.net.ssl.trustStore=${ACTIVEMQ_HOME}/conf/client.ts \
 exec:java -Dexec.mainClass=org.apache.activemq.book.ch4.Consumer \
 -Dexec.args="ssl://localhost:61617 CSCO ORCL"

...

ORCL 65.71 65.78 up
ORCL 66.07 66.14 up
```

```
ORCL 65.93 65.99 down
CSCO 23.30 23.33 up
```

. . .

Again, note the use of the JSSE system properties in bold. Now both clients can communicate with the broker using the encrypted network channels provided by the SSL transport connector.

Working with the default certificate, keystore, and truststore is okay for development purposes, but for a production system, it's highly recommended that you create and use your own certificates. You can even disable ciphers that you may not be using. In most cases, you'll need to purchase an appropriate SSL certificate from the trusted certificate authority.

CREATING YOUR OWN SSL RESOURCES

For development purposes, you'll want to create your own self-signed certificates. The rest of this section will lead you through the process of creating and sharing self-signed certificates. For that purpose the keytool will be used—the command-line tool for managing keystores that's distributed with Java.

First, you must create a keystore and a certificate for the broker. Here's an example of this using the keytool that comes with the JDK:

```
$ keytool -genkey -alias broker -keyalg RSA -keystore mybroker.ks
Enter keystore password:  test123
What is your first and last name?
  [Unknown]:  Dejan Bosanac
What is the name of your organizational unit?
  [Unknown]:  Chapter 4
What is the name of your organization?
  [Unknown]:  ActiveMQ in Action
What is the name of your City or Locality?
  [Unknown]:  Belgrade
What is the name of your State or Province?
  [Unknown]:
What is the two-letter country code for this unit?
  [Unknown]:  RS
Is CN=Dejan Bosanac, OU=Chapter 3, O=ActiveMQ in Action,
  L=Belgrade, ST=Unknown, C=RS correct?
  [no]:  yes

Enter key password for <broker>
 (RETURN if same as keystore password):
```

The keytool application prompts you to enter certificate data and create a keystore with the certificate in it. In this case we've created a keystore file named mybroker.ks with the password test123.

The next step is to export this certificate from the keystore, so it can be shared with the broker's clients. This is done using the following command:

```
$ keytool -export -alias broker -keystore mybroker.ks -file mybroker_cert
Enter keystore password:  test123
Certificate stored in file <mybroker_cert>
```

This step creates a file named mybroker_cert, containing a broker certificate.

Now you must create a client keystore with the appropriate certificate using a command similar to the one that was used previously to create the broker's keystore:

```
$ keytool -genkey -alias client -keyalg RSA -keystore myclient.ks
What is your first and last name?
  [Unknown]:  Dejan Bosanac
What is the name of your organizational unit?
  [Unknown]:  Chapter 4
What is the name of your organization?
  [Unknown]:  ActiveMQ in Action
What is the name of your City or Locality?
  [Unknown]:  Belgrade
What is the name of your State or Province?
  [Unknown]:
What is the two-letter country code for this unit?
  [Unknown]:  RS
Is CN=Dejan Bosanac, OU=Chapter 3, O=ActiveMQ in Action,
  L=Belgrade, ST=Unknown, C=RS correct?
  [no]:  yes

Enter key password for <client>
  (RETURN if same as keystore password):
```

The result of this command is the myclient.ks file with the appropriate certificate for the client side. Finally, the client truststore must be created and the broker's certificate must be imported into it. Again, keytool is used to achieve this with the following command:

```
$ keytool -import -alias broker -keystore myclient.ts -file mybroker_cert
Enter keystore password:  test123
Owner: CN=Dejan Bosanac, OU=Chapter 3, O=ActiveMQ in Action,
  L=Belgrade, ST=Unknown, C=RS
Issuer: CN=Dejan Bosanac, OU=Chapter 3, O=ActiveMQ in Action,
  L=Belgrade, ST=Unknown, C=RS
Serial number: 484fdc8a
Valid from: Wed Jun 11 16:09:14 CEST 2008 until: Tue Sep 09 16:09:14 CEST 2008
Certificate fingerprints:
  MD5:   04:66:F2:AA:71:3A:9E:0A:3C:1B:83:C0:23:DC:EC:6F
  SHA1:  FB:FA:BB:45:DC:05:9D:AE:C3:BE:5D:86:86:0F:76:84:43:C7:36:D3
Trust this certificate? [no]:  yes
Certificate was added to keystore
```

With this step, all the necessary stores were created and the broker certificate was imported into the keystore. Now the stock portfolio example can use them.

Remember to start the broker using the newly created certificate. One way to do this is to replace the default keystore files and the broker cert in the conf directory with the ones that were just created. For example, if you want to use certificates that come with the example source code, you'd do something like this:

```
$ cp src/main/resources/org/apache/activemq/book/ch4/mybroker.ks \
    ${ACTIVEMQ_HOME}/conf/broker.ks
$ cp src/main/resources/org/apache/activemq/book/ch4/myclient.ks \
```

```
    ${ACTIVEMQ_HOME}/conf/client.ks
$ cp src/main/resources/org/apache/activemq/book/ch4/myclient.ts \
    ${ACTIVEMQ_HOME}/conf/client.ts
```

Another way is to pass the SSL-related system properties to the command used to start our broker. For that we need first to copy certificates with their original names (with prefix my in the name) to the conf/ directory

```
$ cp src/main/resources/org/apache/activemq/book/ch4/mybroker.ks \
    ${ACTIVEMQ_HOME}/conf/
$ cp src/main/resources/org/apache/activemq/book/ch4/myclient.ks \
    ${ACTIVEMQ_HOME}/conf/
$ cp src/main/resources/org/apache/activemq/book/ch4/myclient.ts \
    ${ACTIVEMQ_HOME}/conf/
```

So now we can pass the system property and use a keystore other than default one:

```
${ACTIVEMQ_HOME}/bin/activemq console \
 -Djavax.net.ssl.keyStorePassword=test123 \
 -Djavax.net.ssl.keyStore=${ACTIVEMQ_HOME}/conf/mybroker.ks
```

Finally, we can achieve the same thing with the `<sslContext/>` element in the ActiveMQ configuration file, as shown here:

```
<broker xmlns="http://activemq.apache.org/schema/core"
 brokerName="localhost"
 dataDirectory="${activemq.base}/data">
 <sslContext>
  <sslContext
   keyStore="file:${activemq.base}/conf/mybroker.ks"
   keyStorePassword="test123"/>
 </sslContext>
 <transportConnectors>
  <transportConnector name="ssl"
   uri="ssl://localhost:61617" />
 </transportConnectors>
</broker>
```

and start the broker in the usual manner:

```
${ACTIVEMQ_HOME}/bin/activemq console
 xbean:src/main/resources/org/apache/activemq/book/ch4/activemq-ssl.xml
...
Loading message broker from:
 xbean:src/main/resources/org/apache/activemq/book/ch4/activemq-ssl.xml
 INFO | Using Persistence Adapter:
 AMQPersistenceAdapter(/workspace/apache-activemq-5.3.0/data/localhost)
 INFO | AMQStore starting using directory:
 /workspace/apache-activemq-5.3.0/data/localhost
 INFO | Kaha Store using data directory
 /workspace/apache-activemq-5.3.0/data/localhost/kr-store/state
 INFO | Active data files: []
 INFO | ActiveMQ 5.3.0 JMS Message Broker (localhost) is starting
 INFO | For help or more information please see: http://activemq.apache.org/
 INFO | Kaha Store using data directory
 /workspace/apache-activemq-5.3.0/data/localhost/kr-store/data
```

```
INFO | JMX consoles can connect to
 service:jmx:rmi:///jndi/rmi://localhost:1099/jmxrmi
INFO | Listening for connections at: ssl://localhost:61617
INFO | Connector ssl Started
INFO | ActiveMQ JMS Message Broker
 (localhost, ID:dejan-bosanacs-macbook-pro.local-52935-1265550444721-0:0)
 started
...
```

Now let's see how to reflect these same changes to the clients. If you try to run the client applications with the old certificate file, you'll get the unknown_certificate exception, just as when the client attempted to access the broker without using any certificate. So you'll have to update the command like the following:

```
$ mvn \
 -Djavax.net.ssl.keyStore=${ACTIVEMQ_HOME}/conf/myclient.ks \
 -Djavax.net.ssl.keyStorePassword=test123 \
 -Djavax.net.ssl.trustStore=${ACTIVEMQ_HOME}/conf/myclient.ts \
 exec:java -Dexec.mainClass=org.apache.activemq.book.ch4.Publisher \
 -Dexec.args="ssl://localhost:61617 CSCO ORCL"

...

Sending: {price=65.713356601409, stock=JAVA, offer=65.779069958011, up=true}
  on destination: topic://STOCKS.JAVA
Sending: {price=66.071605671946, stock=JAVA, offer=66.137677277617, up=true}
  on destination: topic://STOCKS.JAVA
Sending: {price=65.929035001620, stock=JAVA, offer=65.994964036622, up=false}
  on destination: topic://STOCKS.JAVA

...
```

The command instructs the publisher to use the newly created client stores. After these changes, the stock portfolio application works again.

ENABLING AND DISABLING SSL CIPHERS

The SSL cipher suites for the ActiveMQ SSL transport are provided by the JVM. For specific information about these cipher suites, see the documentation on the Sun JSSE provider (http://mng.bz/7TYe). The Sun JSSE provider supports a long list of cipher suites, and these are utilized in their default preference order. In some situations, there can be a need to disable certain ciphers. Examples of such situations include the discovery of a vulnerability in a particular cipher or a requirement to support only certain ciphers. To make it easy to enable/disable cipher suites, starting in ActiveMQ 5.4.0, a new option for the SSL transport named `transport.enabledCipherSuites` is available. Here's an example of this new option:

```
<transportConnectors>
   <transportConnector
   name="ssl"
   uri="ssl://localhost:61617?
 transport.enabledCipherSuites=SSL_RSA_WITH_RC4_128_SHA" />
</transportConnectors>
```

Please note that the `uri` attribute shown here has been split into two lines for the purpose of readability. This is only for readability and will cause the configuration to break if left in this manner. If you use the configuration example, make sure to combine the two lines that are held within the quotes.

In the preceding example, the SSL_RSA_WITH_RC4_128_SHA cipher suite is the only one that's been enabled on the ActiveMQ SSL transport. Additional cipher suites can be enabled using a comma-separated list. The purpose of this new option is for added security as it allows only certain cipher suites to be enabled. This can be handy in environments that consider some cipher suites too weak to leave them enabled, such as the Payment Card Industry (PCI).

> **NOTE** To test which cipher suites are enabled, a Perl script named ssl-cipher-check.pl is available (http://mng.bz/Ko7k). This script was inspired by the Payment Card Industry Data Security Standard (PCI DSS) for preventing credit card fraud (see http://mng.bz/8cYo). The script is easy to use and makes performing a check for weak ciphers extremely easy.

Not everyone will need to disable SSL cipher suites, but if you do, this new option for the SSL transport will make the task easy.

4.3.5 *Hypertext Transfer Protocol (HTTP/HTTPS)*

In many environments, firewalls are configured to allow only basic services such as web access and email. So how can ActiveMQ be used in such an environment? This is where the HTTP transport comes into play.

Hypertext Transfer Protocol (HTTP) was originally designed to transmit hypertext (HTML) pages over the web. It uses TCP as an underlying network protocol and adds some additional logic for communication between browsers and web servers. After the first boom of the internet, web infrastructure and the HTTP protocol in particular found a new role in supporting *web services*, commonly used these days to exchange information between applications. The main difference is that in the case of web services, XML-formatted data is transmitted using the HTTP protocol rather than HTML data.

ActiveMQ implements the *HTTP transport connector*, which provides for the exchange of XML-formatted messages with the broker using the HTTP protocol. This is what allows ActiveMQ to bypass strict firewall rules. By using the HTTP protocol that runs on the standard web port number (80), ActiveMQ can use an existing hole in the firewall, so to speak.

The URI syntax of this transport connector is as follows:

`http://hostname:port``?key=value`

Secure HTTP (HTTP over SSL or HTTPS) is also supported by this transport:

`https://hostname:port``?key=value`

Note the slight difference in the scheme used by the two examples based on whether SSL is needed. Let's walk through an example configuration to see how to run the examples using the HTTP transport. The transport connectors section of the XML configuration in this case looks similar to those used in previous sections, but with the HTTP scheme:

```
<transportConnectors>
 <transportConnector name="tcp"
  uri="tcp://localhost:61616?trace=true"/>
 <transportConnector name="http"
  uri="http://localhost:8080?trace=true" />
</transportConnectors>
```

Note that there are two transports configured here: one for the TCP transport and one for the HTTP transport, which listens to port 8080.

In order to run the clients using the HTTP transport protocol, one dependency must be added to the classpath. The HTTP transport is located in the ActiveMQ optional module, so you'll have to add it to the application's classpath (along with appropriate dependencies). Using Maven, you'll need to add the following dependency to the pom.xml file:

```
<dependency>
    <groupId>org.apache.activemq</groupId>
    <artifactId>activemq-optional</artifactId>
    <version>5.4.1</version>
</dependency>
```

This will include `activemq-optional` module and all its dependencies to the classpath. In case you don't use Maven to manage your classpath, be sure to include all of these JARs into your classpath:

```
$ACTIVEMQ_HOME/lib/optional/activemq-optional-<version>.jar
$ACTIVEMQ_HOME/lib/optional/commons-httpclient-<version>.jar
$ACTIVEMQ_HOME/lib/optional/xstream-<version>.jar
$ACTIVEMQ_HOME/lib/optional/xmlpull-<version>.jar
```

Finally, the stock portfolio publisher is ready to be run using the HTTP transport:

```
$ mvn exec:java -Dexec.mainClass=org.apache.activemq.book.ch4.Publisher \
-Dexec.args="http://localhost:8080 CSCO ORCL"

...

Sending: {price=65.713356601409, stock=JAVA, offer=65.779069958011, up=true}
  on destination: topic://STOCKS.JAVA
Sending: {price=66.071605671946, stock=JAVA, offer=66.137677277617, up=true}
  on destination: topic://STOCKS.JAVA
Sending: {price=65.929035001620, stock=JAVA, offer=65.994964036622, up=false}
  on destination: topic://STOCKS.JAVA

...
```

As stated previously, when using the HTTP transport, all broker-to-client communication is performed by sending XML messages. This type of communication can have an impact on the overall system performance compared to the use of the TCP transport with the OpenWire protocol (which is tuned specifically for messaging purposes). So if performance is a concern, you're best to stick to the TCP transport and find some other workaround for the firewall issues.

So far this chapter has covered protocols used to connect brokers and clients using the network stack in the operating system. As an alternative, ActiveMQ was designed to be embedded in a Java application. This allows client-to-broker communication to take place locally in the JVM, instead of via the network. In order to support this kind of intra-VM communication, ActiveMQ provides a special protocol named the *VM protocol*.

4.4   Connecting to ActiveMQ inside the virtual machine (VM connector)

The *VM transport connector* is used by Java applications to launch an embedded broker and connect to it. Use of the VM transport means that no network connections are created between clients and the embedded broker. Communication is performed through direct method invocations of the broker object. Because the network stack isn't employed, performance improves significantly. The broker is started when the first connection is created using the VM protocol. All subsequent VM transport connections from the same virtual machine will connect to the same broker.

A broker created using the VM protocol doesn't lack any of the standard ActiveMQ features. So, for example, the broker can be configured with other transport connectors as well. When all clients that use the VM transport to the broker close their connections, the broker will automatically shut down.

The URI syntax for the VM transport is as follows:

```
vm://brokerName?key=value
```

The broker name plays an important role in the VM transport connector URI by uniquely identifying the broker. For example, you can create two different embedded brokers by specifying different broker names. This is the only required difference.

Transport options are set using the query part of the URI, the same as the previously discussed transports. The complete reference for this connector can be found at the ActiveMQ website (http://mng.bz/716b).

The important thing about options for the VM transport protocol is that you can use them to configure the broker to some extent. Options whose name begins with the prefix `broker.` are used to tune the broker. For example, the following URI starts up a broker with persistence disabled (message persistence is explained in chapter 5):

```
vm://broker1?marshal=false&broker.persistent=false
```

There's also an alternative URI syntax that can be used to configure an embedded broker:

```
vm:broker:(transportURI,network:networkURI)/brokerName?key=value
```

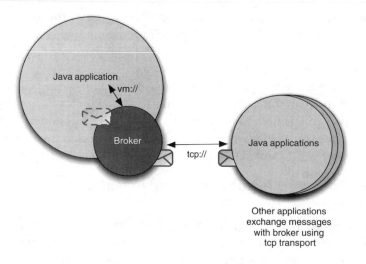

Other applications
exchange messages
with broker using
tcp transport

Figure 4.4   Application exchanges messages with embedded broker using vm transport

The complete reference of the broker URI can be found at the ActiveMQ website (http://mng.bz/FNos).

As you can see, this kind of URI can be used to configure additional transport connectors. Take a look at the following URI, for example:

```
vm:broker:(tcp://localhost:6000)?brokerName=embeddedbroker&persistent=false
```

Here, we've defined an embedded broker named `embeddedBroker` and also configured a TCP transport connector that listens for connections on port 6000. Finally, persistence is also disabled in this broker. Figure 4.4 can help you better visualize this example configuration. This figure demonstrates that clients connecting to the broker from within the application that embeds the broker will use the VM transport, whereas external applications connect to that embedded broker using the TCP connector, just as they would in the case of any standalone broker.

An embedded broker using an external configuration file can be achieved using the `brokerConfig` transport option and by specifying the URI for the activemq.xml file. Here's an example:

```
vm://localhost?brokerConfig=xbean:activemq.xml
```

The example will locate the activemq.xml file in the classpath using the `xbean:` protocol. Using this approach, an embedded broker can be configured just like a standalone broker using the XML configuration.

Now the stock portfolio publisher can be started with an embedded broker using the following command:

```
$ mvn exec:java -Dexec.mainClass=org.apache.activemq.book.ch4.Publisher \
-Dexec.args="vm://localhost CSCO ORCL"

...

Sending: {price=65.713356601409, stock=JAVA, offer=65.779069958011, up=true}
  on destination: topic://STOCKS.JAVA
```

```
Sending: {price=66.071605671946, stock=JAVA, offer=66.137677277617, up=true}
   on destination: topic://STOCKS.JAVA
Sending: {price=65.929035001620, stock=JAVA, offer=65.994964036622, up=false}
   on destination: topic://STOCKS.JAVA
```

...

Note that the publisher works just fine without having to start an external broker.

One obvious advantage of the VM transport is improved performance for client-to-broker communication. Also, you'll have only one Java application to run (one JVM) instead of two, which can ease your deployment process. This also means that there's one fewer Java process to manage. So, if you plan to use the broker mainly from one application, maybe you should consider using the embedded broker. Embedding ActiveMQ is covered in detail in chapter 8.

On the other hand, if too many Java applications that use embedded brokers exist, maintenance problems may arise when trying to consistently configure each broker as well as back up the data. In such situations, it's always easier to create a small cluster of standalone brokers instead of using embedded brokers.

Having one ActiveMQ broker to serve all your application needs works well for most situations. But some environments need advanced features, such as high availability and larger scalability. This is typically achieved using what's known as a *network of brokers*. In the following section you'll learn about networks of brokers and *network connectors* used to configure those networks.

4.5 Network connectors

A network of brokers creates a cluster composed of multiple ActiveMQ instances that are interconnected to meet more advanced messaging scenarios. Various topologies for broker networks, their purpose, and their configuration details are explained in detail in chapter 10. The previous section discussed transport connectors that provide client-to-broker communications, whereas this section will discuss *network connectors* that provide broker-to-broker communications.

Network connectors are channels that are configured between brokers so that those brokers can communicate with one another. A network connector is a unidirectional channel by default. A given broker communicates in one direction by only forwarding messages it receives to the brokers on the other side of the connection. This setup is commonly referred to as a *forwarding bridge*. In some situations, you may want to create a bidirectional communication channel between brokers—a channel that communicates not only outward to the brokers on the other side of the connection, but also receives messages from other brokers on that same channel. ActiveMQ supports this kind of bidirectional connector, which is usually referred to as a *duplex connector*. Figure 4.5 shows one example of a network of brokers that contains both a forwarding bridge and duplex connectors.

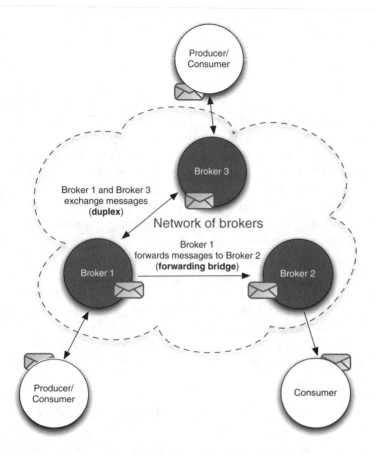

Figure 4.5   An example of a complex network of brokers topology

Network connectors are configured through the ActiveMQ XML configuration file in a fashion similar to the configuration of transport connectors. Let's take a look at an example configuration:

```
<networkConnectors>
  <networkConnector name="default-nc" uri="multicast://default"/>
</networkConnectors>
```

As you can see, networks of brokers are configured using the <networkConnectors> element. This element contains the configuration for one or more connectors using the <networkConnector> element. As was the case with transport connectors, the mandatory attributes for the <networkConnector> element are the name and the uri. All other attributes are optional and are used to configure additional features on the connector, as you'll see in a moment.

In the rest of this chapter, various ActiveMQ protocols and techniques that are used to configure and connect to a network of brokers will be presented and discussed. But before we dive in, there's one more important ActiveMQ concept we should explain known as *discovery*. In general, discovery is a process of detecting remote broker services. Clients usually want to discover all available brokers. Brokers, on the other hand, usually want to find other available brokers so they can establish a network of brokers.

When you want to configure a network of brokers, the first obvious question is, do you know the exact network address of each broker in the network? If the answer is yes, then you can proceed configuring your network statically and also connect your clients to predefined broker URIs. This situation is more often seen in production environments where you want to have total control of all resources. Section 4.5.1 explains how you can set up and use static networks. It starts with explaining the *static* protocol used to connect multiple brokers together. Then, we'll explain a *failover* protocol that allows clients to connect to one of the brokers in the network and also utilize reconnection logic.

In case clients and brokers don't know each other's network addresses, they must use some kind of a discovery mechanism to dynamically locate the available brokers. This kind of setup is more often found in development environments, as it's much easier to set up and maintain. Discovery agents and the protocols they use are explained in section 4.5.2. You'll learn how IP multicast is used by brokers to advertise their services and locate other available brokers, using the *multicast* connector. Also, we'll see how clients use the multicast connector to discover brokers using a *discovery* connector.

We'll also dive into the *peer* connector, which makes creating a network of embedded brokers a very simple task. Finally, we'll see how the *fanout* connector enables clients to send messages to multiple brokers. Let's begin with static networks.

4.5.1 Static networks

The first approach to configuring and connecting to a network of brokers is through the use of statically configured URIs—configuring a list of broker URIs available for connection. The only prerequisite is that you know the addresses of all the brokers you want to use. Once you have these URIs, you need to know how to use them in a configuration. So let's look at the connector available to create a static networks of brokers.

STATIC CONNECTOR

The *static network connector* is used to create a static configuration of multiple brokers in a network. This protocol uses a composite URI—a URI that contains other URIs. A composite URI consists of multiple broker addresses or URIs that are on the other end of the network connection.

Here's the URI syntax for the static protocol:

```
static:(uri1,uri2,uri3,...)?key=value
```

You can find the complete reference for this transport at the ActiveMQ website (http://mng.bz/r74v).

Now take a look at the following configuration example:

```
<networkConnectors>
  <networkConnector name="local network"
    uri="static://(tcp://remotehost1:61616,tcp://remotehost2:61616)"/>
</networkConnectors>
```

Assuming that this configuration is for the broker on the `localhost` and that brokers on hosts `remotehost1` and `remotehost2` are up and running, you'll notice the following messages when you start the local broker:

```
...
INFO  DiscoveryNetworkConnector  - Establishing network connection between
      from vm://localhost to tcp://remotehost1:61616
INFO  TransportConnector         - Connector vm://localhost Started
INFO  DiscoveryNetworkConnector  - Establishing network connection between
      from vm://localhost to tcp://host2:61616
INFO  DemandForwardingBridge     - Network connection between vm://
      localhost#0
      and tcp://remotehost1:61616 has been established.
INFO  DemandForwardingBridge     - Network connection between vm://
      localhost#2
      and tcp://remotehost2:61616 has been established.
...
```

The output indicates that the broker on the `localhost` has successfully configured a *forwarding bridge* with two other brokers running on two remote hosts. In other words, messages sent to the local broker will be forwarded to brokers running on `remotehost1` and `remotehost2`, but only if there's demand for those messages from a consumer.

The best way to understand this is to walk through the use of static networks using the stock portfolio example with a network of brokers. Figure 4.6 provides a perspective of the broker topology used in this example.

In the diagram, the two brokers are networked. The brokers utilize a network connector with a URI using the static protocol. A consumer is attached to a destination on BrokerB, which creates demand for messages across the network connector. When the producer sends messages to the same destination on BrokerA, they'll be forwarded to the broker where there's demand. In this case, BrokerA forwards messages to BrokerB. The following example will walk through this basic use case.

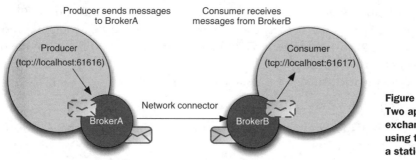

**Figure 4.6
Two applications
exchange messages
using two brokers in
a static network.**

To make this example work, first we need to start these two networked brokers. Let's start with BrokerB:

```
<broker xmlns="http://activemq.apache.org/schema/core"
  brokerName="BrokerB"
  dataDirectory="${activemq.base}/data">

  <transportConnectors>
    <transportConnector name="openwire" uri="tcp://localhost:61617" />
  </transportConnectors>

</broker>
```

This simple configuration starts a broker that listens on port 61617. We can start this broker with the following command:

```
${ACTIVEMQ_HOME}/bin/activemq console \
xbean:src/main/resources/org/apache/activemq/book/ch4/brokerA.xml
```

Now it's time to configure BrokerA:

```
<broker xmlns="http://activemq.apache.org/schema/core"
  brokerName="BrokerA"
  dataDirectory="${activemq.base}/data">

  <transportConnectors>
    <transportConnector name="openwire" uri="tcp://localhost:61616" />
  </transportConnectors>
  <networkConnectors>
    <networkConnector uri="static:(tcp://localhost:61617)" />
  </networkConnectors>

</broker>
```

Besides the transport connector listening on port 61616, it defines a network connector that connects to BrokerB. In a separate console window, you can start this broker like this:

```
${ACTIVEMQ_HOME}/bin/activemq console \
xbean:src/main/resources/org/apache/activemq/book/ch4/brokerB.xml
```

Now that we have both brokers up and running, let's run the stock portfolio example. First we'll start our publisher and connect it to BrokerA:

```
$ mvn exec:java -Dexec.mainClass=org.apache.activemq.book.ch4.Publisher \
-Dexec.args="tcp://localhost:61616 CSCO ORCL"

...

Sending: {price=65.713356601409, stock=JAVA, offer=65.779069958011, up=true}
  on destination: topic://STOCKS.JAVA
Sending: {price=66.071605671946, stock=JAVA, offer=66.137677277617, up=true}
  on destination: topic://STOCKS.JAVA
Sending: {price=65.929035001620, stock=JAVA, offer=65.994964036622, up=false}
  on destination: topic://STOCKS.JAVA

...
```

This is practically the same command was used with the earlier TCP connector example. Now start the consumer and connect it to BrokerB:

```
$ mvn exec:java -Dexec.mainClass=org.apache.activemq.book.ch4.Consumer \
-Dexec.args="tcp://localhost:61617 CSCO ORCL"

...

ORCL 65.71 65.78 up
ORCL 66.07 66.14 up
ORCL 65.93 65.99 down
CSCO 23.30 23.33 up


...
```

Using this setup, messages are published to BrokerA. These messages are then forwarded to BrokerB, where they're received by the consumer. The overall functionality of this example hasn't been changed and both the publisher and the consumer behave the same as the previous single broker example. The only difference is that the publisher and the consumer are now connecting to different brokers that are networked using the static protocol.

From this simple example you can conclude that this particular configuration can help you in situations when you need your distributed clients to benefit from the performance advantages of communicating with the local broker instead of a remote one.

EXAMPLE USE OF THE STATIC PROTOCOL

Configuring broker networks can be difficult depending on the situation. Use of the static protocol allows for an explicit notation that a network should exist. Consider a situation where clients in remote offices are connecting to a broker in the home office. Depending on the number of clients in each remote office, you may wind up with far too many wide area network connections into the home office. This can cause an unnecessary burden on the network. To minimize connections, you may want to place a broker in each remote office and allow a static network connection between the remote office broker and the home office broker. Not only will this minimize the number of network connections between the remote offices and the home office, but it'll allow the client applications in the remote offices to operate more efficiently. The removal of the long haul connection over the wide area network means less latency and therefore less waiting for the client application.

FAILOVER PROTOCOL

In all the examples so far, the clients have been configured to connect to only one specific broker. But what should you do in case you can't connect to the desired broker or your connection fails at the later stage? Your clients have two options: either they'll die gracefully or try to connect to the same or some other broker and resume their work. As you can probably guess, the stock portfolio example runs using the protocols described thus far and aren't immune to network problems and unavailable brokers. That's where protocols such as *failover* come in to implement automatic reconnection. Similar to the case with the network connectors, there are two ways to provide a list of suitable brokers to which the client can connect. In the first case, you provide a static list of available brokers. This is the approach used by the *failover transport connector*. In the second case, dynamic discovery of the available brokers is used. This will be explained later in the chapter. This section will examine the failover transport connector.

The URI syntax for the failover connector is similar to the previous static network connector URI. There are actually two available forms to the failover URI:

```
failover:(uri1,...,uriN)?key=value
```

or

```
failover:uri1,...,uriN
```

The complete reference of this protocol can be found at the ActiveMQ website (http://mng.bz/u58s).

By default, this protocol uses a random algorithm to choose one of the underlying connectors. If the connection fails (both on startup or at a later stage), the transport will pick another URI and try to make a connection. A default configuration also implements *reconnection delay logic*, meaning that the transport will start with a 10ms delay for the first reconnection attempt and double this time for any subsequent attempt up to 30000ms. Also, the reconnection logic will try to reconnect indefinitely. Of course, all reconnection parameters can be reconfigured according to your needs using the appropriate transport options.

Recall the theoretical static network of brokers that was defined in the previous section. In that example, all messages sent to the local broker could be forwarded to the brokers located on `remotehost1` and `remotehost2`. Because all messages could be sent to both of these brokers, those messages can be consumed from either broker. The same is true here. The only difference is that the failover transport will automatically attempt a reconnect in the event of a broker failover. To experience the use of this transport, run the stock portfolio consumer and configure it to connect to the brokers using the failover connector:

```
$ mvn exec:java -Dexec.mainClass=org.apache.activemq.book.ch4.Consumer \
-Dexec.args="failover:(tcp://remotehost1:61616,tcp://
    remotehost2:61616) CSCO ORCL"
```

The beauty of this solution is that it requires no changes to the application in order to add support for automatic reconnection in the event of a broker failure.

Now let's see the failover connector at work. Imagine that the random algorithm in the failover transport has chosen to connect the consumer to the broker on `host1`. You can expect that the consumer will print the following log message during the startup:

```
org.apache.activemq.transport.failover.FailoverTransport$1 iterate INFO: \
Successfully reconnected to tcp://host1:61616
```

As we already said, all messages sent by the publisher to the local broker will be forwarded to the broker on `host1` and received by the consumer. Now try to simulate a broker failure by shutting down the broker on `host1`. The consumer will print the following log message:

```
org.apache.activemq.transport.failover.FailoverTransport handleTransportFailu
    re
WARNING: Transport failed,
  attempting to automatically reconnect due to: java.io.EOFException
java.io.EOFException
 at java.io.DataInputStream.readInt(DataInputStream.java:375)
 at org.apache.activemq.openwire.OpenWireFormat.unmarshal(
    OpenWireFormat.java:268
 )
 at org.apache.activemq.transport.tcp.TcpTransport.readCommand(
    TcpTransport.java:192
 )
 at org.apache.activemq.transport.tcp.TcpTransport.doRun(
    TcpTransport.java:184
 )
 at org.apache.activemq.transport.tcp.TcpTransport.run(
    TcpTransport.java:172
 )
 at java.lang.Thread.run(Thread.java:619)
org.apache.activemq.transport.failover.FailoverTransport$1 iterate
 INFO: Successfully reconnected to tcp://host2:61616
```

Notice the initial exception noting the failure, followed by the log message about reconnecting to another broker. This means that the consumer has successfully connected to the other broker and you can see that it resumed its normal operation without any assistance.

EXAMPLE USE OF THE FAILOVER PROTOCOL

Due to its reconnection capabilities, it's highly advisable that you use the failover protocol for all clients, even if a client will only be connecting to a single broker. For example, the following URI will try to reestablish a connection to the same broker in the event that the broker shuts down for any reason:

```
failover:(tcp://localhost:61616)
```

The advantage of this is that clients don't need to be manually restarted in the case of a broker failure (or maintenance, and so forth). As soon as the broker becomes available again the client will automatically reconnect. This means far more robustness for your applications by simply utilizing a feature of ActiveMQ.

The failover transport connector plays an important role in achieving advanced functionalities such as high availability and load balancing as will be explained in chapter 12.

4.5.2 *Dynamic networks*

Thus far we've seen how to set up broker networks and connect to them by explicitly specifying broker URIs (both transport and network connectors). As you'll see in this section, ActiveMQ implements several mechanisms that can be used by brokers and clients to find each other and establish necessary connections.

MULTICAST CONNECTOR

IP multicast is a network technique used for easy transmission of data from one source to a group of interested receivers (one-to-many communications) over an IP network. One of the fundamental concepts of IP multicast is the so-called *group address*. The group address is an IP address in the range of `224.0.0.0` to `239.255.255.255` used by both sources and receivers. Sources use this address as a destination for their data, whereas receivers use it to express their interest in data from that group.

When IP multicast is configured, ActiveMQ brokers use the multicast protocol to advertise their services and locate the services of other brokers for the purpose of creating networks of brokers. Clients, on the other hand, use multicast to locate brokers and establish a connection with them. This section discusses how brokers use multicast; the use of multicast by a client will be discussed later.

The URI syntax for the multicast protocol is as follows:

`multicast://ipadaddress:``port?key=value`

This is no different than the previous URIs with the exception of the scheme portion.

Here's a snippet from the default ActiveMQ configuration that makes use of multicast:

```
<broker xmlns="http://activemq.apache.org/schema/
   core" brokerName="multicast"
       dataDirectory="${activemq.base}/data">

  <networkConnectors>
      <networkConnector name="default-nc" uri="multicast://default"/>
  </networkConnectors>

  <transportConnectors>
      <transportConnector name="openwire" uri="tcp://localhost:61616"
                          discoveryUri="multicast://default"/>
  </transportConnectors>

</broker>
```

In the example, the group name *default* is used instead of a specific IP address. There are two important things achieved with this configuration snippet. First, the transport connector's `discoveryUri` attribute is used to advertise this transport's URI on the default group. All clients interested in finding an available broker would use this connector. This will be demonstrated in the following section.

Next, the `uri` attribute of the network connector is used to search for available brokers and to create a network with them. In this case, the broker acts like a client and uses multicast for lookup purposes. You can find a complete reference of this protocol at the ActiveMQ website (http://mng.bz/14yJ).

Now that you know how to configure discovery on the broker side, I'm sure you're wondering where you might use this protocol.

EXAMPLE USE OF THE MULTICAST PROTOCOL

The multicast protocol is somewhat different from the TCP protocol. The difference is the automatic discovery of other brokers instead of using a static list of brokers. Use of

Preventing automatic broker discovery

When developing in a team environment it's possible (and quite probable) that two or more ActiveMQ instances will automatically connect to one another and begin consuming one another's messages. Here are some recommendations for preventing this situation from occurring:

1 *Remove the discoveryUri portion of the openwire transport connector*—The transport connector whose name is *openwire* is configured by default to advertise the broker's TCP transport using multicast. This allows other brokers to automatically discover it and connect to it if necessary.

Here's the OpenWire transport connector definition from the conf/activemq.xml configuration file:

```
<transportConnector name="openwire" uri="tcp://localhost:61616"
    discoveryUri="multicast://default"/>
```

To stop the broker from advertising the TCP transport URI via multicast, change the definition to remove the `discoveryUri` attribute so it looks like this:

```
<transportConnector name="openwire" uri="tcp://localhost:61616" />
```

2 *Comment out/remove the default-nc network connector*—The network connector named *default-nc* utilizes the multicast transport to automatically and dynamically discover other brokers. To stop this behavior, comment out/remove the default-nc network connector so that it won't automatically discover other brokers.

Here's the default-nc network connector definition from the conf/activemq.xml configuration file:

```
<networkConnector name="default-nc" uri="multicast://default"/>
```

To disable this network connector, comment it out so it looks like this:

```
<!--networkConnector name="default-nc" uri="multicast://default"/-->
```

3 *Give the broker a unique name*—The default configuration for ActiveMQ in the conf/activemq.xml file provides a broker name of localhost as shown:

```
<broker xmlns="http://acti vemq.apache.org/schema/core"
    brokerName="localhost"
        dataDirectory="${activemq.base}/data">
```

In order to uniquely identify your broker instance, change the `brokerName` attribute from localhost to something unique such as in the following example:

```
<broker xmlns="http://activemq.apache.org/schema/core"
    brokerName="broker1234"
        dataDirectory="${activemq.base}/data">
```

This is especially handy when searching through log files to see which brokers are taking certain actions.

the multicast protocol is common where brokers are added and removed frequently, and in cases where brokers may have their IP addresses changed frequently. In these cases, instead of reconfiguring each broker manually for every change, it's often easier to utilize a discovery protocol.

One disadvantage to using the multicast protocol is that discovery is automatic. If there are brokers that you don't want to be automatically added to a given group, you must be careful in setting up the initial configuration of the broker network. Careful segmentation of broker networks is important, as you don't want messages to wind up in a broker network where they don't belong. Another disadvantage of the multicast protocol is that it can be excessively chatty on the network. For this reason, many network administrators won't allow its use. Please check with your network administrator before taking the time to configure a network using the multicast protocol.

As IP multicast can be used for discovery on the broker side, there's a similar discovery protocol for the client side.

DISCOVERY PROTOCOL

The *discovery transport connector* is on the client side of the ActiveMQ multicast functionality. This protocol is basically the same as the failover protocol in its behavior. The only difference is that it'll use multicast to discover available brokers and randomly choose one to connect to.

The syntax of this protocol is

```
discovery:(discoveryAgentURI)?key=value
```

Its complete reference could be found at the ActiveMQ website (http://mng.bz/96wI).

Using the multicast broker configuration explained earlier, you can run the broker with the following command:

```
${ACTIVEMQ_HOME}/bin/activemq console \
xbean:src/main/resources/org/apache/activemq/book/ch4/
activemq-multicast.xml
```

Once the broker is started, run the stock portfolio publisher with the following command:

```
$ mvn -e exec:java \
-Dexec.mainClass=org.apache.activemq.book.ch4.Publisher \
-Dexec.args="discovery:(multicast://default) CSCO ORCL"
```

You'll notice the following log messages at the application startup:

```
Jun 18, 2008 2:13:18 PM
 org.apache.activemq.transport.discovery.DiscoveryTransport onServiceAdd
 INFO: Adding new broker connection URL: tcp://localhost:61616
Jun 18, 2008 2:13:19 PM
 org.apache.activemq.transport.failover.FailoverTransport doReconnect
 INFO: Successfully connected to tcp://localhost:61616

...

Sending: {price=65.713356601409, stock=JAVA, offer=65.779069958011, up=true}
  on destination: topic://STOCKS.JAVA
Sending: {price=66.071605671946, stock=JAVA, offer=66.137677277617, up=true}
  on destination: topic://STOCKS.JAVA
Sending: {price=65.929035001620, stock=JAVA, offer=65.994964036622, up=false}
  on destination: topic://STOCKS.JAVA

...
```

These messages tell you that the publisher client has successfully used multicast to discover and connect to the local broker.

PEER PROTOCOL

As we've seen before, networks of brokers and embedded brokers are useful concepts that allow you to fit brokers to your infrastructure needs. Of course, it's theoretically possible to create networks of embedded brokers, but this would be quite cumbersome to configure manually. This is why ActiveMQ provides the *peer transport connector,* as it allows you to more easily network embedded brokers. The peer connector is a utility transport that is a superset of a VM connector that creates a *peer-to-peer* network of embedded brokers.

The URI syntax of this protocol is as follows:

peer://peergroup/brokerName?key=value

You can find its complete reference at the ActiveMQ website (http://mng.bz/bIaH).

When started with the peer protocol URI, the application will automatically start an embedded broker (just as was the case with the VM protocol), but will also configure the broker to establish network connections to other brokers in the local network with the same group name.

Let's walk through a demonstration of this using the stock portfolio example with the peer protocol. In this case, both the publisher and the consumer will use their own embedded brokers that will be networked automatically. Figure 4.7 provides a better perspective of this solution.

Advise the stock portfolio publisher to create its own embedded broker using group1 like this:

```
$ mvn -e exec:java -Dexec.mainClass=org.apache.activemq.book.ch4.Publisher \
-Dexec.args="peer://group1 CSCO ORCL"

...

Sending: {price=65.713356601409, stock=JAVA, offer=65.779069958011, up=true}
  on destination: topic://STOCKS.JAVA
Sending: {price=66.071605671946, stock=JAVA, offer=66.137677277617, up=true}
  on destination: topic://STOCKS.JAVA
Sending: {price=65.929035001620, stock=JAVA, offer=65.994964036622, up=false}
  on destination: topic://STOCKS.JAVA

...
```

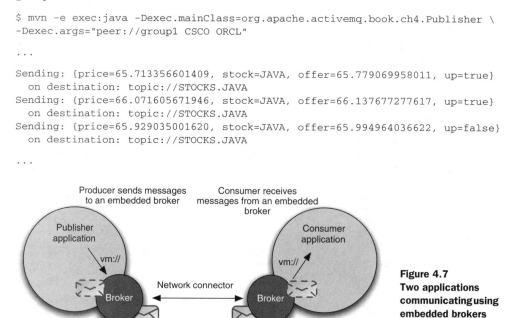

Figure 4.7
Two applications
communicating using
embedded brokers
over peer protocol

Also advise the stock portfolio consumer to create its own embedded broker using
group1 like this:

```
$ mvn -e exec:java -Dexec.mainClass=org.apache.activemq.book.ch4.Consumer \
-Dexec.args="peer://group1 CSCO ORCL"

...

ORCL 65.71 65.78 up
ORCL 66.07 66.14 up
ORCL 65.93 65.99 down
CSCO 23.30 23.33 up

...
```

The two commands start two embedded brokers (one for each application) and create a peer-to-peer broker network named group1 between these two brokers. All messages sent to one broker will be available in the other broker as well as any other
brokers that might join group1. Note that the overall system operates as if these two
applications were using the same centralized broker.

EXAMPLE USE OF THE PEER PROTOCOL
Consider an application that resides on the laptop of a field sales representative who
often disconnects from the company network but still needs the application to run
successfully in a disconnected mode. This is a common scenario where the client
application needs to continue working regardless of whether the network is available.
This is a case where the peer protocol can be utilized for an embedded broker to
allow the application on the laptop to keep running successfully. In reality, while in
disconnected mode, the application is simply sending messages to the local broker,
where they're queued up to be sent at a later time when the network is available again.
The sales rep can still log client calls, visits, and so on while the laptop is disconnected
from the network. When the laptop is again connected to the network, all of the
queued messages will be sent along based on the demand from consuming clients.

FANOUT CONNECTOR
Fanout is another utility connector used by clients to simultaneously connect to multiple brokers and replicate operations to those brokers. The URI syntax of this protocol
is as follows:

fanout:(fanoutURI)?key=value

You can find its complete reference at the ActiveMQ website (http://mng.bz/J7i0).
    The fanoutURI can utilize either a static URI or a multicast URI. Consider the fol-
lowing example:

```
fanout:(static:(tcp://host1:61616,tcp://host2:61616,tcp://host3:61616))
```

In figure 4.8, the client will try to connect to three brokers statically defined using the
static protocol
    The same effect could be accomplished by simply using the following URI:

```
fanout:(multicast://default)
```

This assumes that the brokers are configured to use multicast to advertise their transport connectors.

By default, the fanout protocol will wait until it connects to at least two brokers and won't replicate commands to queues (only topics). Both of these features are, of course, configurable with appropriate transport options.

Finally, there are a couple of things you should be aware of if you plan to use the fanout protocol. First of all, it's not recommended for consuming messages. Its only purpose is to produce messages to multiple brokers. Also, if the brokers you're using are in the same network of brokers, it's likely that certain consumers will receive duplicate messages. So basically, the fanout protocol is only recommended for publishing messages to multiple nonconnected brokers.

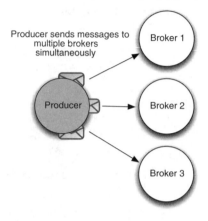

Figure 4.8   Producer sends messages to multiple brokers using the fanout protocol

With the fanout protocol, we come to the end of the discussion on networks of brokers and network connectors. For reference purposes, table 4.2 provides a summary of all the protocols covered in this section.

Table 4.2   Summary of protocols used to network brokers

Protocol	Description
Static	Used for defining networks of brokers with known addresses
Failover	Used to provide reconnection logic for clients to the network of brokers or a single broker
Multicast	Used for defining dynamic networks of brokers (broker addresses are not statically defined)
Discovery	Used by clients to connect to dynamic network of brokers
Peer	Used to easily connect multiple embedded brokers
Fanout	Used to produce messages to multiple unconnected brokers

In this section we saw that ActiveMQ isn't just a standalone message broker; it can be used to create complex networks and thus allow you to achieve good scalability and availability of your messaging infrastructure.

4.6   Summary

Connectivity options for ActiveMQ are extremely important, and one of the first items that users encounter. The format of ActiveMQ URIs is designed to be easy to understand and it dramatically simplifies connectivity. This connectivity extends not only to clients via transport connectors, but also to other brokers via network connectors. Embedded brokers and networks of brokers were briefly introduced and will be discussed in detail in chapters 8 and 10. Also of importance are the reconnection protocols and discovery agents that demonstrate the true power of ActiveMQ connectivity options. Knowing the types of connectors and the essence of particular protocols is important when you choose the overall topology of your messaging system. Another important feature in ActiveMQ is message persistence, which will be discussed in the next chapter.

5

ActiveMQ message storage

This chapter covers

- How messages are stored in ActiveMQ for both queues and topics
- The four styles of message stores provided with ActiveMQ
- How ActiveMQ caches messages for consumers
- How to control message caching using subscription recovery policies

The JMS specification supports two types of message delivery: persistent and nonpersistent. A message delivered with the persistent delivery property must be logged to stable storage. For nonpersistent messages, a JMS provider must make best efforts to deliver the message, but it won't be logged to stable storage.

ActiveMQ supports both of these types of message delivery and can also be configured to support message recovery, an in-between state where messages are cached in memory. ActiveMQ supports a pluggable strategy for message storage and provides storage options for in-memory, file-based, and relational databases.

Persistent messages are used if you want messages to always be available to a message consumer after they've been delivered to the broker, even if that consumer isn't running when the message was sent. Once a message has been consumed and acknowledged by a message consumer, it's typically deleted from the broker's message store.

Nonpersistent messages are typically used for sending notifications or real-time data. You should use nonpersistent messages when performance is critical and guaranteed delivery of the message isn't required.

This chapter will first examine why messages are stored differently for queues and topics. We'll then look at all four different message stores available to ActiveMQ, and why and when to use them for your application. Finally we'll look at how ActiveMQ can be configured to temporarily cache messages for retrieval by message consumers at a later point in time. The flexibility offered by ActiveMQ for caching messages is unique, allowing fine control of message retrieval for your application.

This chapter will provide a detailed guide to message persistence. In order to lay the groundwork for this, first we'll examine the storage of messages for JMS destinations.

5.1 *How are messages stored by ActiveMQ?*

It's important to gain some basic knowledge of the storage mechanisms for messages in an ActiveMQ message store. This will aid in configuration and provide an awareness of what takes place in the ActiveMQ broker during the delivery of persistent messages. Messages sent to queues and topics are stored differently, because there are some storage optimizations that can be made with topics that don't make sense with queues, as we'll explain.

Storage for queues is straightforward—messages are basically stored in first in, first out order (FIFO). See figure 5.1 for a depiction of this. One message is dispatched to a single consumer at a time. Only when that message has been consumed and acknowledged can it be deleted from the broker's message store.

For durable subscribers to a topic, each consumer gets a copy of the message. In order to save storage space, only one copy of a message is stored by the broker. A durable subscriber object in the store maintains a pointer to its next stored message and dispatches a copy of it to its consumer as shown in figure 5.2. The message store is implemented in this manner because each durable subscriber could be consuming messages at different rates or they may not all be running at the same time. Also,

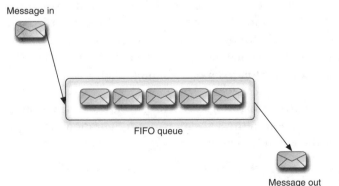

Message in

FIFO queue

Message out

Figure 5.1   First in, first out message storage for queues

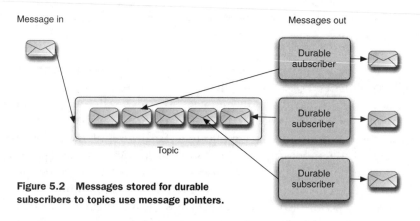

Figure 5.2   Messages stored for durable subscribers to topics use message pointers.

because every message can potentially have many consumers, a message can't be deleted from the store until it's been successfully delivered to every interested durable subscriber.

Every message store implementation for ActiveMQ supports storing messages for both queues and topics, though obviously the implementation differs between storage types. For example, the memory store holds all messages in memory.

Throughout the rest of this chapter, more details about configuring the different ActiveMQ message stores and their advantages and disadvantages will be explained.

5.2   *The KahaDB message store*

The recommended message store for general-purpose messages since ActiveMQ version 5.3 is KahaDB. This is a file-based message store that combines a transactional journal, for reliable message storage and recovery, with good performance and scalability.

The KahaDB store is a file-based, transactional store that's been tuned and designed for the fast storage of messages. The aim of the KahaDB store is to be easy to use and as fast as possible. Its use of a file-based message database means there's no prerequisite for a third-party database. This message store enables ActiveMQ to be downloaded and running in literally minutes. In addition, the structure of the KahaDB store has been streamlined especially for the requirements of a message broker.

The KahaDB message store uses a transactional log for its indexes and only uses one index file for all its destinations. It's been used in production environments with 10,000 active connections, each connection having a separate queue. The configurability of the KahaDB store means that it can be tuned for most usage scenarios, from high throughput applications (for example, trading platforms), to storing large amounts of messages (for example, GPS tracking).

To enable the KahaDB store for ActiveMQ, you need to configure the <persistenceAdapter> element in the activemq.xml configuration file. Here's a minimal configuration for the KahaDB message store:

```
<broker brokerName="broker" persistent="true" useShutdownHook="false">
...
```

```
    <persistenceAdapter>
    <kahaDB directory="activemq-data" journalMaxFileLength="16mb"/>
    </persistenceAdapter>
...
</broker>
```

If you want to embed an ActiveMQ broker inside an application, the message store can also be configured programmatically. Here's an example of a programmatic configuration for KahaDB:

```
public class EmbeddedBrokerUsingAMQStoreExample {

    BrokerService createEmbeddedBroker() throws Exception {        Initialize
                                                                    ActiveMQ
        BrokerService broker = new BrokerService();                 broker
        File dataFileDir = new File("target/amq-in-action/kahadb");

        KahaDBStore kaha = new KahaDBStore();
        kaha.setDirectory(dataFileDir);                     Create instance
                                                            of KahaDB
        // Using a bigger journal file                      message store
        kaha.setJournalMaxFileLength(1024*100);

        // small batch means more frequent and smaller writes
        kaha.setIndexWriteBatchSize(100);
        // do the index write in a separate thread
        kaha.setEnableIndexWriteAsync(true);                Instruct broker
                                                            to use KahaDB
        broker.setPersistenceAdapter(kaha);                 store
        //create a transport connector
        broker.addConnector("tcp://localhost:61616");       Create transport
        //start the broker                                  connector to expose
        broker.start();              Start broker           broker to clients

        return broker;
    }
}
```

Although the example seems small, it's enough to create an ActiveMQ broker using the KahaDB message store and listen for ActiveMQ clients connecting over TCP. For more information about embedding ActiveMQ, see chapter 8.

In order to better understand its use and configuration, it's important to examine the internals of the KahaDB message store.

5.2.1 The KahaDB message store internals

The KahaDB message store is the fastest of all the provided message store implementations. Its speed is the result of the combination of a fast transactional journal comprised of data log files, the highly optimized indexing of message IDs, and in-memory message caching. Figure 5.3 provides a high-level diagram of the KahaDB message store.

The diagram provides a view of the three distinct parts of the KahaDB message store including the following:

- *The data logs* act as a message journal, which consists of a rolling log of messages and commands (such as transactional boundaries and message deletions) stored in data files of a certain length. When the maximum length of the currently used data file has been reached, a new data file is created. All the messages in a data file are reference counted, so that once every message in that data file is no longer required, the data file can be removed or archived. In the data logs, messages are only appended to the end of the current data file, so storage is fast.

- *The cache* holds messages temporarily if there are active consumer(s) for the messages. If

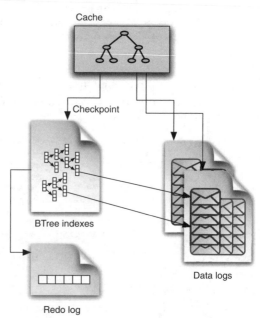

Figure 5.3   In KahaDB messages are stored in indexed log files and cached for performance.

there are active consumers, messages are dispatched at the same time they're scheduled to be stored. If messages are acknowledged in time, they don't need to be written to disk.

- *The BTree indexes* hold references to the messages in the data logs that are indexed by their message ID. The indexes maintain the FIFO data structure for queues and the durable subscriber pointers to their topic messages. The redo log is used only if the ActiveMQ broker hasn't shut down cleanly, and are used to insure the integrity of the BTree index is maintained.

The KahaDB uses different files on disk for its data logs and indexes, so in the next section we'll show a typical KahaDB directory structure.

5.2.2   *The KahaDB message store directory structure*

When you start an ActiveMQ broker configured to use a KahaDB store, a directory will automatically be created in which the persistent messages are stored. This directory structure is shown in figure 5.4.

Inside of the KahaDB directory, the following directory and file structures can be found:

- *db log files*—KahaDB stores messages into data log files named *db-<Number>.log* of a predefined size. When a data log is full, a new one will be created, and the log number incremented. When there are no more references to any of the messages in the data log file, it'll be deleted or archived.

- *archive directory*—This exists only if archiving is enabled. The archive is used to store data logs that are no longer needed by KahaDB, making it possible to replay messages from the archived data logs at a later point. If archiving isn't enabled (the default), data logs that are no longer in use are deleted from the file system.

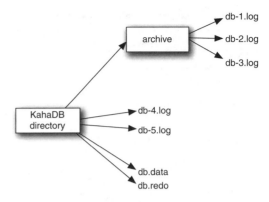

- *db.data*—This file contains the persistent BTree indexes to the messages held in the message data logs.

Figure 5.4   The KahaDB message store directory structure

- *db.redo*—This is the redo file, used for recovering the BTree indexes if the KahaDB message store starts after a hard stop.

Now that we've covered the basics of the KahaDB store, the next step is to review its configuration.

5.2.3   *Configuring the KahaDB message store*

The KahaDB message store can be configured in the activemq.xml file. Its configuration options control the different tuning parameters, as described in table 5.1.

Table 5.1   Configuration options available for the KahaDB message store

Property name	Default value	Description
directory	activemq-data	Directory path used by KahaDB
indexWriteBatchSize	1000	Number of index pages to write in a batch to disk
indexCacheSize	10000	Number of index pages cached in memory
enableIndexWriteAsync	false	If set, will asynchronously write indexes
journalMaxFileLength	32mb	A hint to set the maximum size of each of the message data logs
enableJournalDiskSyncs	true	Ensures every nontransactional journal write is followed by a disk sync (JMS durability requirement)
cleanupInterval	30000	Time (ms) before checking for and discarding/moving message data logs that are no longer used

Table 5.1 Configuration options available for the KahaDB message store *(continued)*

Property name	Default value	Description
checkpointInterval	5000	Time (ms) before checkpointing the journal
ignoreMissingJournalfiles	false	If enabled, will ignore a missing message log file
checkForCorruptJournalFiles	false	If enabled, on startup will validate that the message data logs haven't been corrupted.
checksumJournalFiles	false	If enabled, will provide a checksum for each message data log
archiveDataLogs	false	If enabled, will move a message data log to the archive directory instead of deleting it
directoryArchive	null	Defines the directory to move data logs to when all the messages they contain have been consumed
databaseLockedWaitDelay	10000	Time (ms) before trying to acquire the database lock (used by shared master/slave)
maxAsyncJobs	10000	Maximum number of asynchronous messages that will be queued awaiting storage (should be the same as the number of concurrent MessageProducers)
concurrentStoreAndDispatchTransactions	true	Enables the dispatching of messages to interested clients to happen concurrently with transaction storage
concurrentStoreAndDispatchTopics	true	Enables the dispatching of topic messages to interested clients to happen concurrently with message storage
concurrentStoreAndDispatchQueues	true	Enables the dispatching of queue messages to interested clients to happen concurrently with message storage

ActiveMQ provides a pluggable API for message stores, and there are three additional implementations to KahaDB that are shipped with ActiveMQ:

- *The AMQ message store*—A file-based message store designed for performance
- *The JDBC message store*—A message store based on JDBC
- *The Memory message store*—A memory-based message store

We'll look at the use cases and configuration for these additional message stores in the next three sections. We'll start with the AMQ message store, which like the KahaDB message store is a file-based implementation. It predates KahaDB, but because of its performance characteristics, it can make sense to use the AMQ store instead of KahaDB, provided the number of persistent destinations is relatively low.

5.3 The AMQ message store

The AMQ message store, like KahaDB, is a combination of a transactional journal for reliable persistence (to survive system crashes) and high-performance indexes, which makes this store the best option when message throughput is the main requirement for an application. But because it uses two separate files for every index, and there's an index per destination, the AMQ message store shouldn't be used if you intend to use thousands of queues per broker. Also, recovery can be slow if the ActiveMQ broker isn't shut down cleanly. This is because all the indexes need to be rebuilt, which requires the broker to traverse all its data logs to accurately build the indexes again.

In the next section, we'll briefly examine the internals of the AMQ message store, which are similar to the components of KahaDB.

5.3.1 The AMQ message store internals

The main components of the AMQ message store are similar to that of the KahaDB message store, in that there's a cache, message data logs, and a reference store for accessing the data logs in order. Figure 5.5 provides a high-level diagram of the AMQ message store.

The diagram provides a view of the three distinct parts of the AMQ message store:

- *The data logs*—These act as a message journal.
- *The cache*—This holds messages for fast retrieval in memory after they've been written to the data logs.
- *The reference store*—This holds references to the messages in the journal that are indexed by their message ID.

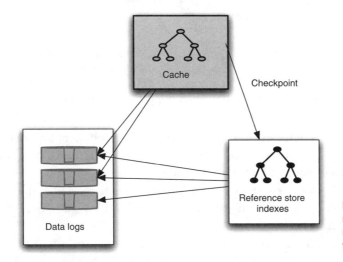

Figure 5.5 In the AMQ store messages are stored in referenced log files and cached for performance.

It's important to understand the file-based directory structure used by the ActiveMQ message store. This will help with the configuration and also with problem identification when using ActiveMQ.

5.3.2   *The AMQ message store directory structure*

When you start ActiveMQ with the AMQ message store configured, a directory will automatically be created in which the persistent messages are held. The AMQ message store directory contains subdirectories for all the brokers that are running on the machine. For this reason it's strongly recommended that each broker use a unique name. In the default configuration for ActiveMQ, the broker name is *localhost,* which needs to changed to something unique. This directory structure is represented in figure 5.6—the AMQ store directory structure.

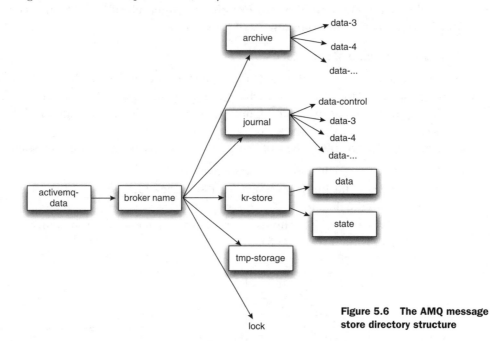

Figure 5.6   The AMQ message store directory structure

The following directories and files can be found inside the data directory of an ActiveMQ broker:

- *A lock file*—Ensures that only one broker can access this data at any given time. The lock is commonly used for hot standby purposes where more than one broker with the same name will exist on the same system.
- *A temp-storage directory*—Used for storing nonpersistent messages that can no longer be stored in broker memory. These messages are typically awaiting delivery to a slow consumer.
- *The kr-store*—The directory structure used by the reference (index) part of the AMQ message store. It uses the Kaha reference store by default (Kaha is part of

the ActiveMQ core library) to index and store references to messages in the data logs. There are two distinct parts to the kr-store:

* *The data directory*—Contains the indexes and collections used to reference the messages held in the data logs. This data directory is deleted and rebuilt as part of recovery, if the broker hasn't shut down cleanly. You can force recovery by manually deleting this directory before starting the broker.

* *The state directory*—Holds information about durable topic consumers. The journal itself doesn't hold information about consumers, so when it's recovered it has to retrieve information about the durable subscribers first to accurately rebuild its database.

- *The journal directory*—Contains the data files for the data logs, and a data-control file that holds some meta information. The data files are reference counted, so when all the contained messages are delivered, a data file can be deleted or archived.

- *The archive directory*—Exists only if archiving is enabled. Its default location can be found next to the journal. It makes sense to use a separate partition or disk. The archive is used to store data logs from the journal directory, which are moved here instead of being deleted. This makes it possible to replay messages from the archive at a later point. To replay messages, move the archived data logs (or a subset) to a new journal directory and start a new broker pointed to the location of this directory. It'll automatically replay the data logs in the journal.

Now that the basics of the AMQ message store have been covered, the next step is to review its configuration.

5.3.3   Configuring the AMQ message store

The AMQ store configuration allows the user to change its basic behaviour around indexing, checkpoint intervals, and the size of the journal data files. These items and many more can be customized through the use of properties. The key properties for the AMQ store are shown in table 5.2.

Table 5.2   Configuration properties for the AMQ message store

Property name	Default value	Description
directory	activemq-data	The directory path used by the AMQ message store.
useNIO	true	NIO provides faster write-through to the systems disks.
syncOnWrite	false	Syncs every write to disk.
syncOnTransaction	true	Syncs every transaction to disk.
maxFileLength	32mb	The maximum size of the message journal data files before a new one is used.

Table 5.2   Configuration properties for the AMQ message store *(continued)*

Property name	Default value	Description
persistentIndex	true	Persistent indexes are used. If false, an in-memory HashMap is used.
maxCheckpointMessageAddSize	4kb	The maximum memory used for a transaction before writing to disk.
cleanupInterval	3000(ms)	Time before checking which journal data files are still required.
checkpointInterval	20000(ms)	Time before moving cached message IDs to the reference store indexes.
indexBinSize	1024	The initial number of hash bins to use for indexes.
indexMaxBinSize	16384	The maximum number of hash bins to use.
directoryArchive	archive	The directory path used by the AMQ message store to place archived journal files.
archiveDataLogs	false	If true, journal files are moved to the archive instead of being deleted.
recoverReferenceStore	true	Recovers the reference store if the broker isn't shut down cleanly; this errs on the side of extreme caution.
forceRecoverReferenceStore	false	Forces a recovery of the reference store.

Here's an example of using the properties from table 5.2 in an ActiveMQ XML configuration file:

```xml
<?xml version="1.0" encoding="UTF-8"?>
<beans>
  <broker xmlns="http://activemq.apache.org/schema/core">
    <persistenceAdapter>
        <amqPersistenceAdapter
          directory="target/Broker2-data/activemq-data"
          syncOnWrite="true"
          indexPageSize="16kb"
          indexMaxBinSize="100"
          maxFileLength="10mb" />
    </persistenceAdapter>
  </broker>
</beans>
```

This is but a small example of a customized configuration for the AMQ store using the available properties.

The AMQ store, like the KahaDB store, enables users to get up and running quickly, as there are no external dependencies on other databases. But when you want to run an ActiveMQ broker and use an already established relational database, you need to use a JDBC message store.

5.4   *The JDBC message store*

The flexibility of the ActiveMQ pluggable message store API allows for many different implementation choices. The oldest and more common store implementation uses JDBC for messaging persistence.

The most common reason why so many organizations choose the JDBC message store is because they already have expertise administering relational databases. JDBC persistence is definitely not superior in performance to the aforementioned message store implementations. The fact of the matter is that many businesses have invested in the use of relational databases so they prefer to make full use of them.

But the use of a *shared* database is particularly useful for making a redundant master/slave topology out of multiple brokers. When a group of ActiveMQ brokers is configured to use a shared database, they'll all try to connect and grab a lock in the lock table, but only one will succeed and become the master. The remaining brokers will be slaves, and will be in a wait state, not accepting client connections until the master fails. This is a common deployment scenario for ActiveMQ, which will be covered in more detail in chapter 10.

When using the JDBC message store, the default JDBC driver used in ActiveMQ is Apache Derby. But many other relational databases are supported.

5.4.1   *Databases supported by the JDBC message store*

Just about any database with a JDBC driver can be used. Though this isn't an exhaustive list, the JDBC store has been shown to operate with the following relational databases:

- Apache Derby
- MySQL
- PostgreSQL
- Oracle
- SQL Server
- Sybase
- Informix
- MaxDB

Some users prefer to use a relational database for message persistence simply because of the ability to query the database to examine messages. The following sections will discuss this topic.

Using Apache Derby ActiveMQ

As mentioned, Apache Derby is the default database used with the JDBC store. Not only is it written in 100% Java, but it's also designed to be embeddable. Derby offers a full feature set, performs well, and provides a small footprint. But there's one caveat with the use of Derby that should be passed along to ActiveMQ users. Derby can be tough on the garbage collector in the JVM. Because so much churn takes place with the storing and deleting of messages in the database, experience has proven that putting Derby in its own JVM instance allows ActiveMQ to perform much better. The reason for this comes down to the fact that ActiveMQ and Derby will no longer be competing for the same JVM resources.

5.4.2   *The JDBC message store schema*

The JDBC message store uses a schema consisting of three tables. Two of the tables are used to hold messages, and the third is used as a lock table to ensure that only one ActiveMQ broker can access the database at one time. Here's a detailed breakdown of these tables.

The message table, shown in table 5.3, is by default named ACTIVEMQ_MSGS and is defined as follows.

Table 5.3   The columns of the ACTIVEMQ_MSGS SQL table

Column name	Default type	Description
ID	INTEGER	The sequence ID used to retrieve the message.
CONTAINER	VARCHAR(250)	The destination of the message.
MSGID_PROD	VARCHAR(250)	The ID of the message producer.
MSGID_SEQ	INTEGER	The producer sequence number for the message. This together with the MSGID_PROD is equivalent to the JMS-MessageID.
EXPIRATION	BIGINT	The time in milliseconds when the message will expire.
MSG	BLOB	The serialized message itself.

Messages are broken down and stored into the ACTIVEMQ_MSGS table for both queues and topics.

There's a separate table for holding durable subscriber information and an ID to the last message the durable subscriber received. This information is held in the ACTIVEMQ_ACKS table, which is shown in table 5.4.

Table 5.4   The columns of the ACTIVEMQ_ACKS SQL table

Column name	Default type	Description
CONTAINER	VARCHAR(250)	The destination of the message
SUB_DEST	VARCHAR(250)	The destination of the durable subscriber (can be different from the container if using wildcards)
CLIENT_ID	VARCHAR(250)	The client ID of the durable subscriber
SUB_NAME	VARCHAR(250)	The subscriber name of the durable subscriber
SELECTOR	VARCHAR(250)	The selector of the durable subscriber
LAST_ACKED_ID	Integer	The sequence ID of last message received by this subscriber

For durable subscribers, the LAST_ACKED_ID sequence is used as a simple pointer into the ACTIVEMQ_MSGS and enables messages for a particular durable subscriber to be easily selected from the ACTIVEMQ_MSGS table.

The lock table, called ACTIVEMQ_LOCK, is used to ensure that only one ActiveMQ broker instance can access the database at one time. If an ActiveMQ broker can't grab the database lock, that broker won't initialize fully, and will wait until the lock becomes free, or it's shut down. The table structure of the lock table is defined in table 5.5.

Table 5.5 The columns of the ACTIVEMQ_LOCK SQL table

Column name	Default type	Description
ID	INTEGER	A unique ID for the lock
Broker Name	VARCHAR(250)	The name of the ActiveMQ broker that has the lock

Now that we've explained the structure of the database tables used by the JDBC store, we can walk through some examples of configuring JDBC message stores, which we look at in the next section.

5.4.3 Configuring the JDBC message store

Configuring the default JDBC message store is straightforward. As stated previously, the default JDBC store uses Apache Derby in the broker configuration as shown:

```
<beans>
  <broker brokerName="test-broker"
    persistent="true"
    xmlns="http://activemq.apache.org/schema/core">

    <persistenceAdapter>
      <jdbcPersistenceAdapter dataDirectory="activemq-data"/>
    </persistenceAdapter>

  </broker>
</beans>
```

The preceding configuration sets the persistence adaptor for the ActiveMQ broker to be the JDBC message store (which uses Apache Derby by default) and sets the data directory to be used by the embedded Apache Derby instance.

One of the key properties on the JDBC persistence adapter (the interface onto the JDBC message store) is the `dataSource` property. This property defines a factory from which connections to a relational database are created. Configuring the `dataSource` object enables the JDBC persistence adaptor to use physical databases other than the default. Here's an example of an ActiveMQ configuration for the JDBC message store using the MySQL database:

```
<?xml version="1.0" encoding="UTF-8"?>
<beans>
  <broker brokerName="test-broker"
    persistent="true"
    xmlns="http://activemq.apache.org/schema/core">

    <persistenceAdapter>
```

```
      <jdbcPersistenceAdapter dataSource="#mysql-ds"/>
   </persistenceAdapter>
</broker>

<bean id="mysql-ds"
  class="org.apache.commons.dbcp.BasicDataSource"
  destroy-method="close">
 <property name="driverClassName" value="com.mysql.jdbc.Driver"/>
 <property name="url"
   value="jdbc:mysql://localhost/activemq?relaxAutoCommit=true"/>
 <property name="username" value="activemq"/>
 <property name="password" value="activemq"/>
 <property name="maxActive" value="200"/>
 <property name="poolPreparedStatements" value="true"/>
</bean>

</beans>
```

The preceding example uses the Apache Commons DBCP BasicDataSource to wrap the MySQL JDBC driver for connection pooling. In the example, the driverClassName is the name of the JDBC driver to use. Some properties that you can configure are passed directly to the database driver itself. For example, maxActive is a property for the MySQL database connector, which tells the database how many active connections to hold open at one time.

Just as a point of comparison, here's an example of a configuration to use the Oracle database:

```
<?xml version="1.0" encoding="UTF-8"?>
<beans>
  <broker brokerName="test-broker"
    persistent=true
    xmlns="http://activemq.apache.org/schema/core">

    <persistenceAdapter>
      <jdbcPersistenceAdapter dataSource="#oracle-ds"/>
    </persistenceAdapter>
  </broker>

 <bean id="oracle-ds" class="org.apache.commons.dbcp.BasicDataSource"
   destroy-method="close">
    <property name="driverClassName"
      value="oracle.jdbc.driver.OracleDriver"/>
    <property name="url" value="jdbc:oracle:thin:@localhost:1521:AMQDB"/>
    <property name="username" value="scott"/>
    <property name="password" value="tiger"/>
    <property name="maxActive" value="200"/>
    <property name="poolPreparedStatements" value="true"/>
 </bean>

</beans>
```

This example uses the Apache Commons DBCP BasicDataSource to wrap the Oracle JDBC driver for connection pooling.

Now that some example configurations for the JDBC message store have been shown, you might ask, when is it best to use this type of persistence?

5.4.4　Using the JDBC message store with the ActiveMQ journal

Though the performance of the JDBC message store isn't wonderful, it can be improved through the use of the ActiveMQ journal. The journal ensures the consistency of JMS transactions. Because it incorporates fast message writes with caching technology, it can significantly improve the performance of the ActiveMQ broker.

Here's an example configuration using the journal with JDBC (aka journaled JDBC). In this case, Apache Derby is being used.

```
<?xml version="1.0" encoding="UTF-8"?>
<beans>
  <broker brokerName="test-broker"
    xmlns="http://activemq.apache.org/schema/core">

    <persistenceFactory>
      <journalPersistenceAdapterFactory
        journalLogFiles="4"
        journalLogFileSize="32768"
        useJournal="true"
        useQuickJournal="true"
        dataSource="#derby-ds"
        dataDirectory="activemq-data" />
    </persistenceFactory>

  </broker>

  <bean id="derby-ds" class="org.apache.derby.jdbc.EmbeddedDataSource">
    <property name="databaseName" value="derbydb"/>
    <property name="createDatabase" value="create"/>
  </bean>

</beans>
```

The journal can be used with any JDBC datasource, but it's important to know when it should and shouldn't be used.

The journal offers considerable performance advantages over the use of a standard JDBC message store, especially when the JDBC database is co-located on the same machine as the ActiveMQ broker. The only time when it's not possible to use the journal is in a shared database master/slave configuration. Because messages from the master may be stored locally in the journal before they've been committed to the database, using the journal in this configuration could lead to lost messages if the master failed because the journal isn't replicated.

We've covered message storage in relational databases with some example configurations. In the next section we'll look at the memory store, which doesn't persist messages.

5.5　The memory message store

The memory message store holds all persistent messages in memory. No active caching is involved, so you have to be careful that both the JVM and the memory limits you set for the broker are large enough to accommodate all the messages that may exist in this message store at one time.

The memory message store can be useful if you know that the broker will only store a finite amount of messages, which will typically be consumed quickly. But it really comes into its own for small test cases, where you want to prove interaction with a JMS broker, but don't want to incur the cost of a message store start time, or the hassle of cleaning up the message store after the test has finished.

5.5.1   Configuring the memory store

Configuring the memory store is simple. The memory store is the implementation used when the broker property named `persistent` is set to false (the default is true). Here's an example of configuration which enables use of the ActiveMQ message store:

```
<?xml version="1.0" encoding="UTF-8"?>
<beans>
    <broker brokerName="test-broker"
            persistent="false"
            xmlns="http://activemq.apache.org/schema/core">
        <transportConnectors>
            <transportConnector uri="tcp://localhost:61635"/>
        </transportConnectors>
    </broker>

</beans>
```

By setting the `persistent` attribute on the broker element to false, this effectively tells the broker not to persist messages to long-term storage. Instead, the ActiveMQ broker will hold messages in memory until the messages are either consumed or the ActiveMQ broker is shut down.

Embedding an ActiveMQ broker with the memory store is easy. The following example starts a broker with the memory store:

```
import org.apache.activemq.broker.BrokerService;

public void createEmbeddedBroker() throws Exception {

    BrokerService broker = new BrokerService();
    //configure the broker to use the Memory Store
    broker.setPersistent(false);

    //Add a transport connector
    broker.addConnector("tcp://localhost:61616");

    //now start the broker
    broker.start();
}
```

Note the bold text that sets persistence to false on the broker object. This is equivalent to the previous XML configuration example.

There are currently no utilities to change from one type of ActiveMQ message store to another. If you want to change message stores for an application, it's recommended that you only do so on a new ActiveMQ broker, or wait until your application has consumed all the messages sent, then close down the ActiveMQ broker, reconfigure it for a new message store, and restart it.

This concludes the discussion of the various message store implementations for message persistent in ActiveMQ. Another topic that bears some discussion regarding message persistence is a more specialized case for caching messages in the ActiveMQ broker for nondurable topic subscribers.

5.6　*Caching messages in the broker for consumers*

Although one of the most important aspects of message persistence is that the messages will survive in long-term storage, there are a number of cases where messages are required to be available for consumers that were disconnected from the broker, but persisting the messages in a database is too slow. Real-time data delivery of pricing information for a trading platform is a good example. But typically real-time data applications use messages that are only valid for a finite amount of time, often less than a minute. So it's pointless to persist them to survive a system outage because new messages will arrive soon.

ActiveMQ supports the caching of messages for these types of systems using message caching in the broker by using something called a *subscription recovery policy*. This configurable policy is used for deciding which types of messages should be cached, how many, and for how long. In the rest of this section we'll explain how message caching works in ActiveMQ and how to configure the different types of subscription recovery policies that are available.

5.6.1　*How message caching for consumers works*

The ActiveMQ message broker caches messages in memory for every topic that's used. The only types of topics that aren't supported are temporary topics and ActiveMQ advisory topics. Caching of messages in this way isn't handled for queues, as the normal operation of a queue is to hold every message sent to it.

Messages that are cached by the broker are only dispatched to a topic consumer if the consumer is retroactive, and never to durable topic subscribers.

Topic consumers are marked as being retroactive by a property set on the destination when the topic consumer is created. Here's an example:

```
import org.apache.activemq.ActiveMQConnectionFactory;
import javax.jms.Connection;
import javax.jms.ConnectionFactory;
import javax.jms.MessageConsumer;
import javax.jms.Session;
import javax.jms.Topic;

    public void createRetroactiveConsumer() throws JMSException{

        ConnectionFactory fac = new ActiveMQConnectionFactory();
        Connection connection = fac.createConnection();
        connection.start();                              Mark consumers
                                                         to be retroactive
        Session session =
            connection.createSession(false,Session.AUTO_ACKNOWLEDGE);
        Topic topic =
            session.createTopic("TEST.TOPIC?consumer.retroactive=true");
```

```
        MessageConsumer consumer = session.createConsumer(topic);
}
```

On the broker side, the message caching is controlled by a *destination policy* called a subscriptionRecoveryPolicy. The default subscription recovery policy used in the broker is a FixedSizeSubscriptionRecoveryPolicy. Let's walk through the different subscription recovery policies that are available.

5.6.2 *The ActiveMQ subscription recovery policies*

There are a number of different policies that allow for fine-tuning the duration and type of messages that are cached for nondurable topic consumers. Each policy type is explained here.

THE ACTIVEMQ FIXED SIZE SUBSCRIPTION RECOVERY POLICY

This policy limits the number of messages cached for the topic based on the amount of memory they use. This is the default subscription recovery policy in ActiveMQ. You can choose to have the cache limit applied to all topics, or on a topic-by-topic basis. The properties available are shown in table 5.6.

Table 5.6   Configuration properties for a fixed size subscription recovery policy

Property name	Default value	Description
maximumSize	6553600	The memory size in bytes for this cache
useSharedBuffer	true	If true, the amount of memory allocated will be used across all topics

THE ACTIVEMQ FIXED COUNT SUBSCRIPTION RECOVERY POLICY

This policy limits the number of messages cached by the topic based on a static count. Only one property is available, as listed in table 5.7.

Table 5.7   Configuration properties for a fixed count subscription recovery policy

Property name	Default value	Description
maximumSize	100	The number of messages allowed in the topics cache

THE ACTIVEMQ QUERY-BASED SUBSCRIPTION RECOVERY POLICY

This policy limits the number of messages cached based on a JMS property selector that's applied to each message. Only one property is available, as shown in table 5.8.

Table 5.8   Configuration properties for a query-based subscription recovery policy

Property name	Default value	Description
query	null	Caches only messages that match the query

THE ACTIVEMQ TIMED SUBSCRIPTION RECOVERY POLICY

This policy limits the number of messages cached by the topic based on an expiration time that's applied to each message. Note that the expiration time on a message is independent from the `timeToLive` that's set by the `MessageProducer`. The configuration properties for a timed subscription policy are shown in table 5.9.

Table 5.9   Configuration properties for a timed subscription recovery policy

Property name	Default value	Description
recoverDuration	60000	The time in milliseconds to keep messages in the cache

THE ACTIVEMQ LAST IMAGE SUBSCRIPTION RECOVERY POLICY

This policy holds only the last message sent to a topic. It can be useful for real-time pricing information—where a price per topic is used, you might only want the last price that's sent to that topic. There are no configuration properties for this policy.

THE ACTIVEMQ NO SUBSCRIPTION RECOVERY POLICY

This policy disables message caching for topics. There are no properties to configure for this policy.

5.6.3   *Configuring the subscription recovery policy*

You can configure the `subscriptionRecoveryPolicy` for either individual topics, or you can use wildcards, in the ActiveMQ broker configuration. An example configuration is shown here:

```
<?xml version="1.0" encoding="UTF-8"?>
<beans>
  <broker brokerName="test-broker"
          persistent="true"
          useShutdownHook="false"
          deleteAllMessagesOnStartup="true"
          xmlns="http://activemq.apache.org/schema/core">
    <transportConnectors>
      <transportConnector uri="tcp://localhost:61635"/>
    </transportConnectors>
    <destinationPolicy>
      <policyMap>
        <policyEntries>
          <policyEntry topic="Topic.FixedSizedSubs.">
            <subscriptionRecoveryPolicy>
              <fixedSizeSubscriptionRecoveryPolicy maximumSize="2000000"
                useSharedBuffer="false"/>
            </subscriptionRecoveryPolicy>
          </policyEntry>

          <policyEntry topic="Topic.LastImageSubs.">
            <subscriptionRecoveryPolicy>
              <lastImageSubscriptionRecoveryPolicy/>
            </subscriptionRecoveryPolicy>
          </policyEntry>
```

◁ **Fixed size recovery policy for Topic.FixedSizeSubs.>**

◁ **Last image recovery for Topic.LastImageSubs.>**

```
        <policyEntry topic="Topic.NoSubs.>">
          <subscriptionRecoveryPolicy>
            <noSubscriptionRecoveryPolicy/>
          </subscriptionRecoveryPolicy>
        </policyEntry>

        <policyEntry topic="Topic.TimedSubs.>">
          <subscriptionRecoveryPolicy>
            <timedSubscriptionRecoveryPolicy recoverDuration="25000"/>
          </subscriptionRecoveryPolicy>
        </policyEntry>
      </policyEntries>
    </policyMap>
  </destinationPolicy>
</broker>

</beans>
```

<- No recovery policy for Topic.LastImageSubs.>

<- Time limited recovery policy for Topic.TimedSubs.>

5.7   Summary

This chapter began by discussing how messages are stored differently for queues and topics. Then the various message store implementations were explained and discussed, including their configuration and when to use each. You should have a good understanding about the two types of file-based message stores that you can use with ActiveMQ—the AMQ message store and the KahaDB message store—and their trade-offs between performance and scalability. We also covered the JDBC message store, which is an option if you want to use an existing relational database and the ActiveMQ memory message store.

Finally we discussed the special case for caching messages in the broker for nondurable topic consumers. This section explained why caching is required, when it makes sense to use this feature, and the flexibility ActiveMQ provides in configuring the message caches.

In the next chapter, we'll look at authentication of users of ActiveMQ and how to restrict access to destinations using authorization.

Securing ActiveMQ

6

This chapter covers

- How to use authentication in ActiveMQ
- How to use authorization in ActiveMQ
- How to create a custom security plug-in for ActiveMQ
- Using certificate-based security with ActiveMQ

Securing access to the message broker and its destinations is a common concern. For this reason, ActiveMQ provides a flexible and customizable security model that can be adapted to the security mechanisms used in your environment.

Before we begin our discussion about security with ActiveMQ, a brief review of some basic terms related to security and how they fit into the ActiveMQ security model is in order.

Authentication is the process used to verify the integrity of an entity or a user that's requesting access to a secured resource. Some common forms of authentication include plain-text passwords, one-time password devices, smart cards, or Kerberos, just to name a few. ActiveMQ provides simple authentication and JAAS (Java Authentication and Authorization Service) authentication, as well as an API for writing custom authentication plug-ins. Upon successful authentication, access to the system is granted, but access to perform operations using the system resources may require specific authorization.

Authorization is the process used to determine the access rights of a user or an entity to a secured resource. Authorization depends upon authentication to prevent unauthorized users from entering the system, but authorization determines whether a user has the privileges to perform certain actions. For example, does user X have the necessary permissions to execute program Y on system Z? Such privileges are often referred to as *access control lists* (ACLs) and determine who or what can access a given resource to perform a given operation. In ActiveMQ, authentication involves restricting access to various operations including the ability to publish to a destination, to consume from a destination, to create a destination, or to delete a destination.

We'll start this chapter by describing authentication plug-ins. We'll see how we can set authentication directly in XML configuration by using the *simple authentication plug-in* or by using the JAAS API. Next, it's time to deal with authorization. We'll cover the *authorization plug-in*, which in conjunction with the authentication plug-ins allows us to define a fine-grained security access to broker clients. Besides this standard per-client authorization, ActiveMQ allows you to do authorization on the message level, as we'll see next. If none of these built-in security mechanisms works for you, you can always build your own. We'll demonstrate this process by building a custom security plug-in that authenticates the clients based on their IP address. The final section of this chapter will deal with certificate-based security. We'll expand on our SSL example used in chapter 4 and see how you can authenticate and authorize clients based on their SSL certificates.

So, after reading this chapter, you'll be able to secure the broker and integrate it fully with your existing security infrastructure. Now let's look at some practical examples of ActiveMQ security configurations.

6.1   *Authentication*

All security concepts in ActiveMQ are implemented as plug-ins. This allows for easy configuration and customization via the `<plugin>` element of the ActiveMQ XML configuration file. Two plug-ins are available in ActiveMQ to authenticate users:

- *Simple authentication plug-in*—Handles credentials directly in the XML configuration file or in a properties file
- *JAAS authentication plug-in*—Implements the JAAS API and provides a more powerful and customizable authentication solution

Let's review these two authentication plug-ins.

6.1.1   *Configuring the simple authentication plug-in*

The easiest way to secure the broker is through the use of authentication credentials placed directly in the broker's XML configuration file. Such functionality is provided by the simple authentication plug-in that's part of ActiveMQ. The following listing provides an example of using this plug-in.

Listing 6.1 Configuring the simple authentication plug-in

```
<broker ...>

  <plugins>
    <simpleAuthenticationPlugin>
      <users>
        <authenticationUser username="admin" password="password"
          groups="admins,publishers,consumers"/>
        <authenticationUser username="publisher" password="password"
          groups="publishers,consumers"/>
        <authenticationUser username="consumer" password="password"
          groups="consumers"/>
        <authenticationUser username="guest" password="password"
          groups="guests"/>
      </users>
    </simpleAuthenticationPlugin>
  </plugins>

</broker>
```

Four authentication users with their groups

By using this simple configuration snippet, four users can now access ActiveMQ. Obviously, for authentication purposes, each user must have a username and a password. Additionally, the `groups` attribute provides a comma-separated list of groups to which the user belongs. This information is used for authorization purposes, as will be seen shortly.

The best way to understand this configuration is to use it with the stock portfolio example. First, the broker must be started using the configuration file defined earlier:

```
${ACTIVEMQ_HOME}/bin/activemq console \
xbean:src/main/resources/org/apache/activemq/book/ch6/activemq-simple.xml
```

Now run the stock publisher and you should see the following exception:

```
$ mvn exec:java \
-Dexec.mainClass=org.apache.activemq.book.ch3.portfolio.Publisher \
-Dexec.args="CSCO ORCL"
...
Exception in thread "main"
javax.jms.JMSException: User name or password is invalid.
 ...
```

The preceding exception is expected because a security plug-in is activated but the authentication credentials haven't yet been defined in the publisher client. To fix this exception, modify the publisher to add a username and password. The following snippet provides an example of this:

```
private String username = "publisher";
private String password = "password";

public Publisher() throws JMSException {
    factory = new ActiveMQConnectionFactory(brokerURL);
    connection = factory.createConnection(username, password);
    connection.start();
```

```
    session = connection.createSession(false,
    Session.AUTO_ACKNOWLEDGE);
    producer = session.createProducer(null);
}
```

As the preceding snippet shows, the only necessary change is to define a username and a password that are then used as parameters to the call to the `create-Connection()` method. Compiling and running the modified publisher will now yield the proper behavior, as shown in the following output:

```
$ mvn exec:java \
-Dexec.mainClass=org.apache.activemq.book.ch6.Publisher
-Dexec.args="CSCO ORCL"
...
Sending: {price=35.25020234334, stock=ORCL, offer=35.28545254568,
up=true} on destination: topic://STOCKS.ORCL
Sending: {price=35.018408299624, stock=ORCL, offer=35.053426707924,
up=false} on destination: topic://STOCKS.ORCL
Sending: {price=34.722966908601, stock=ORCL, offer=34.75768987551,
up=false} on destination: topic://STOCKS.ORCL
Sending: {price=1.651542629939308, stock=CSCO, offer=1.653194172569,
up=true} on destination: topic://STOCKS.CSCO
Sending: {price=34.598719623046, stock=ORCL, offer=34.63331834266,
up=false} on destination:topic://STOCKS.ORCL
Sending: {price=34.43900856142, stock=ORCL, offer=34.47344756998,
up=false} on destination: topic://STOCKS.ORCL
Sending: {price=1.6580787335090, stock=CSCO, offer=1.659736812242,
up=true} on destination: topic://STOCKS.CSCO
Sending: {price=34.458768559093, stock=ORCL, offer=34.49322732765,
up=true} on destination: topic://STOCKS.ORCL
Sending: {price=1.6547727745488, stock=CSCO, offer=1.6564275473233,
up=false} on destination:topic://STOCKS.CSCO
Sending: {price=1.665375738897, stock=CSCO, offer=1.6670411146368,
up=true} on destination: topic://STOCKS.CSCO
Published '10' of '10' price messages
...
```

Note in the output that our producer successfully connects to the broker and sends messages.

Unfortunately, with the simple authentication plug-in, passwords are stored (and transferred) as clear text, which impacts the security of the broker. But even plain-text passwords prevent unauthorized clients from interacting with the broker, and in some environments this is all that's needed. Additionally, you can consider using the simple authentication plug-in in combination with the SSL transport, which will at least solve the problem of sending plain passwords over the network.

For environments that need a more secure installation and/or for environments that already have an existing security infrastructure with which ActiveMQ will need to integrate, the JAAS plug-in may be more appropriate.

6.1.2 Configuring the JAAS plug-in

A detailed explanation of JAAS is beyond the scope of this book. Instead, this section will briefly introduce JAAS basic concepts and demonstrate how to create a `Properties-LoginModule` that can be used to achieve the same functionality as the simple security plug-in using JAAS. For more detailed information about JAAS, please refer to the JAAS documentation (http://mng.bz/BvvB).

JAAS provides *pluggable authentication*, which means ActiveMQ will use the same authentication API regardless of the technique used to verify user credentials (a text file, a relational database, LDAP, and so on). All that's required is an implementation of the `javax.security.auth.spi.LoginModule` interface (http://mng.bz/8zLV) and a configuration change to ActiveMQ. Fortunately, ActiveMQ comes with implementations of some modules that can authenticate users using properties files, LDAP, and SSL certificates, which will be enough for many use cases. Because JAAS login modules follow a specification, one advantage of them is that they're relatively straightforward to configure. The best way to understand a login module is by walking through a configuration. For this task, the login module that works with properties files will be used.

The first step in this task is to identify the `PropertiesLoginModule` so that ActiveMQ is made aware of it. To do so, you must create a file named login.config that contains a standardized format for configuring JAAS users and groups (http://mng.bz/IIEB). Here are the contents of the file:

```
activemq-domain {
    org.apache.activemq.jaas.PropertiesLoginModule required
        debug=true
        org.apache.activemq.jaas.properties.user="users.properties"
        org.apache.activemq.jaas.properties.group="groups.properties";
};
```

The login.config file shown here contains a few different items for configuring a JAAS module. The `activemq-domain` is the predominant item in this file and it contains all the configuration for the login module. First is the fully qualified name of the `PropertiesLoginModule` and the trailing notation identifying it as required. This means that the authentication can't continue without this login module. Second is a line to enable debug logging for the login module; this is optional. Third is the `org.apache.activemq.jaas.properties.user` property, which points to the users.properties file. Fourth is the `org.apache.activemq.jaas.properties.group` property, which points to the groups.properties file. Once this is all defined, the two properties files must be created.

> **NOTE** The `PropertiesLoginModule` used in this section is an implementation of a JAAS login module, and it comes with ActiveMQ.

Defining user credentials in the properties files is simple. The users.properties file defines each user in a line-delimited manner along with its password, as shown:

```
admin=password
publisher=password
```

```
consumer=password
guest=password
```

The groups.properties file defines group names in a line-delimited manner as well. But each group contains a comma-separated list of its users as shown:

```
admins=admin
publishers=admin,publisher
consumers=admin,publisher,consumer
guests=guest
```

Once these files are created, the JAAS plug-in must be defined in the ActiveMQ XML configuration file. The following is an example of this necessary change:

```
...
<plugins>
  <jaasAuthenticationPlugin configuration="activemq-domain" />
</plugins>
...
```

The example is shortened for readability and only shows the necessary change to enable the JAAS login module. As you can see, the JAAS plug-in only needs the name of the JAAS domain in the login.config file. ActiveMQ will locate the login.config file on the classpath (an alternative to this is to use the `java.security.auth.login.config` system property for the location of the login.config file). To test out the JAAS login module that was just created, start up ActiveMQ using these changes. Here's the command to use:

```
${ACTIVEMQ_HOME}/bin/activemq console \
-Djava.security.auth.login.config=\
src/main/resources/org/apache/activemq/book/ch6/login.config \
xbean:src/main/resources/org/apache/activemq/book/ch6/activemq-jaas.xml
...
Loading message broker from:
xbean:src/main/resources/org/apache/activemq/book/ch6/activemq-jaas.xml
 INFO | PListStore:
/Users/bsnyder/amq/apache-activemq-5.4.1/data/localhost/tmp_storage
started
 INFO | Using Persistence Adapter: KahaDBPersistenceAdapter
[/Users/bsnyder/amq/apache-activemq-5.4.1/data/localhost/KahaDB]
 INFO | JMX consoles can connect to service:
jmx:rmi:///jndi/rmi://localhost:1099/jmxrmi
 INFO | ActiveMQ 5.4.1 JMS Message Broker (localhost) is starting
 INFO | For help or more information please see:
http://activemq.apache.org/
 INFO | Scheduler using directory:
/Users/bsnyder/amq/apache-activemq-5.4.1/data/localhost/scheduler
 INFO | JobSchedulerStore:
/Users/bsnyder/amq/apache-activemq-5.4.1/data/localhost/scheduler
started
 INFO | Listening for connections at: tcp://localhost:61616
 INFO | Connector openwire Started
 INFO | ActiveMQ JMS Message Broker
(localhost, ID:mongoose.local-61955-1289966951514-0:0) started
```

The broker has been secured just like the previous section where simple authentication was used, only now the JAAS standard was used. Now we can start our stock portfolio publisher that uses proper credentials and expect it to be able to access the broker:

```
mvn exec:java \
-Dexec.mainClass=org.apache.activemq.book.ch6.Publisher \
-Dexec.args="CSCO ORCL"
...
Sending: {price=44.84266119470, stock=ORCL, offer=44.88750385590,
up=true} on destination: topic://STOCKS.ORCL
Sending: {price=44.5575471806, stock=ORCL, offer=44.60210472778,
up=false} on destination: topic://STOCKS.ORCL
Sending: {price=44.49794307251, stock=ORCL, offer=44.54244101559,
up=false} on destination: topic://STOCKS.ORCL
Sending: {price=44.48574009628, stock=ORCL, offer=44.530225836380,
up=false} on destination: topic://STOCKS.ORCL
Sending: {price=55.89763705357, stock=CSCO, offer=55.953534690630,
up=true} on destination: topic://STOCKS.CSCO
Sending: {price=44.09643970531, stock=ORCL, offer=44.140536145020,
up=false} on destination: topic://STOCKS.ORCL
Sending: {price=44.20879151845, stock=ORCL, offer=44.25300030997,
up=true} on destination: topic://STOCKS.ORCL
Sending: {price=44.38257378288, stock=ORCL, offer=44.426956356664,
up=true} on destination: topic://STOCKS.ORCL
Sending: {price=44.660334580924, stock=ORCL, offer=44.704994915505,
up=true} on destination: topic://STOCKS.ORCL
Sending: {price=44.77852477644, stock=ORCL, offer=44.8233033012,
up=true} on destination: topic://STOCKS.ORCL
Published '10' of '10' price messages
...
```

As we can see, the JAAS plug-in provides exactly the same functionality as the simple authentication plug-in. But it does so using the standardized Java mechanism, meaning you can use it to plug in any existing security policies you use inside your organization.

In addition to the ability to authenticate access to the broker services, ActiveMQ also provides the ability to authorize specific operations at a fine-grained level. The next section explores this topic thoroughly.

6.2   *Authorization*

To build upon authentication, consider a use case requiring more fine-grained control over clients to authorize certain tasks. In most stock trading applications, only specific applications can write to a given destination. After all, you wouldn't want any old application publishing stock prices to the STOCKS.* destinations. Only an authenticated *and* authorized application should have this ability.

For this reason, ActiveMQ provides two levels of authorization: operation-level authorization and message-level authorization. These two types of authorization provide a more detailed level of control than simple authentication. This section discusses these two types of authorization and walks through some examples to demonstrate each.

6.2.1   *Destination-level authorization*

There are three types of user-level operations with JMS destinations:

- *Read*—The ability to receive messages from the destination
- *Write*—The ability to send messages to the destination
- *Admin*—The ability to administer the destination

Through these well-known operations, you can control the ability to perform the operations. Using the ActiveMQ XML configuration file, such authorization can be easily defined. Take a look at the following listing to add some operation-specific authorization to some destinations.

Listing 6.2   Configuring destination-level authorization

```
...
<plugins>
  <jaasAuthenticationPlugin
       configuration="activemq-domain" />
    <authorizationPlugin>
      <map>
        <authorizationMap>
          <authorizationEntries>
            <authorizationEntry topic=">"
              read="admins" write="admins" admin="admins" />
            <authorizationEntry topic="STOCKS.>"
             read="consumers" write="publishers"              Authorization entry for
             admin="publishers" />                            STOCKS.> destinations

             <authorizationEntry topic="STOCKS.ORCL"
               read="guests" />
            <authorizationEntry topic="ActiveMQ.Advisory.>"
              read="admins,publishers,consumers,guests"
              write="admins,publishers,consumers,guests"
              admin="admins,publishers,consumers,guests" />
          </authorizationEntries>
        </authorizationMap>
      </map>
    </authorizationPlugin>
</plugins>
...
```

In the listing, the JAAS authorization plug-in has been defined and pointed at the `activemq-domain` configuration in the login.config file. It has also been provided with a map of authorization entries. When configuring the map of authorization entries, the first task is to define the destination to be secured. This is achieved through the use of either a `topic` or a `queue` attribute on the entry. The next task is to declare which users and/or groups have privileges for operations on that destination.

A handy feature is the ability to define the destination value using *wildcards*. For example, `STOCKS.>` means the entry applies to all destinations in the `STOCKS` path recursively. You can find more information on wildcards in chapter 11. Also, the authorization operations will accept either a single group or a comma-separated list of groups as a value.

Considering this explanation, the configuration used in the previous example can be translated as follows:

- Users from the *admins* group have full access to all topics
- *Consumers* can consume and *publishers* can publish to the destinations in the STOCKS path
- *Guests* can only consume from the STOCKS.ORCL topic

The previous example uses an additive model, where all operations on a topic have been restricted to administrators only. Beyond this, specific operations on specific destinations are added as needed.

In order to start the broker to test out both the JAAS authentication plug-in as well as the authorization entries, use the following command to start the broker:

```
${ACTIVEMQ_HOME}/bin/activemq console \
-Djava.security.auth.login.config=\
src/main/resources/org/apache/activemq/book/ch6/login.config
xbean:src/main/resources/org/apache/activemq/book/ch6/\
activemq-authorization.xml
...
xbean:src/main/resources/org/apache/activemq/book/ch6/\
activemq-authorization.xml
 INFO | PListStore:
/Users/bsnyder/amq/apache-activemq-5.4.1/data/localhost/tmp_storage
 started
 INFO | Using Persistence Adapter: KahaDBPersistenceAdapter
[/Users/bsnyder/amq/apache-activemq-5.4.1/data/localhost/KahaDB]
 INFO | JMX consoles can connect to service:
jmx:rmi:///jndi/rmi://localhost:1099/jmxrmi
 INFO | ActiveMQ 5.4.1 JMS Message Broker (localhost) is starting
 INFO | For help or more information please see:
http://activemq.apache.org/
 INFO | Scheduler using directory:
/Users/bsnyder/amq/apache-activemq-5.4.1/data/localhost/scheduler
 INFO | JobSchedulerStore:
/Users/bsnyder/amq/apache-activemq-5.4.1/data/localhost/scheduler
started
 INFO | Listening for connections at: tcp://localhost:61616
 INFO | Connector openwire Started
 INFO | ActiveMQ JMS Message Broker
(localhost, ID:mongoose.local-62861-1289968271876-0:0) started
```

Note the use of the java.security.auth.login.config system property to point to the login.config file. This ensures that ActiveMQ can locate the file for its use.

Now let's see how introduction of authorization affects JMS clients. We'll demonstrate our authorization setup by trying to consume from the stock topics. As we were doing for the publisher example in the previous section, we'll modify our original stock portfolio consumer and make it pass an appropriate connection username and password. For example, in order to try consuming from the STOCKS.ORCL topic as guest, we should add the following to the consumer (marked as bold):

```
... private String username = "guest";
private String password = "password";
public Consumer() throws JMSException {
  factory = new ActiveMQConnectionFactory(brokerURL);
  connection = factory.createConnection(username, password);
  connection.start();
  session =
    connection.createSession(false,Session.AUTO_ACKNOWLEDGE);
}
...
```

Credentials have been added so that the consumer can create a connection to the broker using an appropriate username and password. The modified consumer can be found in the `org.apache.activemq.book.ch6.Consumer` class. Now we can run our example and see how authorization configuration at the broker affects the client. First start the publisher using the following command:

```
$ mvn exec:java \
-Dexec.mainClass=org.apache.activemq.book.ch6.Publisher \
-Dexec.args="CSCO ORCL"
...
Sending: {price=24.07337784180, stock=ORCL, offer=24.0974512196,
up=true} on destination: topic://STOCKS.ORCL
Sending: {price=73.49647952723, stock=CSCO, offer=73.5699760067,
up=false} on destination: topic://STOCKS.CSCO
Sending: {price=24.282731805343, stock=ORCL, offer=24.307014537149,
up=true} on destination: topic://STOCKS.ORCL
Sending: {price=74.1916498091, stock=CSCO, offer=74.265841458,
up=true} on destination: topic://STOCKS.CSCO
Sending: {price=24.350683304888, stock=ORCL, offer=24.375033988192,
up=true} on destination: topic://STOCKS.ORCL
Sending: {price=24.46113711010, stock=ORCL, offer=24.485598247216,
up=true} on destination: topic://STOCKS.ORCL
Sending: {price=24.219079287873, stock=ORCL, offer=24.243298367160,
up=false} on destination: topic://STOCKS.ORCL
Sending: {price=24.282977831328, stock=ORCL, offer=24.307260809160,
up=true} on destination: topic://STOCKS.ORCL
Sending: {price=24.33344653108, stock=ORCL, offer=24.35777997761,
up=true} on destination: topic://STOCKS.ORCL
Sending: {price=73.86498266780, stock=CSCO, offer=73.93884765047,
up=false} on destination: topic://STOCKS.CSCO
Published '10' of '10' price messages
...
```

Now let's see what happens when we try to access different destinations with guest user credentials. For example, if you instruct it to consume messages from STOCKS.CSCO topic, you'll see the following exception:

```
$ mvn exec:java \
-Dexec.mainClass=org.apache.activemq.book.ch6.Consumer \
-Dexec.args="STOCKS.CSCO"
...
Exception in thread "main"
javax.jms.JMSException: User guest is not authorized to read from:
topic://STOCKS.CSCO ...
```

This is exactly what we expected to happen. Consuming from the STOCKS.CSCO topic is restricted due to the authorization settings in listing 6.2. But the authorization configuration does allow guests to consume from the STOCKS.ORCL topic as shown in the following example:

```
$ mvn exec:java \
-Dexec.mainClass=org.apache.activemq.book.ch6.Consumer \
-Dexec.args="STOCKS.ORCL"
...
ORCL 9.66 9.67 down
ORCL 9.70 9.71 up
ORCL 9.80 9.81 up
ORCL 9.83 9.84 up
ORCL 9.80 9.81 down
ORCL 9.75 9.76 down
ORCL 9.81 9.82 up
ORCL 9.88 9.89 up
ORCL 9.80 9.81 down
ORCL 9.84 9.85 up
ORCL 9.84 9.85 up
ORCL 9.86 9.87 up
ORCL 9.95 9.96 up
ORCL 10.03 10.04 up
ORCL 10.03 10.04 down
...
```

As you can see, the authorization settings allowed only read access to the STOCKS.ORCL topic for users that belong to the guests group.

These simple examples demonstrate how easy it is to secure ActiveMQ destinations and assign different security levels to various users and groups. But what if defining the access levels per destination isn't enough for your application's needs? Luckily, ActiveMQ allows you to do a message-based authorization as well.

6.2.2 Message-level authorization

So far in this chapter, we've covered broker-level authentication and authorization. But as you can see, authorization was granted or denied in the process of creating a connection to the broker. In some situations you might want to authorize access to only particular messages in a destination. In this section, we'll examine such message-level authorization.

We'll implement a simple authorization plug-in that allows only applications running on the same host as the broker (the localhost) to consume messages. The first thing we need to do is to create an implementation of the org.apache.activemq.security.MessageAuthorizationPolicy interface, as shown in the following listing.

Listing 6.3 Implementation of `MessageAuthorizationPolicy` interface

```
public class AuthorizationPolicy implements MessageAuthorizationPolicy {

  private static final Log LOG =
      LogFactory.getLog(AuthorizationPolicy.class);

  public boolean isAllowedToConsume(ConnectionContext context,
```

```
        Message message) {
      LOG.info(context.getConnection().getRemoteAddress());
      String remoteAddress = context.getConnection().getRemoteAddress();

      if (remoteAddress.startsWith("/127.0.0.1")) {
        LOG.info("Permission to consume granted");
        return true;
      } else {
        LOG.info("Permission to consume denied");
        return false;
      }
    }
  }
}
```

Method for message-level authentication

As you can see, the `MessageAuthorizationPolicy` interface is simple and defines only one method named `isAllowedToConsume()`. This method has access to the message in question and the context of the connection in which the message will be consumed. In this example, the remote address property for a connection is used (via the call to the `Connection.getRemoteAddress()` method) to distinguish a remote consumer from a local consumer. The `isAllowedToConsume()` method then determines whether the read operation is allowed for the given consumer. Of course, this implementation is arbitrary. You can use any message property or even some message content to make the determination. The implementation of this method is meant to be a simple example.

Now this policy must be installed and configured in the ActiveMQ broker. The first and most obvious step is to compile this class and package it in an appropriate JAR. Place this JAR into the lib/ directory of the ActiveMQ distribution and the policy is ready to be used. You can do that by building and copying the book examples JAR:

```
$ mvn clean install
...
$ cp target/activemq-in-action-examples.jar ${ACTIVEMQ_HOME}/lib/
```

Second, the policy must be configured to create an instance of the `Authorization-Policy` class in the ActiveMQ XML configuration file. Using the Spring beans–style XML inside the `<messageAuthorizationPolicy>` element, the `AuthorizationPolicy` class is instantiated when the broker starts up. Here's an example of this configuration:

```
...
<messageAuthorizationPolicy>
  <bean
    class="org.apache.activemq.book.ch6.AuthorizationPolicy"
    xmlns="http://www.springframework.org/schema/beans" />
</messageAuthorizationPolicy>
...
```

The only step left is to start up ActiveMQ and test out the new policy. Here's the command to start up the broker using the appropriate configuration file:

```
${ACTIVEMQ_HOME}/bin/activemq console\
xbean:src/main/resources/org/apache/activemq/book/ch6/activemq-policy.xml
...
```

```
Loading message broker from:
xbean:src/main/resources/org/apache/activemq/book/ch6/activemq-policy.xml
...
22:19:23,532 |  INFO | PListStore:
/Users/bsnyder/amq/apache-activemq-5.4.1/data/localhost/tmp_storage
started
22:19:23,692 |  INFO | JMX consoles can connect to service:
jmx:rmi:///jndi/rmi://localhost:1099/jmxrmi
22:19:23,717 |  INFO | Using Persistence Adapter: KahaDBPersistenceAdapter
[/Users/bsnyder/amq/apache-activemq-5.4.1/data/localhost/KahaDB]
22:19:23,815 | DEBUG | loading
22:19:23,847 |  INFO | ActiveMQ 5.4.1 JMS Message Broker (localhost) is
starting
22:19:23,848 |  INFO | For help or more information please see:
http://activemq.apache.org/
22:19:23,990 |  INFO | Scheduler using directory:
/Users/bsnyder/amq/apache-activemq-5.4.1/data/localhost/scheduler
22:19:24,037 | DEBUG | loading
22:19:24,039 | DEBUG | loading
22:19:24,041 |  INFO | JobSchedulerStore:
/Users/bsnyder/amq/apache-activemq-5.4.1/data/localhost/scheduler started
22:19:24,081 |  INFO | Listening for connections at: tcp://localhost:61616
22:19:24,081 |  INFO | Connector openwire Started
22:19:24,083 |  INFO | ActiveMQ JMS Message Broker
(localhost, ID:mongoose.local-64256-1289971163870-0:0) started
...
```

If you run the examples from chapter 3 now on the host on which your broker is running, you'll see that everything works in the same manner as it did with the original configuration. The producer produces messages:

```
$ mvn exec:java \
-Dexec.mainClass=org.apache.activemq.book.ch3.portfolio.Publisher \
-Dexec.args="CSCO ORCL"
...
Sending: {price=94.51516220513759, stock=ORCL, offer=94.60967736734271,
up=true} on destination: topic://STOCKS.ORCL
Sending: {price=94.12582896629408, stock=ORCL, offer=94.21995479526036,
up=false} on destination: topic://STOCKS.ORCL
Sending: {price=52.82279394171494, stock=CSCO, offer=52.87561673565665,
up=false} on destination: topic://STOCKS.CSCO
Sending: {price=93.30370880341836, stock=ORCL, offer=93.39701251222176,
up=false} on destination: topic://STOCKS.ORCL
Sending: {price=94.0890269658999, stock=ORCL, offer=94.1831159928658,
up=true} on destination: topic://STOCKS.ORCL
Sending: {price=52.50790406130471, stock=CSCO, offer=52.56041196536601,
up=false} on destination: topic://STOCKS.CSCO
Sending: {price=94.11072880595002, stock=ORCL, offer=94.20483953475596,
up=true} on destination: topic://STOCKS.ORCL
Sending: {price=52.947263764976896, stock=CSCO, offer=53.000211028741866,
up=true} on destination: topic://STOCKS.CSCO
Sending: {price=94.40912590172766, stock=ORCL, offer=94.50353502762938,
up=true} on destination: topic://STOCKS.ORCL
Sending: {price=95.0802935408136, stock=ORCL, offer=95.1753738343544,
up=true} on destination: topic://STOCKS.ORCL
Published '10' of '10' price messages
...
```

And the consumer receives these stock messages:

```
$ mvn exec:java \
-Dexec.mainClass=org.apache.activemq.book.ch3.portfolio.Consumer \
-Dexec.args="CSCO ORCL"
...
ORCL 94.52 94.61 up
ORCL 94.13 94.22 down
CSCO 52.82 52.88 down
ORCL 93.30 93.40 down
ORCL 94.09 94.18 up
CSCO 52.51 52.56 down
ORCL 94.11 94.20 up
CSCO 52.95 53.00 up
ORCL 94.41 94.50 up
ORCL 95.08 95.18 up
CSCO 52.90 52.96 down
ORCL 95.62 95.71 up
CSCO 53.32 53.37 up
ORCL 95.45 95.55 down
CSCO 53.59 53.64 up
...
```

You can also notice log messages from the policy in the broker's console:

```
INFO | /127.0.0.1:50930
INFO | Permission to consume granted
INFO | /127.0.0.1:50930
INFO | Permission to consume granted
INFO | /127.0.0.1:50930
INFO | Permission to consume granted
INFO | /127.0.0.1:50930
INFO | Permission to consume granted
INFO | /127.0.0.1:50930
INFO | Permission to consume granted
INFO | /127.0.0.1:50930
INFO | Permission to consume granted
```

But, when run from another host (for example, 192.168.10.10), the consumer won't be able to consume messages, as our policy will deny the access. And you'll notice log messages similar to these in the broker's console:

```
INFO | /192.168.10.10:50930
INFO | Permission to consume denied
INFO | /192.168.10.10:50930
INFO | Permission to consume denied
INFO | /192.168.10.10:50930
INFO | Permission to consume denied
INFO | /192.168.10.10:50930
INFO | Permission to consume denied
INFO | /192.168.10.10:50930
INFO | Permission to consume denied
INFO | /192.168.10.10:50930
INFO | Permission to consume denied
```

In this way, we verified that our message-based policy works and enables message consumption only from the local host.

Message-level authorization provides some powerful functionality with endless possibilities. Although a simple example was used here, you can adapt it to any security mechanism used in your project. Just bear in mind that a message authorization policy is executed for every message that flows through the broker. So be careful not to add functionality that could possibly slow down the flow of messages.

In addition to authorization, ActiveMQ provides a special class for tighter control over broker-level operations that's even more powerful. The next section examines and demonstrates just such an example.

6.3 *Building a custom security plug-in*

So far this chapter has focused on the built-in security features in ActiveMQ. Though these features should provide enough functionality for the majority of users, an even more powerful feature is available. As stated previously, the ActiveMQ plug-in API is extremely flexible and the possibilities are endless. The flexibility in this functionality comes from the `BrokerFilter` class. This class provides the ability to intercept many of the available broker-level operations. Broker operations include such items as adding consumers and producers to the broker, committing transactions in the broker, and adding and removing connections to the broker, to name a few. Custom functionality can be added by extending the `BrokerFilter` class and overriding a method for a given operation.

Though the ActiveMQ plug-in API isn't concerned solely with security, implementing a class whose main purpose is to handle a custom security feature is achievable. So if you have security requirements that can't be met using the previous security features, you may want to consider developing a custom solution for your needs. Depending on your needs, two choices are available:

- *Implement a JAAS login module*—There's a good chance that you're already using JAAS in your Java applications. In this case, it's only natural that you'll try to reuse all that work for securing the ActiveMQ broker, too. Since JAAS isn't the main topic of this book, we won't dive any deeper into this topic than we already have.
- *Implement a custom plug-in for handling security*—ActiveMQ provides a flexible generic plug-in mechanism. You can create your own custom plug-ins for just about anything, including custom security plug-ins. So if you have requirements that can't be met by implementing a JAAS module, writing a custom plug-in is the way to go.

In this section we'll describe how to write a simple security plug-in that authorizes broker connections only from a certain set of IP addresses. The concept isn't complex but is good enough to give you a taste of the `BrokerFilter` with an angle toward security.

6.3.1 *Implementing the plug-in*

In order to limit connectivity to the broker based on IP address, we'll create a class named `IPAuthenticationBroker` to override the `BrokerFilter.addConnection()` method. The implementation of this method will perform a simple check of the IP address using a regular expression to determine the ability to connect. The following listing shows the implementation of the `IPAuthenticationBroker` class.

Listing 6.4 `IPAuthenticationBroker` class—custom broker implementation

```
public class IPAuthenticationBroker extends BrokerFilter {

  List<String> allowedIPAddresses;
  Pattern pattern = Pattern.compile("^/([0-9\\.]*):(.*)");
  public IPAuthenticationBroker(Broker next, List<String>
      allowedIPAddresses) {
    super(next);
    this.allowedIPAddresses = allowedIPAddresses;
  }

  public void addConnection(ConnectionContext
      context, ConnectionInfo info) throws Exception {

String remoteAddress = context.getConnection().getRemoteAddress();
    Matcher matcher = pattern.matcher(remoteAddress);

    if (matcher.matches()) {
      String ip = matcher.group(1);
      if (!allowedIPAddresses.contains(ip)) {
        throw new SecurityException("Connecting from IP address "
          + ip + " is not allowed" );
      }
    } else {
      throw new SecurityException("Invalid remote address "
          + remoteAddress);
    }

    super.addConnection(context, info);
  }
}
```

Filter connections based on IP address

The `BrokerFilter` class defines methods that intercept broker operations such as adding a connection, removing a subscriber, and so forth. In the `IPAuthenticationBroker` class, the `addConnection()` method is overridden to create some logic that checks whether the address of a connecting client falls within a list of IP addresses that are allowed to connect. If that IP address is allowed to connect, the call is delegated to the `BrokerFilter. addConnection()` method. If that IP address isn't allowed to connect, an exception is thrown.

One additional item of note in the `IPAuthenticationBroker` class is that its constructor calls the `BrokerFilter`'s constructor. This call serves to set up the chain of interceptors so that the proper cascading will take place through the chain. Don't forget to do this if you create your own `BrokerFilter` implementation.

After the actual plug-in logic has been implemented, the plug-in must be configured and installed. For this purpose, an implementation of the `BrokerPlugin` will be created. The `BrokerPlugin` is used to expose the configuration of a plug-in and also to install the plug-in into the ActiveMQ broker. In order to configure and install the `IPAuthenticationBroker`, the `IPAuthenticationPlugin` class is created as shown in the following listing.

Listing 6.5 `IPAuthenticationPlugin` class—custom plug-in implementation

```
public class IPAuthenticationPlugin implements BrokerPlugin {

  List<String> allowedIPAddresses;

  public Broker installPlugin(Broker broker) throws Exception {     ◁── Create instance of custom class

    return new IPAuthenticationBroker(broker, allowedIPAddresses);
  }

  public List<String> getAllowedIPAddresses() {
    return allowedIPAddresses;
  }

  public void setAllowedIPAddresses(List<String> allowedIPAddresses) {
    this.allowedIPAddresses = allowedIPAddresses;
  }
}
```

The `IPAuthenticationBroker.installPlugin()` method is used to instantiate the plug-in and return a new intercepted broker for the next plug-in in the chain. Note that the `IPAuthenticationPlugin` class also contains getter and setter methods used to configure the `IPAuthenticationBroker`. These setter and getter methods are then available via a Spring beans–style XML configuration in the ActiveMQ XML configuration file (as you'll see in a moment).

6.3.2 *Configuring the plug-in*

Now that we've implemented the plug-in, let's see how we can configure it using the ActiveMQ XML configuration file. The following listing shows how the `IPAuthenticationPlugin` class is used in configuration.

Listing 6.6 Configuring the custom plug-in

```xml
<broker xmlns="http://activemq.apache.org/schema/core"
    brokerName="localhost" dataDirectory="${activemq.base}/data">

    <plugins>
        <bean xmlns="http://www.springframework.org/schema/beans"
          id="ipAuthenticationPlugin"
          class="org.apache.activemq.book.ch6.IPAuthenticationPlugin">
            <property name="allowedIPAddresses">
                <list>
                    <value>127.0.0.1</value>
                </list>
            </property>
```

```
        </bean>
    </plugins>

    <transportConnectors>
        <transportConnector name="openwire"
            uri="tcp://localhost:61616" />
    </transportConnectors>
</broker>
```

Spring beans–style configuration

The `<broker>` element provides the `plugins` element for declaring plug-ins. Using the `IPAuthenticationPlugin`, only those clients connecting from the IP address 127.0.0.1 (the localhost) can actually connect to the broker.

6.3.3   *Testing the plug-in*

All that needs to be done now is to test the plug-in. Here's the command to copy the examples JAR file into place (because it contains the plug-in) and the command to start up ActiveMQ using the `IPAuthenticationPlugin` and the `IPAuthentication-Broker`:

```
$ cp target/activemq-in-action-examples.jar ${ACTIVEMQ_HOME}/lib/
$ {ACTIVEMQ_HOME}/bin/activemq console \
xbean:src/main/resources/org/apache/activemq/book/ch6/activemq-custom.xml
...
Loading message broker from:
xbean:src/main/resources/org/apache/activemq/book/ch6/activemq-custom.xml
...
23:22:46,982 |  INFO | PListStore:
/Users/bsnyder/amq/apache-activemq-5.4.1/data/localhost/tmp_storage
started
23:22:47,156 |  INFO | JMX consoles can connect to service:
jmx:rmi:///jndi/rmi://localhost:1099/jmxrmi
23:22:47,159 |  INFO | Using Persistence Adapter: KahaDBPersistenceAdapter
[/Users/bsnyder/amq/apache-activemq-5.4.1/data/localhost/KahaDB]
23:22:48,033 |  INFO | KahaDB is version 2
23:22:48,083 |  INFO | ActiveMQ 5.4.1 JMS Message Broker (localhost) is
starting
23:22:48,084 |  INFO | For help or more information please see:
http://activemq.apache.org/
23:22:48,234 |  INFO | Scheduler using directory:
/Users/bsnyder/amq/apache-activemq-5.4.1/data/localhost/scheduler
23:22:48,275 |  INFO | JobSchedulerStore:
/Users/bsnyder/amq/apache-activemq-5.4.1/data/localhost/scheduler
started
23:22:48,317 |  INFO | Listening for connections at: tcp://localhost:61616
23:22:48,317 |  INFO | Connector openwire Started
23:22:48,319 |  INFO | ActiveMQ JMS Message Broker
(localhost, ID:mongoose.local-49947-1289974968106-0:0) started
...
```

Now run the client to connect to ActiveMQ from the localhost and everything should be working fine. See the following output:

```
$ mvn exec:java \
-Dexec.mainClass=org.apache.activemq.book.ch3.portfolio.Publisher \
```

```
-Dexec.args="CSCO ORCL"
...
Sending: {price=0.7137712112409276, stock=ORCL, offer=0.7144849824521684,
up=true} on destination: topic://STOCKS.ORCL
Sending: {price=0.7127548328743109, stock=ORCL, offer=0.7134675877071851,
up=false} on destination: topic://STOCKS.ORCL
Sending: {price=0.710497871629952, stock=ORCL, offer=0.711208369501582,
up=false} on destination: topic://STOCKS.ORCL
Sending: {price=0.7167766362460622, stock=ORCL, offer=0.7174934128823083,
up=true} on destination: topic://STOCKS.ORCL
Sending: {price=54.586310464064766, stock=CSCO, offer=54.64089677452883,
up=false} on destination: topic://STOCKS.CSCO
Sending: {price=54.45678231194236, stock=CSCO, offer=54.5112390942543,
up=false} on destination: topic://STOCKS.CSCO
Sending: {price=0.7134830573922482, stock=ORCL, offer=0.7141965404496403,
up=false} on destination: topic://STOCKS.ORCL
Sending: {price=0.7125898470778729, stock=ORCL, offer=0.7133024369249507,
up=false} on destination: topic://STOCKS.ORCL
Sending: {price=0.7106363691848542, stock=ORCL, offer=0.711347005554039,
up=false} on destination: topic://STOCKS.ORCL
Sending: {price=54.99339386523512, stock=CSCO, offer=55.04838725910035,
up=true} on destination: topic://STOCKS.CSCO
Published '10' of '10' price messages
...
```

If a connection attempt is made from any host other than the localhost, you can expect to see the following output including the exception:

```
$ mvn exec:java \
-Dexec.mainClass=org.apache.activemq.book.ch3.portfolio.Publisher \
-Dexec.args="CSCO ORCL"
...
Exception in thread "main"
javax.jms.JMSException: Connecting from IP address 192.168.10.10 is not
allowed
...
```

Although this example was more complex, it serves as a good demonstration of the power provided by the BrokerFilter class. Just imagine how flexible this plug-in mechanism is for integrating with existing custom security requirements. This example was focused on a security example, but many other operations can be customized by using the pattern illustrated here.

6.4   *Certificate-based security*

Earlier in this chapter, we described ActiveMQ plug-ins used to secure the broker by authenticating the clients and authorizing the access to destinations. These plug-ins do their work properly, but they store client credentials using plain user names and passwords. Though this is sufficient for most users and use cases, some organizations prefer to implement security using SSL certificates. We've already discussed the SSL transport and how it uses certificates in chapter 4. In this section we'll expand on that material and show you how the SSL transport (along with supporting plug-in) can be used to secure the broker. We'll see how we can authenticate clients using their certificates, but also how we can give those clients different access rights based on the certificate they use to connect to the broker.

For the example in this section we'll use our stock portfolio publisher and consumer. Just this time, they'll use different certificates which will identify them and give them access to publish and consume from broker destinations.

6.4.1 Preparing certificates

Let's start by creating appropriate certificates. The procedure here is similar to the one we used in chapter 4 for the basic SSL transport setup. We've provided all these certificates in the examples that comes with the book, so you can use them to run the example.

We'll create two certificates: one named `producer` and contained in the myproducer.ks keystore:

```
$ keytool -genkey -alias producer -keyalg RSA -keystore myproducer.ks
Enter keystore password: test123
Re-enter new password: test123
What is your first and last name? [Unknown]: producer
What is the name of your organizational unit? [Unknown]:
Chapter 6
What is the name of your organization? [Unknown]: ActiveMQ in Action
What is the name of your City or Locality? [Unknown]: Belgrade
What is the name of your State or Province? [Unknown]:
What is the two-letter country filename for this unit? [Unknown]: RS
Is CN=producer, OU=Chapter 6, O=ActiveMQ in Action,
L=Belgrade, ST=Unknown, C=RS correct? [no]: yes
Enter key password for <producer> (RETURN if same as keystore password):
```

and another called `consumer` and stored in the myconsumer.ks keystore:

```
$ keytool -genkey -alias consumer -keyalg RSA -keystore myconsumer.ks
Enter keystore password: test123
What is your first and last name? [Unknown]: consumer
What is the name of your organizational unit? [Unknown]: Chapter 6
What is the name of your organization? [Unknown]: ActiveMQ in Action
What is the name of your City or Locality? [Unknown]: Belgrade
What is the name of your State or Province? [Unknown]:
What is the two-letter country code for this unit? [Unknown]: RS
Is CN=consumer, OU=Chapter 6, O=ActiveMQ in Action,
L=Belgrade, ST=Unknown, C=RS correct? [no]: yes
Enter key password for <client> (RETURN if same as keystore password):
```

Note the info of the certificates we create, as we'll use it to grant or deny access to the broker later. Of course, in production environments you should consider keeping certificates in secure locations to provide better security of the whole system.

6.4.2 Creating a truststore

The next thing we need to do is import these certificates into the broker's truststore. But first we need to export them from their keystores. Use the following command to export the producer keystore:

```
$ keytool -export -alias producer -keystore myproducer.ks \
-file producer_cert
Enter keystore password: test123
Certificate stored in file <producer_cert>
```

as well as the following command to export the consumer keystore:

```
$ keytool -export -alias consumer -keystore myconsumer.ks \
-file consumer_cert
Enter keystore password: test123
Certificate stored in file <consumer_cert>
```

Now that the JMS client certificates have been exported, the broker truststore must be created.

Creating a broker truststore and importing producer and consumer certificates is a rather straightforward task. First import the producer certificate into the broker truststore:

```
$ keytool -import -alias producer -keystore mybroker.ts \
-file producer_cert
Enter keystore password:
Re-enter new password:
Owner: CN=producer, OU=Chapter 6, O=ActiveMQ in Action,
L=Belgrade, ST=Unknown, C=RS Issuer: CN=producer, OU=Chapter 6,
O=ActiveMQ in Action, L=Belgrade, ST=Unknown, C=RS
Serial number: 4b6f0cf0
Valid from: Sun Feb 07 19:56:48 CET 2010 until: Sat May 08
20:56:48 CEST 2010
Certificate fingerprints: MD5:
9A:8C:02:17:0D:B1:11:CB:4E:14:63:37:03:F3:31:AD SHA1:
21:3B:A8:15:B8:67:39:28:9C:1B:23:35:E9:9F:30:2C:4C:8D:16:85 Signature
algorithm name: SHA1withRSA Version: 3
Trust this certificate? [no]: yes
Certificate was added to keystore
```

Then import the consumer certificate into the broker truststore:

```
$ keytool -import -alias consumer -keystore mybroker.ts \
-file consumer_cert
Enter keystore password:
Owner: CN=consumer, OU=Chapter 6, O=ActiveMQ in Action,
L=Belgrade, ST=Unknown, C=RS Issuer: CN=consumer, OU=Chapter 6,
O=ActiveMQ in Action, L=Belgrade, ST=Unknown, C=RS
Serial number: 4b6f0ed4
Valid from: Sun Feb 07 20:04:52 CET 2010 until: Sat May 08
21:04:52 CEST 2010 Certificate fingerprints: MD5:
6D:C9:AF:3C:AB:1D:E3:8A:C1:5D:70:71:DE:17:CE:95 SHA1:
73:F6:7B:E9:42:5C:90:EB:6F:4F:8C:CB:9E:DB:59:66:B0:EF:02:2E Signature
algorithm name: SHA1withRSA Version: 3
Trust this certificate? [no]:yes
Certificate was added to keystore
```

After the broker truststore is ready, we need to place it somewhere where we can reference it from the configuration file. This is usually the ${ACTIVEMQ_HOME}/conf/ folder, where all other configuration resources reside. We've provided this truststore with the examples, so all you have to do is to copy it to the right place:

```
$ cp src/main/resources/org/apache/activemq/book/ch6/mybroker.ts \
${ACTIVEMQ_HOME}/conf/
```

Now let's focus on the configuration file and how we can use this truststore to configure ActiveMQ security.

6.4.3 Configuring the broker

The XML configuration file shown in the following listing uses the provided truststore
to instruct the SSL transport which clients are allowed to connect to the broker, and
then uses `jaasCertificateAuthenticationPlugin` (shown in bold) to authorize
their access to broker resources.

Listing 6.7   Configuring certificate-based security

```
...
<broker xmlns="http://activemq.apache.org/schema/core"
  brokerName="localhost"
  dataDirectory="${activemq.base}/data">
  <plugins>
  <jaasCertificateAuthenticationPlugin configuration="activemq-certificate" />
    <authorizationPlugin>
      <map>
        <authorizationMap>
          <authorizationEntries>
            <authorizationEntry topic=">"
              read="admins" write="admins" admin="admins" />
            <authorizationEntry topic="STOCKS.>"
              read="consumers"
              write="publishers" admin="publishers" />
            <authorizationEntry topic="STOCKS.ORCL"
              read="guests" />
            <authorizationEntry topic="ActiveMQ.Advisory.>"
              read="admins,publishers,consumers,guests"
              write="admins,publishers,consumers,guests"
              admin="admins,publishers,consumers,guests" />
          </authorizationEntries>
        </authorizationMap>
      </map>
    </authorizationPlugin>
  </plugins>
  <sslContext>
    <sslContext keyStore="file:${activemq.base}/conf/mybroker.ks"
      keyStorePassword="test123"
      trustStore="file:${activemq.base}/conf/mybroker.ts"
      trustStorePassword="test123"/>
  </sslContext>
  <transportConnectors>
    <transportConnector name="openwire" uri="tcp://localhost:61616"/>
    <transportConnector name="ssl"
      uri="ssl://localhost:61617?needClientAuth=true" />
  </transportConnectors>
</broker>
...
```

A few things are worth noting in this configuration file, as shown in bold. First of all, we added the `trustStore` and `trustStorePassword` properties to the `<sslContext>` configuration, which allows us to use our previously defined broker truststore. Next, we set the `needClientAuth` parameter in the SSL transport URI, which instructs the broker to check connecting client certificates and allow access only to those that are found in the truststore.

6.4.4 Authorization explained

Now that we've covered authentication with certificates, it's time to take care of authorization, and that's why we use `jaasCertificateAuthenticationPlugin`. This plug-in is similar to the JAAS plug-in we used earlier in this chapter. We now configure it to look at `activemq-certificate` configuration in login.config, which should look like this:

```
activemq-certificate {
    org.apache.activemq.jaas.TextFileCertificateLoginModule
    required debug=true
    org.apache.activemq.jaas.textfiledn.user="users.properties"
    org.apache.activemq.jaas.textfiledn.group="groups.properties";
};
```

The login.config file is now different in that it uses `TextFileCertificateLoginModule` instead of `PropertiesLoginModule`, configured using the appropriate properties.

Now it's time to see what the `user.properties` file looks like:

```
admin=password
publisher=password
consumer=password
guest=password
sslconsumer=CN=consumer, OU=Chapter 6, O=ActiveMQ in Action, L=Belgrade,
ST=Unknown, C=RS
sslpublisher=CN=producer, OU=Chapter 6,
O=ActiveMQ in Action, L=Belgrade, ST=Unknown, C=RS
```

As you can see, we added our two certificates as `sslconsumer` and `sslpublisher` users. You may notice that the `user.properties` file is the place where you map your certificate to a certain username, and we used the appropriate info of the certificate to map it to the desired username. Now that we have a username, we can put it in the certain group using `groups.properties` file:

```
admins=admin
publishers=admin,publisher,sslpublisher
consumers=admin,publisher,consumer,sslconsumer
guests=guest
```

Once we have our users in their groups, the `authorizationPlugin` kicks in and authorizes the access to broker's destinations.

6.4.5 Testing it out

Now let's start the broker using the configuration and login.config file from earlier:

```
${ACTIVEMQ_HOME}/bin/activemq console \
-Djava.security.auth.login.config=\
src/main/resources/org/apache/activemq/book/ch6/login.config \
xbean:src/main/resources/org/apache/activemq/book/ch6/activemq-ssl.xml
...
Loading message broker from:
xbean:src/main/resources/org/apache/activemq/book/ch6/activemq-ssl.xml
...
00:15:26,144 |  INFO | PListStore:
/Users/bsnyder/amq/apache-activemq-5.4.1/data/localhost/tmp_storage started
00:15:26,312 |  INFO | Using Persistence Adapter: KahaDBPersistenceAdapter
[/Users/bsnyder/amq/apache-activemq-5.4.1/data/localhost/KahaDB]
00:15:26,387 |  INFO | JMX consoles can connect to service:
jmx:rmi:///jndi/rmi://localhost:1099/jmxrmi
00:15:26,882 |  INFO | KahaDB is version 2
00:15:26,905 |  INFO | ActiveMQ 5.4.1 JMS Message Broker (localhost) is
starting
00:15:26,906 |  INFO | For help or more information please see:
http://activemq.apache.org/
00:15:27,044 |  INFO | Scheduler using directory:
/Users/bsnyder/amq/apache-activemq-5.4.1/data/localhost/scheduler
00:15:27,086 |  INFO | JobSchedulerStore:
/Users/bsnyder/amq/apache-activemq-5.4.1/data/localhost/scheduler started
00:15:27,113 |  INFO | Listening for connections at: tcp://localhost:61616
00:15:27,114 |  INFO | Connector openwire Started
00:15:27,810 |  INFO | Listening for connections at:
ssl://localhost:61617?needClientAuth=true
00:15:27,811 |  INFO | Connector ssl Started
00:15:27,820 |  INFO | ActiveMQ JMS Message Broker
(localhost, ID:mongoose.local-51704-1289978126925-0:0) started
...
```

The broker is ready, so let's now see how clients behave depending on which certificate they use. For example, if we try to access the broker with the original certificate used in chapter 4, we can expect that access will be denied, as that certificate isn't in the broker's truststore.

```
$ mvn -Djavax.net.ssl.keyStore=\
src/main/resources/org/apache/activemq/book/ch4/myclient.ks \
-Djavax.net.ssl.keyStorePassword=test123 \
-Djavax.net.ssl.trustStore=${ACTIVEMQ_HOME}/conf/myclient.ts \
-Djavax.net.ssl.trustStorePassword=test123 exec:java
-Dexec.mainClass=org.apache.activemq.book.ch4.Publisher \
-Dexec.args="ssl://localhost:61617 CSCO ORCL"
...
No user for client certificate: CN=Dejan Bosanac,
OU=Chapter 4, O=ActiveMQ in Action, L=Belgrade, ST=Unknown,
C=RS
...
```

Note that we're using the client truststore from the original SSL example here, since nothing has changed regarding certificates on the broker side.

Now let's start it with the appropriate certificate and see how it works:

```
$ mvn -Djavax.net.ssl.keyStore=\
src/main/resources/org/apache/activemq/book/ch6/myproducer.ks \
-Djavax.net.ssl.keyStorePassword=test123 \
-Djavax.net.ssl.trustStore=${ACTIVEMQ_HOME}/conf/myclient.ts \
-Djavax.net.ssl.trustStorePassword=test123 exec:java \
-Dexec.mainClass=org.apache.activemq.book.ch4.Publisher \
-Dexec.args="ssl://localhost:61617 CSCO ORCL"
...
Sending: {price=22.67337141688392, stock=ORCL, offer=22.696044788300803,
up=true} on destination: topic://STOCKS.ORCL
Sending: {price=22.783456638853973, stock=ORCL, offer=22.806240095492825,
up=true} on destination: topic://STOCKS.ORCL
Sending: {price=35.92652907541019, stock=CSCO, offer=35.96245560448559,
up=false} on destination: topic://STOCKS.CSCO
Sending: {price=35.81608910812595, stock=CSCO, offer=35.851905197234075,
up=false} on destination: topic://STOCKS.CSCO
Sending: {price=35.49430393012775, stock=CSCO, offer=35.52979823405787,
up=false} on destination: topic://STOCKS.CSCO
Sending: {price=22.613210876407855, stock=ORCL, offer=22.63582408728426,
up=false} on destination: topic://STOCKS.ORCL
Sending: {price=22.584893337535, stock=ORCL, offer=22.607478230872534,
up=false} on destination: topic://STOCKS.ORCL
Sending: {price=35.81521985692496, stock=CSCO, offer=35.85103507678188,
up=true} on destination: topic://STOCKS.CSCO
Sending: {price=35.8020033885887, stock=CSCO, offer=35.837805391977284,
up=false} on destination: topic://STOCKS.CSCO
Sending: {price=22.570064862430183, stock=ORCL, offer=22.59263492729261,
up=false} on destination: topic://STOCKS.ORCL
Published '10' of '10' price messages
...
```

As expected, the publisher successfully sends stock portfolio updates to the broker in this case. Now let's see how to start a consumer with a proper certificate:

```
$ mvn -Djavax.net.ssl.keyStore=\
src/main/resources/org/apache/activemq/book/ch6/myconsumer.ks \
-Djavax.net.ssl.keyStorePassword=test123 \
-Djavax.net.ssl.trustStor${ACTIVEMQ_HOME}/conf/myclient.ts \
-Djavax.net.ssl.trustStorePassword=test123 exec:java \
-Dexec.mainClass=org.apache.activemq.book.ch4.Consumer \
-Dexec.args="ssl://localhost:61617 CSCO ORCL"
...
ORCL 82.20 82.28 up
CSCO 88.52 88.61 down
CSCO 89.10 89.19 up
ORCL 81.90 81.98 down
ORCL 81.16 81.24 down
CSCO 89.84 89.93 up
ORCL 81.19 81.27 up
ORCL 81.38 81.46 up
CSCO 90.14 90.23 up
ORCL 81.03 81.12 down
ORCL 80.71 80.79 down
ORCL 80.01 80.09 down
ORCL 79.51 79.59 down
CSCO 90.52 90.61 up
```

```
ORCL 79.52 79.60 up
ORCL 78.77 78.85 down
...
```

Finally, we can test that our authorization settings work fine. As you can see from our broker configuration, consumers shouldn't be allowed to send messages to our stock-related topics. So if you try to do it, the operation should fail:

```
$ mvn -Djavax.net.ssl.keyStore=\
src/main/resources/org/apache/activemq/book/ch6/myconsumer.ks \
-Djavax.net.ssl.keyStorePassword=test123 \
-Djavax.net.ssl.trustStore=${ACTIVEMQ_HOME}/conf/myclient.ts \
-Djavax.net.ssl.trustStorePassword=test123 exec:java \
-Dexec.mainClass=org.apache.activemq.book.ch4.Publisher \
-Dexec.args="ssl://localhost:61617 CSCO ORCL"
...
role="bold">User CN=consumer, OU=Chapter 6, O=ActiveMQ in Action,
L=Belgrade, ST=Unknown, C=RS is not authorized to write to:
topic://STOCKS.CSCO
...
```

In this section, we learned how to leverage what we knew about the SSL transport (and configuring certificates) and with a bit of work configured certificate-based security for the ActiveMQ broker. This brings ActiveMQ security to an entirely new level and makes it a perfect fit for organizations with tight security requirements.

6.5   *Summary*

In this chapter, the ActiveMQ broker was secured from non-authenticated and non-authorized access. For the most simple purposes, you can use the ActiveMQ simple authentication plug-in, allowing you to define security credentials directly into the configuration file. The ActiveMQ JAAS plug-ins provide the ability to utilize the standardized Java login modules via simple configuration, allowing you to authenticate users from various sources, such as LDAP, properties files, and so on. Additionally, custom JAAS login modules can be created for use with other authentication or authorization schemes such as Kerberos, NTLM, NIS, and so forth.

Operation-level authorization was also demonstrated for more fine-grained control over destinations. Next we demonstrated message-level authorization by creating a custom policy to control consumption of a given message. Then we demonstrated the ActiveMQ plug-in mechanism through the customized IP-based authentication example. Finally, we demonstrated how to configure the broker for certificate-based security.

ActiveMQ provides some powerful security mechanisms, as seen in this chapter. Hopefully the process for utilizing these solutions is more clear after walking through the examples.

With this chapter, we've finished the first part of the book that explained ActiveMQ basics and various concepts regarding configuring the broker. In the following part of the book, we'll concentrate more on how to write applications that utilize ActiveMQ. In particular, the following chapter focuses on topics such as embedding ActiveMQ in your Java applications and using the Spring framework to write JMS-oriented applications.

Part 3

Using ActiveMQ to build messaging applications

Now that you have the basics under your belt, it's time to start building applications that utilize ActiveMQ. The asynchronous nature of messaging tends to be foreign to most developers because they're used to using synchronous calls in the applications they build. Using asynchronous calls in your applications requires a different style of thinking and a different set of APIs.

Part 3 explores the topic-building applications that utilize messaging with ActiveMQ. Building applications using the Spring Framework is popular in the Java community, and this is the first topic we cover. We quickly follow up with integrating ActiveMQ with application servers. This section covers the use of ActiveMQ with Tomcat, Jetty, Geronimo, and JBoss application servers. Not only do we explore Java development in part 3, but other languages as well, including Ruby, Python, Perl, PHP, C#, C/C++, and more.

Creating Java applications with ActiveMQ

This chapter covers

- Embedding ActiveMQ in Java applications
- Embedding ActiveMQ using Spring
- Creating request/reply applications
- Writing JMS clients using Spring

Thus far the book has concentrated on ActiveMQ as a software application. Most of the information we've presented has concerned the internal structure of ActiveMQ and how its components can be configured. But apart from basic JMS examples, using ActiveMQ in your applications hasn't been discussed. This chapter is dedicated to explaining how to create applications with ActiveMQ.

One of the things you might want to do with ActiveMQ is to *embed* it into your application. Since ActiveMQ is written in Java, it can naturally be integrated in another Java application. As you'll see, you can configure the broker using either Java code or XML (via the Spring Framework). A fully configured broker can serve clients from the same application (using the VM protocol) as well as clients from remote applications to exchange messages over the network. This scenario is depicted in figure 7.1.

145

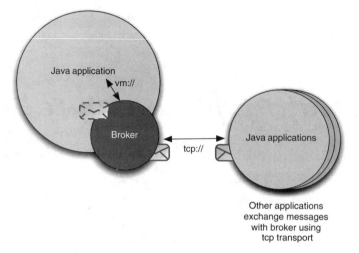

Figure 7.1   **Local and remote applications exchange messages with an embedded broker.**

Other applications exchange messages with broker using tcp transport

The first section of this chapter will explore various techniques available for embedding ActiveMQ in your Java applications. The second section will explain how to embed ActiveMQ using Spring. You'll see how to configure ActiveMQ using both pure Spring XML and custom namespaces, as well as the standard ActiveMQ XML via Apache XBean (http://mng.bz/EAfX). This will be followed by a discussion of some advanced programming techniques that include ActiveMQ. This is a vast topic and we'll dig into two common use cases. We'll also take a look at how to create a request/reply system using JMS and ActiveMQ. We'll discuss advantages of such a system over the traditional client-server architecture.

Finally, you'll learn about using Spring JMS to simplify the creation of JMS clients with ActiveMQ. Using the stock portfolio sample application, we'll use Spring JMS to set up connections, consumers, and producers in a quick manner. To begin, let's discuss embedding ActiveMQ in your applications. There's no single correct way to embed ActiveMQ. The method you choose will probably depend on your application design.

7.1   *Embedding ActiveMQ using Java*

Although most developers today use some kind of framework for composing their applications, it's always good to start with plain old Java. In this section we'll initialize and configure ActiveMQ using its Java APIs. You'll see how to use the `BrokerService` class to configure a broker using nothing but pure Java code.

Next, we'll describe how you can configure your broker using custom configuration XML files. We'll use the `BrokerFactory` class to achieve this and you'll learn how you can use regular configuration files to embed the broker in your Java applications. After this section you'll be able to embed ActiveMQ with any configuration in your Java applications.

7.1.1 Embedding ActiveMQ using the BrokerService

When using plain old Java to set up your broker, the `org.apache.activemq.broker.`
`BrokerService` class is one starting point. This class is used to configure the broker
and manage its entire lifecycle. The best way to demonstrate the usage of the `Broker-`
`Service` class is with an appropriate example. Let's start with a broker configuration
we used in chapter 6 to configure a simple authentication plug-in and see how we can
achieve the same functionality with plain old Java code. For starters, let's take a look at
the well-known XML configuration example shown here.

Listing 7.1 Configure ActiveMQ with security plug-ins using XML

```xml
<broker xmlns="http://activemq.apache.org/schema/core"
  brokerName="myBroker"
  dataDirectory="${activemq.base}/data">

 <transportConnectors>
  <transportConnector name="openwire"
   uri="tcp://localhost:61616" />
 </transportConnectors>

 <plugins>
   <simpleAuthenticationPlugin>
     <users>
       <authenticationUser username="admin"
                           password="password"
                           groups="admins,publishers,consumers"/>
       <authenticationUser username="publisher"
                           password="password"
                           groups="publishers,consumers"/>
       <authenticationUser username="consumer"
                           password="password"
                           groups="consumers"/>
       <authenticationUser username="guest"
                           password="password"
                           groups="guests"/>
     </users>
   </simpleAuthenticationPlugin>
 </plugins>
</broker>
```

Listing 7.1 uses the standard ActiveMQ XML to define a broker instance with a name
and data directory, as well as one transport connector and one plug-in. Now look at the
same configuration using plain old Java and the `BrokerService` as shown next.

Listing 7.2 Configure ActiveMQ with security plug-ins using Java

```java
public static void main(String[] args) throws Exception {

  BrokerService broker = new BrokerService();
  broker.setBrokerName("myBroker");
  broker.setDataDirectory("data/");            ⟵ Instantiate
                                                 and configure
  SimpleAuthenticationPlugin authentication =    BrokerService
     new SimpleAuthenticationPlugin();
```

```
    List<AuthenticationUser> users =
        new ArrayList<AuthenticationUser>();

    users.add(new AuthenticationUser("admin",
                                     "password",
                                     "admins,publishers,consumers"));
    users.add(new AuthenticationUser("publisher",
                                     "password",
                                     "publishers,consumers"));
    users.add(new AuthenticationUser("consumer",
                                     "password",
                                     "consumers"));
    users.add(new AuthenticationUser("guest",
                                     "password",
                                     "guests"));
    authentication.setUsers(users);

    broker.setPlugins(new BrokerPlugin[]{authentication});   ◁── Add SimpleAuthentication Plugin
    broker.addConnector("tcp://localhost:61616");            ◁── Add transport connector
    broker.start();                        ◁── Start broker

    System.out.println();
    System.out.println("Press any key to stop the broker");
    System.out.println();

    System.in.read();
}
```

As you can see, listing 7.2 instantiates the BrokerService and configures the broker-Name and dataDirectory properties. Next the SimpleAuthenticationPlugin is added to the BrokerService via the setPlugins() method. Then a transport connector is added to the BrokerService via the addConnector() method. Finally the start() method is used to start the BrokerService instance. Now your broker is fully initialized using just plain old Java code; no XML configuration files were used. To see this class in action, execute it as shown in this listing.

Listing 7.3   Run the pure Java example of the BrokerService

```
$ mvn exec:java \
 -Dexec.mainClass=org.apache.activemq.book.ch7.broker.Broker \
 -Dlog4j.configuration=file:src/main/java/log4j.properties
...
[INFO] [exec:java {execution: default-cli}]
INFO | Using Persistence Adapter: AMQPersistenceAdapter(data/localhost)
INFO | AMQStore starting using directory: data/localhost
INFO | Kaha Store using data directory data/localhost/kr-store/state
INFO | AMQPersistenceAdapter        - Active data files: []
INFO | ActiveMQ 5.4.1 JMS Message Broker (localhost) is starting
INFO | For help or more information please see: http://activemq.apache.org/
INFO | Kaha Store using data directory data/localhost/kr-store/data
INFO | Listening for connections at: tcp://localhost:61616
INFO | Connector tcp://localhost:61616 Started
INFO | JMX consoles can connect to
  service:jmx:rmi:///jndi/rmi://localhost:1099/jmxrmi
```

```
INFO  | ActiveMQ JMS Message Broker
   (localhost, ID:dejanb-63935-1269536159457-0:0) started
Press any key to stop the broker
...
```

One important thing to note in listing 7.3 is that you should always add your plug-ins before connectors; otherwise they won't be initialized. Also, any connectors added after the broker has been started won't be properly started either.

The `BrokerService` class is useful when you want to use plain old Java for the broker configuration. This method is useful for many situations where you don't need an externally customizable configuration. In many applications, you'll want to be able to initialize the broker using the same configuration files used to configure standalone instances of the ActiveMQ broker. For that purpose ActiveMQ provides the utility `org.apache.activemq.broker.BrokerFactory` class.

7.1.2 Embedding ActiveMQ using the BrokerFactory

The `BrokerFactory` class is a utility that makes it easy to create a broker instance simply using an ActiveMQ URI. Depending on the broker URI scheme, the `BrokerFactory` locates the appropriate factory and uses it to create an instance of the `BrokerService` class. The most widely used factory is the `XBeanBrokerFactory` class and is configured by simply passing the XBean-style of URI. An example of an XBean broker URI is shown next:

```
xbean:/path/to/activemq.xml
```

This example URI tells the `BrokerFactory` to use the `XBeanBrokerFactory` and the path following the colon to create the broker instance.

Now, let's look at the following listing. The `BrokerFactory` can instantiate the `BrokerService` class using the standard ActiveMQ XML configuration file as shown.

Listing 7.4 Using the `BrokerFactory` with an XML configuration

```java
public class Factory {

 public static void main(String[] args) throws Exception {
  System.setProperty("activemq.base", System.getProperty("user.dir"));

  String configUri =
    "xbean:target/classes/org/apache/activemq/book/ch6/activemq-simple.xml"

  URI brokerUri = new URI(configUri);

  BrokerService broker = BrokerFactory.createBroker(brokerUri);
  broker.start();

  System.out.println();
  System.out.println("Press any key to stop the broker");
  System.out.println();

  System.in.read();
 }

}
```

As you can see in listing 7.4, the `BrokerFactory.createBroker()` method uses a configuration URI to create the `BrokerService` instance. Note that the configuration URI used in listing 7.4 is the `xbean:` URI scheme. This tells the broker factory to search for the given XML configuration file in the classpath or somewhere on the file system. To illustrate this example in action, the following listing shows how to execute it.

> **Listing 7.5 Run the example of the `BrokerFactory`**

```
$ mvn exec:java \
 -Dexec.mainClass=org.apache.activemq.book.ch7.broker.Factory \
 -Dlog4j.configuration=file:src/main/java/log4j.properties
...
[INFO] [exec:java {execution: default-cli}]
INFO | Using Persistence Adapter: AMQPersistenceAdapter(data/localhost)
INFO | AMQStore starting using directory: data/localhost
INFO | Kaha Store using data directory data/localhost/kr-store/state
INFO | Active data files: []
INFO | ActiveMQ 5.4.1 JMS Message Broker (localhost) is starting
INFO | For help or more information please see: http://activemq.apache.org/
INFO | Kaha Store using data directory data/localhost/kr-store/data
INFO | Listening for connections at: tcp://localhost:61616
INFO | Connector openwire Started
INFO | ActiveMQ JMS Message Broker
   (localhost, ID:dejanb-65001-1269594442403-0:0) started

Press any key to stop the broker
...
```

You can also use the `broker:` URI scheme for simple broker configuration performed completely via the configuration URI. See the following example URI:

```
broker:(tcp://localhost:61616,network:static:tcp://remotehost:61616)
?persistent=false&useJmx=true
```

This single URI contains enough configuration to start up a broker, including both network and transport connectors; persistence has been disabled and JMX has been explicitly enabled. For more information, see the complete URI reference on the ActiveMQ website (http://mng.bz/FNos).

As mentioned earlier, most Java developers use some kind of framework to compose their applications. Since the Spring Framework (http://www.springframework.org/) is the most popular framework used today, let's examine how to configure and use ActiveMQ as a component in a Spring application.

7.2 *Embedding ActiveMQ using Spring*

ActiveMQ is developed with Spring in mind. In fact, ActiveMQ uses a Spring XML configuration file by default. This makes it easy to embed an ActiveMQ broker in Spring-enabled applications. This section will explore numerous methods for utilizing ActiveMQ with Spring. Although there are advantages and disadvantages to some methods, and some are recommended more than others, no single method is the best one. The decision on which method to use typically can be made by considering your application and system architecture, the skill set of your developers, and the difficulty to maintain the solution once it's deployed to your production systems.

7.2.1 *Pure Spring XML*

The first style of Spring configuration to examine is what's known as a *pure Spring configuration.* A pure Spring configuration is characterized by the style of the XML. It uses the standard Spring `<bean id="..." class="...">` style of XML in the configuration file. This style of XML is widely known because Spring is so ubiquitous and it's easy to understand.

Using a pure Spring XML syntax is easy to do with ActiveMQ. All you have to do is define the `BrokerService` as a bean and any dependencies in the Spring configuration file. The following listing shows the same broker configuration that was shown in listing 7.2.

Listing 7.6 A pure Spring configuration for ActiveMQ

```
<beans>
  <bean id="admins" class="org.apache.activemq.security.AuthenticationUser">
    <constructor-arg index="0" value="admin" />
    <constructor-arg index="1" value="password" />
    <constructor-arg index="2" value="admins,publisher,consumers" />
  </bean>

  <bean id="publishers"
    class="org.apache.activemq.security.AuthenticationUser">
    <constructor-arg index="0" value="publisher" />
    <constructor-arg index="1" value="password" />
    <constructor-arg index="2" value="publisher,consumers" />
  </bean>

  <bean id="consumers"
    class="org.apache.activemq.security.AuthenticationUser">
    <constructor-arg index="0" value="consumer" />
    <constructor-arg index="1" value="password" />
    <constructor-arg index="2" value="consumers" />
  </bean>

  <bean id="guests" class="org.apache.activemq.security.AuthenticationUser">
    <constructor-arg index="0" value="guest" />
    <constructor-arg index="1" value="password" />
    <constructor-arg index="2" value="guests" />
  </bean>

  <bean id="simpleAuthPlugin"
    class="org.apache.activemq.security.SimpleAuthenticationPlugin">
    <property name="users">
      <util:list>
        <ref bean="admins" />
        <ref bean="publishers" />
        <ref bean="consumers" />
        <ref bean="guests" />
      </util:list>
    </property>
```

```
      </bean>

      <bean id="broker" class="org.apache.activemq.broker.BrokerService"
        init-method="start" destroy-method="stop">
        <property name="brokerName" value="myBroker" />
        <property name="persistent" value="false" />
        <property name="transportConnectorURIs">
          <list>
            <value>tcp://localhost:61616</value>
          </list>
        </property>
        <property name="plugins">
          <list>
            <ref bean="simpleAuthPlugin"/>
          </list>
        </property>
      </bean>

  </beans>
```

As noted, the broker configuration in listing 7.6 follows exactly the same broker configuration that was shown in listing 7.2. The difference between these two configurations is that listing 7.2 directly makes use of the ActiveMQ Java API, and listing 7.6 indirectly uses the ActiveMQ Java API by way of the Spring container and a pure Spring style of XML. There's no distinct advantage necessarily; this is just another available option. Even if you use the standard ActiveMQ XML in the config file, you can still use the standard Spring XML syntax in that file as well.

To start up ActiveMQ using this style of configuration, use the SpringConfig class as shown next.

Listing 7.7   Start ActiveMQ using a pure Spring XML syntax

```
$ mvn exec:java \
-Dexec.mainClass=org.apache.activemq.book.ch7.broker.SpringConfig
...
13:27:42,125 |  INFO | Loading XML bean definitions from class path
resource [org/apache/activemq/book/ch7/pure-spring.xml]
13:27:42,366 |  INFO | Bean factory for application context
[org.springframework.context.support.
ClassPathXmlApplicationContext@20edbca8]:
org.springframework.beans.factory.support.
DefaultListableBeanFactory@7c959fa1
13:27:42,418 |  INFO | Pre-instantiating singletons in
org.springframework.beans.factory.support.
DefaultListableBeanFactory@7c959fa1:
defining beans
[admins,publishers,consumers,guests,simpleAuthPlugin,broker];
root of factory hierarchy
13:27:42,719 |  INFO | Using Persistence Adapter: MemoryPersistenceAdapter
13:27:42,721 |  INFO | ActiveMQ 5.4.1 JMS Message Broker (myBroker) is
starting
13:27:42,721 |  INFO | For help or more information please see:
http://activemq.apache.org/
```

```
13:27:43,224 | INFO | Listening for connections at:
tcp://mongoose.local:61616
13:27:43,225 | INFO | Connector tcp://mongoose.local:61616 Started
13:27:43,227 | INFO | ActiveMQ JMS Message Broker
(myBroker, ID:mongoose.local-50630-1282246062743-0:0) started

Press any key to stop the broker
```

The `SpringConfig` class is a simple class that uses the Spring `ClassPathXml-ApplicationContext` (http://mng.bz/71U2) in a main method to read in the pure Spring config and start the ActiveMQ broker. A slight variation on this style of startup is to use the `BrokerFactoryBean` that's provided with ActiveMQ.

7.2.2 Using the BrokerFactoryBean

It's common in enterprise Java development to use Spring factory beans (http://mng.bz/h0OJ) to expose beans that are themselves factories. The purpose of Spring factory beans is to instantiate a factory that requires a complex configuration. The use of the factory bean replaces writing a bunch of complex XML, and it hooks right into the Spring container. The `org.apache.activemq.xbean.BrokerFactoryBean` class does this job for ActiveMQ. Using the `BrokerFactoryBean` is easier than creating and maintaining your own class for this purpose. An ActiveMQ broker can be started up using the `BrokerFactoryBean` class as shown next.

Listing 7.8 ActiveMQ XML configuration for projects using Spring syntax

```
<beans>
 <bean id="broker"
  class="org.apache.activemq.xbean.BrokerFactoryBean">
  <property name="config"
   value="org/apache/activemq/book/ch6/activemq-simple.xml"/>      ◁── XML
                                                                         configuration
  <property name="start" value="true" />     ◁─┐ Decide whether to
 </bean>                                          start a broker
</beans>
```

Note in listing 7.8 that the XML to configure the `BrokerFactoryBean` is minimal. It uses a property named `config` to point to the standard ActiveMQ XML configuration file that was described in earlier chapters and a property named `start` to instruct Spring to invoke the start method on the factory bean after it's initialized (this starts up the ActiveMQ broker instance). You can also disable this feature and simply start the broker manually if you wish. To execute this example, see the following listing.

Listing 7.9 Start ActiveMQ using the `BrokerFactoryBean`

```
$ mvn exec:java \
-Dexec.mainClass=\
org.apache.activemq.book.ch7.spring.BrokerFactoryBeanExample \
-Dlog4j.configuration=file:src/main/java/log4j.properties \
-Dexec.args="src/main/resources/org/apache/activemq/book/ch7/spring-1.0.xml"
...
[INFO] [exec:java {execution: default-cli}]
```

```
Starting broker with the following configuration:
 src/main/resources/org/apache/activemq/book/ch7/spring-1.0.xml
INFO | Using Persistence Adapter:
 AMQPersistenceAdapter(data/localhost)
INFO | AMQStore starting using directory:
 data/localhost
INFO | Kaha Store using data directory
 data/localhost/kr-store/state
INFO | Active data files: []
INFO | ActiveMQ 5.4.1 JMS Message Broker (localhost) is starting
INFO | For help or more information please see:
http://activemq.apache.org/
INFO | Kaha Store using data directory
 data/localhost/kr-store/data
INFO  ManagementContext            - JMX consoles can connect to
 service:jmx:rmi:///jndi/rmi://localhost:1099/jmxrmi
INFO | Listening for connections at: tcp://localhost:61616
INFO | Connector openwire Started
INFO |ActiveMQ JMS Message Broker
 (localhost, ID:wfh-dejanb-65076-1269595139615-0:0) started
Sending: {price=22.74502068626, stock=JAVA, offer=22.767765706954,
up=true}
 on destination: topic://STOCKS.JAVA
Sending: {price=65.23301909637, stock=IONA, offer=65.29825211547,
up=true}
 on destination: topic://STOCKS.IONA
Sending: {price=65.09672311118, stock=IONA, offer=65.16181983429,
up=false}
 on destination: topic://STOCKS.IONA
Sending: {price=64.84016157839, stock=IONA, offer=64.90500173997,
up=false}
 on destination: topic://STOCKS.IONA
Sending: {price=22.560415476111, stock=JAVA, offer=22.582975891587,
up=false}
 on destination: topic://STOCKS.JAVA
Sending: {price=64.43834994393, stock=IONA, offer=64.50278829387,
up=false}
 on destination: topic://STOCKS.IONA
Sending: {price=22.583510723322, stock=JAVA, offer=22.606094234045,
up=true}
 on destination: topic://STOCKS.JAVA
...
```

In listing 7.9, you should see that the broker is started using the `BrokerFactoryBean` via the Spring configuration and stock price messages are being sent to the broker.

In addition to the `BrokerFactoryBean`, you can also use XBean with Spring.

7.2.3 *Using Apache XBean with Spring*

By default, ActiveMQ uses Spring and Apache XBean (http://mng.bz/EAfX) for its internal configuration purposes. Therefore all activemq.xml files we used in previous chapters to configure various features of ActiveMQ are basically Spring configuration files, powered by an XBean custom XML schema. XBean provides the ability to define and use a custom XML syntax that's much more compact than the standard Spring XML syntax. Although Spring provides the ability to do this now, such features weren't available when ActiveMQ was created (Spring only supported DTDs at the time).

The following listing shows an example of a simple Java application using Spring and XBean.

Listing 7.10   The XBeanBroker class

```
package org.apache.activemq.book.ch7.xbean;

import org.apache.activemq.book.ch6.Publisher;
import org.apache.xbean.spring.context.FileSystemXmlApplicationContext;

public class XBeanBroker {

 public static void main(String[] args) throws Exception {
    if (args.length == 0) {
     System.err.println("Please define a configuration file!");
     return;
    }                                                          Define
                                                               configuration file
    String config = args[0];
    System.out.println(
      "Starting broker with the following configuration: " + config
    );
    System.setProperty("activemq.base",          Set base        Initialize
        System.getProperty("user.dir"));          property        application
    FileSystemXmlApplicationContext                              context
      context = new FileSystemXmlApplicationContext(config);

    Publisher publisher = new Publisher();                    Send
    for (int i = 0; i < 100; i++) {                           messages
      publisher.sendMessage(new String[]{"JAVA", "IONA"});
    }

 }

}
```

Listing 7.10 accepts an argument for the path to the XML configuration file, sets the `activemq.base` system property, and instantiates a Spring application context using the XML configuration file. Then the publisher is instantiated and used to send a simple message 100 times. That's the entire application. Everything else that's needed is handled by ActiveMQ and the Spring Framework. Please note that the application context class used in this example is from XBean, not the Spring Framework. This example can be run using the command shown in the following listing.

Listing 7.11   Start ActiveMQ Using XBean with Spring

```
$ mvn exec:java \
-Dexec.mainClass=org.apache.activemq.book.ch7.xbean.XBeanBroker \
-Dlog4j.configuration=file:src/main/java/log4j.properties \
-Dexec.args= \
"src/main/resources/org/apache/activemq/book/ch6/activemq-simple.xml"
...
```

```
[INFO] [exec:java {execution: default-cli}]
Starting broker with the following configuration:
 src/main/resources/org/apache/activemq/book/ch6/activemq-simple.xml
INFO | Using Persistence Adapter:
 AMQPersistenceAdapter(data/localhost)
INFO | AMQStore starting using directory: data/localhost
INFO | Kaha Store using data directory data/localhost/kr-store/state
INFO | Active data files: []
INFO | ActiveMQ 5.4.1 JMS Message Broker (localhost) is starting
INFO | For help or more information please see:
http://activemq.apache.org/
INFO | Kaha Store using data directory data/localhost/kr-store/data
INFO | JMX consoles can connect to
 service:jmx:rmi:///jndi/rmi://localhost:1099/jmxrmi
INFO | Listening for connections at: tcp://localhost:61616
INFO | Connector openwire Started
INFO | ActiveMQ JMS Message Broker
 (localhost, ID:dejanb-65363-1269596340878-0:0) started
Sending: {price=53.794098159875, stock=IONA, offer=53.847892258035,
up=false}
 on destination: topic://STOCKS.IONA
Sending: {price=53.489740886575, stock=IONA, offer=53.543230627461,
up=false}
 on destination: topic://STOCKS.IONA
Sending: {price=53.5342708859, stock=IONA, offer=53.58780515680,
up=true}
 on destination: topic://STOCKS.IONA
Sending: {price=53.86122035252, stock=IONA, offer=53.91508157288,
up=true}
 on destination: topic://STOCKS.IONA
Sending: {price=54.15343454330, stock=IONA, offer=54.207587977851,
up=true}
 on destination: topic://STOCKS.IONA
Sending: {price=49.27384513708, stock=JAVA, offer=49.323118982218,
up=false}
 on destination: topic://STOCKS.JAVA
Sending: {price=53.83373859262, stock=IONA, offer=53.8875723312,
up=false}
 on destination: topic://STOCKS.IONA
Sending: {price=53.933391780045, stock=IONA, offer=53.98732517182,
up=true}
 on destination: topic://STOCKS.IONA
...
```

The broker that's started behaves the same as the previously defined examples.

In addition to the compact XML syntax provided by XBean, Spring also support XML namespaces.

7.2.4   *Using a custom XML namespace with Spring*

All recent versions of the Spring Framework allow developers to utilize a custom XML schema. ActiveMQ provides a custom XML schema to configure ActiveMQ via the Spring configuration file. The following listing demonstrates how to configure ActiveMQ using its custom Spring schema via an XML namespace.

Listing 7.12   ActiveMQ XML configuration using Spring 2.x (and newer)

```
<beans xmlns="http://www.springframework.org/schema/beans"
 xmlns:amq="http://activemq.apache.org/schema/core"
 xmlns:xsi="http://www.w3.org/2001/XMLSchema-instance"
 xsi:schemaLocation="http://www.springframework.org/schema/beans
 http://www.springframework.org/schema/beans/spring-beans-2.0.xsd
 http://activemq.apache.org/schema/core
 http://activemq.apache.org/schema/core/activemq-core.xsd">

 <amq:broker
  brokerName="localhost" dataDirectory="${activemq.base}/data">

  <amq:transportConnectors>
   <amq:transportConnector name="openwire"
    uri="tcp://localhost:61616" />
  </amq:transportConnectors>
  <amq:plugins>
   <amq:simpleAuthenticationPlugin>
    <amq:users>
     <amq:authenticationUser username="admin"
                             password="password"
                             groups="admins,publishers,consumers"/>
     <amq:authenticationUser username="publisher"
                             password="password"
                             groups="publishers,consumers"/>
     <amq:authenticationUser username="consumer"
                             password="password"
                             groups="consumers"/>
     <amq:authenticationUser username="guest"
                             password="password"
                             groups="guests"/>
    </amq:users>
   </amq:simpleAuthenticationPlugin>
  </amq:plugins>
 </amq:broker>

</beans>
```

> Define namespace prefix and URI

> Define URI and location of XSD

As you can see in listing 7.12, first a prefix is declared that will be used throughout the XML document to reference element types from the custom schema. The prefix that's commonly used for ActiveMQ is amq. Second is the URI to the right of the prefix, which in this case is http://activemq.apache.org/schema/core. The prefix is used to reference the URI from within the XML document. Third, the URI is used as an identifier to point to the actual location of the XML schema document (XSD) via the schemaLocation attribute. For example, when the <amq:broker> element is used, the amq prefix serves as an alias to the URI and the URI points to the XSD where the broker element can be found.

Once the XML namespace is declared, we're free to define our broker-related beans using the custom XML syntax. In this particular example we've configured the broker as it was configured in our previously used chapter 6 example, with the simple authentication plug-in. Now the Spring broker can be started as shown next.

Listing 7.13   Start ActiveMQ using a configuration with a custom XML namespace

```
$ mvn -e exec:java \
-Dexec.mainClass=org.apache.activemq.book.ch7.spring.SpringBroker \
-Dlog4j.configuration=file:src/main/java/log4j.properties \
-Dexec.args=\
src/main/resources/org/apache/activemq/book/ch7/spring-2.0.xml
...
[INFO] [exec:java {execution: default-cli}]
Starting broker with the following configuration:
 src/main/resources/org/apache/activemq/book/ch7/spring-2.0.xml
INFO | Using Persistence Adapter:
 AMQPersistenceAdapter(${activemq.base}/data/localhost)
INFO | AMQStore starting using directory: data/localhost
INFO | Kaha Store using data directory data/localhost/kr-store/state
INFO | Active data files: []
INFO | ActiveMQ 5.4.1 JMS Message Broker (localhost) is starting
INFO | For help or more information please see: http://activemq.apache.org/
INFO | Kaha Store using data directory data/localhost/kr-store/data
INFO | JMX consoles can connect
 to service:jmx:rmi:///jndi/rmi://localhost:1099/jmxrmi
INFO | Listening for connections at: tcp://localhost:61616
INFO | Connector openwire Started
INFO | ActiveMQ JMS Message Broker
 (localhost, ID:dejanb-65324-1269595874364-0:0) started
Sending: {price=83.53568740848, stock=IONA, offer=83.61922309589, up=true}
 on destination: topic://STOCKS.IONA
Sending: {price=84.15670625187, stock=IONA, offer=84.24086295812, up=true}
 on destination: topic://STOCKS.IONA
Sending: {price=83.64752134809, stock=IONA, offer=83.7311688694, up=false}
 on destination: topic://STOCKS.IONA
Sending: {price=83.33023218494, stock=IONA, offer=83.41356241712, up=false}
 on destination: topic://STOCKS.IONA
Sending: {price=84.05476877613, stock=IONA, offer=84.13882354490, up=true}
 on destination: topic://STOCKS.IONA
Sending: {price=57.75764610250, stock=JAVA, offer=57.815403748606, up=true}
 on destination: topic://STOCKS.JAVA
Sending: {price=84.3813034823, stock=IONA, offer=84.46568478585, up=true}
 on destination: topic://STOCKS.IONA
Sending: {price=84.77874758495, stock=IONA, offer=84.86352633253, up=true}
 on destination: topic://STOCKS.IONA
...
```

The example shown in listing 7.13 uses the most common type of XML configuration file. So although this is nothing new, it's something that many developers don't fully understand.

Now that we've examined and demonstrated various styles of configuration examples for ActiveMQ, it's time to shift gears a bit to look at a common use of ActiveMQ: creating an application that uses a common JMS paradigm known as *request/reply*.

7.3   *Implementing request/reply with JMS*

As described in earlier chapters, messaging is all about the decoupling of senders from receivers. Messages are sent by one process to a broker, and messages are received from a broker by a different process in an asynchronous manner. One style of system architecture that can be implemented using JMS is known as *request/reply*. From a high level, a request/reply scenario involves an application that sends a message (the request) and expects to receive a message in return (the reply). Traditionally, such a system design was implemented using a client-server architecture, with the server and the client communicating in a synchronous manner across a network transport (TCP, UDP, and so on). This style of architecture certainly has scalability limitations, and it's difficult to distribute it further. That's where messaging enters the picture—to provide the ability to design a system that can easily scale much further via a messaging-based request/reply design. Some of the most scalable systems in the world are implemented using asynchronous processing like that being demonstrated in this example.

The diagram shown in figure 7.2 depicts an overview of the request/reply paradigm. Note that the client consists of both a producer and a consumer, and the worker also consists of both a producer and a consumer. These two entities are both explained next.

First, the producer creates a request in the form of a JMS message and sets a couple of important properties on the message—the correlation ID (set via the `JMS-CorrelationID` message property) and the reply destination (set via the `JMSReplyTo` message property). The correlation ID is important, as it allows requests to be correlated with replies if there are multiple outstanding requests. The reply destination is where the reply is expected to be delivered (usually a temporary JMS destination since it's much more resource friendly). The client then configures a consumer to listen on the reply destination.

Second, a worker receives the request, processes it, and sends a reply message using the destination named in the `JMSReplyTo` property of the request message. The reply message must also set `JMSCorrelationID` using the correlation ID from the orig-

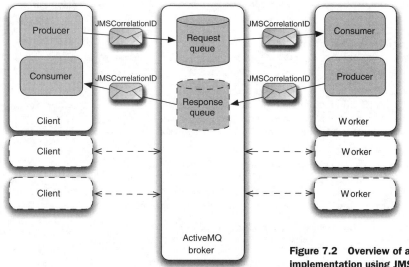

Figure 7.2 Overview of a request/reply implementation using JMS

inal request. When the client receives this reply message, it can then properly associate it with the original request.

Now comes the interesting part—to demonstrate how this architecture can be highly scalable. Imagine that a single worker isn't enough to handle the load of incoming requests. No problem: just add additional workers to handle the load. Those workers can even be distributed across multiple hosts—this is the most important aspect of scaling this design. Because the workers aren't contending for the same resources on the same host, the only limit is the maximum throughput of messages through the broker, which is much higher than you can achieve with any classic client-server setup. Furthermore, ActiveMQ can be scaled both vertically and horizontally, as discussed in part 4. Let's now take a look at a simple implementation of request/reply.

7.3.1 Implementing the server and the worker

The first piece of the system on which to focus is the message broker. Get the broker up and running so that it's ready for connections when both sides are started up. An embedded broker will be used for this example because it's easy to demonstrate. The second piece of the system to get running is the worker. The worker is composed of a message listener that consumes the message and sends a response. Even though this is a simple implementation, it'll provide you enough information to use it with your systems. So take a look at the server implementation.

> **Listing 7.14 Create a broker, a consumer, and a producer for the request/reply example**

```
...
public void start() throws Exception {
  createBroker();
  setupConsumer();
}

private void createBroker() throws Exception {        ⟵——— Start broker
  broker = new BrokerService();
  broker.setPersistent(false);
  broker.setUseJmx(false);
  broker.addConnector(brokerUrl);
  broker.start();
}

private void setupConsumer() throws JMSException {        ⟵——— Set up consumer
  ActiveMQConnectionFactory connectionFactory
      = new ActiveMQConnectionFactory(brokerUrl);

  Connection connection;
  connection = connectionFactory.createConnection();
  connection.start();
  session = connection.createSession(false, Session.AUTO_ACKNOWLEDGE);
  Destination adminQueue = session.createQueue(requestQueue);

  producer = session.createProducer(null);
  producer.setDeliveryMode(DeliveryMode.NON_PERSISTENT);

  consumer = session.createConsumer(adminQueue);
```

```
  consumer.setMessageListener(this);
 }
 public void stop() throws Exception {          ◁─── Stop server
  producer.close();
  consumer.close();
  session.close();
  broker.stop();
 }
...
```

As you can see, the `start()` method calls one method to create and start an embedded broker, and another method to create and start up the worker. The `createBroker()` method uses the `BrokerService` class to create an embedded broker. The `setupConsumer()` method creates all the necessary JMS objects for receiving and sending messages including a connection, a session, a destination, a consumer, and a producer. The producer is created without a default destination, because it'll send messages to destinations that are specified in each message's `JMSReplyTo` property .

Taking a closer look at the listener, note how it handles the consumption of each request as shown next.

Listing 7.15 The message listener for the request/reply example

```
...
 public void onMessage(Message message) {
  try {
   TextMessage response = this.session.createTextMessage();
   if (message instanceof TextMessage) {
    TextMessage txtMsg = (TextMessage) message;
    String messageText = txtMsg.getText();
    response.setText(handleRequest(messageText));      ◁─── Handle request
   }

   response.setJMSCorrelationID(message.getJMSCorrelationID());  ◁┐ Assign
                                                                   │ correlation
   producer.send(message.getJMSReplyTo(), response);      ◁┐     │ ID
  } catch (JMSException e) {                  Send response │
   e.printStackTrace();
  }
 }

 public String handleRequest(String messageText) {
  return "Response to '" + messageText + "'";
 }
...
```

The listener creates a new message, assigns the appropriate correlation ID, and sends a message to the reply-to queue. Simple stuff, but still important. Although this message listener isn't earth shattering in its implementation, it demonstrates the basic steps necessary to complete the task of the worker. Any amount of extra processing or database access could be added to the listener in your systems depending on the requirements.

Starting the server is rather obvious: create an instance of it and call the `start()` method. All of the server functionality is housed in the main method, as shown in the following listing.

Listing 7.16 Starting the server for the request-reply example

```
...
public static void main(String[] args) throws Exception {
  Server server = new Server();
  server.start();

  System.out.println();
  System.out.println("Press any key to stop the server");
  System.out.println();

  System.in.read();

  server.stop();
}
...
```

Once the server is started and the worker is running, everything is ready to accept requests from the client.

7.3.2 *Implementing the client*

The job of the client is to initiate requests to the broker. This is where the whole request/reply process begins, and is typically triggered by one of your business processes. This process could be to accept an order, fulfill an order, integrate various business systems, or buy or sell a financial position. Whatever the case may be, request-reply begins by sending a message.

Sending a message to the broker requires the standard connection, session, destination, and producer which are all created in the client by the `start()` method. This is all shown in the following listing.

Listing 7.17 Methods for starting and stopping the request/reply client

```
...
public void start() throws JMSException {
  ActiveMQConnectionFactory connectionFactory =
    new ActiveMQConnectionFactory(brokerUrl);
  connection = connectionFactory.createConnection();
  connection.start();
  session = connection.createSession(false, Session.AUTO_ACKNOWLEDGE);
  Destination adminQueue = session.createQueue(requestQueue);

  producer = session.createProducer(adminQueue);
  producer.setDeliveryMode(DeliveryMode.NON_PERSISTENT);

  tempDest = session.createTemporaryQueue();
  consumer = session.createConsumer(tempDest);

  consumer.setMessageListener(this);
}
```

```
public void stop() throws JMSException {
 producer.close();
 consumer.close();
 session.close();
 connection.close();
 }
...
```

The producer sends a message to the request queue and then the consumer listens on the newly created temporary queue. Now it's time to implement an actual logic for the client, as shown next.

Listing 7.18   Implementation of logic for request/reply client

```
...
public void request(String request) throws JMSException {       ◁── Send request
  System.out.println("Requesting: " + request);
  TextMessage txtMessage = session.createTextMessage();
  txtMessage.setText(request);

  txtMessage.setJMSReplyTo(tempDest);

  String correlationId = UUID.randomUUID().toString();
  txtMessage.setJMSCorrelationID(correlationId);
  this.producer.send(txtMessage);
 }

public void onMessage(Message message) {                       ◁── Wait for reply
  try {
   System.out.println("Received response for: "
     + ((TextMessage) message).getText());
  } catch (JMSException e) {
   e.printStackTrace();
  }
 }
...
```

The `request()` method shown in listing 7.18 creates a message with the request content, sets the `JMSReplyTo` property to the temporary queue, and sets the correlation ID—these three items are important. Although the correlation ID in this case uses a random UUID, just about any ID generator can be used. Now we're ready to send a request.

Just like starting the server was a simple main method, the same is true of the client as shown in the next listing.

Listing 7.19   Starting the request/reply client

```
...
 public static void main(String[] args) throws Exception {
  Client client = new Client();
  client.start();
  int i = 0;
  while (i++ < 10) {
   client.request("REQUEST-" + i);
  }
```

```
Thread.sleep(3000); //wait for replies
client.stop();
}
...
```

As explained earlier, this is a simple implementation. So upon starting up the client, 10 requests are sent to the broker. Now it's time to actually run the example.

7.3.3   *Running the request/reply example*

Running the example requires two terminals: one for the server and one for the client. The server needs to be started first. The server is implemented in a class named `Server` and the client is implemented in a class named `Client`. Because each of these classes is initiated via a main method, it's easy to start each one. The following listing demonstrates starting up the server class.

Listing 7.20   Start up the server for the request/reply example

```
$ mvn exec:java -Dexec.mainClass=org.apache.activemq.book.ch7.sync.Server
...
INFO | Using Persistence Adapter: MemoryPersistenceAdapter
INFO | ActiveMQ 5.4.1 JMS Message Broker (localhost) is starting
INFO | For help or more information please see:
  http://activemq.apache.org/
INFO | Listening for connections at:
  tcp://dejan-bosanacs-macbook-pro.local:61616
INFO | Connector tcp://dejan-bosanacs-macbook-pro.local:61616 Started
INFO | ActiveMQ JMS Message Broker
  (localhost, ID:dejanb-57522-1271170284460-0:0) started

Press any key to stop the server

INFO | ActiveMQ Message Broker
  (localhost, ID:dejanb-57522-1271170284460-0:0) is shutting down
INFO | Connector tcp://dejan-bosanacs-macbook-pro.local:61616 Stopped
INFO | ActiveMQ JMS Message Broker
  (localhost, ID:dejanb-57522-1271170284460-0:0) stopped
...
```

When the server is started up, then it's time to start up the client and begin sending requests. The following listing shows how to start up the client.

Listing 7.21   Start up the client for the request/reply example

```
$ mvn exec:java -Dexec.mainClass=org.apache.activemq.book.ch7.sync.Client
...
Requesting: REQUEST-1
Requesting: REQUEST-2
Requesting: REQUEST-3
Requesting: REQUEST-4
Requesting: REQUEST-5
Requesting: REQUEST-6
Requesting: REQUEST-7
Requesting: REQUEST-8
Requesting: REQUEST-9
```

```
Requesting: REQUEST-10
Received response for: Response to 'REQUEST-1'
Received response for: Response to 'REQUEST-2'
Received response for: Response to 'REQUEST-3'
Received response for: Response to 'REQUEST-4'
Received response for: Response to 'REQUEST-5'
Received response for: Response to 'REQUEST-6'
Received response for: Response to 'REQUEST-7'
Received response for: Response to 'REQUEST-8'
Received response for: Response to 'REQUEST-9'
Received response for: Response to 'REQUEST-10'
...
```

Note that when the client is started, 10 requests are sent to initiate the request/reply process and 10 replies are received back from the worker. Although it's not glorious, the power in this simple request/reply example will become evident when you apply it to your own business processes.

Using the request/reply pattern, envision that there are thousands of requests entering the broker every second from many clients, all distributed across many hosts. In a production system, more than just a single broker instance would be used for the purposes of redundancy, failover, and load balancing. These brokers would also be distributed across many hosts. The only way to handle this many requests would be to use many workers. Producers can always send messages much faster than a consumer can receive and process them, so lots of workers would be needed, all of them spread out across many hosts as well. The advantage of using many workers is that each one can go up and down at will, and the overall system itself isn't affected. The producers and workers would continue to process messages, and even if one of them crashed, it wouldn't affect the system. This is exactly how many large-scale systems can handle such a tremendous load—through the use of asynchronous messaging like that demonstrated by the request/reply pattern.

The JMS API can be tedious, as it requires you to write a lot of code for initializing all the necessary JMS objects such as connections, sessions, producers, consumers, and so forth. This is where the Spring Framework provides a lot of benefit. It helps you to remove such boilerplate code by supplying a more cogent API and by simplifying the overall configuration.

7.4   *Writing JMS clients using Spring*

ActiveMQ uses the Spring Framework to ease the various aspects of client-to-broker communication, but the Spring Framework goes much further, with its API and container designed specifically for JMS messaging. Together, ActiveMQ and Spring make an excellent JMS development platform, making many common tasks extremely easy to accomplish. Some of the tasks to be covered in this section include

- *Configuring JMS connections*—ActiveMQ provides classes that can be used to configure URLs and other parameters of connections to brokers. The connection factory could later be used by your application to get the appropriate connection.

- *Configuring JMS destinations*—ActiveMQ destination objects can be configured simply as beans representing JMS destinations used by your producers and consumers.
- *Defining JMS consumers*—Spring provides helper classes that allow you to easily configure a message listener container and hook message listeners to it.
- *Implementing JMS producers*—Spring also provides helper bean classes for creating new producers.

In the following sections, these tasks will be demonstrated and the portfolio application will be changed to use all benefits of the ActiveMQ and Spring integration.

7.4.1 Configuring JMS connections

As seen in the previous examples, the first step in creating a JMS application is to create a connection to the ActiveMQ broker. The `ActiveMQConnectionFactory` is a factory that creates an `ActiveMQConnection`, both of which can be easily used with Spring. The following snippet shows how to define an `ActiveMQConnectionFactory` using a Spring XML config:

```
<bean id="jmsConnectionFactory"
   class="org.apache.activemq.ActiveMQConnectionFactory">
 <property name="brokerURL" value="tcp://localhost:61616" />
 <property name="userName" value="admin" />
 <property name="password" value="password" />
</bean>
```

In the snippet, note the properties that are configured on the `ActiveMQConnectionFactory`.

In some use cases a pool of connections is necessary in order to achieve a desired performance. For this purpose, ActiveMQ provides the `PooledConnectionFactory` class, which maintains a pool of JMS connections and sessions. Here's an example Spring XML configuration for the `PooledConnectionFactory`:

```
<bean id="pooledJmsConnectionFactory"
   class="org.apache.activemq.pool.PooledConnectionFactory"
   destroy-method="stop">
 <property name="connectionFactory" ref="jmsConnectionFactory" />
</bean>
```

Only one property is configured on the `PooledConnectionFactory` in this case—the `connectionFactory` property. The `connectionFactory` property is used to define the underlying connection factory to the ActiveMQ broker that'll be used by the pooled connection factory. In this case we've used our previously defined `jmsConnectionFactory` bean.

Since the pooled connection factory has a dependency on the Apache Commons Pool project (http://mng.bz/j3PV), you'll need to add the JAR to the classpath. Or, if you use Maven for your project management, just add the following dependency to the `pom.xml` file:

```
<dependency>
 <groupId>commons-pool</groupId>
 <artifactId>commons-pool</artifactId>
 <version>1.4</version>
</dependency>
```

The preceding XML defines a Maven dependency on the commons-pool-1.4.jar file, and even fetches it for you automatically.

Once the JMS connection has been defined, you can move on to defining the JMS destinations, producers, and consumers.

7.4.2 Configuring JMS destinations

JMS destinations can be predefined in the activemq.xml file using the `ActiveMQTopic` and `ActiveMQQueue` classes. The following snippet contains two new topic definitions to be used in the portfolio example:

```
<bean id="cscoDest" class="org.apache.activemq.command.ActiveMQTopic">
  <constructor-arg value="STOCKS.CSCO" />
</bean>

<bean id="orclDest" class="org.apache.activemq.command.ActiveMQTopic">
  <constructor-arg value="STOCKS.ORCL" />
</bean>
```

As you can see, these classes use constructor injection for setting a desired destination name on the `ActiveMQTopic` class. Predefining topics isn't required in ActiveMQ, but it can be handy for environments where the broker requires clients to authenticate for various operations. For more information about client authentication, see chapter 6. Now that a connection and a couple of destinations exist, you can begin sending and receiving messages.

7.4.3 Creating JMS consumers

The next two sections touch upon basic use of Spring JMS (http://mng.bz/I0Pe) for creating consumers and producers, as it makes creating JMS consumers and producers incredibly easy. Although Spring JMS provides some powerful features, these two sections won't dive into deep details, since this is outside of the scope of this book. Instead, we'll show some of the basic concepts to get you up and running quickly with the portfolio example. For more information on Spring JMS, consult the Spring documentation.

The basic abstraction for receiving messages in Spring is the message listener container (MLC: see http://mng.bz/LJti). The MLC design provides an intermediary between your message listener and broker to handle connections, threading, and more, leaving you to worry only about your business logic that lives in the listener. In the following listing, the portfolio message listener from chapter 3 is used by two message listener containers for the two destinations that were defined in the previous section.

Listing 7.22   Defining two Spring message listener containers and a message listener

```
<!-- The message listener -->
<bean id="portfolioListener"
  class="org.apache.activemq.book.ch3.portfolio.Listener">
</bean>

<!-- Spring DMLC -->
<bean id="cscoConsumer"
class="org.springframework.jms.listener.DefaultMessageListenerContainer">
    <property name="connectionFactory" ref="jmsConnectionFactory" />
    <property name="destination" ref="cscoDest" />
    <property name="messageListener" ref="portfolioListener" />
</bean>

<!-- Spring DMLC -->
<bean id="orclConsumer"
class="org.springframework.jms.listener.DefaultMessageListenerContainer">
    <property name="connectionFactory" ref="jmsConnectionFactory" />
    <property name="destination" ref="orclDest" />
    <property name="messageListener" ref="portfolioListener" />
</bean>
```

Each MLC instance in listing 7.22 requires a connection factory, a destination, and a message listener. So all you have to do is to implement a message listener bean and leave everything else to the Spring MLC. Note that in this example we've used the plain (not pooled) connection factory. This is because no connection pooling is needed for this simple example. This example uses the Spring `DefaultMessage-ListenerContainer` (DMLC), which is the most commonly used MLC. Although numerous other properties on the DMLC can be configured, this example is using only the basics. When these two DMLC instances start up, they'll be ready to receive messages and hand them off to the message listener.

Now let's send some messages to ActiveMQ.

7.4.4   Creating JMS producers

As was the case for receiving messages, Spring also provides conveniences for sending messages. The crucial abstraction for sending messages is the Spring `JmsTemplate` class. The `JmsTemplate` follows the standard template pattern to provide a convenience class for sending messages.

One of the most common ways to send a message using Spring is by implementing the Spring `MessageCreator` interface and utilizing it with the appropriate `send()` method of the `JmsTemplate` class. The following listing demonstrates this by implementing all message creation logic borrowing the stock portfolio publisher from chapter 3.

Listing 7.23   Implementation of a `MessageCreator` for sending messages using Spring

```
public class StockMessageCreator
          implements MessageCreator {

  private int MAX_DELTA_PERCENT = 1;
```

```
private Map<Destination, Double> LAST_PRICES
  = new Hashtable<Destination, Double>();

Destination stock;

public StockMessageCreator(Destination stock) {
 this.stock = stock;
}

public Message createMessage(Session session) throws JMSException {
 Double value = LAST_PRICES.get(stock);
 if (value == null) {
  value = new Double(Math.random() * 100);
 }

 // lets mutate the value by some percentage
 double oldPrice = value.doubleValue();
 value = new Double(mutatePrice(oldPrice));
 LAST_PRICES.put(stock, value);
 double price = value.doubleValue();

 double offer = price * 1.001;

 boolean up = (price > oldPrice);
 MapMessage message = session.createMapMessage();
 message.setString("stock", stock.toString());
 message.setDouble("price", price);
 message.setDouble("offer", offer);
 message.setBoolean("up", up);
 System.out.println(
    "Sending: " + ((ActiveMQMapMessage)message).getContentMap()
  + " on destination: " + stock
 );
 return message;
}

protected double mutatePrice(double price) {
 double percentChange = (2 * Math.random() * MAX_DELTA_PERCENT)
    - MAX_DELTA_PERCENT;

 return price * (100 + percentChange) / 100;
}

}
```

The `MessageCreator` interface defines only the `createMessage()` method, which returns a JMS message. Here, we've implemented some logic for creating random stock prices, and we're creating an appropriate JMS map message to hold all of the relevant data. To send the message, the `JmsTemplate`'s `send()` method will utilize the `StockMessageCreator` as shown next.

> **Listing 7.24 JMS publisher implementation in Spring**

```
public class SpringPublisher {

private JmsTemplate template;
private int count = 10;
private int total;
private Destination[] destinations;
```

```java
private HashMap<Destination,StockMessageCreator>
    creators = new HashMap<Destination,StockMessageCreator>();

public void start() {
 while (total < 1000) {
  for (int i = 0; i < count; i++) {
   sendMessage();
  }
  total += count;
  System.out.println("Published '" + count + "' of '"
    + total + "' price messages");
  try {
  Thread.sleep(1000);
  } catch (InterruptedException x) {
  }
 }
}

protected void sendMessage() {
 int idx = 0;
  while (true) {
   idx = (int)Math.round(destinations.length * Math.random());
    if (idx < destinations.length) {
     break;
    }
  }
  Destination destination = destinations[idx];
  template.send(destination, getStockMessageCreator(destination));

}
private StockMessageCreator getStockMessageCreator(Destination dest) {
 if (creators.containsKey(dest)) {
  return creators.get(dest);
 } else {
  StockMessageCreator creator = new StockMessageCreator(dest);
  creators.put(dest, creator);
  return creator;
 }
}

 // getters and setters goes here
}
```

Send with JmsTemplate (annotation pointing to `template.send(...)` line)

The important thing to note in listing 7.24 is how the send() method uses the message creator. Everything else in this example is the same as in the original stock portfolio publisher from chapter 3. Now you have all the necessary components to publish messages to ActiveMQ using Spring. All that's left to be done is to configure it properly as demonstrated in the following listing.

Listing 7.25   JMS publisher configuration in Spring

```xml
<!-- Spring JMS Template -->
<bean id="jmsTemplate" class="org.springframework.jms.core.JmsTemplate">
  <property name="connectionFactory" ref="pooledJmsConnectionFactory" />
</bean>
```

```
<bean id="stockPublisher"
  class="org.apache.activemq.book.ch7.spring.SpringPublisher">
  <property name="template" ref="jmsTemplate" />
  <property name="destinations">
    <list>
      <ref local="cscoDest" />
      <ref local="orclDest" />
    </list>
  </property>
</bean>
```

The snippet in listing 7.25 shows an instance of the Spring `JmsTemplate` and the publisher. The publisher simply needs a reference to the JMS destinations being used, and the `JmsTemplate` requires a connection factory.

> **NOTE** The pooled connection factory is used with the `JmsTemplate`. This is important because the `JmsTemplate` is designed for use with Java EE containers in mind, which typically provide connection pooling capabilities as required by the Java EE specifications. Every call to the `JmsTemplate.send()` method creates and destroys all the JMS resources (connections, consumers, and producers). So if you're not using a Java EE container, make sure to use a pooled connection factory for sending messages with the `JmsTemplate`.

The connections and destinations are defined; the consumers and producer have been created. Now let's run the example.

7.4.5 Putting it all together

After implementing all pieces of the example, the application should be ready to run. Take a look at the following listing to see the main method that will execute the example.

Listing 7.26 The main method for the Spring example

```
public class SpringClient {

 public static void main(String[] args) {
  BrokerService broker = new BrokerService();
  broker.addConnector("tcp://localhost:61616");
  broker.setPersistent(false);
  broker.start();                                    ⟵  Start broker

  FileSystemXmlApplicationContext context =
    new FileSystemXmlApplicationContext(
      "src/main/resources/org/apache/activemq/book/ch7/spring-client.xml"
    );                                               ⟵  Initialize Spring clients
  SpringPublisher publisher =
    (SpringPublisher)context.getBean("stockPublisher");
  publisher.start();
 }

}
```

This simple class starts a minimal ActiveMQ broker configuration and initializes the Spring application context to start the JMS clients.

The example can be run from the command line using the following command.

Listing 7.27 Run the Spring example

```
$ mvn exec:java \
-Dexec.mainClass=org.apache.activemq.book.ch7.spring.SpringClient \
-Dlog4j.configuration=file:src/main/java/log4j.properties
...
Sending: {price=65.958996694, stock=CSCO, offer=66.0249556914, up=false}
  on destination: topic://STOCKS.CSCO
topic://STOCKS.IONA 79.97 80.05 down
Sending: {price=80.67595675108, stock=ORCL, offer=80.7566327078, up=true}
  on destination: topic://STOCKS.ORCL
topic://STOCKS.JAVA 65.96 66.02 down
Sending: {price=65.63333898492, stock=CSCO, offer=65.69897232391, up=false}
  on destination: topic://STOCKS.CSCO
topic://STOCKS.IONA 80.68 80.76 up
Sending: {price=80.50525969261, stock=ORCL, offer=80.58576495231, up=false}
  on destination: topic://STOCKS.ORCL
topic://STOCKS.JAVA 65.63 65.70 down
Sending: {price=81.2186806051, stock=ORCL, offer=81.29989928577, up=true}
  on destination: topic://STOCKS.ORCL
topic://STOCKS.IONA 80.51 80.59 down
Sending: {price=65.48960846536, stock=CSCO, offer=65.5550980738, up=false}
  on destination: topic://CSCO
topic://STOCKS.IONA 81.22 81.30 up
topic://STOCKS.JAVA 65.49 65.56 down
...
```

As you can see, both producer and consumer print their messages to standard output as the example runs.

In this section, you used Spring to augment the stock portfolio example application from chapter 3. You were able to reuse most of the original logic, but this time you used some Spring utilities to simplify the example a lot. As stated previously, this example simply touched on the basics of using Spring JMS. If you'd like more information about Spring JMS, see the documentation (http://mng.bz/I0Pe).

7.5   Summary

In this chapter, you've seen how ActiveMQ can be viewed not only as a separate Java infrastructure application, but also as a Java module that can be easily integrated in your Java applications. Offering a wide range of flexibility, ActiveMQ can be configured with plain Java code or by using XML configuration files.

You've also seen how ActiveMQ can play well with the Spring Framework, both in terms of integrating brokers in Java applications and simplifying the implementation of JMS clients.

We covered some advanced programming techniques with ActiveMQ as well. The request/reply pattern was explained in terms of the benefits it brings to your application's architecture and how to implement it using ActiveMQ. Lastly, we revisited the portfolio example from chapter 3 in order to refactor it to use Spring JMS. Though only the basics of Spring JMS were demonstrated here, its capabilities are powerful and incredibly streamlined, and we encourage you to read more about it for your applications.

The next chapter focuses on ActiveMQ integration options with various Java EE containers. You'll see how ActiveMQ can be used in conjunction with Java application servers such as Apache Geronimo and Apache Tomcat, for example, and how to use JNDI.

Integrating ActiveMQ
with application servers

8

This chapter covers

- Integrating ActiveMQ with Apache Tomcat
- Integrating ActiveMQ with Jetty
- Integrating ActiveMQ with Apache Geronimo
- Integrating ActiveMQ with JBoss
- Understanding ActiveMQ and JNDI

Up to this point, most of the examples in the book have utilized a standalone instance of ActiveMQ: ActiveMQ was started up in its own JVM. Then chapter 7 demonstrated multiple ways to embed ActiveMQ inside a Java application, including the use of the ActiveMQ Java APIs as well as using a Spring Framework XML configuration. This style of integration is common, but the aim of this chapter is different. The goal of this chapter is to demonstrate the use of an application server's features for integrating third-party middleware.

The term *application server* is overloaded, but in the most general sense, application servers provide a container architecture that accepts the deployment of an application and provides an environment in which it can run. This chapter focuses on Java application servers, of which there are two types. The first type of application server implements the Java Servlet specification (http://mng.bz/cmMj) and is known as a *web container*. Apache Tomcat and Jetty both fall into the category of web containers. The second type of application server implements the Java EE family of specifications (http://mng.bz/NTSk) and is known as a *Java EE container*. Apache Geronimo and JBoss both fall into the category of Java EE containers. We chose these four application servers for this chapter because they're popular and freely available. ActiveMQ can also be integrated with commercial application servers such as WebLogic and WebSphere using the same strategies used in this chapter.

When deploying ActiveMQ to an application server, two major tasks need to be completed—starting the broker and providing access to the JMS destinations. There are different approaches to solving both of these problems. One option to handle both tasks is to use the Spring Framework. The strategy used in chapter 7 demonstrated that Spring can be used to start ActiveMQ and to provide access to the JMS destinations. But since we already demonstrated that approach, a different approach will be used this chapter.

ActiveMQ provides a unique feature that allows a broker to be created via the ActiveMQ JMS connection factory. By creating an ActiveMQ connection factory using a URI for a broker that doesn't yet exist, the JMS connection will create an instance of the broker. So this means that the creation of the broker is dependent upon the ability to create the ActiveMQ connection. JMS connections are created from a connection factory that's registered with the application server. For this purpose, Java application servers provide a JNDI (Java Naming and Directory Interface) implementation that can be used to expose objects to be used by applications deployed to the container. Objects such as JDBC drivers, JMS resources, transaction managers, and so forth can be configured to be accessed using the JNDI API. This is the approach that will be used with the web containers.

Both Apache Tomcat and Jetty support two different styles of configuration for objects in JNDI: local JNDI and global JNDI. Local JNDI is used to configure objects that will only be exposed to a specific application, whereas global JNDI is used to expose objects to any application in the entire web container. We'll use each style of JNDI configuration to demonstrate the creation of the JMS resources. To situate these differences in JNDI configuration and to demonstrate the use of each in Tomcat and Jetty, there are two different flavors of the sample web application. These are available in the example source code and are named `jms-webapp-local` and `jms-webapp-global`.

Both Apache Geronimo and JBoss support JNDI, but this will only be used to register the JMS resources. The ActiveMQ broker won't be started by the creation of a JMS connection. To start up the ActiveMQ broker and integrate it with Geronimo and JBoss, this chapter will utilize a *J2EE Connector Architecture* (http://mng.bz/fXU9) resource adapter, also known as *JCA*. To situate the difference in integration details between the two Java EE containers reviewed here, two different flavors of the sample web application are available in the example source code and are named `jms-webapp-geronimo` and `jms-webapp-jboss`.

Although four sample web application projects are used in this chapter, the core of each application is exactly the same. The reason why there are four copies of the same application is to support the different deployment styles being used. Before proceeding with the actual integrations, it's a good idea to take a high-level look at the sample web application.

8.1   *The sample web application*

To demonstrate the sample integrations in this chapter, a simple web application is used to prove that each integration is successful. There are four copies of this web application that are each customized for various environments. Each web application is small and utilizes only the ActiveMQ broker, a JMS connection factory, and a JMS queue. Figure 8.1 provides a look at the directory structure for the sample web application.

As you can see, the structure of this is fairly standard for a Maven-based Java web application. Though the screenshot in figure 8.1 shows the project structure for the `jms-webapp-local` application, the directory structure for the other instances of the application is only slightly different. Each web application uses the Spring Framework's web framework features, which reduces the complexity of building a web application. To understand how the web application works, it's best to examine some of the major items found in a standard Java web application.

The relevant portions of the web application that are pertinent to the exercises in this chapter are the web.xml file, the Spring application context, and the `JmsMessage-SenderService` class. The following listing shows the relevant portion of the web.xml file.

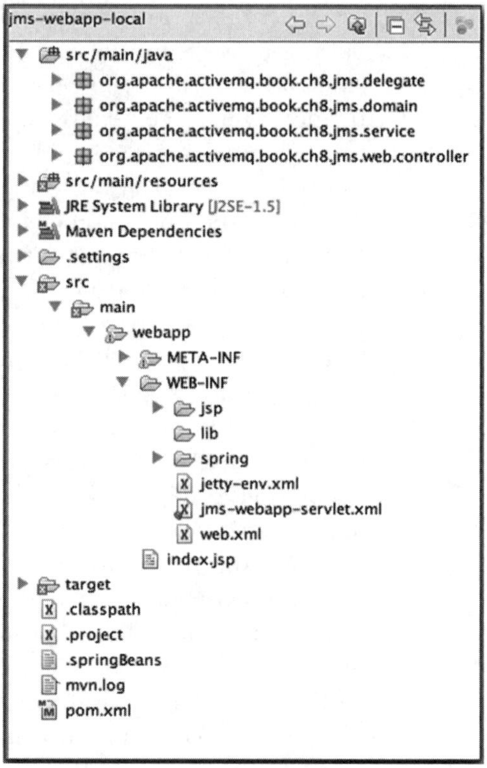

Figure 8.1   The project structure for the sample web application that demonstrates local JNDI configuration

---

Listing 8.1   The web.xml file

```
...
<resource-ref>
  <description>JMS Connection</description>
  <res-ref-name>jms/ConnectionFactory</res-ref-name>
  <res-type>org.apache.activemq.ActiveMQConnectionFactory</res-type>
```

```
  <res-auth>Container</res-auth>
</resource-ref>

<resource-ref>
  <res-ref-name>jms/FooQueue</res-ref-name>
  <res-type>javax.jms.Queue</res-type>
  <res-auth>Container</res-auth>
</resource-ref>
...
```

The <resource-ref> elements in the web.xml reference the JNDI resources that are registered with the application server. This configuration makes those resources available to the web application. This configuration will only change for the Geronimo integration, which uses the standard <message-destination-ref> element instead of a <resource-ref> for the JMS queue.

The other relevant configuration file from the web application is the Spring application context, shown next.

Listing 8.2   The Spring application context file

```
...
<jee:jndi-lookup id="connectionFactory"
  jndi-name="java:comp/env/jms/ConnectionFactory"
  cache="true"
  resource-ref="true"
  lookup-on-startup="true"
  expected-type="org.apache.activemq.ActiveMQConnectionFactory"
  proxy-interface="javax.jms.ConnectionFactory" />

<jee:jndi-lookup id="fooQueue"
  jndi-name="java:comp/env/jms/FooQueue"
  cache="true"
  resource-ref="true"
  lookup-on-startup="true"
  expected-type="org.apache.activemq.command.ActiveMQQueue"
  proxy-interface="javax.jms.Queue" />

<bean id="jmsMessageBean"
  class="org.apache.activemq.book.ch8.jms.domain.JmsMessage" />

<bean id="messageSenderService"
  class="org.apache.activemq.book.ch8.jms.service.JmsMessageSenderService"
  p:connectionFactory-ref="connectionFactory"
  p:queue-ref="fooQueue" />
...
```

The Spring application context shown in listing 8.2 is an XML configuration file for the Spring Framework: see http://www.springframework.org. (Please also note that Spring's p-namespace http://mng.bz/dLT9 is being used in the configuration.) The <jee:jndi-lookup> elements utilize Spring to perform a JNDI lookup of the noted resources. These resources are then injected into the messageSenderService Java bean (the values are inserted via setter methods) after it's instantiated by Spring. The messageSenderService is then used by the web application to send a JMS message. Listing 8.3 shows the source code for the JmsMessageSenderService bean.

Listing 8.3   The JmsMessageSenderService class

```
public class JmsMessageSenderService {

  private JmsTemplate jmsTemplate;

  public void sendMessage(final JmsMessage bean)
    throws JMSException {

      if (bean.isPersistent()) {
        jmsTemplate.setDeliveryPersistent(bean.isPersistent());
      }

      if (0 != bean.getTimeToLive()) {
        jmsTemplate.setTimeToLive(bean.getTimeToLive());
      }

      jmsTemplate.send(new MessageCreator() {
        public Message createMessage(Session session)
          throws JMSException {

            TextMessage message =
              session.createTextMessage(bean.getMessagePayload());

            if (bean.getReplyTo() != null &&
                !bean.getReplyTo().equals("")) {
              ActiveMQQueue replyToQueue =
                new ActiveMQQueue(bean.getReplyTo());
              message.setJMSReplyTo(replyToQueue);
            }
            return message;
        }
      });
  }

  public void setJmsTemplate(JmsTemplate jmsTemplate) {
    this.jmsTemplate = jmsTemplate;
  }

}
```

The JmsMessageSenderService bean is kept simple so that it only focuses on the task of sending the JMS message. This class uses the Spring JmsTemplate and an anonymous MessageCreator to easily send the JMS message.

There's only one web page in this web application and it's deliberately uncomplicated. This is because the web application is only necessary to test the integration and nothing more. To add further detail to it would only complicate matters and detract from the real purpose of the chapter.

To better understand the flow of a JMS message through these classes, take a look at figure 8.2.

Here's a brief explanation of the illustrated steps:

Step 1 The `JmsMessageSenderService` implements an anonymous Spring `Message-`
`Creator` to create the message.

Step 2 The `JmsMessageSenderService` uses the
Spring `JmsTemplate` to send the message
to ActiveMQ.

Step 3 The Spring `DefaultMessageListener-`
`Container` consumes the message and
hands it off to the `JmsMessageDelegate`.

Step 4 The `JmsMessageDelegate` bean processes
the message (it outputs the message payload).

The `JmsMessageSenderService` is completely iso-
lated from the Spring `DefaultMessageListener-`
`Container` and the `JmsMessageDelegate` bean. Any
messages sent to ActiveMQ by the `JmsMessage-`
`SenderService` have no bearing on whether the
`DefaultMessageListenerContainer` is actually
online and ready to consume. In fact, the `Jms-`
`MessageSenderService` and the Spring `Default-`
`MessageListenerContainer` could easily be split
out of this application so as to reside in completely
different processes and it wouldn't change the functionality of this application. This is a perfect albeit
small example of the asynchronous messaging provided by ActiveMQ.

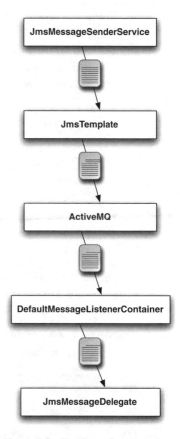

**Figure 8.2   The flow of a message
through the classes in the sample
web application**

The steps in figure 8.2 are all hid-
den behind the scenes of the single
page in the sample web application
shown in 8.3.

When sending a message using the
page shown in figure 8.3, a small message appears briefly on the page and
then fades away quickly to indicate that
the message was sent. This is just a san-
ity check to show some activity in the
web application. These are the only visi-
ble features in the web application.
Everything else happens behind the
scenes.

**Figure 8.3   A screenshot of the only page in the
web application demonstrates that it's
intentionally simplistic.**

These are only the portions of the web application that are apropos to the integration of ActiveMQ with application servers. To get a better look at the details of this sample web application, and to actually deploy it yourself to test your own integrations as you work through the examples, download the example source code for the book.

The four versions of the sample web application for this chapter are

- *jms-webapp-geronimo*—Used to demonstrate ActiveMQ integration with Geronimo
- *jms-webapp-global*—Used to demonstrate ActiveMQ integration with Tomcat and Jetty using global JNDI
- *jms-webapp-jboss*—Used to demonstrate ActiveMQ configuration and deployment with JBoss
- *jms-webapp-local*—Used to demonstrate ActiveMQ integration with Tomcat and Jetty using local JNDI

NOTE   The local JNDI configuration example and the global JNDI configuration example can't be deployed at the same time. This will cause classloader issues and will prevent ActiveMQ from being deployed correctly. Make sure to only deploy one style of configuration at a time.

Before proceeding with this chapter, you need to build all four of these examples. This can be achieved using the Maven command shown next.

Listing 8.4   Build the examples

```
[amq-in-action-example-src] $ cd chapter8/
[chapter8] $ mvn clean install
[INFO] Scanning for projects...
[INFO] Reactor build order:
[INFO]    jms-webapp-geronimo
[INFO]    jms-webapp-global
[INFO]    jms-webapp-jboss
[INFO]    jms-webapp-local
[INFO]    ActiveMQ In Action Examples Chapter 8
...
[INFO]
[INFO]
[INFO] ------------------------------------------------------------------
-----
[INFO] Reactor Summary:
[INFO] ------------------------------------------------------------------
-----
[INFO] jms-webapp-geronimo ...................................
SUCCESS [4.787s]
[INFO] jms-webapp-global ....................................
SUCCESS [1.265s]
[INFO] jms-webapp-jboss .....................................
SUCCESS [8.278s]
[INFO] jms-webapp-local .....................................
SUCCESS [2.359s]
[INFO] ActiveMQ In Action Examples Chapter 8 ................
```

```
SUCCESS [1.911s]
[INFO] ------------------------------------------------------------------
-----
[INFO] ------------------------------------------------------------------
-----
[INFO] BUILD SUCCESSFUL
[INFO] ------------------------------------------------------------------
-----
[INFO] Total time: 18 seconds
[INFO] Finished at: Mon Apr 26 13:24:31 MDT 2010
[INFO] Final Memory: 19M/35M
[INFO] ------------------------------------------------------------------
-----
```

Note that the output in listing 8.4 has been elided slightly. As long as you see the BUILD SUCCESSFUL message, the examples were built correctly and a WAR file for each one should now exist in each project's target directory. This WAR file can then be deployed to the appropriate application server and used to test the ActiveMQ integration.

> **NOTE** Although this chapter describes in detail the changes necessary for each application server, all of these changes have already been made in each of the projects. Just make sure to download the source code for the book to get these example projects.

Now that you have an overview of the sample applications, you're ready to walk through the integrations. The first application server with which to integrate ActiveMQ is Apache Tomcat.

8.2   *Integrating with Apache Tomcat*

Apache Tomcat is arguably the most widely used Java web container available today. Tomcat is used for both development and production throughout the world because it's extremely robust, highly configurable, and commercially supported by a number of companies. Because of its widespread use, Tomcat provides facilities for integrating third-party resources such as JDBC data sources, JMS connection factories, and so on, and making them JNDI accessible. In this section, we'll show you how to integrate ActiveMQ with Apache Tomcat. You'll need to download Apache Tomcat 6.0.26 (http://mng.bz/75qc) and expand it on your computer.

Tomcat offers two styles of configuration for JNDI resources: local JNDI context and global JNDI context. Configuring a *local* JNDI resource means that the resource is only available to a particular web application deployed to Tomcat. Configuring a resource in the *global* JNDI context means that the resource is available to any web application deployed to Tomcat. The configuration for each type of JNDI style is different, so let's review both.

> **NOTE** The sample applications for the local JNDI configuration and the global JNDI configuration can't be deployed at the same time. This will cause classloader issues and will prevent ActiveMQ from being deployed correctly. Make sure to only deploy one of the sample applications at a time.

8.2.1 *Using local JNDI to integrate ActiveMQ with Tomcat*

The local JNDI configuration restricts the availability of resources to the application where they're defined. With this style of configuration for Tomcat, the JNDI resources are defined in a file named META-INF/context.xml. The following listing shows the context.xml file.

Listing 8.5 The Tomcat context.xml file

```
<Context reloadable="true">
    <Resource auth="Container"
            name="jms/ConnectionFactory"
            type="org.apache.activemq.ActiveMQConnectionFactory"
            description="JMS Connection Factory"
            factory="org.apache.activemq.jndi.JNDIReferenceFactory"
            brokerURL="vm://localhost?brokerConfig=xbean:activemq.xml"
            brokerName="MyActiveMQBroker"/>

    <Resource auth="Container"
            name="jms/FooQueue"
            type="org.apache.activemq.command.ActiveMQQueue"
            description="JMS queue"
            factory="org.apache.activemq.jndi.JNDIReferenceFactory"
            physicalName="FOO.QUEUE"/>
</Context>
```

Listing 8.5 is specific to Tomcat. The first element is named jms/Connection-Factory—it defines an ActiveMQ connection factory and takes advantage of features in ActiveMQ to start an instance of the broker via the connection factory. The second element named jms/FooQueue defines a JMS queue in ActiveMQ. This configuration file lives with the web application and is automatically picked up by Tomcat to configure the resources. Tomcat makes them available via a standard JNDI lookup to the sample web application.

> **NOTE** The $TOMCAT_HOME variable is being used to generically reference the Tomcat installation directory. This isn't something that you must set in your environment.

To test the local JNDI resources, use the following steps:

Step 1 Copy the jms-webapp-local/target/jms-webapp.war file to the $TOMCAT_HOME/ webapps directory.

Step 2 Start up Tomcat:

```
$ cd $TOMCAT_HOME
$ ./bin/catalina.sh run
Using CATALINA_BASE:   /opt/apache-tomcat-6.0.26
Using CATALINA_HOME:   /opt/apache-tomcat-6.0.26
Using CATALINA_TMPDIR: /opt/apache-tomcat-6.0.26/temp
Using JRE_HOME:
/System/Library/Frameworks/JavaVM.framework/Versions/
CurrentJDK/Home
Using CLASSPATH:       /opt/apache-tomcat-6.0.26/bin/bootstrap.jar
...
```

```
INFO  - BrokerService              - ActiveMQ 5.4.1 JMS Message
Broker (FooBroker) is starting
...
Apr 8, 2010 9:03:03 PM org.apache.catalina.startup.Catalina start
INFO: Server startup in 3542 ms
```

You can see in the output that ActiveMQ is actually using the activemq.xml configuration file because the brokerName FooBroker is being used. Passing the run argument to the catalina.sh script will cause Tomcat to start up so that its output will appear in the terminal. The ability to see the output is helpful as noted earlier, and will also help you to verify the message receipt in a few steps.

As noted at the beginning of the chapter, this configuration takes advantage of a unique feature in ActiveMQ. This feature allows an ActiveMQ broker to be started simply by creating a connection factory and passing it a broker URI. The connection factory attempts to connect to a broker at the URI, and if one doesn't exist, it'll start one up. As you can see, this is a handy feature in ActiveMQ.

Step 3 Visit http://localhost:8080/jms-webapp and use the web page to send a message. See figure 8.4 for an example of what you should see.

Step 4 To verify the message send, check the terminal to see that the consumer received the message. See the following output:

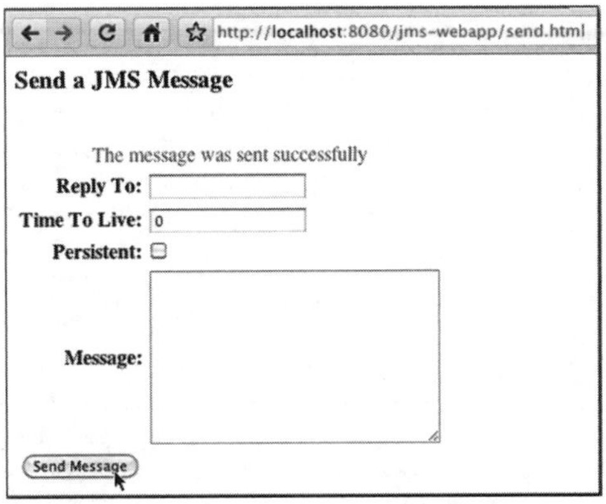

Figure 8.4   Upon sending a JMS message using the web application, a message appears in the web application and then fades away to let you know that the message was sent successfully.

```
...
INFO: Server startup in 3306 ms
INFO  - SingleConnectionFactory        - Established shared
JMS Connection:
ActiveMQConnection {id=ID:mongoose.local-55759-1270249165283-2:1,
clientId=null,
started=false}
INFO  - JmsMessageDelegate        - Consumed message with payload:
This is a test message
```

Note the output from the terminal—specifically, the final line that's a log message from the JmsMessageDelegate bean. This line indicates that the message has been consumed, and you see the message payload is being output.

The local configuration of the ActiveMQ resources is a great approach because these resources are contained with the web application. Nothing in Tomcat itself needs to be changed or configured, which is different from the way that resources are configured for global JNDI.

8.2.2   *Using global JNDI to integrate ActiveMQ with Tomcat*

The global JNDI configuration in Tomcat is also easy to use. It just requires a bit of additional configuration and copying some JARs into the Tomcat lib directory. The advantage of global JNDI is that the resources are available to any web applications that are deployed to Tomcat. In this style of configuration, the JNDI resources are defined in configuration files that live with the Tomcat application server named conf/server.xml and conf/context.xml. The following listing shows the relevant portion of the server.xml file.

Listing 8.6   The Tomcat server.xml file

```
<GlobalNamingResources>
...
  <Resource auth="Container"
    name="jms/ConnectionFactory"
    type="org.apache.activemq.ActiveMQConnectionFactory"
    description="JMS Connection Factory"
    factory="org.apache.activemq.jndi.JNDIReferenceFactory"
    brokerURL="vm://localhost?brokerConfig=xbean:conf/activemq.xml"
    brokerName="MyActiveMQBroker"/>

  <Resource auth="Container"
    name="jms/FooQueue"
    type="org.apache.activemq.command.ActiveMQQueue"
    description="A sample queue"
    factory="org.apache.activemq.jndi.JNDIReferenceFactory"
    physicalName="FOO.QUEUE"/>

...
</GlobalNamingResources>
```

The <Resource> elements in the server.xml file shown in listing 8.6 register the JNDIReferenceFactory object with Tomcat for creating the noted object types—the ActiveMQConnectionFactory and the ActiveMQQueue. Again, ActiveMQ is unique in the fact that a full broker instance can be created by creating an ActiveMQ-ConnectionFactory. The brokerURL attribute is used to pass the broker URI, which allows any of the supported transports (TCP, VM, and so forth) to be used. It also supports the optional brokerConfig parameter used to point to a configuration file for the ActiveMQ instance that's being started.

The next file to be changed is the context.xml file; the relevant additions are shown next.

Listing 8.7   The Tomcat context.xml file

```
<Context>
...
  <ResourceLink global="jms/ConnectionFactory"
    name="jms/ConnectionFactory" />

  <ResourceLink global="jms/FooQueue"
    name="jms/FooQueue" />

...
</Context>
```

The <ResourceLink> elements define a link to the resources that are defined in the global JNDI context and expose these resources to all web applications deployed in this instance of Tomcat.

To test the global JNDI resource configurations, use the following steps:

Step 1 Copy the following JARs into the $TOMCAT_HOME/lib directory:

- activemq-all-5.4.1.jar
- aopalliance-1.0.jar
- commons-logging-1.1.1.jar
- geronimo-j2ee-management_1.0_spec-1.0.jar
- geronimo-jms_1.1_spec-1.1.1.jar
- geronimo-jta_1.0.1B_spec-1.1.1.jar
- log4j-1.2.14.jar
- org.osgi.core-4.1.0.jar
- spring-aop-2.5.6.jar
- spring-beans-2.5.6.jar
- spring-context-2.5.6.jar
- spring-context-support-2.5.6.jar
- spring-core-2.5.6.jar
- spring-jms-2.5.6.jar
- spring-tx-2.5.6.jar
- spring-web-2.5.6.jar
- spring-webmvc-2.5.6.jar

The easiest place to get these JARs is from the jms-webapp-local project that was used for the local JNDI configuration *after* that project is built. After running the Maven command to build the jms-webapp-local project, take a look in the jms-webapp-local/target/jms-webapp/WEB-INF/lib/ directory for these JARs. Simply copy the JARs from that directory into the $TOMCAT_HOME/lib directory.

Step 2 After making changes to the configuration files as noted, they must be included in the WAR file. To build the jms-webapp-global project and create a new WAR file, from the command line, run the following Maven command:

```
$ cd jms-webapp-global
$ mvn clean install
...
[INFO] Scanning for projects...
[INFO] -----------------------------------------------------------------
-----
[INFO] Building jms-webapp-global
[INFO]    task-segment: [clean, install]
[INFO] -----------------------------------------------------------------
-----
...
[INFO] -----------------------------------------------------------------
-----
[INFO] BUILD SUCCESSFUL
[INFO] -----------------------------------------------------------------
-----
...
```

After running this command, a WAR file will exist in the target directory.

Step 3 Copy the jms-webapp-global/activemq.xml file to $TOMCAT_HOME/conf/activemq.xml. This makes the ActiveMQ configuration file available on the classpath.

Step 4   Copy the jms-webapp-global/target/jms-webapp.war to the $TOMCAT_HOME/
webapps directory. This deploys the example web application.

Step 5   Start up Tomcat using the following command:

```
$ cd $TOMCAT_HOME
$ ./bin/catalina.sh run
Using CATALINA_BASE:   /opt/apache-tomcat-6.0.26
Using CATALINA_HOME:   /opt/apache-tomcat-6.0.26
Using CATALINA_TMPDIR: /opt/apache-tomcat-6.0.26/temp
Using JRE_HOME:
/System/Library/Frameworks/JavaVM.framework/Versions/CurrentJDK/Home
Using CLASSPATH:
/opt/apache-tomcat-6.0.26/bin/bootstrap.jar
...
INFO  - BrokerService              - ActiveMQ 5.4.1 JMS Message
Broker (FooBroker) is starting
...
Apr 9, 2010 8:54:59 PM org.apache.catalina.startup.Catalina start
INFO: Server startup in 3365 ms
```

Again, you can see that ActiveMQ is using the activemq.xml configuration file based
on the output stating that the FooBroker is starting.

Step 6   Visit http://localhost:8080/jms-webapp and send a message.

Step 7   To confirm a successful message send, check the terminal for the following
output:

```
...
INFO: Server startup in 3365 ms
INFO  - SingleConnectionFactory    - Established shared
JMS Connection:
ActiveMQConnection {id=ID:mongoose.local-49429-1270868098091-2:1,
clientId=null,started=false}
INFO  - JmsMessageDelegate         - Consumed message with payload:
This is a test message
```

In the output shown, note that the last line of output from the JmsMessageDelegate
bean shows the message payload that was consumed by the JmsMessageDelegate
bean.

For some projects, configuring ActiveMQ to use the Tomcat global JNDI context is
appropriate because there may be multiple projects that need access to those
resources. In some situations, it makes sense to control ActiveMQ from within the
Tomcat process. The disadvantage is that Tomcat and ActiveMQ are now contending
for the same resources inside of the same JVM. For some projects, this isn't a problem,
and is therefore an acceptable trade-off.

   But Tomcat isn't the only viable open source web container. Jetty is a formidable
alternative.

8.3   *Integrating with Jetty*

The Jetty web container has been around for a long time and is reliable. It's small, fast, and has an active community of developers. Jetty provides many of the same features as Tomcat because they're both based on the Java Servlet spec, but the implementation of each is unique.

Jetty is essentially a toolkit for building a web container and it can be customized in many ways. Out of the box, Jetty is bare-bones, but it comes with a handful of configuration files so that many different combinations of services can be started in Jetty. This level of customization is intentional and allows for extreme flexibility. Jetty Hightide is one distribution of Jetty, with a set of services enabled by default. Jetty Hightide is best described by its documentation:

> *Hightide is an optimized, versioned distribution of the Jetty open source web container. It comes pre-integrated with a number of services usually only found in J2EE application servers, or which you would otherwise have to craft together yourself: JNDI, an XA transaction service, a JMS message fabric, and a JDBC accessible database. Thanks to Jetty's lightweight, pluggable architecture, Hightide allows you to easily choose which of these services you want to use, or even replace them with others.*

In this section, ActiveMQ will be integrated with Jetty Hightide using both a local JNDI configuration and a global JNDI configuration. Download Jetty Hightide 7.0.2.v20100331 (http://mng.bz/Sk6u) from the Codehaus for this section and expand it on your computer.

Jetty offers three styles of configuration for JNDI resources: local, global to all applications deployed in Jetty, and global to all applications deployed in the JVM. There are differences in these styles of JNDI configuration, some of which can be controlled via a Jetty feature that provides the ability to scope JNDI resources to a specific context. Jetty's JNDI scoping is powerful and will be used in this section, but only minimally. For a deeper understanding of Jetty's ability to scope JNDI resources, see the Jetty global JNDI information (http://mng.bz/x67C). The two styles of JNDI configuration that we'll demonstrate here are local JNDI and global JNDI. These two styles of JNDI configuration are similar to those in Tomcat, but the configuration format is unique to Jetty.

> **NOTE** The sample applications for the local JNDI configuration and the global JNDI configuration can't be deployed at the same time. This will cause classloader issues and will prevent ActiveMQ from being deployed correctly. Please make sure to only deploy one of the sample applications at a time.

8.3.1   *Using local JNDI to integrate ActiveMQ with Jetty*

Jetty's local JNDI configuration also limits the availability of those resources to the application where they're defined. The JNDI resources are defined in a file that lives with the web application named WEB-INF/jetty-env.xml, which is shown next.

Listing 8.8 The Jetty jetty-env.xml file

```
<Configure id='jms-webapp-wac'
  class="org.foo.mortbay.jetty.webapp.WebAppContext">

  <New id="connectionFactory"
    class="org.mortbay.jetty.plus.naming.Resource">
    <Arg>
      <Ref id='jms-webapp-wac' />
    </Arg>
    <Arg>jms/ConnectionFactory</Arg>
    <Arg>
      <New class="org.apache.activemq.ActiveMQConnectionFactory">
        <Arg>vm://localhost?brokerConfig=xbean:activemq.xml</Arg>
      </New>
    </Arg>
  </New>

  <New id="fooQueue" class="org.mortbay.jetty.plus.naming.Resource">
    <Arg>jms/FooQueue</Arg>
    <Arg>
      <New class="org.apache.activemq.command.ActiveMQQueue">
        <Arg>FOO.QUEUE</Arg>
      </New>
    </Arg>
  </New>

</Configure>
```

The configuration in listing 8.8 is specific to Jetty, and it tells Jetty to make the three resources available via a standard JNDI lookup from the sample web application. Note that listing 8.8 contains the ActiveMQ connection factory definition and an ActiveMQ queue definition. The reference to the `jms-webapp-wac` context identifier limits the availability of these resources to this web app context (the local context).

> **NOTE** The `$JETTY_HOME` variable is being used to generically reference the Jetty Hightide installation directory. This isn't something that you must set in your environment.

To test the local JNDI resource configuration in Jetty, use the following steps:

Step 1 Copy the jms-webapp-local/target/jms-webapp.war file to the $JETTY_HOME/ webapps directory.

Step 2 Start up Jetty Hightide using the following command:

```
$ cd $JETTY_HOME
$ java -jar ./start.jar
2010-04-08 21:06:51.994:INFO::Logging to StdErrLog::DEBUG=false via
org.eclipse.jetty.util.log.StdErrLog
...
INFO  - BrokerService                      - ActiveMQ 5.4.1 JMS Message
Broker (FooBroker) is starting
...
2010-04-08 21:07:01.995:INFO::Started SelectChannelConnector@0.0.0.0:8080
```

The output indicates that ActiveMQ is using the activemq.xml configuration file because the `brokerName` FooBroker is specified in that file. Again, as noted at the beginning of the chapter, this configuration is taking advantage of a unique feature in ActiveMQ. This feature allows an ActiveMQ broker to be started by creating a connection factory and passing it a broker URI. The connection factory attempts to connect to a broker at the URI and if one doesn't exist, it'll start one up.

Step 3 Visit http://localhost:8080/jms-webapp and use the web page shown in figure 8.4 to send a message.

Step 4 Confirm that the message is sent successfully by checking the terminal to see the output shown:

```
...
2010-04-08 21:07:01.995:INFO::Started SelectChannelConnector@0.0.0.0:8080
INFO  - SingleConnectionFactory      - Established shared JMS Connection:
ActiveMQConnection {id=ID:mongoose.local-61512-1270782421187-2:1,
clientId=null,started=false}
INFO  - JmsMessageDelegate           - Consumed message with payload:
This is a test message
```

Note the output from Jetty. The log message from the `JmsMessageDelegateListener` bean indicates that the message was consumed and the message payload is being logged.

This demonstrates that configuring a local JNDI context for the ActiveMQ resources is also supported by Jetty. Nothing in the Jetty application server requires any changes, because the configuration is housed with the sample web application. The alternative to the local JNDI context is a global JNDI context.

8.3.2 *Using global JNDI to integrate ActiveMQ with Jetty*

Jetty's global JNDI configuration requires a different configuration, but the configuration XML is nearly the same as the local JNDI configuration XML. The difference is that it must reside in a different location. For this demonstration, the global JNDI configuration has been placed in the etc/jetty.xml file as shown next.

Listing 8.9 The Jetty jetty.xml file

```
...
    <New id="connectionFactory"
      class="org.eclipse.jetty.plus.jndi.Resource">
      <Arg>
        <Ref id="Server"/>
      </Arg>
      <Arg>jms/ConnectionFactory</Arg>
      <Arg>
        <New class="org.apache.activemq.ActiveMQConnectionFactory">
          <Arg>vm://localhost?brokerConfig=xbean:etc/activemq.xml</Arg>
        </New>
      </Arg>
    </New>
```

```
<New id="fooQueue" class="org.eclipse.jetty.plus.jndi.Resource">
  <Arg>jms/FooQueue</Arg>
  <Arg>
    <New class="org.apache.activemq.command.ActiveMQQueue">
      <Arg>FOO.QUEUE</Arg>
    </New>
  </Arg>
</New>

<New id="fooTopic" class="org.eclipse.jetty.plus.jndi.Resource">
  <Arg>jms/FooTopic</Arg>
  <Arg>
    <New class="org.apache.activemq.command.ActiveMQTopic">
      <Arg>FOO.TOPIC</Arg>
    </New>
  </Arg>
</New>
...
```

Note that listing 8.9 is only slightly different than the XML for the local JNDI configuration in Jetty. The difference is the first <Arg> element that references Server—the entire Jetty server. This is an example of Jetty's scoping feature that tells Jetty to expose this resource to the Server object—the entire server (which is defined in the same file).

To validate the definition of the global JNDI resources in Jetty, use the following steps:

Step 1 Create the following new directory: $JETTY_HOME/lib/ext/activemq.

Step 2 Copy the following list of JARs into the directory that you created in step 1:

- activemq-all-5.4.1.jar
- aopalliance-1.0.jar
- commons-logging-1.1.1.jar
- geronimo-j2ee-management_1.0_spec-1.0.jar
- geronimo-jms_1.1_spec-1.1.1.jar
- log4j-1.2.14.jar
- org.osgi.core-4.1.0.jar
- spring-aop-2.5.6.jar
- spring-beans-2.5.6.jar
- spring-context-2.5.6.jar
- spring-context-support-2.5.6.jar
- spring-core-2.5.6.jar
- spring-jms-2.5.6.jar
- spring-tx-2.5.6.jar
- spring-web-2.5.6.jar
- spring-webmvc-2.5.6.jar
- xbean-spring-3.4.3.jar

Again, the quickest way to grab these JARs is from the jms-webapp-local project *after* it's built. After building the project with Maven, you'll be able to find the JARs in the jms-webapp-local/target/jms-webapp/WEB-INF/lib/ directory. Just copy them to the $JETTY_HOME/lib/ext/activemq directory.

Step 3 To build the jms-webapp-global project and create the WAR file, from the command line, run the following Maven command:

```
$ mvn clean install
...
[INFO] Scanning for projects...
```

```
[INFO] ------------------------------------------------------------
-----
[INFO] Building jms-webapp-global
[INFO]    task-segment: [clean, install]
[INFO] ------------------------------------------------------------
-----
...
[INFO] ------------------------------------------------------------
-----
[INFO] BUILD SUCCESSFUL
[INFO] ------------------------------------------------------------
-----
...
```

After running this command, a WAR file will exist in the target directory.

Step 4 Copy the jms-webapp-global/activemq.xml file to $JETTY_HOME/etc/ activemq.xml to make it available on the classpath.

Step 5 Copy the jms-webapp-global/target/jms-webapp.war to $JETTY_HOME/ webapps. This will deploy the example web application.

Step 6 Start up Jetty using the following command:

```
$ java -jar start.jar
2010-04-11 21:41:23.253:INFO::Logging to StdErrLog::DEBUG=false
via org.eclipse.jetty.util.log.StdErrLog
...
INFO  - BrokerService                - ActiveMQ 5.4.1 JMS Message
Broker (FooBroker) is starting
...
2010-04-11 21:41:33.116:INFO::Started SelectChannelConnector@0.0.0.0:8080
```

You can see from the output of the broker startup above that ActiveMQ is using the activemq.xml configuration file because the brokerName FooBroker is specified in that file.

Step 7 Visit http://localhost:8080/jms-webapp and use the page shown in figure 8.4 to send a message.

Step 8 Verify that the message is sent and consumed successfully by checking the terminal to see the following output:

```
...
2010-04-11 21:41:33.116:INFO::Started SelectChannelConnector@0.0.0.0:8080
INFO  - SingleConnectionFactory       - Established shared JMS Connection:
ActiveMQConnection {id=ID:mongoose.local-61512-1270782421187-2:1,
clientId=null,started=false}
INFO  - JmsMessageDelegate            - Consumed message with payload:
This is a test message
```

Again, note the output from where Jetty is running. The output from the Jms-MessageDelegateListener bean demonstrates that the message was consumed.

The global JNDI configuration for Jetty offers the same advantages provided by Tomcat. If multiple applications deployed to a single Jetty instance need access to the JNDI resources, this is a good option.

Tomcat and Jetty are two examples of web containers with which ActiveMQ integrates well. Beyond web containers are full-fledged Java EE application servers such as Apache Geronimo and JBoss.

8.4 *Integrating with Apache Geronimo*

The Apache Geronimo application server is a fully certified Java EE 5 runtime that uses many leading open source projects for various aspects of the application server. In fact, Geronimo is more of a toolkit for creating a customized application server distribution with only the components you need.

By default, there are three different distributions of Geronimo depending on your needs:

1 *Java EE Certified*—A fully certified Java EE 5 distribution utilizing the two major open source web containers:
  - Geronimo with Jetty 7
  - Geronimo with Tomcat 6
2 *Little-G*—A distribution that provides a web container and a subset of Geronimo modules:
  - Geronimo with Jetty 7
  - Geronimo with Tomcat 6
3 *Micro-G*—A distribution that allows you to build your own custom application server from the ground up. You decide what components to include via the Geronimo deployer.

Geronimo offers a wide variety of options, but we'll use Little-G 2.2 with Tomcat 6 for this chapter because it doesn't have ActiveMQ already installed (whereas the Java EE certified runtime does include ActiveMQ). So download Little-G 2.2 with Tomcat 6 from the Geronimo downloads page (http://mng.bz/DaoR) and expand it on your computer.

In this section, we'll deploy the ActiveMQ plug-in for Geronimo and register the ActiveMQ JMS resources with the Geronimo JNDI provider using the Geronimo web console. After these steps are complete, the sample application for Geronimo (the `jms-webapp-geronimo` project) can be deployed.

8.4.1 *Installing Geronimo and configuring the ActiveMQ plug-in in Geronimo*

After expanding the archive, move into the directory that's created and start up Geronimo as shown in the following listing.

Listing 8.10   Start up Geronimo

```
$ cd ./geronimo-tomcat6-minimal-2.2
$ ./bin/start-server
Launching Geronimo Server...
Booting Geronimo Kernel (in Java 1.6.0_15)...
...
```

```
Startup completed in 6.431s seconds
  Listening on Ports:
    1099 0.0.0.0 RMI Naming
    8009 0.0.0.0 Tomcat Connector AJP TomcatAJPConnector
    8080 0.0.0.0 Tomcat Connector HTTP BIO TomcatWebConnector
    8443 0.0.0.0 Tomcat Connector HTTPS BIO TomcatWebSSLConnector
    9999 0.0.0.0 JMX Remoting Connector
Geronimo Server started in 0:00:08.787

  Started Application Modules:
    WAR: org.apache.geronimo.configs/remote-deploy-tomcat/2.2/car

  Web Applications:
    /remote-deploy

Geronimo Application Server started
```

As Geronimo starts up, it displays output to show what components are being started. These are all components that are included with Little-G by default. Note that ActiveMQ isn't included in the output. Now it's time to use the Geronimo deployer to install ActiveMQ.

The Geronimo deployer is a command-line tool for querying and installing Geronimo plug-ins. Start the Geronimo deployer and use its search-plugins function to view a list of all the available plug-ins.

```
$ ./bin/deploy.sh --user system --password manager \
search-plugins http://geronimo.apache.org/plugins/geronimo-2.2

Using GERONIMO_HOME:   /opt/geronimo-tomcat6-minimal-2.2
Using GERONIMO_TMPDIR: var/temp
Using JRE_HOME:
<no category>
  1:      ActiveMQ web console on Jetty (2.2)
  2:      ActiveMQ web console on Tomcat (2.2)
  3:      Geronimo Plugins, Clustering :: Plugin Farm Datasource (2.2)
  4:      Geronimo Plugins, UDDI : Database (2.2)
Administration
  5:      Geronimo Plugins, Console :: Debug Views (Jetty) (2.2)
...
 12:      Geronimo Plugins, Console :: System Database (Jetty) (2.2)
 13:      Geronimo Plugins, Console :: System Database (Tomcat) (2.2)
 14: Geronimo Plugins, Console :: Tomcat (2.2)
 15:      Geronimo Plugins, OpenEJB :: Jetty (2.2)
JMS
 88: Geronimo Plugins, ActiveMQ v5 :: Broker (2.2)
 89: Geronimo Plugins, ActiveMQ v5 :: Console (Jetty) (2.2)
 90: Geronimo Plugins, ActiveMQ v5 :: Console (Tomcat) (2.2)
 91: Geronimo Plugins, ActiveMQ v5 :: Resource Adapter (2.2)
JavaEE
 92:      Geronimo Framework, Configs :: JavaEE Specs (2.2)
...

Install Services [enter a comma separated list of numbers or 'q' to quit]:
```

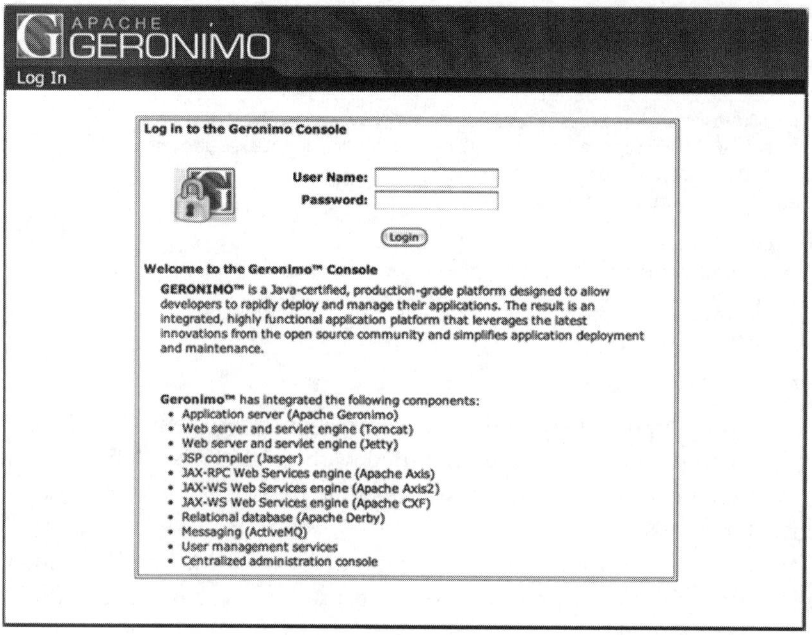

Figure 8.5   The Geronimo console simplifies the configuration and management of Geronimo.

NOTE   When the Geronimo deployer is started, it requires a username and a password. The default username is *system* and the default password is *manager*. Note that these are passed in as arguments to the deployer.

Although much of the output from the deployer has been elided to save space, you can see by the list of 142 different plug-ins that there's a large choice. But the only plug-ins needed for this chapter are in bold—plug-ins 14, 88, and 91. Plug-in 14 is the Geronimo console, a web-based console for managing Geronimo. The Geronimo console will make it easy to set up the JMS resources. Plug-in 88 is the ActiveMQ message broker. Plug-in 91 is the ActiveMQ resource adapter, which allows ActiveMQ to integrate with a Java EE server.

Note that the last line of output from the deployer is actually a prompt that allows you to enter a comma-separated list of plug-ins (by number) to install. At the prompt, type 14,88,91 and press Enter. Here's the output that you'll see when you do this:

```
...
Install Services [enter a comma separated list of numbers or
'q' to quit]: 14,88,91
Checking for status every 1000ms:
Downloading org.apache.geronimo.plugins/console-tomcat/2.2/car (40%)
Downloading org.apache.pluto/pluto-portal-driver/1.1.6/jar
Downloading org.apache.pluto/pluto-container/1.1.6/jar
Downloading org.apache.pluto/pluto-descriptor-impl/1.1.6/jar
Downloading commons-beanutils/commons-beanutils/1.7.0/jar
```

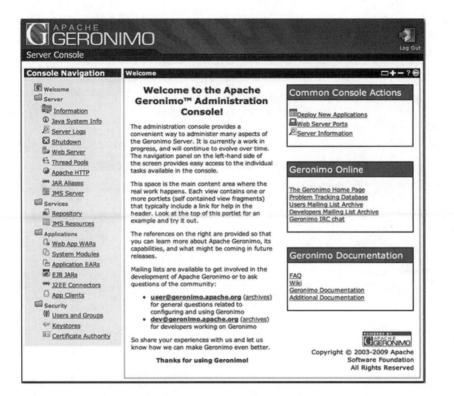

Figure 8.6   The Geronimo console provides the ability to manage ActiveMQ (the JMS Server) and the ActiveMQ resources (JMS Resources).

```
Downloading org.apache.portals/portlet-api_1.0_spec/1.0/jar
Downloading org.springframework/spring-core/2.5.6/jar
Downloading org.springframework/spring-context/2.5.6/jar
...

**** Installation Complete!
...
Downloaded 22983 kB in 52s (441 kB/s)
```

The output has been truncated, but as long as you see the Installation Complete! message, that means that the three ActiveMQ plug-ins have been installed successfully. The easiest way to check this is to open a browser and visit http://localhost:8080/ console to view the Geronimo console. You should see the page shown in figure 8.5.

To log in, use the same credentials that were used with the Geronimo deployer (the default username is *system* and the password is *manager*). Upon logging in to the Geronimo console, you'll see the page shown in figure 8.6.

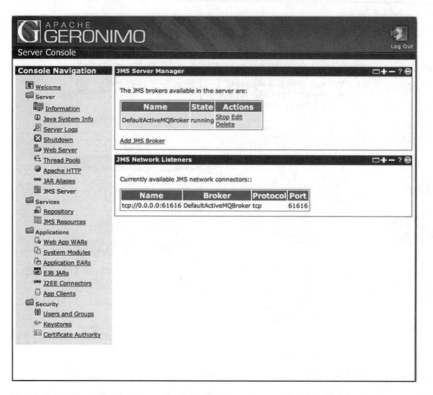

Figure 8.7   The Geronimo console simplifies the management of the ActiveMQ configuration.

Note the links on right side of figure 8.6. The figure named JMS Server allows you to manage the ActiveMQ configuration, as shown in 8.7.

Although the Geronimo console makes managing the ActiveMQ configuration easy, for this chapter it's easiest to utilize the default configuration for the broker. But the default configuration for the JMS resources in Geronimo is a different story.

8.4.2   *Configuring the ActiveMQ JMS resources in Geronimo*

The JMS resources for ActiveMQ (the JMS connection and the JMS destination) need to be customized to match the resources that are configured in the sample application. To do this, click on the link in the web console named JMS Resources and you'll see the page displayed in figure 8.8.

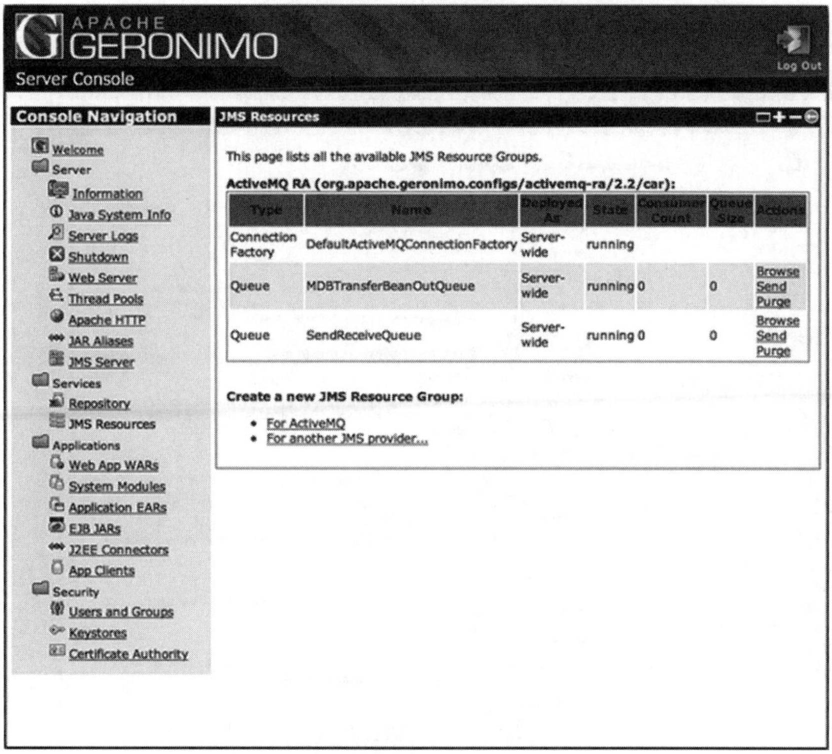

Figure 8.8 The Geronimo console also simplifies the management of JMS resources.

As you can see, a default JMS resource group is already configured. The default JMS resources in Geronimo aren't named in a manner that's compatible with the sample application, so you'll need to create a new resource group. To do this, click on the link named For ActiveMQ. You'll be presented with the page shown in figure 8.9. Enter a name for the resource group. For this example, the resource group is named Foo-Group. Then just scroll to the bottom of that page and click the Next button.

The next page allows you to create JMS connection factories and JMS destinations. This page is shown in figure 8.10.

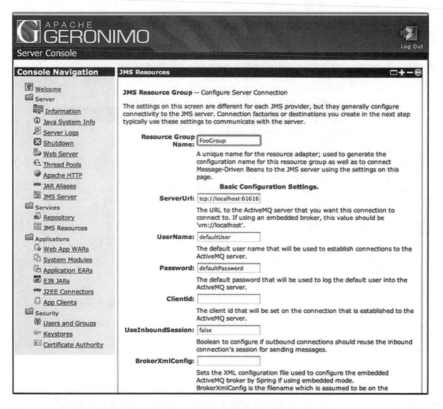

Figure 8.9   Accept the default values when configuring the ActiveMQ resource adapter's server connection.

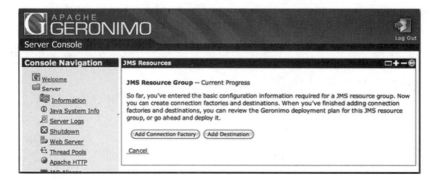

Figure 8.10   Use the Geronimo console to create a JMS connection factory and a JMS destination for ActiveMQ.

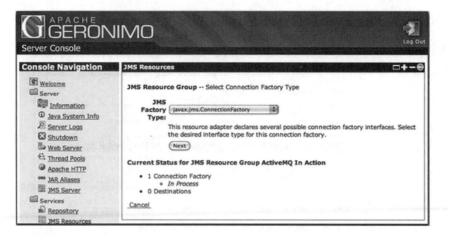

Figure 8.11 Easily create a JMS connection factory for ActiveMQ via the Geronimo console.

Click the Add Connection Factory button. In the next page, leave the default type of `javax.jms.ConnectionFactory` as shown in figure 8.11 and click the Next button.

The next page allows for some customizations of the JMS connection factory as shown in figure 8.12.

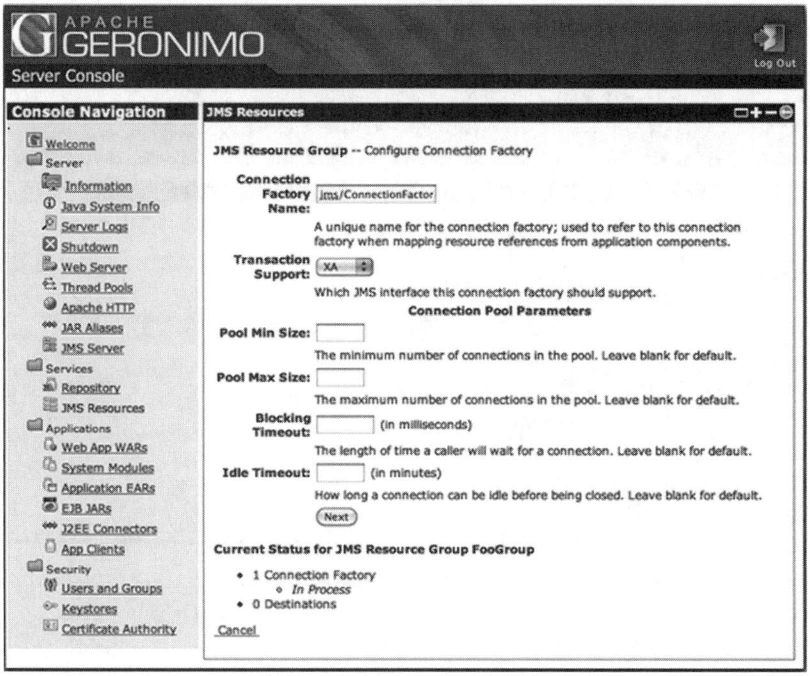

Figure 8.12 Use the Geronimo console to configure the connection factory.

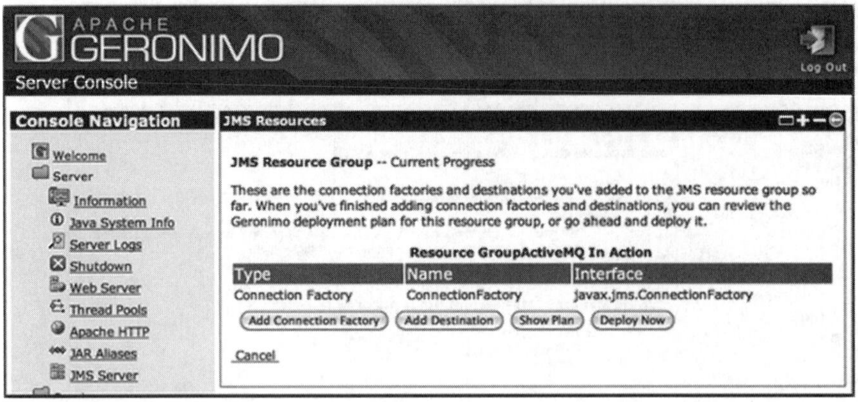

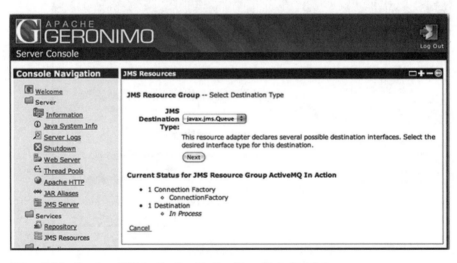

Figure 8.13   The connection factory has been created successfully.

Make sure to name the connection factory `ConnectionFactory` and set the transaction support to None. Then click the Next button. This will take you back to the page that allows you to create JMS resources. But now the new connection factory should be listed, as shown in figure 8.13.

Now click the Add Destination button to create a JMS destination. This will show a page that allows the choice of destination type, as shown in figure 8.14. Make sure that `javax.jms.Queue` is selected, and click the Next button to customize the queue.

Figure 8.14   Create a JMS destination that's of type javax.jms.Queue.

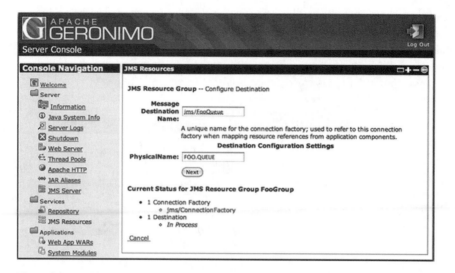

Figure 8.15 Customize the destination using the Geronimo console.

On the next page, make sure to enter FooQueue in the Message Destination Name field and FOO.QUEUE in the Physical Name field, as shown in figure 8.15.

The queue will be fetched from the JNDI context as FooQueue, but the actual name of the queue that will be used by the sample web application is FOO.QUEUE. Now click the Next button. This will take you back to the page that allows you to create JMS resources again. Only now the new connection factory and the new queue should be listed, as shown in figure 8.16.

Now the JMS resource group is ready to be deployed. To do this, click the Deploy Now button. Geronimo will deploy the ActiveMQ resource adapter and take you back to the initial JMS resource group page. The difference now is that the FooGroup resource group is listed, as shown in figure 8.17.

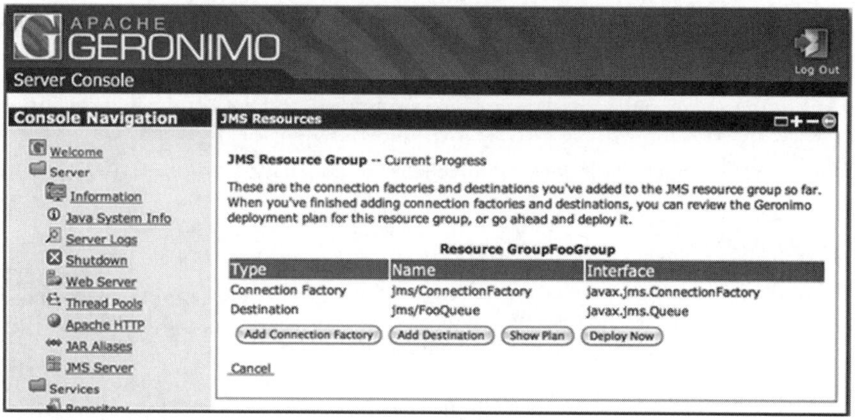

Figure 8.16 Now the connection factory and the destination have been created and are ready to be deployed.

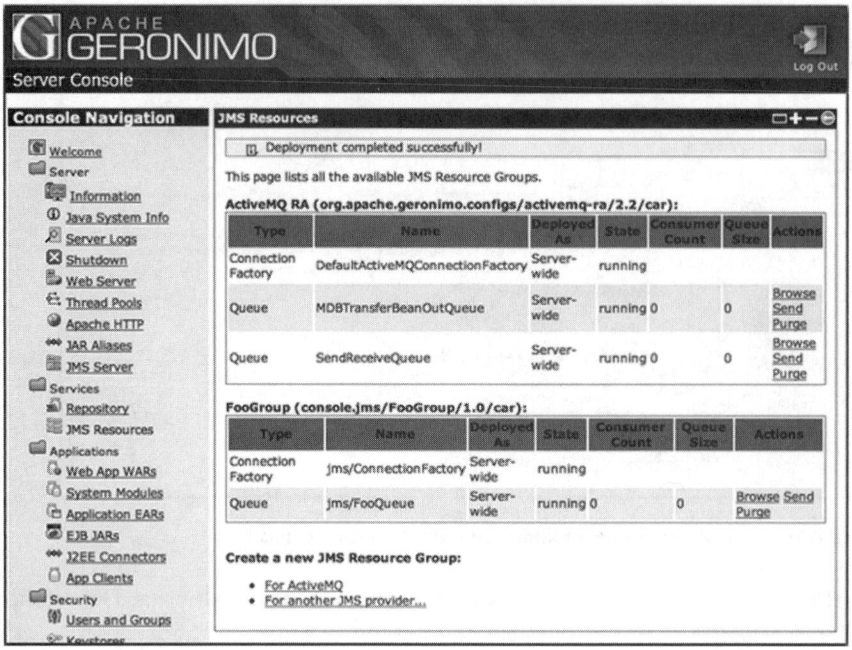

Figure 8.17   Now the FooGroup JMS resource group has been created and deployed.

Now that the JMS resources have been created, you can move on to deploying the sample web application to test them out.

8.4.3   *Preparing the sample application for deployment in Geronimo*

For this deployment example, a copy of the `jms-webapp-local` project will be used that's named `jms-webapp-geronimo`. Java EE application servers provide different environments in which to deploy applications, so some tweaks to support this environment are necessary:

Step 1   Create a file named src/main/webapp/WEB-INF/geronimo-web.xml as shown next.

Listing 8.11   The geronimo-web.xml file

```
<web-app xmlns="http://geronimo.apache.org/xml/ns/j2ee/web-2.0.1">

    <environment>
      <moduleId>
        <groupId>org.apache.activemq.book</groupId>
        <artifactId>jms-webapp</artifactId>
        <version>1.0-SNAPSHOT</version>
        <type>war</type>
      </moduleId>
      <dependencies>
      <!-- Depend upon the custom JMS resources group -->
        <dependency>
          <groupId>console.jms</groupId>
```

```
         <artifactId>FooGroup</artifactId>
         <version>1.0</version>
         <type>car</type>
       </dependency>
     </dependencies>
     <!-- Filter out the following items from the parent classloader -->
     <hidden-classes>
       <filter>org.springframework.</filter>
       <filter>META-INF/spring</filter>
     </hidden-classes>
   </environment>

   <context-root>/jms-webapp</context-root>

</web-app>
```

The geronimo-web.xml file is specific to Geronimo. It provides some specific instructions to Geronimo. The `<moduleId>` element is used to identify the WAR file that's being deployed to Geronimo. The `<dependency>` element tells Geronimo that it requires the JMS resources group that was created earlier in this section. Without the connection factory and the destination that were created as part of that resources group, the sample application won't function properly. The `<hidden-classes>` element tells Geronimo not to expose any classes in the packages listed, because they may already exist in the classloader of the application server that's exposed to the web application. This is something that should happen automatically and will probably be corrected in the near term based on a JIRA issue that was created to point this out. Once this is fixed, the `<hidden-classes>` element will no longer be needed to hide the Spring classes that are part of the activemq-broker Geronimo plug-in.

Step 2 Instead of using the `<resource-ref>` element to define the JMS queue in the web.xml file, Geronimo requires that the `<message-destination-ref>` element be used. The `<message-destination-ref>` element is defined in the DTD for the web.xml. The following listing shows the change necessary to the jms-webapp-geronimo/src/main/webapp/WEB-INF/web.xml file.

Listing 8.12   Change to the web.xml file for Geronimo

```
...
  <message-destination-ref>
    <message-destination-ref-name>jms/FooQueue</message-destination-ref-name>
    <message-destination-type>javax.jms.Queue</message-destination-type>
    <message-destination-usage>Produces</message-destination-usage>
    <message-destination-link>jms/FooQueue</message-destination-link>
  </message-destination-ref>

  <!--
  <resource-ref>
    <res-ref-name>jms/FooQueue</res-ref-name>
    <res-type>javax.jms.Queue</res-type>
    <res-auth>Container</res-auth>
    <res-sharing-scope>Shareable</res-sharing-scope>
  </resource-ref>
  -->
...
```

Step 3 Because ActiveMQ is made available by the activemq-broker Geronimo plug-in, `jms-webapp-geronimo` doesn't package the ActiveMQ JAR or its dependencies in the WAR file. To prevent the ActiveMQ dependencies from being included in the WAR file by the Maven build process, in the pom.xml file, add the `<scope>provided</scope>` element to the ActiveMQ dependency, the XBean dependency, and the Log4J dependency, as shown in bold in the following listing.

Listing 8.13   Maven dependency changes for Geronimo

```
...
    <dependency>
     <groupId>org.apache.activemq</groupId>
     <artifactId>activemq-core</artifactId>
     <version>${activemq-version}</version>
     <scope>provided</scope>
     <exclusions>
       <exclusion>
         <groupId>org.apache.activemq</groupId>
         <artifactId>activeio-core</artifactId>
       </exclusion>
       <exclusion>
         <groupId>org.apache.camel</groupId>
         <artifactId>camel-core</artifactId>
       </exclusion>
       <exclusion>
         <artifactId>activemq-protobuf</artifactId>
         <groupId>org.apache.activemq.protobuf</groupId>
       </exclusion>
       <exclusion>
         <artifactId>commons-net</artifactId>
         <groupId>commons-net</groupId>
       </exclusion>
     </exclusions>
    </dependency>
    <dependency>
       <groupId>org.apache.xbean</groupId>
       <artifactId>xbean-spring</artifactId>
       <version>3.4.3</version>
       <scope>provided</scope>
    </dependency>
    <dependency>
       <groupId>log4j</groupId>
       <artifactId>log4j</artifactId>
       <version>1.2.14</version>
       <scope>provided</scope>
    </dependency>
...
```

Note the `<scope>provided</scope>` element in bold in listing 8.13. Excluding these JARs from inclusion in the WAR file prevents any classloader clashes that may result if those dependencies were included.

Step 4 The last thing you need to change in the sample web application is the type on the connection factory in the Spring configuration file. Edit the jms-webapp-geronimo/src/main/webapp/WEB-INF/spring/jms-context.xml   file to change the connection factory type from `org.apache.activemq.Active-MQConnectionFactory` to `org.apache.activemq.ra.ActiveMQConnection-Factory`. This is needed because the connection factory that's being used here is from the ActiveMQ resource adapter, not the standard connection factory.

All of the application-specific changes already exist in the `jms-webapp-geronimo` project. Make sure to download the example source code for the book to see this sample project.

8.4.4   *Deploying and verifying the sample application in Geronimo*

To validate the definition of the JNDI resources in Geronimo using the `jms-webapp-geronimo` project, follow these steps:

Step 1 To build the project and create the WAR file, from the command line, run the following Maven command:

```
$ cd jms-webapp-geronimo
$ mvn clean install
...
[INFO] Scanning for projects...
[INFO] -------------------------------------------------------------
-----
[INFO] Building jms-webapp-global
[INFO]    task-segment: [clean, install]
[INFO] -------------------------------------------------------------
-----
...
[INFO] -------------------------------------------------------------
-----
[INFO] BUILD SUCCESSFUL
[INFO] -------------------------------------------------------------
-----
...
```

Step 2 In one terminal, start up Geronimo using the following command:

```
$ cd $GERONIMO_HOME
$ ./bin/start-server
Launching Geronimo Server...
Booting Geronimo Kernel (in Java 1.6.0_15)...
...
Module 33/36 org.apache.geronimo.configs/activemq-broker/2.2/car
started in  1.248s
Module 34/36 org.apache.geronimo.configs/activemq-ra/2.2/car
started in   .350s
Module 35/36 org.apache.geronimo.plugins/activemq-console-tomcat/2.2/car
started in   .264s
```

```
Module 36/36 console.jms/FooGroup/1.0/car
started in   .111s
Startup completed in 17.753s seconds
  Listening on Ports:
    1099 0.0.0.0 RMI Naming
    1527 0.0.0.0 Derby Connector
    8009 0.0.0.0 Tomcat Connector AJP TomcatAJPConnector
    8080 0.0.0.0 Tomcat Connector HTTP BIO TomcatWebConnector
    8443 0.0.0.0 Tomcat Connector HTTPS BIO TomcatWebSSLConnector
    9999 0.0.0.0 JMX Remoting Connector
   61616 0.0.0.0 ActiveMQ Transport Connector

  Started Application Modules:
    EAR: org.apache.geronimo.plugins/console-tomcat/2.2/car
    RAR: console.jms/FooGroup/1.0/car
    RAR: org.apache.geronimo.configs/activemq-ra/2.2/car
    RAR: org.apache.geronimo.configs/system-database/2.2/car
    WAR: org.apache.geronimo.configs/remote-deploy-tomcat/2.2/car

  Web Applications:
   /console
   /console-base
   /remote-deploy

Geronimo Application Server started
Geronimo Server started in 0:00:21.997
```

Although some output has been eliminated to save space, the FooGroup that holds the JMS resources is deployed, and the necessary ActiveMQ plug-ins for Geronimo are deployed.

Step 3 In a second terminal, deploy the jms-webapp-geronimo/target/jms-webapp. war using the command-line deployer as shown:

```
$ $GERONIMO_HOME/bin/deploy.sh --user system --password manager deploy \
/path/to/jms-webapp-global/target/jms-webapp.war
Using GERONIMO_HOME:   /opt/geronimo-tomcat6-minimal-2.2
Using GERONIMO_TMPDIR: var/temp
Using JRE_HOME:
    Deployed org.apache.activemq.book/jms-webapp/1.0-SNAPSHOT/war @
    /jms-webapp
```

> **NOTE** The $GERONIMO_HOME variable is being used to generically reference the Geronimo installation directory. This isn't something that you must set in your environment.

Note the output from Geronimo letting you know that the WAR file has been successfully deployed. Go back to the terminal where Geronimo was started, and you should see the following output beyond the server startup:

```
...
INFO  - ContextLoader                  - Root WebApplicationContext:
initialization started
INFO  - XmlWebApplicationContext       - Refreshing
org.springframework.web.context.support.
XmlWebApplicationContext@6156ee8e: display name [Root
```

```
WebApplicationContext]; startup date [Sun Apr 25 11:04:23
MDT 2010]; root of context hierarchy
INFO  - XmlBeanDefinitionReader      - Loading XML bean definitions
from ServletContext resource [/WEB-INF/spring/jms-context.xml]
INFO  - XmlWebApplicationContext     - Bean factory for application
context [org.springframework.web.context.support.
XmlWebApplicationContext@6156ee8e]:
org.springframework.beans.factory.support.
DefaultListableBeanFactory@21606a56
INFO  - DefaultListableBeanFactory   - Pre-instantiating singletons
in org.springframework.beans.factory.support.
DefaultListableBeanFactory@21606a56: defining beans
[connectionFactory,fooQueue,singleConnectionFactory,jmsTemplate,
messageSenderService,jmsMessageDelegate,myMessageListener,
org.springframework.jms.listener.DefaultMessageListenerContainer#0];
root of factory hierarchy
INFO  - ContextLoader                - Root WebApplicationContext:
initialization completed in 379 ms
INFO  - DispatcherServlet            - FrameworkServlet 'jms-webapp':
initialization started
INFO  - XmlWebApplicationContext     - Refreshing
org.springframework.web.context.support.
XmlWebApplicationContext@6c164690: display name [WebApplicationContext
for namespace 'jms-webapp-servlet']; startup date [Sun Apr 25 11:04:23
MDT 2010]; parent: org.springframework.web.context.support.
XmlWebApplicationContext@6156ee8e
INFO  - XmlBeanDefinitionReader      - Loading XML bean definitions
from ServletContext resource [/WEB-INF/jms-webapp-servlet.xml]
INFO  - XmlWebApplicationContext     - Bean factory for application
context [org.springframework.web.context.support.
XmlWebApplicationContext@6c164690]:
org.springframework.beans.factory.support.
DefaultListableBeanFactory@39fe9830
INFO  - DefaultListableBeanFactory   - Pre-instantiating singletons
in org.springframework.beans.factory.support.
DefaultListableBeanFactory@39fe9830: defining beans
[jmsMessageSenderController,org.springframework.context.annotation.
internalCommonAnnotationProcessor,org.springframework.context.
annotation.internalAutowiredAnnotationProcessor,org.springframework.
context.annotation.internalRequiredAnnotationProcessor,
org.springframework.web.servlet.mvc.annotation.
AnnotationMethodHandlerAdapter#0,org.springframework.web.servlet.
view.InternalResourceViewResolver#0]; parent: org.springframework.
beans.factory.support.DefaultListableBeanFactory@21606a56
INFO  - DispatcherServlet            - FrameworkServlet
'jms-webapp': initialization completed in 203 ms
```

The output shown is the initialization of the `jms-webapp-geronimo` project web application, including the startup of the Spring application context.

You can also check the deployment via the Geronimo console as shown in figure 8.18. You can see that the sample web application has been deployed and is the first item listed in the Component Name column.

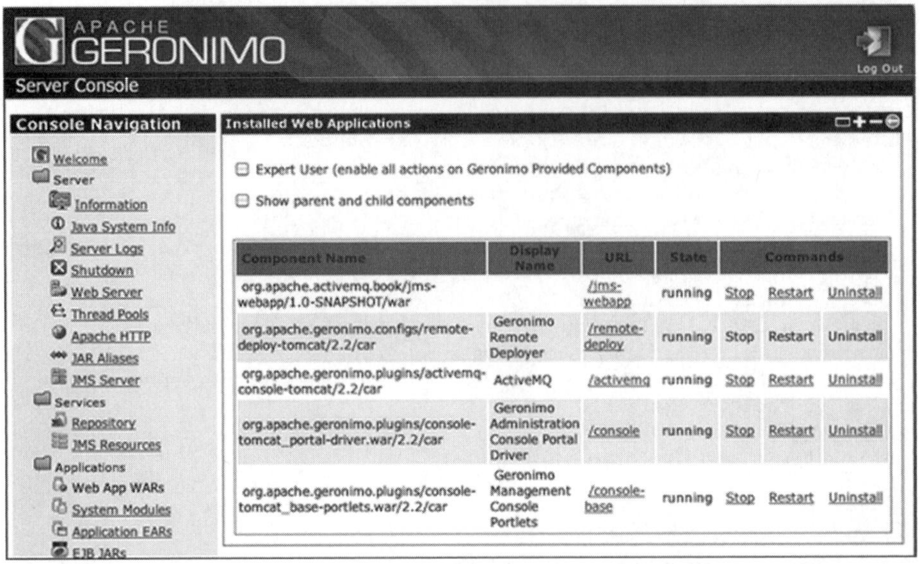

Figure 8.18   Note that the information provided in the `<moduleId>` element is used to identify the web application when it's deployed to Geronimo.

Step 4   Visit http://localhost:8080/jms-webapp and use the page shown in figure 8.4 to send a message.

Step 5   Verify that you can send a message from the sample web application and that it's consumed successfully by checking the terminal to see the following output:

```
...
INFO  - SingleConnectionFactory      - Established shared JMS Connection:
org.apache.activemq.ra.ManagedConnectionProxy@7f1a594c
INFO  - JmsMessageDelegate            - Consumed message with payload:
This is a test message
```

As you can see, deploying ActiveMQ to Geronimo is rather straightforward. This is due to the ease of using the Geronimo console, which provides a nice UI for creating the JMS resources instead of hacking an XML file with which you may not be familiar.

But Geronimo isn't the only open source application server available today. JBoss has been around for more than 10 years and is also widely used.

8.5   *Integrating with JBoss*

The JBoss application server is also a Java EE–certified application server. In fact, JBoss was the first widely used open source Java application server. JBoss (the company) has come a long way and offers many more projects than just the application server today, including projects around the web interface, different programming models, myriad services, application servers, management, the cloud, and many different tools.

You need to download two items for this section:

- JBoss 5.1.0 GA can be downloaded from the JBoss application server downloads page (http://mng.bz/172k). Download and expand the archive.
- The ActiveMQ JCA resource adapter can be downloaded using the following URL: http://mng.bz/JTHl.

In this section, we'll configure the ActiveMQ JCA resource adapter to be started by JBoss, and customize the sample web application so that it can be deployed to JBoss.

8.5.1 Installing JBoss and configuring the ActiveMQ resource adapter in JBoss

Installing JBoss is simple: download and expand the JBoss zip file. This will create a directory for JBoss that contains everything needed to run it. Once this is complete, you need to configure the ActiveMQ resource adapter.

The ActiveMQ resource adapter is a JCA resource adapter implementation that's needed in order to integrate ActiveMQ with JBoss. After downloading the ActiveMQ resource adapter using the URL shown earlier, move into the JBoss deploy directory to expand it as shown:

```
$ cd $JBOSS_HOME/server/default/deploy
$ mkdir ./activemq-ra.rar
$ cd ./activemq-ra.rar
$ jar xf /path/to/activemq-ra-5.4.1.jar
$ $ ls -1
META-INF
activeio-core-3.1.2.jar
activemq-core-5.4.1.jar
activemq-protobuf-1.0.jar
activemq-ra-5.4.1.jar
aopalliance-1.0.jar
broker-config.xml
commons-logging-1.1.jar
commons-logging-api-1.1.jar
commons-net-2.0.jar
derby-10.1.3.1.jar
geronimo-j2ee-management_1.0_spec-1.0.jar
geronimo-j2ee-management_1.1_spec-1.0.1.jar
kahadb-5.4.1.jar
log4j-1.2.14.jar
log4j.properties
org.osgi.core-4.1.0.jar
spring-beans-2.5.6.jar
spring-context-2.5.6.jar
spring-core-2.5.6.jar
spring-osgi-core-1.2.1.jar
spring-osgi-io-1.2.1.jar
xbean-spring-3.6.jar
```

Expanding the ActiveMQ resource adapter into this directory will allow it to be more easily customized. Once the resource adapter customization is completed, you can JAR up the directory so that it's ready for production deployment.

NOTE The $JBOSS_HOME variable is being used to generically reference the JBoss installation directory. This isn't something that you must set in your environment.

To begin customizing the ActiveMQ resource adapter to start up an embedded ActiveMQ instance, you need to make some changes to META-INF/ra.xml as shown in the following steps:

Step 1 Change the ServerUrl from using the TCP transport URI (tcp://localhost: 61616) to use the VM transport URI (vm://localhost). Note that the VM transport is right beneath the TCP transport, but it's commented out. Swap the comment between the two transports as shown next.

Listing 8.14 Change the ServerUrl in the ra.xml file

```
<config-property>
    <description>
        The URL to the ActiveMQ server that you want this connection to
        connect to. If using an embedded broker, this value should be
        'vm://localhost'.
    </description>
    <config-property-name>ServerUrl</config-property-name>
    <config-property-type>java.lang.String</config-property-type>
    <!--<config-property-value>tcp://localhost:61616</config-property-value>-->
<config-property-value>vm://localhost</config-property-value>
</config-property>
```

Since ActiveMQ will be embedded inside the same JVM process as JBoss, it's more efficient to use the VM transport than the TCP transport.

Step 2 Further down in the ra.xml file, you'll find the BrokerXmlConfig. Because the ActiveMQ resource adapter is embedding the broker within JBoss, it's logical to provide a configuration file for the broker. For this integration example, the easiest way to do this to use the xbean factory to load the broker-config. xml file from the classpath. Add the xbean:broker-config.xml line to the empty <config-property-value> element as shown.

Listing 8.15 Change the BrokerXmlConfig in the ra.xml file

```
<config-property>
    <description>
        Sets the XML configuration file used to configure the embedded
        ActiveMQ broker via Spring if using embedded mode.

        BrokerXmlConfig is the filename which is assumed to be on the
        classpath unless a URL is specified. So a value of foo/bar.xml
        would be assumed to be on the classpath whereas file:dir/file.xml
```

```
                  would use the file system. Any valid URL string is supported.

                </description>
                <config-property-name>BrokerXmlConfig</config-property-name>
                <config-property-type>java.lang.String</config-property-type>
                <config-property-value>xbean:broker-config.xml</config-property-value>
                <!--
                  To use the broker-config.xml from the root for the RAR
                    <config-property-value>
                      xbean:broker-config.xml
                    </config-property-value>
                  To use an external file or url location
                    <config-property-value>
                      xbean:file:///amq/config/jee/broker-config.xml
                    </config-property-value>
                -->
</config-property>
```

Now that the ActiveMQ resource adapter has been told to load the broker-config.xml file, this file needs to be customized.

Step 3   The broker-config.xml is just another name for the ActiveMQ XML configuration file. A basic one is already provided in the activemq-ra directory. You can customize this to your liking, but the one used for this section is shown next.

Listing 8.16   The broker-config.xml

```
<beans xmlns="http://activemq.apache.org/schema/core">

  <!-- shutdown hook is disabled as RAR classloader may be gone at
  shutdown -->
  <broker brokerName="FooBroker" useJmx="true" useShutdownHook="false">

      <managementContext>
        <!-- use appserver provided context instead of creating one,
             for jboss use: -Djboss.platform.mbeanserver -->
        <managementContext createConnector="false"/>
      </managementContext>

      <persistenceAdapter>
        <kahaDB directory="/var/activemq/activemq-data/kahadb"/>
      </persistenceAdapter>

      <transportConnectors>
        <transportConnector uri="tcp://0.0.0.0:61616"/>
      </transportConnectors>

  </broker>
</beans>
```

Notice the change to the broker-config.xml file to add the `brokerName` attribute to the `<broker>` element to uniquely identify the broker.

Although many other options may be configured in the ActiveMQ resource adapter for further customization, these changes will suffice for the sample web application to be deployed.

8.5.2   *Configuring the ActiveMQ JMS resources in JBoss*

A JBoss-specific resource adapter deployment descriptor needs to be configured to register the ActiveMQ resources in JNDI. The loading of the ActiveMQ resource adapter and registration of the JMS resources in JNDI take place in a file that has been named activemq-ds.xml. This file is shown in the following listing.

Listing 8.17   The activemq-ds.xml file

```
<?xml version="1.0" encoding="UTF-8"?>

<!DOCTYPE connection-factories
    PUBLIC "-//JBoss//DTD JBOSS JCA Config 1.5//EN"
    "http://www.jboss.org/j2ee/dtd/jboss-ds_1_5.dtd">

<connection-factories>

    <tx-connection-factory>
        <jndi-name>jms/ConnectionFactory</jndi-name>
        <xa-transaction/>
        <track-connection-by-tx/>
        <rar-name>activemq-ra.rar</rar-name>
        <connection-definition>
          javax.jms.ConnectionFactory
        </connection-definition>
        <ServerUrl>vm://localhost</ServerUrl>
        <min-pool-size>1</min-pool-size>
        <max-pool-size>10</max-pool-size>
        <blocking-timeout-millis>30000</blocking-timeout-millis>
        <idle-timeout-minutes>3</idle-timeout-minutes>
    </tx-connection-factory>

    <mbean code="org.jboss.resource.deployment.AdminObject"
      name="activemq.queue:name=fooQueue">
        <attribute name="JNDIName">jms/FooQueue</attribute>
        <depends optional-attribute-name="RARName">
          jboss.jca:service=RARDeployment,name='activemq-ra.rar'
        </depends>
        <attribute name="Type">javax.jms.Queue</attribute>
        <attribute name="Properties">PhysicalName=FOO.QUEUE</attribute>
    </mbean>

</connection-factories>
```

JBoss automatically loads any file whose name is *-ds.xml from the deploy directory at startup. In the case of the activemq-ds.xml file, the JMS resources (the JMS connection factory and the JMS destination) are configured and each one is linked to activemq.ra. This file needs to live in the $JBOSS_HOME/server/default/deploy directory so that it will be loaded when JBoss starts up.

8.5.3   *Preparing the sample application for deployment in JBoss*

Now it's time to make some changes to the sample web application so that it can be deployed to JBoss. For this, we'll use a copy of the `jms-webapp-local` project named `jms-webapp-jboss`.

Step 1 Begin by adding a new jms-webapp-jboss/src/main/webapp/WEB-INF/jboss-web.xml file to the sample application as shown next.

Listing 8.18   The jboss-web.xml file

```xml
<?xml version="1.0" encoding="UTF-8"?>

<!DOCTYPE jboss-web PUBLIC "-//JBoss//DTD Web Application 5.0//EN"
        "http://www.jboss.org/j2ee/dtd/jboss-web_5_0.dtd">

<jboss-web>
  <context-root>/jms-webapp</context-root>

  <resource-ref>
    <res-ref-name>jms/ConnectionFactory</res-ref-name>
    <jndi-name>java:jms/ConnectionFactory</jndi-name>
  </resource-ref>

  <resource-ref>
    <res-ref-name>jms/FooQueue</res-ref-name>
    <jndi-name>jms/FooQueue</jndi-name>
  </resource-ref>
</jboss-web>
```

This is a file that is specific to JBoss and is needed to map the JMS resources to the proper JNDI context. Once this file is in place, one additional change needs to be made to the sample web application.

Step 2 Evidently there's a clash between the JBoss Log4J configuration and a Log4J configuration in any application that's deployed to JBoss. You'll need to create a Log4J `RepositorySelector` implementation. This is easy enough because a sample is provided in the JBoss wiki. Take a look at Log4jRepositorySelector (http://mng.bz/Fd16) to get a copy of the class. Create the org.jboss.repositoryselectorexample package and create the sample class in there by literally cutting/pasting the example. Without this custom Log4J `RepositorySelector`, the jms-webapp will begin to start up and then throw the following error:

```
09:08:48,345 INFO  [TomcatDeployment] deploy, ctxPath=/jms-webapp
09:08:48,740 INFO  [[/jms-webapp]] Set web app root system property:
'webapp.root' = [/opt/jboss-5.1.0.GA/server/default/tmp/
5c4o039-9vh4op-g8hfa3el-1-g8hfb8we-9r/jms-webapp.war/]
09:08:48,745 INFO  [[/jms-webapp]] Initializing log4j from
[/opt/jboss-5.1.0.GA/server/default/tmp/
5c4o039-9vh4op-g8hfa3el-1-g8hfb8we-9r/jms-webapp.war/WEB-INF/classes/
log4j.xml]
ERROR: invalid console appender config detected,
console stream is looping
```

By adding the custom Log4J `RepositorySelector` to the application, you'll avoid this error.

Step 3 Now you need to make sure to change the sample web application's connection factory type. Edit the jms-webapp-jboss/src/main/webapp/WEB-INF/spring/jms-context.xml file to change the connection factory type from org.apache.

activemq.ActiveMQConnectionFactory to org.apache.activemq.ra.Active-MQConnectionFactory. Again, this is needed because the connection factory that's being used here is from the ActiveMQ resource adapter, not the standard connection factory.

Step 4 In order to work with the JBoss <tx-connection-factory> used in the activemq-ds.xml file, you'll need to enable support for transactions in the Spring configuration file for the sample web application. To do this, edit the jms-webapp-jboss/src/main/webapp/WEB-INF/spring/jms-context.xml file to add the following items in bold:

```
...
  <tx:jta-transaction-manager />

  <jms:listener-container
    container-type="default"
    connection-factory="singleConnectionFactory"
    acknowledge="auto"
    transaction-manager="transactionManager">
    <jms:listener destination="FOO.QUEUE" ref="myMessageListener" />
  </jms:listener-container>
...
```

Note that the JTA transaction manager has been added and a reference to it has been added to the listener-container. This allows the sample application to play nicely with the JBoss resource adapter configuration that uses transactions.

Step 5 The sample web application utilizes the Spring Framework to load a Spring application context. Evidently there's an incompatibility between the Spring Framework and the JBoss Virtual File System (VFS). The Spring Framework can load an application context from a file system without issue, but loading it from the JBoss Virtual File System presents a problem. To work around this issue, JBoss created a project named Snowdrop (http://mng.bz/pkx6). To use Snowdrop to work around this problem, follow the instructions in section 2.1, "The VFS-supporting application contexts," at http://mng.bz/wyob. The necessary changes that are already available in the jms-webapp-jboss/src/main/webapp/WEB-INF/web.xml file are shown here in bold:

```
...
<context-param>
 <param-name>contextClass</param-name>
 <param-value>
  org.jboss.spring.vfs.context.VFSXmlWebApplicationContext
 </param-value>
 </context-param>

<listener>
  <listener-class>
    org.springframework.web.context.ContextLoaderListener
  </listener-class>
</listener>

<servlet>
```

```
      <servlet-name>jms-webapp</servlet-name>
      <servlet-class>
        org.springframework.web.servlet.DispatcherServlet
      </servlet-class>
      <init-param>
      <param-name>contextClass</param-name>
      <param-value>
       org.jboss.spring.vfs.context.VFSXmlWebApplicationContext
      </param-value>
      </init-param>
       <load-on-startup>1</load-on-startup>
   </servlet>
   ...
```

The Snowdrop JAR also needs to be added to the pom.xml file. This change already exists in the jms-webapp-jboss/pom.xml file, as shown here:

```
   ...
      <dependency>
        <groupId>org.jboss.snowdrop</groupId>
        <artifactId>snowdrop-vfs</artifactId>
        <version>1.0.0-GA</version>
      </dependency>
   ...
```

Please note that all of the changes described in this section already exist in the `jms-webapp-jboss` sample web application so that it can be successfully deployed to JBoss. Download the example source code for the book to see this example.

8.5.4 *Deploying and verifying the sample application in JBoss*

To validate the deployment of the sample application in JBoss using the `jms-webapp-jboss` project, follow these steps:

Step 1 Build the project and create the WAR file, using the following Maven command from the command line:

```
$ mvn clean install
...
[INFO] Scanning for projects...
[INFO] -------------------------------------------------------------
-----
[INFO] Building jms-webapp-global
[INFO]    task-segment: [clean, install]
[INFO] -------------------------------------------------------------
-----
...
[INFO] -------------------------------------------------------------
-----
[INFO] BUILD SUCCESSFUL
[INFO] -------------------------------------------------------------
-----
...
```

After running this command, a WAR file will exist in the target directory.

Step 2 Copy the jms-webapp-jboss/target/jms-webapp.jar file to the JBoss deploy
directory:

```
$ cp jms-webapp-jboss/target/jms-webapp.jar \
$JBOSS_HOME/server/default/deploy/
```

Step 3 Start up JBoss using the following command:

```
$ $ ./bin/run.sh
==================================================================

  JBoss Bootstrap Environment

  JBOSS_HOME: /opt/jboss-5.1.0.GA

  JAVA: java

  JAVA_OPTS: -Dprogram.name=run.sh -Xms128m -Xmx512m
-XX:MaxPermSize=256m -Dorg.jboss.resolver.warning=true
-Dsun.rmi.dgc.client.gcInterval=3600000
-Dsun.rmi.dgc.server.gcInterval=3600000

  CLASSPATH: /opt/jboss-5.1.0.GA/bin/run.jar

==================================================================

12:11:02,699 INFO  [ServerImpl] Starting JBoss (Microcontainer)...
...
[5.1.0.GA (build: SVNTag=JBoss_5_1_0_GA date=200905221634)]
Started in 2m:6s:566ms
```

Some of the output here has been elided to save space, but the important part is
toward the end where the sample web application is started up.

Step 4 Visit http://localhost:8080/jms-webapp and use the page shown in figure 8.4
to send a message.

Step 5 Now you just need to verify that a message can be sent from the sample web
application and that it's consumed by checking the terminal to see the following output:

```
12:13:22,372 INFO  [JmsMessageDelegate] Consumed message with payload:
This is a test message
```

As long as you see your test message in the terminal output, you know it worked as it
should.

Integrating ActiveMQ with JBoss is also easy to do when you know the steps to take. The
real difference is that you're required to manually edit XML configuration files instead
of working through the configuration via a nice web UI. Also, deploying the sample
web application to JBoss requires some additional customization to the application.
This is common when working with a Java EE application server, since each one
requires its own custom configuration file and possibly more deployment descriptors.

One last topic that's typically of concern when using ActiveMQ with Java EE containers is JNDI. The next section covers this topic in its entirety.

8.6 *ActiveMQ and JNDI*

So far this chapter has demonstrated how to configure the ActiveMQ administrative objects (the `ConnectionFactory` and `Destination` objects) for each container that was covered. This entailed a style of configuration for the `ConnectionFactory` and `Destination` objects that was *specific to each container* so that they were made accessible via JNDI to the sample web application. The sample web application then used Spring to look up those objects via JNDI in order to interact with ActiveMQ. The following listing shows an example of the Spring JNDI lookup.

Listing 8.19   Spring JNDI lookup from sample web app

```
...
  <jee:jndi-lookup id="connectionFactory"
    jndi-name="java:comp/env/jms/ConnectionFactory"
    cache="true"
    resource-ref="true"
    lookup-on-startup="true"
    expected-type="org.apache.activemq.ActiveMQConnectionFactory"
    proxy-interface="javax.jms.ConnectionFactory">
  </jee:jndi-lookup>

  <jee:jndi-lookup id="fooQueue"
    jndi-name="java:comp/env/jms/FooQueue"
    cache="true"
    resource-ref="true"
    lookup-on-startup="true"
    expected-type="org.apache.activemq.command.ActiveMQQueue"
    proxy-interface="javax.jms.Queue">
  </jee:jndi-lookup>
...
```

The configuration in listing 8.19 uses the Spring framework to perform a JNDI lookup of the `ConnectionFactory` and the `Destination` objects. Because the JNDI provider for each application server has already been configured (see the earlier sections related to the different application servers), this simple Spring configuration is powerful—it makes easy work of performing JNDI lookups. And the sample web application was always deployed locally to the application server where the JNDI provider is running, making the JNDI lookup a local call. But what if the JMS client isn't deployed locally to an application server?

8.6.1 *Client-side JNDI configuration*

Although the example in this chapter didn't make use of it, ActiveMQ also provides the ability to configure a locally accessible, client-side JNDI context for retrieving JMS administrative objects. This isn't required to be used, but is provided because JNDI is so commonly used.

An important point to understand about ActiveMQ and JNDI is that ActiveMQ doesn't provide a remotely accessible JNDI provider—a JNDI provider where the JMS administered objects are configured on the server side and made available for remote lookup by an application running on a different host. Instead, ActiveMQ provides a simple in-memory JNDI context over a simple hash map. To configure a remotely accessible JNDI, you'll need to use a third-party JNDI provider, for example, a Java EE container's JNDI provider (which was shown throughout this chapter).

ACTIVEMQ JNDI SUPPORT

ActiveMQ provides support for a locally accessible JNDI context on the client side. With this style of configuration, the client-side JNDI configuration makes use of a URI to access a remote ActiveMQ broker when the connection factory is created. The best way to understand this style of configuration is to review an example.

If an ActiveMQ instance is running on host A and a Java client application is running on host B, and you want to look up a connection factory via JNDI to access the remote ActiveMQ instance from the Java application, then you need to configure a JNDI context in the Java application. An example jndi.properties file is shown next.

Listing 8.20   An example jndi.properties file

```
#
# This is an example jndi.properties file for use with ActiveMQ. To make use of
# the locally available ActiveMQ JNDI provider place this file in the classpath
# of the client application.
#

#
# The java.naming.factory.initial property is a standard JNDI system
# property
# (http://java.sun.com/products/jndi/tutorial/beyond/env/context.html)
# that is used to specify the InitialContextFactory implementation to
# use. In this instance, the ActiveMQInitialContextFactory is used to
# provide a locally available context factory.
#
java.naming.factory.initial = \
org.apache.activemq.jndi.ActiveMQInitialContextFactory

#
# The JNDI names for the connection factories to be registered in JNDI.
# These are the name that should be used to lookup the connection
# factories in JNDI.
#
connectionFactoryNames = remotePublisherConnectionFactory, \
remoteConsumerConnectionFactory

#
# Configure the connection factory for publishers. For more information
# on available properties, see the ActiveMQConnectionFactory class.
#
connection.remotePublisherConnectionFactory.brokerURL = tcp://hostA:61616
connection.remotePublisherConnectionFactory.username = publisher
connection.remotePublisherConnectionFactory.username = password

#
# Configure the connection factory for consumers. For more information
# on available properties, see the ActiveMQConnectionFactory class.
#
```

```
connection.remoteConsumerConnectionFactory.username = tcp://hostA:61616
connection.remoteConsumerConnectionFactory.username = consumer
connection.remoteConsumerConnectionFactory.username = password

#
# Define a JMS queue destination to be registered in JNDI. The format
# for specifying JMS queue is queue.<logical name> = <physical name>
# where <logical name> is whatever you like and <physical name> is the
# actual queue name referenced by ActiveMQ.
#
queue.MyTestQueue = TEST.FOO

#
# Define a JMS topic destination to be registered in JNDI. The format for
# specifying a JMS topic is topic.<logical name> = <physical name> where
# <logical name> is whatever you like and <physical name> is the actual
# topic name referenced by ActiveMQ.
#
topic.someTopicName = GREEN.DEMO.TOPIC
```

To use the jndi.properties file shown in listing 8.20, it must be placed in the classpath of the client application. The first property defined is the standard java.naming. factory.initial property. This is a standard system property for configuring JNDI. It's used to note the implementation of the `InitialContextFactory` interface to use. The example is using the `ActiveMQInitialContextFactory`, so that class must be available on the classpath.

The `connectionFactoryNames` property is used to specify the names of the connection factories that will be created and placed in the JNDI tree. In listing 8.20, the names `remotePublisherConnectionFactory` and `remoteConsumerConnection-Factory` were used. This means that to resolve either one of these connection factories, these two names would be used in a JNDI lookup. Here's a snippet of the code to be used to look up one of them:

```
...
Context ctx = new InitialContext();
ConnectionFactory factory = (ConnectionFactory)
    ctx.lookup("remotePublisherConnectionFactory");
...
```

Each connection factory can also be configured in the jndi.properties file by specifying the property name to be set. In listing 8.20, the brokerURL, the username, and the password are being set. Numerous other properties can be set on a connection factory, so take a look at the properties available in the `ActiveMQConnectionFactory` class.

The last items to be specified in listing 8.20 are a couple JMS destinations. The format for defining destinations is shown in the example. As you can see, the logical name has no bearing on the physical name; it's an alias to the destination to be used when performing a JNDI lookup of the destination. Here's a snippet demonstrating a JNDI lookup for the queue destination:

```
...
Context ctx = new InitialContext();
```

```
Queue myTestQueue = (Queue) ctx.lookup("MyTestQueue");
...
```

And here's an example JNDI lookup for the topic destination:

```
...
Context ctx = new InitialContext();
Topic myTopic = (Topic) ctx.lookup("someTopicName");
...
```

This client-side configuration of the locally accessible `InitialContextFactory` provided by ActiveMQ is powerful and useful. Its major unique quality is that it's not remotely accessible. This is one reason why all of the previous examples utilized the JNDI provider supplied by each application server. The other reason that the application server's JNDI provider was used is because it is a best practice to have a single system of record for the JNDI configuration.

8.7   *Summary*

Though deployment to an application server requires more initial configuration than simply starting up a standalone ActiveMQ broker, in some environments the long-term benefit of allowing ActiveMQ to be managed in the same JVM process is a better trade-off. And ActiveMQ isn't limited to integration with open source application servers. In the interest of saving space for this chapter, we didn't include integration with commercial application servers. Make no mistake, integrating ActiveMQ with commercial application servers is not only possible, it's popular. The most common form of deploying ActiveMQ to commercial Java EE servers is through the use of the ActiveMQ resource adapter, as shown in this chapter when configuring both Geronimo and JBoss.

Also, JNDI is widely used for the storage of preconfigured JMS administrative objects. Most of the examples in this chapter use the JNDI provider that's supplied by the application server. The last section of this chapter briefly reviewed the ActiveMQ client-side JNDI configuration.

No matter whether you're running a standalone ActiveMQ broker or one that's embedded in a Java application or even an application server, managing ActiveMQ is still possible via a JMX tool such as JConsole. ActiveMQ can use an existing MBean server or even create its own if necessary. In deploying the sample web application throughout this chapter, the ActiveMQ JMX capabilities were left enabled (the default setting) and were accessible via JConsole. For more information on administration and monitoring of ActiveMQ, see chapter 14.

Now that you've seen how to integrate ActiveMQ with various application servers, the next chapter will transition to a new topic: using ActiveMQ with programming languages other than Java.

ActiveMQ messaging
for other languages

This chapter covers

- Using scripting languages via STOMP
- Exploring ActiveMQ NMS with C#
- Exploring ActiveMQ CMS with C++
- Using the ActiveMQ REST API
- Using the ActiveMQ Ajax API

Thus far we've been focused on ActiveMQ as a JMS broker and explored various ways of using it in Java environment. But ActiveMQ is more than just a JMS broker. It provides an extensive list of connectivity options, so it can be seen as a general messaging solution for a variety of development platforms. In this chapter we'll cover all ActiveMQ aspects related to providing messaging services to different platforms. We'll start by exploring the *STOMP* (*Streaming Text Orientated Messaging Protocol*) protocol, which due to its simplicity plays an important role in messaging for scripting languages. Examples in Ruby, Python, PHP, and Perl will demonstrate the ease of messaging with STOMP and ActiveMQ. Next, we'll focus on writing clients for C++ and .NET platforms with appropriate examples. Finally, we'll see how

ActiveMQ could be used in the Web environment through its *REST* and *Ajax* APIs. By the end of this chapter, you'll see that ActiveMQ isn't just another Java message broker, but rather a general messaging platform for various environments. Before we go into details on specific platforms, we have to define the examples we'll be using throughout this chapter.

9.1 Adapting the stock portfolio example

In chapter 3, we defined a stock portfolio example that uses map messages to exchange data between producers and consumers. For the purpose of this chapter, we'll modify this original example and make it a better fit for environments described here. Instead of map messages, we'll exchange XML data in text messages, as that's the more natural way of communication in some of these environments, such as dynamic languages. So we'll create a Java message producer that sends text messages with appropriate XML data. Through the rest of the chapter, we'll implement appropriate consumers for each of the platforms described, which will show us how to connect the specified platform with Java in an asynchronous way.

For starters, we have to modify our publisher to send XML data in text messages instead of map messages. The only thing we have to change from our original publisher is the `createStockMessage()` method. Listing 9.1 shows the method that creates an appropriate XML representation of desired data and creates a `TextMessage` instance out of it.

Listing 9.1 Modified stock portfolio publisher that sends messages as XML payloads

```
protected Message createStockMessage(String stock, Session session)
  throws JMSException, XMLStreamException {
    Double value = LAST_PRICES.get(stock);
    if (value == null) {
        value = new Double(Math.random() * 100);
    }

    // lets mutate the value by some percentage
    double oldPrice = value.doubleValue();
    value = new Double(mutatePrice(oldPrice));
    LAST_PRICES.put(stock, value);
    double price = value.doubleValue();

    double offer = price * 1.001;

    boolean up = (price > oldPrice);

    StringWriter res = new StringWriter();              ⟵── Create XML data
    XMLStreamWriter writer =
      XMLOutputFactory.newInstance().createXMLStreamWriter(res);
    writer.writeStartDocument();
    writer.writeStartElement("stock");
    writer.writeAttribute("name", stock);
    writer.writeStartElement("price");
    writer.writeCharacters(String.valueOf(price));
    writer.writeEndElement();
```

```
        writer.writeStartElement("offer");
        writer.writeCharacters(String.valueOf(offer));
        writer.writeEndElement();

        writer.writeStartElement("up");
        writer.writeCharacters(String.valueOf(up));
        writer.writeEndElement();
        writer.writeEndElement();
        writer.writeEndDocument();                          │ Create text
                                                         ◁─┘ message
        TextMessage message = session.createTextMessage();
        message.setText(res.toString());
        return message;
    }
```

As you can see, we've used a simple StAX API (http://mng.bz/0S2s) to create an XML representation of our stock data. Next, we created a text message and used the set-Text() method to associate this XML to the message.

Now we can start our publisher in the standard manner:

```
$ mvn exec:java -Dexec.mainClass=org.apache.activemq.book.ch9.Publisher \
  -Dexec.args="IONA JAVA"
```

and expect the following output:

```
Sending: <?xml version="1.0" ?>
  <stock name="JAVA">
    <price>81.987225215383</price><offer>82.069212440599</offer>
    <up>false</up>
  </stock>
on destination: topic://STOCKS.JAVA
Sending: <?xml version="1.0" ?><stock name="IONA">
  <price>16.2205230479432</price><offer>16.236743570991</offer>
  <up>false</up>
</stock>
on destination: topic://STOCKS.IONA
Sending: <?xml version="1.0" ?><stock name="JAVA">
  <price>82.70353458512</price><offer>82.786238119706</offer><up>true</up>
</stock>
on destination: topic://STOCKS.JAVA
Sending: <?xml version="1.0" ?><stock name="IONA">
  <price>16.264366325962</price><offer>16.280630692288</offer><up>true</up>
</stock>
on destination: topic://STOCKS.IONA
Sending: <?xml version="1.0" ?><stock name="JAVA">
  <price>83.341791666986</price><offer>83.425133458653</offer><up>true</up>
</stock>
on destination: topic://STOCKS.JAVA
Sending: <?xml version="1.0" ?><stock name="JAVA">
  <price>83.891272205115</price><offer>83.975163477321</offer><up>true</up>
</stock>
on destination: topic://STOCKS.JAVA
```

As expected, the publisher sends a series of XML-formatted text messages to different ActiveMQ topics. As they're ready to be consumed, it's time to see how we can consume them using different programming languages and platforms.

9.2   *Messaging for scripting languages*

In chapter 3, we explained various network protocols used for communication between ActiveMQ and clients. But what we didn't discuss there is that choosing the right network protocol is just one side of the story. An equally important aspect of communication is finding the right way to serialize your messages over the network, or picking the *wire protocol*. ActiveMQ can support different wire protocols, and comes with two of them implemented by default. This makes messaging with ActiveMQ adaptable to various programming environments, as we'll see in the rest of this chapter.

For all transport connectors we covered thus far, ActiveMQ uses the *OpenWire* (http://mng.bz/u2eT) protocol to exchange messages between brokers and clients. OpenWire is designed to be an efficient binary protocol in terms of network bandwidth and performance. This makes it an ideal choice for communication with so-called native clients usually written in Java, C, or C#. But all this efficiency comes at a cost, and in this case it's the complexity of implementation.

STOMP (Streaming Text Oriented Messaging Protocol), on the other hand, is designed with entirely different requirements in mind. It's a simple text-oriented protocol, similar to HTTP. You can see it as HTTP adapted to the messaging realm. This implies that it's easy to implement the STOMP client in an arbitrary programming language. It's even possible to communicate with the broker through the telnet session using STOMP, as we'll see in a moment.

In the following section we'll cover the basics of STOMP to give you an idea of how it works and what you can expect from it. After that, we'll write stock portfolio consumers in some of the most popular scripting (dynamic) languages used today, such as Ruby and Python. It's a long section, but after reading it you'll be fully ready to use asynchronous messaging in almost any programming language. Of course, after reading the basics, you can jump to the language of your choice.

We won't explain the STOMP protocol in detail here, and you're advised to take a look at the protocol specification (http://mng.bz/JAUH) if you're interested in this topic. But let's walk through some basics, just to get a feel for what's happening under the hood.

9.2.1   *STOMP protocol basics*

Clients and brokers communicate with each other by exchanging *frames*, textual representation of messages. Frames could be delivered over any underlying network protocol, but it's usually TCP. Every frame consists of three basic elements: *command*, *headers*, and *body*, as shown in the following snippet:

```
SEND
destination:/queue/a

hello queue a
^@
```

The command part of the frame identifies what kind of operation should take place. In this example, the SEND frame is used to send a message to the broker, but you can also

- CONNECT or DISCONNECT from the broker
- SUBSCRIBE or UNSUBSCRIBE from a destination
- BEGIN, COMMIT, or ABORT a transaction
- ACK (acknowledge) messages

These commands are self-explanatory and represent common functionalities expected to be found in any messaging system. We'll see them in action through examples in the coming sections.

Headers are used to specify additional properties for each command, such as the destination where a message is sent in the preceding example. Headers are basically key-value pairs, separated by a colon (:) character. Every header should be written in a separate line (of course, our example contains only one header).

The blank line indicates the end of the headers section and start of an optional body section. In case of the SEND command, the body section contains an actual message we want to send. Finally the frame is ended by the ASCII null character (^@).

After explaining the basic structure of frames, let's go to STOMP sessions. The following shows how easy it is to create a regular telnet session and use it to send and receive messages from the command line.

Listing 9.2 Using ActiveMQ via telnet and STOMP

```
$ telnet localhost 61613
Trying 127.0.0.1...
Connected to localhost.
Escape character is '^]'.
CONNECT
login:system
passcode:manager

^@
CONNECTED
session:ID:dejan-laptop-36961-1221552914772-4:0

SEND
destination:/queue/a

hello queue a
^@

SUBSCRIBE
destination:/queue/a

^@
MESSAGE
message-id:ID:dejan-laptop-36961-1221552914772-4:0:-1:1:1
destination:/queue/a
timestamp:1221553047204
expires:0
priority:0

hello queue a
```

```
UNSUBSCRIBE
destination:/queue/a

^@

DISCONNECT

^@
Connection closed by foreign host
```

As you can see, the usual session starts by connecting to the broker (with appropriate credentials provided). The broker will acknowledge successful connection by sending the CONNECTED frame back to the client. After creating a successful connection, the client can send messages using the SEND frame similar to the one we just described. If it wants to receive messages, it should subscribe to the desired destination. From that moment on, messages from the subscribed destination will be pushed asynchronously to the client. When the client is finished with consuming messages, it should unsubscribe from the destination. Finally, the client should disconnect from the broker to terminate the session.

You've probably noticed that we started the destination name with the /queue/ prefix, which naturally suggests that the desired destination is a message queue. STOMP doesn't define any semantics regarding destination names, and specifies it only as a string value that's specific to the server implementation. ActiveMQ implements the syntax we've seen in our example, where prefixes /queue/ or /topic/ define the type of the destination, while the rest is interpreted as the destination name. So the value /queue/a used in the previous example interprets as "queue named a." Having said all this, we can conclude that you should be careful when dealing with destination names starting with the / character. For example, you should use value /queue//a if you want to access the queue named /a.

9.2.2 *Configuring STOMP transport*

Now that we've learned the basics of the STOMP protocol, let's see how we can configure ActiveMQ to enable this kind of communication with its clients. The configuration shown in the following listing defines two transport connectors: one that allows connections over the TCP connector (and uses OpenWire wire protocol) and another one that uses STOMP.

Listing 9.3   Configure STOMP and TCP transport connectors used in examples

```
<broker xmlns="http://activemq.apache.org/schema/core"
 brokerName="localhost" dataDirectory="${activemq.base}/data">

 <transportConnectors>
  <transportConnector name="openwire"
   uri="tcp://localhost:61616" />

<transportConnector name="stomp"
   uri="stomp://localhost:61613" />
 </transportConnectors>

</broker>
```

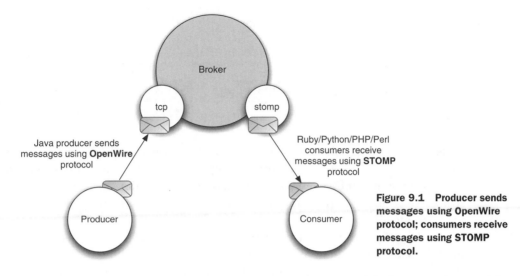

Figure 9.1   Producer sends messages using OpenWire protocol; consumers receive messages using STOMP protocol.

So all you have to do to is to define a transport connector with the stomp keyword for a URI schema and you're ready to go.

Now let's see how to implement consumers of our stock portfolio data in some of the most popular scripting languages. Figure 9.1 illustrates examples we'll build in the rest of this section.

9.2.3   *Ruby STOMP consumer*

We all witnessed the rising popularity of *Ruby on Rails* web development framework, which marked Ruby as one of the most popular dynamic languages today. The asynchronous messaging with STOMP and ActiveMQ brings one more tool to the Ruby and Rails developers' toolbox, making it possible to tackle a whole new range of problems. More information on how to install the STOMP client for Ruby can be found at http://mng.bz/605u. Once you've installed and configured your Ruby environment, you can write the stock portfolio consumer as shown next.

Listing 9.4   Stock portfolio consumer written in Ruby

```
#!/usr/bin/ruby

require 'rubygems'
require 'stomp'                                                    Define
require 'xmlsimple'                                                connection

@conn = Stomp::Connection.open '', '', 'localhost', 61613, false   ◁┘
@count = 0

@conn.subscribe "/topic/STOCKS.JAVA", { :ack =>"auto" }      ◁──── Subscribe
@conn.subscribe "/topic/STOCKS.IONA", { :ack =>"auto" }
while @count < 100
 @msg = @conn.receive                    ◁──── Receive message
 @count = @count + 1
 if @msg.command == "MESSAGE"
```

```
    @xml = XmlSimple.xml_in(@msg.body)
    $stdout.print "#{@xml['name']}\t"
    $stdout.print "#{'%.2f' % @xml['price']}\t"
    $stdout.print "#{'%.2f' % @xml['offer']}\t"
    $stdout.print "#{@xml['up'].to_s == 'true'?'up':'down'}\n"
  else
    $stdout.print "#{@msg.command}: #{@msg.body}\n"
  end
end
@conn.disconnect
```

Basically, all STOMP clients provide wrapper functions (methods) for creating basic STOMP frames and sending to (or reading from) TCP sockets. Let's explain it in detail with some Ruby examples. All examples that follow in other languages are structured similarly to this example (and any new concepts will be described as they are introduced).

In this example, we first created a connection with a broker using the open() method. This is equivalent to opening a TCP socket and sending the CONNECT frame to the broker. Besides the usual connection parameters, such as username, password, host, and port, we've provided one extra argument at the end of this method call. This parameter specifies whether the client will be *reliable*—will it try to reconnect until it successfully connects to the broker? In this example, we set the reliable parameter to false, which means it will raise an exception in case of a connection failure.

After the connection is created, we can subscribe to desired topics, using the subscribe() method. In this example, note that we've passed the additional ack header, which defines the way messages are acknowledged. The STOMP protocol defines two acknowledgment modes:

- *auto*—The broker will mark the message as delivered right after the client consumes it.
- *client*—The broker will consider the message delivered only after the client explicitly acknowledges it with an ACK frame.

The auto mode is the default and you don't have to include any headers if you plan to use it. In this example, we've specifically used it for demonstration purposes. The client acknowledgment mode is explained later in section 9.7.

Now let's receive some messages. We can do this using the receive() method, which reads frames from the TCP socket and parses them. As you can see, we don't have any logic implemented to acknowledge messages, as we're using the auto-acknowledgment mode.

The rest of the code is dedicated to XML parsing and printing. Now you can run the code and expect the following output (of course, the publisher described at the start of the chapter should be running):

```
 ruby consumer.rb
IONA 34.53 34.57 up
JAVA 37.61 37.65 down
JAVA 37.55 37.59 down
JAVA 37.56 37.60 up
```

```
IONA 34.84 34.88 up
JAVA 37.83 37.87 up
JAVA 37.83 37.87 up
JAVA 38.05 38.09 up
JAVA 38.14 38.18 up
IONA 35.06 35.10 up
JAVA 38.03 38.07 down
JAVA 37.68 37.72 down
JAVA 37.55 37.59 down
JAVA 37.59 37.62 up
IONA 35.21 35.25 up
IONA 35.12 35.15 down
JAVA 37.26 37.30 down
```

If you like Rails-like frameworks, you can also check out the ActiveMessaging project (http://mng.bz/5f80), which attempts to "bring simplicity and elegance of Rails development to messaging."

Now let's see how to implement the same stock portfolio data consumer in Python.

9.2.4 *Python STOMP consumer*

Python is another extremely popular and powerful dynamic language, often used in a wide range of software projects. As you can see from the list of STOMP Python clients (http://mng.bz/Qnl6), you can use a variety of libraries in your projects. For the basic implementation of our stock portfolio consumer we've chosen the stomp.py implementation you can find at the following web address: http://mng.bz/d0t2.

For starters we'll create a helper script, called book.py, which will contain helper classes and methods for all our Python examples as shown next.

Listing 9.5 Python helper script containing useful functions

```python
from xml.etree.ElementTree import XML

def printXml(text):
    xml = XML(text)

    print "%s\t%.2f\t%.2f\t%s" % (
        xml.get("name"),
        eval(xml.find("price").text),
        eval(xml.find("offer").text),
        "up" if xml.find("up").text == "True" else "down"
        )
```

For now, this script only contains one method (called `printXml()`), which parses and prints our stock portfolio XML data.

The following listing shows a Python script that receives XML-formatted stock data and uses the `printXml()` function to parse and print it on the screen.

Listing 9.6 Stock portfolio consumer written in Python

```python
#!/usr/bin/env python

import time, sys
from elementtree.ElementTree import ElementTree, XML
```

```
from book import printXml

import stomp

class MyListener(object):                                    ◁——— Message listener
    def on_error(self, headers, message):
        print 'received an error %s' % message

    def on_message(self, headers, message):
        printXml(message)

conn = stomp.Connection()

conn.add_listener(MyListener())                              ◁——— Add listener
conn.start()
conn.connect()

conn.subscribe(destination='/topic/STOCKS.JAVA', ack='auto')    ◁┐ Subscribe to
conn.subscribe(destination='/topic/STOCKS.IONA', ack='auto')     ┘ destination


time.sleep(60);

conn.disconnect()
```

As you can see, the Python client implements an asynchronous JMS-like API with message listeners, rather than using synchronous message receiving philosophy used by other STOMP clients. This code sample defines a simple message listener that parses the XML text message (using our printXml() function) and prints the desired data on the standard output. Then, similar to the Java examples, it creates a connection, adds a listener, starts a connection, and finally subscribes to the desired destinations.

When started, this example will produce output similar to the following:

```
python consumer.py
IONA 52.21 52.26 down
JAVA 91.88 91.97 down
IONA 52.09 52.14 down
JAVA 92.16 92.25 up
JAVA 91.44 91.53 down
IONA 52.17 52.22 up
JAVA 90.81 90.90 down
JAVA 91.46 91.55 up
JAVA 90.69 90.78 down
IONA 52.33 52.38 up
JAVA 90.45 90.54 down
JAVA 90.51 90.60 up
JAVA 91.00 91.09 up
```

This is consistent with what we had for the Ruby client.

MESSAGING WITH PYACTIVEMQ

As we said before, a few other Python clients can exchange messages with ActiveMQ. One specially interesting client is the *pyactivemq* project (http://mng.bz/ErKS), which we'll cover in this section. The interesting thing about this project is that it's basically a Python wrapper around the ActiveMQ C++ library (described a bit later) which supports both STOMP and OpenWire protocols and provides excellent performance for your Python applications. Since it wraps the ActiveMQ C++ library, it requires a special installation procedure, so be sure to check the project site for information relevant to your platform.

Let's now create a full stock portfolio example using pyactivemq and see how it can be used over the STOMP and OpenWire protocols. For starters, we need to add a few more helper functions to our helper script, as shown next.

Listing 9.7 Extending helper script for pyactivemq usage

```python
import random
from xml.etree.ElementTree import Element, SubElement, XML, tostring

def printXml(text):
    xml = XML(text)

    print "%s\t%.2f\t%.2f\t%s" % (
        xml.get("name"),
        eval(xml.find("price").text),
        eval(xml.find("offer").text),
        "up" if xml.find("up").text == "True" else "down"
        )

def mutatePrice(price):                              ◁──── Mutates price
    MAX_DELTA_PERCENT = 1
    percentChange = (2 * random.random()
        * MAX_DELTA_PERCENT) - MAX_DELTA_PERCENT

    return price * (100 + percentChange) / 100;
                                                     │ Formats stock
def createXml(oldPrice, price):                      ◁─ data as XML
    stock = Element("stock")
    stock.set("name", "JAVA")
    priceElem = SubElement(stock, "price")
    priceElem.text = str(price)

    offer = SubElement(stock, "offer")
    offer.text = str(price * 1.001)

    up = SubElement(stock, "up")
    up.text = str(oldPrice > price)

    return stock
```

As you can see, there are two new functions which are basically the same as those in our original Java stock portfolio producer example. Now, let's put it all together.

Listing 9.8 Stock portfolio producer written with pyactivemq

```python
import pyactivemq, time, sys, random
from pyactivemq import ActiveMQConnectionFactory
from book import mutatePrice, printXml, createXml
from xml.etree.ElementTree import Element, SubElement, XML, tostring

class MessageListener(pyactivemq.MessageListener):

    def onMessage(self, message):
        printXml(message.text)
```

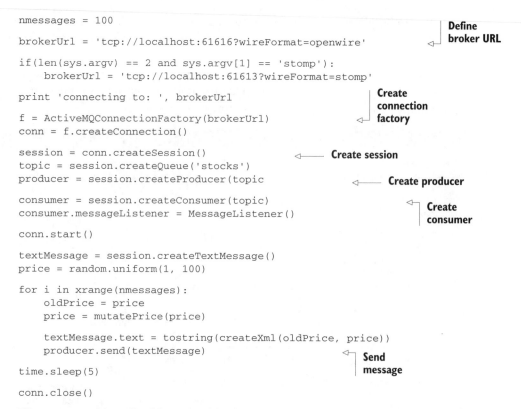

```
nmessages = 100

brokerUrl = 'tcp://localhost:61616?wireFormat=openwire'          ◁  Define
                                                                     broker URL

if(len(sys.argv) == 2 and sys.argv[1] == 'stomp'):
    brokerUrl = 'tcp://localhost:61613?wireFormat=stomp'

print 'connecting to: ', brokerUrl                        ⎤  Create
                                                          ⎮  connection
f = ActiveMQConnectionFactory(brokerUrl)                  ◁  factory
conn = f.createConnection()

session = conn.createSession()            ◁───  Create session
topic = session.createQueue('stocks')
producer = session.createProducer(topic         ◁───  Create producer

consumer = session.createConsumer(topic)             ⎤  Create
consumer.messageListener = MessageListener()         ⎦  consumer

conn.start()

textMessage = session.createTextMessage()
price = random.uniform(1, 100)

for i in xrange(nmessages):
    oldPrice = price
    price = mutatePrice(price)

    textMessage.text = tostring(createXml(oldPrice, price))
    producer.send(textMessage)               ⎤  Send
                                             ⎦  message
time.sleep(5)

conn.close()
```

The *CMS API* (described later in this chapter) defines an API similar to JMS, and since the pyactivemq is just a wrapper around a CMS API implementation, we can expect a JMS-like API for Python. So in this example, we've defined a broker URL, created a connection using a connection factory, and created a session. Next, we create a producer and consumer with an appropriate message listener. Finally, we can create stock portfolio data (with the help of previously defined functions) and send them to the broker.

Now if we run this example, we'll get output similar to the following:

```
$ python stocks.py
connecting to:  tcp://localhost:61616?wireFormat=openwire
JAVA 92.26 92.35 up
JAVA 91.99 92.08 up
JAVA 92.19 92.29 down
JAVA 92.28 92.37 down
JAVA 91.36 91.45 up
JAVA 91.88 91.97 down
JAVA 91.52 91.61 up
JAVA 91.22 91.31 up
```

Note the URL we're connecting to. You can see that we're passing a `wireFormat` parameter, and in this case it configures the client to use the OpenWire protocol to exchange messages. We can change this by passing a `stomp` argument when executing the script.

```
$ python stocks.py stomp
connecting to:  tcp://localhost:61613?wireFormat=stomp
JAVA 19.55 19.57 up
JAVA 19.58 19.60 down
JAVA 19.76 19.78 down
JAVA 19.95 19.97 down
JAVA 20.13 20.15 down
JAVA 20.09 20.11 up
JAVA 20.28 20.30 down
JAVA 20.26 20.28 up
JAVA 20.19 20.21 up
JAVA 20.28 20.30 down
```

Now the `wireFormat` parameter value in our connection URL has changed, configuring the producer and consumer to use STOMP. This shows how easy it is to use both OpenWire and STOMP with just a slight change to the connection URL parameter.

After showing Ruby and Python examples, it's time to focus on old-school scripting languages, such as PHP and Perl, and their STOMP clients.

9.2.5 *PHP STOMP consumer*

Despite the tremendous competition in the web development platform arena, PHP (in combination with Apache web server) is still one of the most frequently used tools for developing web-based applications. The *stompcli* library (http://mng.bz/sgBE) provides an easy way to use asynchronous messaging in PHP applications. The following listing demonstrates how to create a stock portfolio data consumer in PHP.

Listing 9.9   Stock portfolio consumer written in PHP

```php
<?

require_once('Stomp.php');

$stomp = new Stomp("tcp://localhost:61613");

$stomp->connect('system', 'manager');                  ⟵── Create connection

$stomp->subscribe("/topic/STOCKS.JAVA");               ⟵┐ Subscribe to
$stomp->subscribe("/topic/STOCKS.IONA");                │ destinations

$i = 0;
while($i++ < 100) {

    $frame = $stomp->readFrame();                      ⟵── Read messages
    $xml = new SimpleXMLElement($frame->body);
    echo $xml->attributes()->name
        . "\t" . number_format($xml->price,2)
        . "\t" . number_format($xml->offer,2)
        . "\t" . ($xml->up == "true"?"up":"down") . "\n";
    $stomp->ack($frame);                               ⟵┐ Acknowledge
                                                        │ messages

}

$stomp->disconnect();                      ⟵── Disconnect

?>
```

Practically, all STOMP examples look alike; the only thing that differs is the language syntax used to write a particular one. So here we have all the basic elements found in the STOMP examples: creating a connection, subscribing to destinations, reading messages, and finally disconnecting. But we have one slight modification over the previous examples. Here, we've used the *client acknowledgment* of messages, which means that messages will be considered consumed only after the client explicitly acknowledges them. For that purpose we've called the ack() method upon processing of each message.

Now we can run the previous script and expect the following result:

```
php consumer.php
JAVA 50.64 50.69 down
JAVA 50.65 50.70 up
JAVA 50.85 50.90 up
JAVA 50.62 50.67 down
JAVA 50.39 50.44 down
JAVA 50.08 50.13 down
JAVA 49.72 49.77 down
IONA 11.45 11.46 up
JAVA 49.24 49.29 down
IONA 11.48 11.49 up
JAVA 49.22 49.27 down
JAVA 48.99 49.04 down
JAVA 48.88 48.92 down
JAVA 48.49 48.54 down
IONA 11.42 11.43 down
```

As we expected, the script produces output similar to what we've seen in our previous examples. The following section explains a similar example written in another popular old-school scripting language, Perl.

9.2.6   *Perl STOMP consumer*

Perl is one of the first powerful dynamic languages, and as such has a large community of users. The range of development tasks Perl is used for is wide, but it's probably best known as an "ultimate system administrator tool." Therefore, an introduction to asynchronous messaging for Perl gives developers one more powerful tool in their toolbox.

An implementation of the STOMP protocol in Perl can be found in the CPAN Net::Stomp module (http://mng.bz/RA5k). The following listing contains an implementation of the stock portfolio consumer in Perl.

Listing 9.10   Stock portfolio consumer written in Perl

```
use Net::Stomp;
use XML::Simple;


my $stomp =
Net::Stomp->new( { hostname => 'localhost', port => '61613' } );
```

```
$stomp->connect( { login => 'system', passcode => 'manager' } );

$stomp->subscribe(
    {   destination             => '/topic/STOCKS.JAVA',
        'ack'                   => 'client',
        'activemq.prefetchSize' => 1              ◁──── Prefetch size
    }
);
$stomp->subscribe(
    {   destination             => '/topic/STOCKS.IONA',
        'ack'                   => 'client',
        'activemq.prefetchSize' => 1

    }
);

my $count = 0;

while ($count++ < 100) {
  my $frame = $stomp->receive_frame;
  my $xml = XMLin($frame->body);
  print $xml->{name} . "\t" . sprintf("%.2f", $xml->{price}) . "\t";
  print sprintf("%.2f", $xml->{offer}) . "\t";
  print ($xml->{up} eq 'true' ? 'up' : 'down') . "\n";

  $stomp->ack( { frame => $frame } );
}

$stomp->disconnect;
```

The example is practically the same as all our previous examples (especially the PHP one, since the syntax is almost the same). But we've added one feature to this example: the usage of the `activemq.prefetchSize` value when subscribing to the destination.

ActiveMQ uses a *prefetch limit* to determine the number of messages it will pre-send to consumers, so that network is used optimally. This option is explained in more detail in chapter 13, but basically this means that the broker will try to send 1,000 messages to be buffered on the client side. Once the consumer buffer is full, no more messages are sent before some of the existing messages in the buffer get consumed (acknowledged). Though this technique works great for Java consumers, STOMP consumers (and libraries) are usually simple scripts and don't implement any buffers on the client side, so certain problems (such as undelivered messages) could be introduced by this feature. Thus, it's advisable to set the prefetch size to 1 (by providing a specialized `activemq.prefetchSize` header to the SUBSCRIBE command frame) and instruct the broker to send one message at a time.

Now that we have it all explained, let's run our example:

```
$ perl consumer.pl
IONA 69.22 69.29 down
JAVA 22.20 22.22 down
IONA 69.74 69.81 up
JAVA 22.05 22.08 down
IONA 69.92 69.99 up
JAVA 21.91 21.93 down
```

```
JAVA 22.10 22.12 up
JAVA 21.95 21.97 down
JAVA 21.84 21.86 down
JAVA 21.67 21.69 down
IONA 70.60 70.67 up
JAVA 21.70 21.72 up
IONA 70.40 70.47 down
JAVA 21.50 21.52 down
IONA 70.55 70.62 up
JAVA 21.69 21.71 up
```

As you can see, the behavior is the same as with all our other STOMP examples.

With Perl, we conclude our demonstration of STOMP clients and exchanging messages with ActiveMQ using different scripting languages. But STOMP (especially combined with ActiveMQ) is more capable than simply sending and receiving messages. In the following section, we'll go through advanced messaging concepts that makes STOMP and ActiveMQ a powerful combination.

9.2.7   *Advanced messaging with STOMP*

Sending and receiving messages one by one is more than enough for most use cases. But even if you write your clients in scripting languages, you may want to use some advanced messaging concepts. In this section we'll learn how to use STOMP transactions and how you can create ActiveMQ *durable topic subscribers* using your STOMP clients.

UNDERSTANDING STOMP TRANSACTIONS

Besides sending and acknowledging messages one by one, STOMP introduces the concept of transactions, which group multiple SEND and ACK commands. Transactions are well known from SQL and JMS, and we're sure you're familiar with the with atomicity they introduce, as well as transaction-related operations, such as *commit* and *rollback* (*abort*).

So if you want to start a transaction, you need to send a BEGIN frame to the broker, along with the transaction header that contains a transaction ID. For example, the following frame will start a transaction named tx1:

```
BEGIN
transaction:tx1

^@
```

After you're finished with the transaction, you can either commit it or abort it by sending the appropriate frame (COMMIT or ABORT), of course with the transaction ID passed as the transaction header. So the following frame will commit the previously started tx1 transaction and mark the successful send and acknowledgment of all messages in the transaction:

```
COMMIT
transaction:tx1

^@
```

One more important thing is how you send and acknowledge messages in the transaction. In order to mark that the message is sent or acknowledged in the transaction, you need to add a `transaction` header to `SEND` and `ACK` frames that are sent to the broker. Of course, the value of this header must match the valid (started) transaction ID.

So, for example, the following frame states that the appropriate message has been acknowledged in transaction tx1:

```
ACK
destination:/queue/transactions
transaction:tx1
message-id:ID:dejanb.local-62217-1249899600449-6:0:-1:1:3


^@
```

The important thing to note here is that transactions in STOMP are only related to sending `SEND` and `ACK` frames. So there's no concept such as *receiving messages in a transaction* as we have in JMS. This basically means that you can only roll back message acknowledgment, but not the message itself, so the message won't be redelivered to the client. The client application (or STOMP client) is responsible for trying to process those messages again and acknowledging them when they do so.

The following listing demonstrates sending and acknowledging messages using transactions. First we'll send some messages in a transaction.

Listing 9.11 Example of sending messages in a transaction

```php
<?
require_once("Stomp.php");

$con = new Stomp("tcp://localhost:61613");
$con->connect();

$con->begin("tx1");                          ◁─── Begin transaction
for ($i = 1; $i < 3; $i++) {
  $con->send("/queue/transactions", $i,
    array("transaction" => "tx1"));          ◁─── Send messages
}
$con->abort("tx1");                          ◁─── Abort transaction

$con->begin("tx2");                          ◁─── Begin new transaction
echo "Sent messages {\n";
for ($i = 1; $i < 5; $i++) {
 $con->send("/queue/transactions", $i,
  array("transaction" => "tx2"));            ◁─── Send more messages
 echo "\t$i\n";
}
echo "}\n";

$con->commit("tx2");                         ◁─── Commit transaction
?>
```

As you can see, we tried first to send two messages in transaction tx1. Note that we're passing an additional header to the `send()` method in order to send a message in the transaction. But as we aborted transaction tx1, those messages weren't sent to the broker. Then we started another transaction tx2 and sent four messages in it. Finally, we committed transaction tx2 and thus told the broker to accept those messages. If you execute this script, you can expect output similar to this:

```
php transactions_send.php
Sent messages {
  1
  2
  3
  4
}
```

We should now expect to have four messages in the queue. Now let's try to consume those messages using transactions, as shown next.

Listing 9.12 Example of consuming (and acknowledging) messages in transactions

```php
<?php
require_once("Stomp.php");

$con = new Stomp("tcp://localhost:61613");
$con->connect();
$con->setReadTimeout(1);

$con->subscribe("/queue/transactions",                        Subscribe
  array('ack' => 'client','activemq.prefetchSize' => 1 ));    to queue

$con->begin("tx3");
$messages = array();
for ($i = 1; $i < 3; $i++) {
  $msg = $con->readFrame();
  array_push($messages, $msg);                Acknowledge
  $con->ack($msg, "tx3");                     messages
}

$con->abort("tx3");                    Abort transaction

$con->begin("tx4");                            Begin new transaction
if (count($messages) != 0) {
  foreach($messages as $msg) {
    $con->ack($msg, "tx4");          Acknowledge
  }                                  received messages
}
for ($i = 1; $i < 3; $i++) {
  $msg = $con->readFrame();
  $con->ack($msg, "tx4");            Acknowledge
  array_push($messages, $msg);       more messages
}
$con->commit("tx4");                   Commit
                                       transaction
echo "Processed messages {\n";
foreach($messages as $msg) {
  echo "\t$msg->body\n";
}
echo "}\n";
```

```
$frame = $con->readFrame();

if ($frame === false) {
  echo "No more messages in the queue\n";
} else {
  echo "Warning: some messages still in the queue: $frame\n";
}

$con->disconnect();
```

> ◁┐ **Verify no more**
> **messages in queue**

In this script, we've first subscribed to the queue using prefetch size 1 and client acknowledgment. Next we're trying to consume two messages and acknowledge them in a transaction tx3. Note that we're now passing another parameter to the ack() method that identifies the transaction in use. Let's now try to abort the transaction and see what happens. Those two messages won't be marked as received by the broker, and since we're using prefetch size 1, the broker won't send any other messages until we consume these two. So when we start a new transaction tx4, we need first to acknowledge already-received messages before we can start consuming the rest of them. Finally, we're ready to commit the transaction and mark all messages consumed. At the end we can verify there are no more messages left in the queue.

If you run the example, you can expect the following output:

```
$ php transactions_receive.php
Processed messages {
  1
  2
  3
  4
}
No more messages in the queue
```

As you can see, transactions enable us to send and acknowledge messages in atomic operations, which is a crucial requirement for many use cases. Now let's see how ActiveMQ enhances the core Stomp protocol and allows you to use durable topic subscribers.

WORKING WITH DURABLE TOPIC SUBSCRIBERS

As you already know, topic consumers receive messages from the topic while they're subscribed. So if they disconnect and connect again, they'll miss all the messages sent to the topic in the meantime. ActiveMQ's way of dealing with this is by using durable topic subscribers, which can receive all messages retroactively. As STOMP has no notion of queues and topics (and especially durable ones), this is a pure ActiveMQ feature, and an example of STOMP enhancement by ActiveMQ.

In order to create a durable subscriber, we need to do two things. First we need to pass the client ID of the durable subscriber while we're connecting to the broker. We can do that by passing a client-id header in the CONNECT frame, like this:

```
CONNECT
login:
passcode:client-id:test
```

Next, we need to pass the same client ID to the SUBSCRIBE header, but this time using the activemq.subcriptionName header. The following snippet shows the example frame:

```
SUBSCRIBE
destination:/topic/test
ack:client
activemq.subscriptionName:test
activemq.prefetchSize:1
```

Now let's create a durable topic subscriber example. Take a look at the following.

Listing 9.13   Example of using durable topic subscriber with STOMP

```php
<?php
require_once("Stomp.php");

$producer = new Stomp("tcp://localhost:61613");
$consumer = new Stomp("tcp://localhost:61613");
$consumer->setReadTimeout(1);
$consumer->clientId = "test";                      ⟵—— Set client ID

$producer->connect();
$consumer->connect();
$consumer->subscribe("/topic/test");               ⟵—— Subscribe to topic

sleep(1);

$producer->send("/topic/test", "test",
  array('persistent'=>'true'));                     ⟵—— Send message
echo "Message 'test' sent to topic\n";

$msg = $consumer->readFrame();                      ⟵—— Receive message

if ( $msg != null) {
    echo "Message '$msg->body' received from topic\n";
    $consumer->ack($msg);
} else {
    echo "Failed to receive a message\n";
}

sleep(1);
                                                    Unsubscribe
$consumer->unsubscribe("/topic/test");          ⟵  from topic
$consumer->disconnect();
echo "Disconnecting consumer\n";

$producer->send("/topic/test", "test1",
array('persistent'=>'true'));                       Send message while
echo "Message 'test1' sent to topic\n";        ⟵  consumer offline

$consumer = new Stomp("tcp://localhost:61613");
$consumer->clientId = "test";
$consumer->connect();
$consumer->subscribe("/topic/test");                ⟵—— Subscribe again
echo "Reconnecting consumer\n";

$msg = $consumer->readFrame();                       Receive message
                                                ⟵  sent while
                                                     consumer was offline
```

```
if ( $msg != null) {
    echo "Message '$msg->body' received from topic\n";
    $consumer->ack($msg);
} else {
    echo "Failed to receive a message\n";
}

$consumer->unsubscribe("/topic/test");
$consumer->disconnect();
$producer->disconnect();
?>
```

First of all, we create a producer and consumer. Note that we set the `clientId` property to the consumer. If set, this property will be passed to both CONNECT and SUBSCRIBE frames. Next, we subscribe to the topic and send a message to it. As expected, the message is received by the consumer. Now we can unsubscribe the durable consumer and send another message while the consumer is offline. After subscribing again, the consumer will receive the message even if it was offline while the message was sent.

If you run this example, you can expect the following output:

```
$ php durable.php
Message 'test' sent to topic
Message 'test' received from topic
Disconnecting consumer
Message 'test1' sent to topic
Reconnecting consumer
Message 'test1' received from topic
```

With durable topic subscribers, we're coming to the end of the STOMP section. As we've seen, STOMP is designed to be simple to implement and thus easily usable from scripting languages, such as Ruby or PHP. We also said that ActiveMQ Java clients use the optimized binary OpenWire protocol, which provides better performance than STOMP. So it's not surprising to see that clients are more powerful because they can also make use of the OpenWire protocol. These clients will be the focus of the following two sections.

9.3 *Messaging for compiled languages*

The simplicity of STOMP, explained in the previous section, allows us to communicate with the broker from a wide range of scripting languages. But in compiled environments that more resemble the Java platform, you can create complex clients with full use of the OpenWire protocol. In this section we'll cover two APIs similar to JMS:

- NMS (.NET Message Service)
- CMS (C++ Message Service)

We'll dig into the NMS API by writing a stock portfolio consumer in C# and showing how you can run it on the Mono platform. For the CMS API, we'll explain the process of writing message consumers in C++ using one of the examples that come with the ActiveMQ-CPP library, a default implementation of the CMS API. Now let's start with the NMS API.

9.3.1   *Writing a C# consumer (using the NMS API)*

Scripting languages covered in previous sections are mostly used for creating server-side software and internet applications on Unix-like systems. Developers who target the Windows platform, on the other hand, usually choose the .NET Framework as their development environment. The ability to use a JMS-like API (and ActiveMQ in particular) to asynchronously send and receive messages can bring a big advantage for .NET developers. The *NMS API* (*.Net Message Service API*), an ActiveMQ subproject (http://mng.bz/gVn3), provides a standard C# interface to messaging systems. The idea behind NMS is to create a unified messaging API for C#, similar to what JMS API represents to the Java world. Currently, it only supports ActiveMQ and the OpenWire protocol, but providers for other messaging brokers could be easily implemented.

In the rest of this section we're going to implement a stock portfolio consumer in C# and show you how to compile and run it using the Mono project (http://www.mono-project.com/). You can run this example on a standard Windows implementation of .NET as well. For information on how to obtain (and optionally build) the NMS project, please refer to the NMS project site.

Now, let's take a look at the stock portfolio consumer written in C#, shown next.

Listing 9.14   Stock portfolio consumer written in C#

```
System;
using Apache.NMS;
using Apache.NMS.Util;
using Apache.NMS.ActiveMQ;

namespace Apache.NMS.ActiveMQ.Book.Ch8
{
  public class Consumer
  {
    public static void Main(string[] args)
    {
      NMSConnectionFactory NMSFactory =
        new NMSConnectionFactory("tcp://localhost:61616");        Create
      IConnection connection = NMSFactory.CreateConnection();     connection
      ISession session =
        connection.                                     Create session
          CreateSession(AcknowledgementMode.AutoAcknowledge);
      IDestination destination =
        session.GetTopic("STOCKS.JAVA");      Get destination
      IMessageConsumer consumer =                          Create
        session.CreateConsumer(destination);               consumer
      consumer.Listener += new MessageListener(OnMessage);   Assign
      connection.Start();                                    message
      Console.WriteLine("Press any key to quit.");           listener
      Console.ReadKey();
    }                                   Start connection

    protected static void OnMessage(IMessage message)      Message listener
    {
      ITextMessage TextMessage = message as ITextMessage;
```

```
        Console.WriteLine(TextMessage.Text);
      }
    }
}
```

As you can see, the NMS API is practically identical to the JMS API, which can greatly simplify developing and porting message-based applications. First, we created the appropriate connection and session objects. Then we used the session to get the desired destination and created an appropriate consumer. Finally, we're ready to assign a listener to the consumer and start the connection. In this example, we left the listener as simple as possible, so it'll just print XML data we receive in a message.

To compile this example on the Mono platform, you have to use Mono C# compiler gmcs (the one that targets the 2.0 runtime). Run the following command:

```
$ gmcs -r:Apache.NMS.ActiveMQ.dll -r:Apache.NMS.dll Consumer.cs
```

Assuming that you have appropriate NMS DLLs, the preceding command should produce the Consumer.exe binary. We can run this application with the following command:

```
mono Consumer.exe
Press any key to quit.
<?xml version="1.0" ?><stock name="JAVA">
  <price>43.013618508808</price><offer>43.056632127317</offer>
<up>false</up>
</stock>
<?xml version="1.0" ?><stock name="JAVA">
  <price>43.393728710927</price><offer>43.437122439637</offer>
<up>true</up>
</stock>
<?xml version="1.0" ?><stock name="JAVA">
  <price>43.312535068644</price><offer>43.355847603713</offer>
<up>false</up>
</stock>
<?xml version="1.0" ?><stock name="JAVA">
  <price>43.5794191622893</price><offer>43.622998581451</offer>
<up>true</up>
</stock>
<?xml version="1.0" ?><stock name="JAVA">
  <price>43.2687194039433</price><offer>43.3119881233472</offer>
<up>false</up>
</stock>
<?xml version="1.0" ?><stock name="JAVA">
  <price>43.035150760515</price><offer>43.078185911276</offer>
<up>false</up>
</stock>
<?xml version="1.0" ?><stock name="JAVA">
  <price>42.756790699982</price><offer>42.7995474906824</offer>
<up>false</up>
</stock>
```

As this simple example showed, connecting to ActiveMQ from C# is as simple (and practically the same) as from Java. Now let's see what options C++ developers have if they want to use messaging with ActiveMQ.

9.3.2   *Writing a C++ consumer (using the CMS API)*

Although the focus of software developers in recent years has primarily been on languages with virtual machines (such as Java and C#) and dynamic languages (Ruby, for example), a lot of development is still done in "native" C and C++ languages. Similar to NMS, *CMS* (*C++ Messaging Service*) represents a standard C++ interface for communicating with messaging systems.

ActiveMQ-CPP, the current implementation of the CMS interface, supports both OpenWire and STOMP. Although having STOMP in a toolbox could be useful in some use cases, we believe most C++ developers will take the OpenWire route for its better performances.

CMS is also one of the ActiveMQ subprojects, and you can find more info on how to obtain and build it on its homepage: http://mng.bz/X8UZ. In the rest of this section, we'll focus on the simple asynchronous consumer example that comes with the distribution. You can find the original example in the following file: src/examples/consumers/SimpleAsyncConsumer.cpp. We'll modify it to listen and consume messages from one of our stock portfolio topics. Since the overall example is too long for the book format, we'll divide it into a few code listings and explain it section by section.

First of all, our `SimpleAsyncConsumer` class implements two interfaces:

- `MessageListener`—Used to receive asynchronously delivered messages
- `ExceptionListener`—Used to handle connection exceptions

```
class SimpleAsyncConsumer : public ExceptionListener,
                            public MessageListener
```

The `MessageListener` interface defines the `onMessage()` method, which handles received messages. In our example, it boils down to printing and acknowledging the message, as shown next.

Listing 9.15   Implementation of message listener in C++

```
virtual void onMessage( const Message* message ){

    static int count = 0;

    try
    {
        count++;
        const TextMessage* textMessage =
            dynamic_cast< const TextMessage* >( message );
        string text = "";

        if( textMessage != NULL ) {
            text = textMessage->getText();
        } else {
            text = "NOT A TEXTMESSAGE!";
        }

        if( clientAck ) {
            message->acknowledge();
        }
```

```
        printf( "Message #%d Received: %s\n", count, text.c_str() );
    } catch (CMSException& e) {
        e.printStackTrace();
    }
}
```

The `ExceptionListener` interface defines the `onException()` method called when connection problems are detected:

```
virtual void onException( const CMSException& ex AMQCPP_UNUSED) {
    printf("CMS Exception occurred.  Shutting down client.\n");
}
```

As you can see, thus far CMS mimics the JMS API completely, which is great for developers who want to create cross-platform solutions.

The complete code related to creating and running a consumer is located in the `runConsumer()` method. Here, we have all the classic elements of creating a consumer with the appropriate message listener as we've seen in our Java examples. We create connection, session, and destination objects first, and then instantiate a consumer and add this object as a message listener. Take a look at the following listing.

Listing 9.16   Creating message consumer in C++

```
void runConsumer() {

  try {

    ActiveMQConnectionFactory* connectionFactory =          Define
      new ActiveMQConnectionFactory( brokerURI );           connection
                                                            factory

    connection = connectionFactory->createConnection();  <--- Create connection
    delete connectionFactory;
    connection->start();                          <--- Start connection

    connection->setExceptionListener(this);                 Create
                                                            session
    if( clientAck ) {
        session = connection->createSession( Session::CLIENT_ACKNOWLEDGE );
    } else {
        session = connection->createSession( Session::AUTO_ACKNOWLEDGE );
    }

    if( useTopic ) {                               <--- Create destination
        destination = session->createTopic( destURI );
    } else {
        destination = session->createQueue( destURI );
    }

    consumer = session-                                     Create
     ->createConsumer( destination );                      consumer
    consumer->setMessageListener( this );                   Add message
                                                            listener
  } catch (CMSException& e) {
      e.printStackTrace();
  }
}
```

All that's left to be done is to initialize everything and run the application as shown next.

Listing 9.17   Implementation of C++ example's main method

```
int main(int argc AMQCPP_UNUSED, char* argv[] AMQCPP_UNUSED) {

    std::cout << "=====================================================\n";
    std::cout << "Starting the example:" << std::endl;
    std::cout << "-----------------------------------------------------\n";

    std::string brokerURI =
        "tcp://127.0.0.1:61616"
        "?wireFormat=openwire"                ←— Use OpenWire protocol
        "&transport.useAsyncSend=true"
        "&wireFormat.tightEncodingEnabled=true";

    std::string destURI = "STOCKS.JAVA";          ←┐ Use stock portfolio
                                                   ┘ example topic
    bool useTopics = true;

    bool clientAck = false;

    SimpleAsyncConsumer consumer( brokerURI, destURI, useTopics,
      clientAck );

    consumer.runConsumer();

    std::cout << "Press 'q' to quit" << std::endl;
    while( std::cin.get() != 'q') {}

    std::cout << "-----------------------------------------------------\n";
    std::cout << "Finished with the example." << std::endl;
    std::cout << "=====================================================\n";
```

As you can see, we've used the OpenWire protocol in this example. Additionally, you can see that we've configured it to listen on our stock portfolio topics. If you want to try the STOMP connector, just change the value of the wireFormat query parameter to stomp.

Now, we can rebuild the project with

```
$ make
```

and run the example with

```
$ src/examples/simple_async_consumer
=====================================================
Starting the example:
-----------------------------------------------------
Press 'q' to quit
Message #1 Received: <?xml version="1.0" ?><stock name="JAVA">
  <price>54.330145466802</price><offer>54.384475612269</offer>
<up>false</up>
</stock>
Message #2 Received: <?xml version="1.0" ?><stock name="JAVA">
  <price>54.6389203072939</price><offer>54.693559227601</offer>
<up>true</up>
</stock>
```

```
Message #3 Received: <?xml version="1.0" ?><stock name="JAVA">
  <price>54.8289342706613</price><offer>54.883763204931</offer>
<up>true</up>
</stock>
Message #4 Received: <?xml version="1.0" ?><stock name="JAVA">
  <price>54.419095885291</price><offer>54.473514981176</offer>
<up>false</up>
</stock>
Message #5 Received: <?xml version="1.0" ?><stock name="JAVA">
  <price>53.955955907643</price><offer>54.009911863551</offer>
<up>false</up>
</stock>
Message #6 Received: <?xml version="1.0" ?><stock name="JAVA">
  <price>53.740940545121</price><offer>53.794681485666</offer>
<up>false</up>
</stock>
Message #7 Received: <?xml version="1.0" ?><stock name="JAVA">
  <price>54.244855189889</price><offer>54.2991000450797</offer>
<up>true</up>
</stock>
Message #8 Received: <?xml version="1.0" ?><stock name="JAVA">
  <price>53.724159915599</price><offer>53.777884075514</offer>
<up>false</up>
</stock>
Message #9 Received: <?xml version="1.0" ?><stock name="JAVA">
  <price>54.0915041625709</price><offer>54.14559566673</offer>
<up>true</up>
</stock>
Message #10 Received: <?xml version="1.0" ?><stock name="JAVA">
  <price>53.9600727853630</price><offer>54.014032858148</offer>
<up>false</up>
</stock>
```

Thus far we've seen how STOMP can be used to create simple messaging clients for practically any programming language. We've also seen how NMS and CMS subprojects help create more complex, JMS-like APIs for environments that deserve this kind of support. Now let's focus on another important development platform—the web. We'll explore the APIs ActiveMQ provides to web developers, and how they can be used to create next-generation web applications.

9.4 Messaging on the web with ActiveMQ

In the last few years we witnessed the rebirth of the web, usually called *Web 2.0*. The transformation is taking place in two particular aspects of software development:

- *Service-oriented architecture (SOA* and *web services* play an increasingly important role for many software projects. Users demand that software functionality be exposed through some kind of web service interface. One way to achieve this is to introduce RESTful principles to your application architecture, which allows you to expose your application resources over HTTP. ActiveMQ follows these principles by exposing its resources through its *REST API,* as we'll see in a moment.

- It's easy to say that *Asynchronous JavaScript and XML (*Ajax*)* revolutionized web development as we knew it. The possibility of achieving asynchronous communication between the browser and the server (without page reloading) opened many doors for web developers, and provided a way for web applications to become much more interactive. Naturally, you can use ActiveMQ *Ajax API* to communicate directly with the broker from your web browser, which adds even more asynchronous communication possibilities between clients (JavaScript browser code) and servers (back-end server applications).

So with REST and Ajax APIs in its toolbox, ActiveMQ is well suited to be a good player in the web arena. Using asynchronous messaging with standard web tools provides whole new programming concepts to web developers. In the rest of this section we'll explore REST and Ajax APIs. We'll see how you can send and receive messages from the command line by issuing GET and POST HTTP calls. We'll also describe the Ajax stock portfolio consumer that comes with the ActiveMQ distribution, which shows how asynchronous messaging and Ajax can be used together to provide real-time updates in web pages.

9.4.1 *Using the ActiveMQ REST API*

As you probably know, the term *REST* first appeared in Roy T. Fielding's PhD thesis *Architectural Styles and the Design of Network-based Software Architectures* (http://mng.bz/2Xa4). In this work, Fielding explains a collection of network architecture principles that define how to address and manage resources (in general) over the network. In simpler terms, if an application implements a RESTful architecture, it usually means that it exposes its resources using HTTP protocol and in a similar philosophy to those used on the World Wide Web.

The web is designed as a system for accessing documents over the internet. Every resource on the web (HTML page, image, video, and so forth) has a unique address defined by its URL (uniform resource locator). Resources are mutually interlinked and transferred between clients and servers using the HTTP protocol. The HTTP GET method is used to obtain the representation of the resource, and shouldn't be used to make any modifications to it. The POST method, on the other hand, is used to send data to be processed by the server. Apply these principles to your application's resources (destinations and messages in case of a JMS broker), and you've defined a RESTful API. Now let's see how ActiveMQ implements its REST API and how you can use it to send and receive messages from the broker. Figure 9.2 shows how you can connect a Java producer (sending messages using the OpenWire protocol) with almost any consumer that can use standard HTTP connections.

ActiveMQ comes with an embedded web server that starts at the same time your broker starts. This web server is used to provide all necessary web infrastructure for the ActiveMQ broker, including the REST API. By default, the demo application is started at

```
http://localhost:8161/demo
```

and it's also configured to expose the REST API at the following URL:

```
http://localhost:8161/demo/message
```

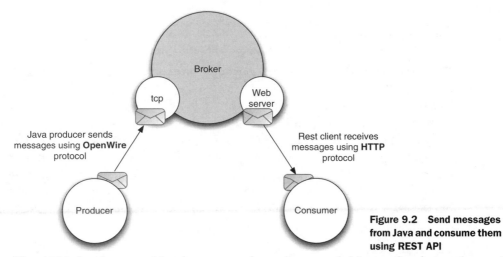

Figure 9.2 Send messages from Java and consume them using REST API

The API is implemented by the org.apache.activemq.web.MessageServlet servlet, and if you wish to configure an arbitrary servlet container to expose the ActiveMQ REST API, you have to define and map this servlet in an appropriate web.xml file (of course, all necessary dependencies should be in your classpath). The following example shows how to configure and map this servlet to the /message path as it is done in the demo application:

```
<servlet>
     <servlet-name>MessageServlet</servlet-name>
     <servlet-class>org.apache.activemq.web.MessageServlet</servlet-class>
     <load-on-startup>1</load-on-startup>
   </servlet>

   <servlet-mapping>
     <servlet-name>MessageServlet</servlet-name>
     <url-pattern>/message/*</url-pattern>
   </servlet-mapping>
```

When configured like this, broker destinations are exposed as relative paths under the defined URI. For example, the STOCKS.JAVA topic is mapped to the following URI:

```
http://localhost:8161/demo/message/STOCKS/JAVA?type=topic
```

As you can see, a path translation is in place, so destination name path elements (separated with .) are adjusted to the web URI philosophy where / is used as a separator. Also, we used the type parameter to define whether we want to access a queue or a topic.

Now we can use GET and POST requests to receive and send messages to destinations (retrospectively). We'll run some simple examples to demonstrate how you can use the REST API to communicate with your broker from the command line. For that we'll use two popular programs that can make HTTP GET and POST method requests from the command line. First we'll use GNU Wget (http://mng.bz/DMf6), a popular tool for retrieving files using HTTP, to subscribe to the desired destination:

```
$ wget -O message.txt \
--save-cookies cookies.txt --load-cookies cookies.txt \
--keep-session-cookies \
http://localhost:8161/demo/message/STOCKS/JAVA?type=topic
```

With this command, we instructed wget to receive the next available message from the
STOCKS.JAVA topic and to save it to the message.txt file. You may also notice that we
keep the HTTP sessions alive between wget calls by saving and sending cookies back to
the server. This is important because the actual consumer API used by the Message-
Servlet is stored in the session. So if you try to receive every message using a new session, you'll spawn a lot of consumers unnecessarily and your requests will probably be
left hanging. Also, if you plan to use multiple REST consumers, it's advisable to set the
prefetch size to 1, just as we did with STOMP consumers. To do that, you have to set
the consumer.prefetchSize initialization parameter value of your message servlet.
The following example shows how to achieve that:

```
<servlet>
  <servlet-name>MessageServlet</servlet-name>
  <servlet-class>
    org.apache.activemq.web.MessageServlet
  </servlet-class>
  <load-on-startup>1</load-on-startup>
  <init-param>
    <param-name>destinationOptions</param-name>
    <param-value>consumer.prefetchSize=1</param-value>
  </init-param>
</servlet>
```

Now, it's time to send some messages to our topic. For that we'll use cUrl (http://
curl.haxx.se/), a popular command-line tool for transferring files using the HTTP
POST method. Take a look at the following command:

```
$ curl -d "body=message" \
  http://localhost:8161/demo/message/STOCKS/JAVA?type=topic
```

Here we've used the -d switch to specify that we want to POST data to the server. As
you can see, the actual content of the message is passed as the body parameter. The
sent message should be received by our previously run consumer.

   This simple example shows how easy it is to use the REST API to do asynchronous
messaging even from the command line. But generally, you should give STOMP a try
(if it's available for your platform) before falling back to the REST API, because it
allows you more flexibility and is much more messaging-oriented.

9.4.2   *Using the ActiveMQ Ajax API*

As we said earlier, the option to communicate with the web server asynchronously
changed how developers thought about web applications. In this section we'll see how
web developers can embrace asynchronous programming even further, by communicating with message brokers directly from JavaScript.

First of all, we should configure our web server to support the ActiveMQ Ajax API. Similar to the `MessageServlet` class used for implementing the REST API, ActiveMQ provides an `AjaxServlet` that implements Ajax support. Figure 9.3 shows how the `AjaxServlet` serves as a mediator between the web browser and the broker. So the JavaScript clients communicate with the servlet, which connects to the broker as a standard JMS client.

The following example shows how to configure it in your web application's WEB-INF/web.xml file:

```xml
<servlet>
  <servlet-name>AjaxServlet</servlet-name>
  <servlet-class>org.apache.activemq.web.AjaxServlet</servlet-class>
</servlet>

<servlet-mapping>
  <servlet-name>AjaxServlet</servlet-name>
  <url-pattern>/amq/*</url-pattern>
</servlet-mapping>
```

Of course, in order to make it work properly you have to put ActiveMQ in your web application's classpath. Now that we have a server side configured and a servlet listening to the requests submitted to the URIs starting with /amq/, we can proceed to implementing the client side of our Ajax application.

First of all, we have to include the amq.js script, which includes all necessary JavaScript libraries for us. Also, we have to point the `amq.uri` variable to the URI our Ajax servlet listens to. The following snippet shows how to achieve this:

```html
<script type="text/javascript" src="amq/amq.js"></script>
<script type="text/javascript">amq.uri='/amq';</script>
```

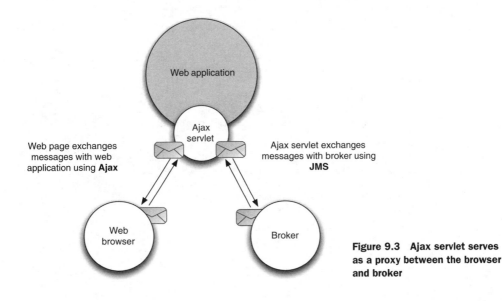

Figure 9.3 **Ajax servlet serves as a proxy between the browser and broker**

The amq.js script defines a JavaScript object named amq, which provides an API for us to send messages and subscribe to ActiveMQ destinations. The following example shows how to send a simple message from our Ajax application:

```
amq.sendMessage("topic://TEST", "message");
```

It can't be much simpler than this: all you have to do is call a sendMessage() method and provide a destination and the text of the message to be sent.

If you wish to subscribe to a certain destination (or multiple destinations), you have to register a callback function that will be called every time a new message is available. This is done with the addListener() method of the amq object, which in addition to a callback function accepts a destination to subscribe to and ID that makes further handling of this listener possible.

The ActiveMQ demo application comes with the stock portfolio example we've used throughout the book, adopted to the web environment. The example contains a servlet that publishes market data and a web page that uses the Ajax API to consume that data. Using this example, we'll show how to consume messages using the Ajax API. Let's take a look at the code shown in the following listing.

Listing 9.18   Consume messages from JavaScript using Ajax API

```
var priceHandler =
{
  _price: function(message)                          Define poll
  {                                                   handler function
    if (message != null) {

      var price = parseFloat(message.getAttribute('bid'))
      var symbol = message.getAttribute('stock')
      var movement = message.getAttribute('movement')
      if (movement == null) {
        movement = 'up'
      }

      var row = document.getElementById(symbol)
      if (row) {
      // perform portfolio calculations
      var value = asFloat(find(row, 'amount')) * price
      var pl = value - asFloat(find(row, 'cost'))

      // now let's update the HTML DOM
      find(row, 'price').innerHTML = fixedDigits(price, 2)
      find(row, 'value').innerHTML = fixedDigits(value, 2)
      find(row, 'pl').innerHTML    = fixedDigits(pl, 2)
      find(row, 'price').className = movement
      find(row, 'pl').className    = pl >= 0 ? 'up' : 'down'
      }
    }
  }
};
```

```
function portfolioPoll(first)
{
   if (first)
   {
     amq.addListener('stocks','topic://STOCKS.*',
       priceHandler._price);                          ◁── Register poll
   }                                                        handler function
}

amq.addPollHandler(portfolioPoll);
```

For starters, we've defined a JavaScript object named `priceHandler` with the `_price()` function we'll use to handle messages. This function finds an appropriate page element and updates its value (or changes its class to show whether it's a positive or negative change). Now we have to register this function to listen to the stock topics. As you can see, we've named our listener `stocks`, set it to listen to all topics in the `STOCKS` name hierarchy, and defined `_price()` as a callback function. You can later remove this subscription (if you wish) by calling the `removeListener()` function of the `amq` object and providing the specified ID (`stocks` in this case).

Now we're ready to run this example. First we're going to start the portfolio publisher servlet by entering the following URL in the browser:

```
http://localhost:8161/demo/portfolioPublish?count=1&refresh=2
&stocks=IBMW&stocks=BEAS&stocks=MSFT&stocks=SUNW
```

The Ajax consumer example is located at the following address:

```
http://localhost:8161/demo/portfolio/portfolio.html
```

After starting it, you can expect a page that looks similar to the one shown in figure 9.4.

The page will dynamically update as messages come to the broker. This simple example shows how Ajax applications can benefit from asynchronous messaging, thus taking dynamic web pages to a whole new level.

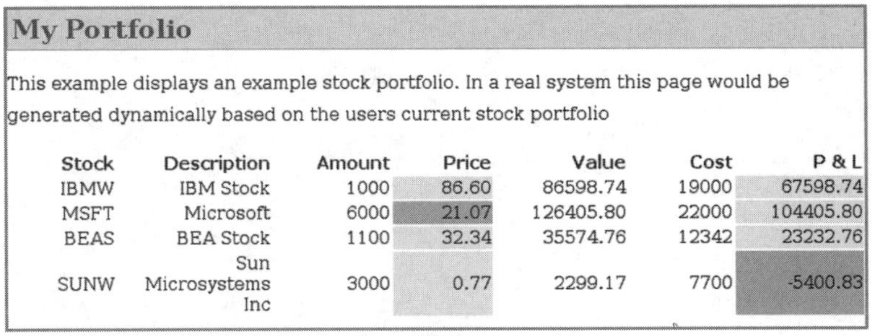

My Portfolio

This example displays an example stock portfolio. In a real system this page would be generated dynamically based on the users current stock portfolio

Stock	Description	Amount	Price	Value	Cost	P & L
IBMW	IBM Stock	1000	86.60	86598.74	19000	67598.74
MSFT	Microsoft	6000	21.07	126405.80	22000	104405.80
BEAS	BEA Stock	1100	32.34	35574.76	12342	23232.76
SUNW	Sun Microsystems Inc	3000	0.77	2299.17	7700	-5400.83

Figure 9.4   Sample output of the Ajax API demo: the look of the web page after a while. Different colors indicate stock movement.

9.5   *Summary*

In this chapter we covered a wide range of technologies (protocols and APIs) which allow developers to connect to ActiveMQ from practically any development platform used today. This implies that ActiveMQ can be seen not only as a JMS broker, but as a whole development platform as well, especially when you add Enterprise Integration Patterns (EIP) to the mix (as we'll see in chapter 13). This wide range of connectivity options makes ActiveMQ an excellent tool for integrating applications written on different platforms in an asynchronous way.

With this chapter, we've finished part 3 of the book, in which we described how you can employ ActiveMQ in your projects. The final part of the book is called "Advanced Features in ActiveMQ" and will dive into a wide range of topics, such as broker topologies, performance tuning, monitoring, and so on. Now that you know all the basics of ActiveMQ, this final part should teach you how to use your ActiveMQ broker instances to the maximum.

We'll start by continuing our discussion started in chapter 3 regarding network connectors. The following chapter discusses various broker topologies and how they can help you implement functionalities such as load balancing and high availability.

Part 4

Advanced features in ActiveMQ

In some environments, it's necessary to utilize multiple brokers in a federated manner. This requires that we understand the various topologies supported by ActiveMQ. And when building applications that utilize messaging, it quickly becomes evident that more advanced features are needed, such as various administrative capabilities, tuning to support larger scale, and monitoring of different aspects of ActiveMQ.

Part 4 presents the enterprise features in ActiveMQ including high availability, networks of ActiveMQ brokers, and scalability, as well as many advanced broker and client features, all of which become necessary in larger enterprise applications. We then move on to discuss performance tuning with ActiveMQ, including the optimization of message producers and consumers. We finish this part with a chapter dedicated to administration and monitoring techniques for ActiveMQ.

Deploying ActiveMQ in the enterprise

10

This chapter covers

- Configuring ActiveMQ for high availability
- Understanding networks of brokers
- Scaling the ActiveMQ via configuration

The first three parts of this book covered how to use ActiveMQ as a messaging and integration platform. This chapter is the first to cover advanced ActiveMQ configuration, so if you're new to messaging or ActiveMQ, you should read the first three parts before reading this chapter.

This chapter will focus on the enterprise deployment of ActiveMQ message brokers, the type of deployments that are used in production environments where applications need to be available without message loss at a 24/7 service level. This chapter will demonstrate how to configure ActiveMQ for high availability so that an ActiveMQ deployment can survive machine or network loss.

For many organizations, application deployment is global, spanning multiple offices across large geographical areas. So we'll show you how ActiveMQ can be

257

used as a reliable global information conduit by using the technique of *store and forward* to pass messages from one geographic location to another.

Finally, we'll examine deploying ActiveMQ for massively concurrent applications, where large numbers of concurrent connections and queues are a requirement. We'll examine the different configuration and deployment options of ActiveMQ and look at the pros and cons for each one.

10.1　*Configuring ActiveMQ for high availability*

When an application is deployed into a production environment, it's important to plan for disaster scenarios—network failures, hardware failures, software failures, or power outages. ActiveMQ can be deployed defensively, to prevent such failures from inhibiting your application in production. Typically you need to run multiple ActiveMQ brokers on different machines, so that if one machine or one ActiveMQ broker fails, a secondary one can take over. Using ActiveMQ terminology, such deployments are known as *master/slave*, where one broker takes the role of the primary or master and there are one or more slave brokers that wait for the master to fail, at which point one will take over to become the new master. The ActiveMQ Java and C++ clients provide a built-in failover transfer, so that they'll automatically switch over from the failed master to the new master without message loss.

ActiveMQ currently supports two different types of master/slave configurations: *shared nothing*, where each ActiveMQ broker has its own unique message storage, and *shared storage*, where multiple ActiveMQ brokers can connect to the shared message store (a relational database or a shared file system) but only one broker will be active at a time. We'll discuss these deployment scenarios in this section.

10.1.1　*Shared nothing master/slave*

A *shared nothing master/slave* refers to a deployment where both the master and the slave have their own message storage. This is probably the easiest option to use for providing high availability of message brokers. A slave is configured to connect to the master broker. Whereas the slave needs a special configuration denoting its special state, the master broker needs no special configuration. There is some optional configuration for the master, which we'll cover at the end of this section.

All message commands (messages, acknowledgements, subscriptions, transactions, and so on) are replicated from the master to the slave as depicted in figure 10.1. Such replication takes place before the master acts upon any command it receives.

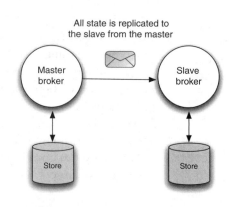

Figure 10.1　A shared nothing master/slave ActiveMQ broker deployment

A slave broker will connect to the master at startup, so ideally the master should be running first. The slave broker won't start any transports (so it can't accept any client or network connections) and won't itself initiate any network connections unless the master fails. A failure of the master is detected by loss of connectivity from the slave to the master.

A shared nothing master/slave configuration does impose some extra overhead on message processing, but this overhead is small considering the benefit that it provides. When a message producer sends a persistent message to the master, it'll wait for a receipt from the master until it can send the next message. The master won't send the receipt until it has replicated the message to the slave, and in turn wait for the slave to finish its processing of the message (which will typically involve the slave persisting it to storage). The master will then process the message (persist it to storage and dispatch it to any interested consumers) before sending back a receipt to the message producer that it has successfully processed the message.

When a master broker fails, the slave has two choices:

- *Shut itself down*—Hence, it's only acting to preserve the state of the master. In this scenario, an administrator will typically have to manually configure the slave to be the master, and configure a new message broker to take the role of the slave.
- *Start up its transports and initiate any network connections*—Hence, the slave automatically becomes the new master.

If the slave broker takes over the role of the master broker, all clients using the failover transport will fail over to the new master. For JMS clients to ActiveMQ, the default transport used by the client's connection is the failover transport and is typically configured to be able to connect to both the master and the slave, as shown:

failover://(tcp://masterhost:61616,tcp://slavehost:61616)?randomize=false

ActiveMQ's shared nothing master/slave configuration has some limitations. A master will only replicate its active state from the time the slave connects to it. So if a client is using the master before the slave is attached, any messages or acknowledgements that have been processed by the master before the slave has attached itself can potentially be lost if the master then fails. You can avoid this by setting the waitForSlave property on the master configuration. This property forces the master to not accept any client connections until a slave broker has attached to it. Other limitations are that a master is allowed to have only one slave, and that a slave itself can't have another slave.

If you already have a running broker that you want to use in a shared nothing master/slave configuration, it's recommended that you first stop that broker, copy all message store files (usually in the data directory) to the slave machine, and, after configuring, restart the master broker and the slave broker. You also need to do the same when introducing a new slave after a master has failed. The shared nothing broker configuration should only be used when you want to ensure that you don't lose messages for your application, but you can afford to have some down time to attach a new slave after the master has failed and the old slave has become the master.

WHEN TO USE SHARED NOTHING MASTER/SLAVE

You should use a shared nothing master/slave configuration in production environments when some down time on failure is acceptable. Manual intervention by an administrator will be necessary after a master fails, as it would be advisable to set up and configure a new slave for the new master after the old master has failed.

Having covered the theory, let's look at how to configure a shared nothing master/slave.

CONFIGURING SHARED NOTHING MASTER/SLAVE

Designating that a broker is a slave is straightforward. You configure a `master-Connector` service that accepts the following parameters:

- *remoteURI*—The URI on which the master broker is listening
- *userName*—Optional username if the master has authentication configured
- *password*—Optional password if the master has authentication configured

The following example of slave configuration shows how to configure the slave broker with a `masterConnector`:

```
<services>
  <masterConnector remoteURI="tcp://remotehost:62001"
    userName="Rob" password="Davies"/>
</services>
```

You'd normally configure the slave to have duplicate transport and network configurations as the master broker.

One additional optional property can be useful for a slave in a shared nothing configuration: the `shutdownOnMasterFailure` property. When this property is enabled, the slave will safely shut down, ensuring no message loss, allowing an administrator to manual set up a new slave. The slave broker properties are shown in table 10.1.

Table 10.1 Slave broker properties

Property name	Default value	Description
shutdownOnMasterFailure	false	The slave will shut down when the master does.

You can designate a broker to be a master without any additional configuration; some optional properties may be useful. The master broker properties are shown in table 10.2.

Table 10.2 Master broker properties

Property name	Default value	Description
waitForSlave	false	The master won't allow any client or network connections until a slave has attached itself.
shutdownOnSlaveFailure	false	If true, the master will shut down if a slave becomes detached. This ensures that a slave is only ever in sync with the master.

In addition to the shared nothing master/slave configuration, ActiveMQ also offers a shared storage master/slave configuration.

10.1.2 *Shared storage master/slave*

Whereas the shared nothing master/slave offers the ability for brokers to remain independent of one another, the *shared storage master/slave* allows many brokers to share the storage mechanism, but only one broker can be live at any given time. Using a shared resource storage will ensure that in the event of a master broker failure, no manual intervention will be required to maintain the integrity of your application in the event of an additional failure. Another benefit is that there's no limitation on the number of slave brokers that can be active at one time with shared storage master/slave.

The ActiveMQ shared storage master/slave configuration comes in two flavors: a relational database or a file system–based storage.

SHARED DATABASE MASTER/SLAVE

If you're already using a relational database for message storage, then providing broker high availability is extremely straightforward. When an ActiveMQ message broker uses a relational database, it grabs an exclusive lock on a table to ensure that no other ActiveMQ broker can access the database at the same time. This is due to the fact that the state of a broker is held in the storage mechanism and is only designed to be used by a single broker at a time. The shared database master/slave configuration is depicted in figure 10.2.

If you're running more than one broker that's trying to access the same database, only the first broker to connect will grab the lock. Any subsequent brokers will

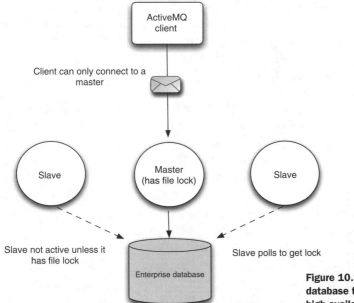

Figure 10.2 Using a shared relational database for ActiveMQ master/slave high availability

poll until they can get access to the lock. While in this polling state, the ActiveMQ broker assumes that it's a slave, so it won't start any transport connections or network connections.

You can run multiple brokers, and only one broker will ever be the master at any given time. All the brokers in this configuration can use the same configuration file, which makes setup easy. If a master broker fails, a slave broker will be able to grab the lock on the database and will then take over as the new master broker. Since all the ActiveMQ brokers are using the same shared database, no additional manual intervention is required to introduce new brokers or remove existing ones.

WHEN TO USE SHARED DATABASE MASTER/SLAVE
Shared database master/slave is an ideal configuration if you're already using an enterprise relational database. Although generally slower than a shared nothing configuration, it requires no additional configuration, and there are no limitations on the number of slave brokers that can be run or when they can be run.

If access to an enterprise database isn't an option, or performance is a consideration, you can use a shared file system instead, where conceptually ActiveMQ brokers can be set up in the same way as the shared database.

SHARED FILE SYSTEM MASTER/SLAVE
An alternative to using a shared database is to use a shared file system. The setup is similar to the shared database master/slave, in that no additional configuration of an ActiveMQ broker is required. Also, there are no limitations on the number of slaves that can be run or when they can be introduced into the system. It's recommended that you use the KahaDB message store, but use an underlying shared file system for the message storage. When the KahaDB message store starts, it'll attempt to grab a file lock, to prevent any other broker from accessing the file-based message store at the same time. The shared file system master/slave configuration is shown in figure 10.3.

Just like the shared database master/slave configuration, there's no restriction on the number of slaves that can be started. The first broker to get the lock on the file store automatically becomes the master, and any brokers that try to connect after that automatically become slaves.

There are some technical restrictions regarding where you can run a shared file system master/slave configuration. The shared file system requires the semantics of a distributed shared file lock. So if you're not using a storage area network (SAN), there are some alternatives such as Network File System (NFS)—available on Mac OS X, OpenVMS, Microsoft Windows (from third parties), Solaris, and AS/400. If you're using Fedora or RedHat Enterprise (5.3 and above), it's recommended you use the Global File System (GFS) 2, which requires a cluster locking protocol, such as *dlm*, the distributed lock manager, which is a Linux kernel module.

WHEN TO USE SHARED FILE SYSTEM MASTER/SLAVE
Using a shared file system is probably the best solution for providing high availability for ActiveMQ to date. It combines the high throughput of KahaDB and the simplicity that you get from using a shared resource. KahaDB is only limited by the performance

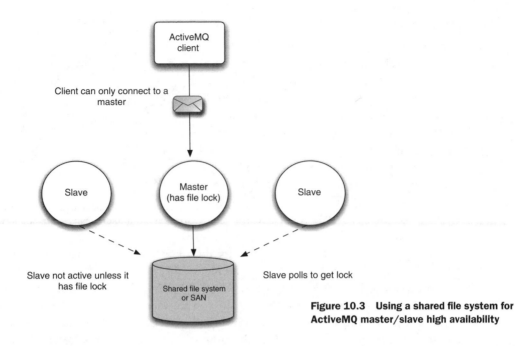

Figure 10.3   Using a shared file system for ActiveMQ master/slave high availability

of the underlying shared file system. The only caveat is that you're restricted to environments that support distributed locking on a shared file system.

So ActiveMQ provides features to make it resilient to failures in production using the shared nothing master/slave and the shared storage master/slave configurations. You should now have a good understanding of the different ActiveMQ high availability options and be able to choose the best configuration for your application's needs.

The next section will examine how to use ActiveMQ to reliably pass messages from broker to broker to support applications that need to use messaging to communicate across geographically distributed locations.

10.2   How ActiveMQ passes messages across a network of brokers

ActiveMQ supports the concept of linking ActiveMQ message brokers together into different topologies, or *networks of brokers* as they're known. Often it's a requirement that geographically dispersed applications need to communicate in a reliable way. This is a situation where having a centralized broker architecture into which all the clients connect isn't the optimal messaging paradigm.

Through the rest of this section, the ActiveMQ store and forward concept will be examined in detail. We'll look at how brokers discover each other in a network and how to configure an ActiveMQ broker to cooperate in a network.

10.2.1 Store and forward

ActiveMQ networks use the concept of *store and forward*, whereby messages are always stored in the local broker before being forwarded across the network to another broker. This means that if messages can't be delivered due to connectivity issues, when the connection is reestablished, a broker will be able to send any undelivered messages across the network connection to the remote broker. By default, a network only operates in a unidirectional manner and logically pushes messages across its network connection, as shown in figure 10.4.

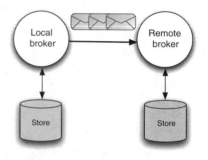

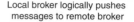
Local broker logically pushes messages to remote broker

Figure 10.4   Passing messages between ActiveMQ brokers using store and forward

When a network is established from a local broker to a remote broker, the remote broker will pass information containing all its durable and active consumers' destinations to the local broker. The local broker uses this information to determine what messages the remote broker is interested in and forward them to the remote broker. It's possible to define filters on the network connection and to always include or exclude messages for a particular destination—we'll cover this in the configuration section later in this chapter.

Having networks operate in one direction allows for networks to be configured for message passing in a one-way fashion. If you want networks to be bidirectional, you can either configure the remote broker with a network connector to point to the local broker, or configure a network connector to be duplex so it sends messages in both directions.

Suppose you have a deployment scenario where you have many supermarkets that need to connect to a back office order system. It would be hard to configure new supermarkets and inflexible for the broker(s) at the back office to be aware of all the remote brokers in each new supermarket. Typically the back office brokers would be located behind a firewall with only a limited number of ports open to accept connections inward, as depicted in figure 10.5.

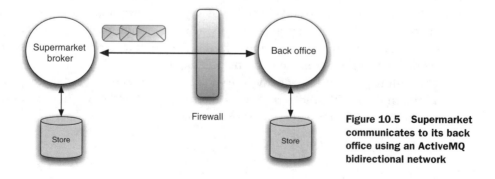

Figure 10.5   Supermarket communicates to its back office using an ActiveMQ bidirectional network

The diagram of the supermarket broker in figure 10.5 requires that the network connector be configured in duplex mode. The single network connection, established from the supermarket broker to the back office, would be able to pass messages in both directions and would behave in the same way as if the back office broker had established a normal network connection back to the supermarket broker.

The configuration for the supermarket broker would include configuration for the network connector that would look something like the following.

Listing 10.1 Configuring a store network broker

```
<networkConnectors>
  <networkConnector uri="static://(tcp://backoffice:61617)"
      name="bridge"
      duplex="true"
      conduitSubscriptions="true"
      decreaseNetworkConsumerPriority="false">
  </networkConnector>
</networkConnectors>
```

Please be aware that the order in which you specify the network connections and the persistence you use in the ActiveMQ broker configuration is important. Always configure networks, persistence, and transports in the following order:

1 *Networks*—They need to be established before the message store.

2 *Message store*—Should be configured before transports.

3 *Transports*—Should be the last in the broker configuration.

An example broker configuration in the correct order is shown next.

Listing 10.2 An example of the correct broker configuration order

```
<?xml version="1.0" encoding="UTF-8"?>
<beans xmlns="http://activemq.apache.org/schema/core">

 <broker brokerName="receiver" persistent="true" useJmx="true">
   <networkConnectors>
    <networkConnector uri="static:(tcp://backoffice:61617)"/>
   </networkConnectors>

   <persistenceAdapter>
     <kahaDB directory = "activemq-data"/>
   </persistenceAdapter>

   <transportConnectors>
    <transportConnector uri="tcp://localhost:62002"/>
   </transportConnectors>
 </broker>

</beans>
```

In large deployment scenarios, it makes sense to combine high availability and network configurations, as shown in figure 10.6.

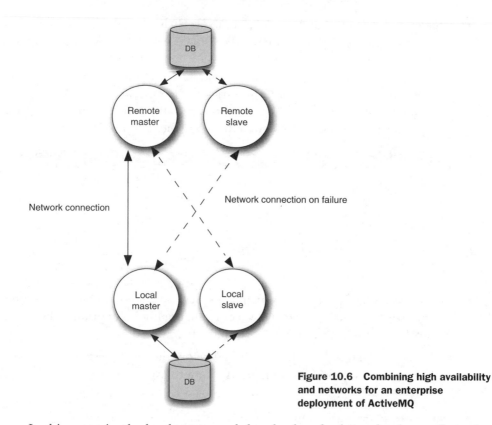

Figure 10.6   Combining high availability and networks for an enterprise deployment of ActiveMQ

In this scenario, the local master and slave brokers both need to be configured to create network connections to both the remote master and the slave to cater to the possibility of the remote master failing. Only when a slave becomes active (becomes the new master) will it start its transports and network connections.

If a network can't establish a connection to a remote broker (as in the case of a remote slave), or the network connection fails, the network will poll the connection until it can establish a connection.

In this section you've seen how store and forward works, as well as message passing over networks, with an example use case of supermarkets communicating with their back office systems. In the next section, we'll look at how brokers in a network discover each other.

10.2.2   *Network discovery*

When a network connection is established to a remote broker, that connection uses a discovery agent to locate the remote broker and (re-)establish that connection. Two main types of network discovery are provided with ActiveMQ:

1   *Dynamic*—Searches for brokers using multicast or rendezvous
2   *Static*—Configured with list of broker URLs with which to establish a connection

Using multicast discovery to create network connections is straightforward. When you start an ActiveMQ broker with a multicast transport on a network connector, it will search for another broker using IP multicast and establish a connection. A network configuration for multicast discovery is shown in the following listing.

Listing 10.3 A network connector using multicast

```
<networkConnectors>
     <networkConnector uri="multicast://default"/>
</networkConnectors>
```

The default name in the `multicast://` URI denotes the group to which the broker belongs. When using multicast discovery, it's strongly recommended that you use a unique group name so that your brokers don't connect to other application brokers unbeknownst to you. Not only can this lead to surprising results, but you can spend a great deal of time chasing a red herring!

There are a couple of limitations with multicast discovery, including the ability to control which brokers are discovered, and the fact that it's usually restricted to the discovery of brokers on the local network segment. This is because IP multicast doesn't extend through routers.

Most of the example configurations used previous to this chapter have used static discovery for establishing networks. Although they require a little more configuration and they wouldn't be suitable for a large number of networks, they're typically used for most deployments. Static discovery accepts a list of broker URIs and will try to connect to the remote brokers in the order they're determined in the list.

For example, to configure the local master broker and the local slave broker to connect to the remote master, but fail over to the remote slave (see figure 10.6), you'd configure the local brokers as shown next.

Listing 10.4 An example network connector

```
<networkConnectors>
  <networkConnector
    uri="static:(tcp://remote-master:61617,tcp://remote-slave:61617)"/>
</networkConnectors>
```

The static network discovery agent can be configured to control which frequency it will try to reestablish a connection with on failure. The configuration properties for the static transport are shown in table 10.3.

Table 10.3 Configuration properties for a static transport

Property name	Default value	Description
`initialReconnectDelay`	1000	The time in milliseconds before attempting to reconnect the network. *This is only used if* `useExponentialBackOff` *isn't enabled.*

Table 10.3   Configuration properties for a static transport *(continued)*

Property name	Default value	Description
maxReconnectDelay	30000	The maximum time in milliseconds that the network will wait before trying to establish a connection after failure. *This is only used if* use-ExponentialBackOff *is enabled.*
useExponentialBackOff	true	If this is enabled, the network will increase the time to wait between each failed attempt to establish a connection.
backOffMultiplier	2	Used in conjunction with useExponential-BackOff, the multiplier to use to increase the time to wait between each new attempt to establish a network connection.

A network connection will always try to establish a connection to a remote broker, so there's no concept of just giving up! You can set the configuration options for the static transport as part of the URI. An example of this is provided in the following listing.

Listing 10.5   An example of configuring the static transport

```
<networkConnectors>
  <networkConnector
    uri="static:(tcp://remote:61617)?useExponentialBackOff=false"/>
</networkConnectors>
```

The multicast and the static discovery mechanisms are shown here, along with some of the trade-offs between them. Many configuration options are available when setting up networks in ActiveMQ; these will be reviewed in more detail in the next section.

10.2.3   Network configuration

Networks by default rely on the remote broker to inform them when the broker is interested in their local messages. For existing active and new message consumers, the destination to which the message consumer is listening is propagated to the local broker's network connection. The local network connection will then subscribe on behalf of the remote broker's message consumers for messages to be forwarded across the network. In order for networks to function properly in a dynamic environment, the broker property advisorySupport needs to be enabled (it's possible to have a statically configured network without enabling advisories). ActiveMQ uses advisory messages to communicate state between brokers (more on this in chapter 14). Because of this, advisory messages are used to forward information about changing message consumers across broker networks as well as clients.

There may not be any active durable subscribers or consumers for an existing destination on the remote broker. So when the network connection is initialized to the remote broker, the remote broker will read through its message store for existing destinations and pass those to the local broker. Then the local broker can forward messages for those destinations as well.

It's important to note that a network will use the name of the broker to create a unique durable subscription proxy on behalf of a remote broker. Hence, if at a later point in time you change the name of the broker, you could lose messages over networks for durable topic subscribers. To avoid this, make sure to use a unique name for the `brokerName` attribute on the `<broker>` element. See the following for a brief example.

Listing 10.6 Make sure to use unique names for the broker

```
<broker xmlns="http://activemq.apache.org/schema/core"
  brokerName="brokerA"
  dataDirectory="${activemq.base}/data">
...
  <networkConnectors>
    <networkConnector
      name="brokerA-to-brokerB" uri="tcp://remotehost:61616" />
  </networkConnectors>
</broker>
```

With a basic understanding of how networks operate, you'll be able to comprehend some of the side effects if you change the default network configuration. A network has several important configuration properties, in addition to the duplex property.

NETWORK PROPERTY: DYNAMICONLY

All networks are dynamic only in the sense that they depend on advisories. The `dynamicOnly` option configures whether inactive durable subs are networked on a restart; with `dynamicOnly=true`, a networked durable sub will not be enabled till it is again activated. The `dynamicOnly` property is false by default.

NETWORK PROPERTY: PREFETCHSIZE

The `prefetchSize` effects message dispatch to forwarding consumers, but message acknowledgement always uses `INDIVIDUAL_ACK` mode on each message receipt. The default value for this property is 1000.

NETWORK PROPERTY: CONDUITSUBSCRIPTIONS

An ActiveMQ message broker will send a copy of a message to every interested consumer of which it's aware, even across networks. But this can be a problem, as the remote broker will send every message it receives to any of its interested consumers. So it's possible to end up with duplicate messages on the remote broker. The `conduitSubscriptions` property is used to inform the network connection that it should treat multiple matching destinations as a single destination to avoid this problem. The `conduitSubscriptions` property is true by default.

NETWORK PROPERTY: EXCLUDEDDESTINATIONS

You can tell the network to exclude certain destinations from passing messages across a network. This property can be used, for example, to prevent destinations that should only be used by local consumers from being propagated to a remote broker. Excluded destinations are denoted inside of the `<excludedDestinations>` element as either a `<queue>` or a `<topic>` element. Each one uses a `physicalName` attribute for the name of the queue or topic to exclude. You can combine a list of excluded destinations, and use wildcards to denote the names of the destinations to exclude, too.

Excluded destinations take priority over both the `<staticallyIncluded-Destinations>` element and `<dynamicallyIncludedDestinations>` element. So if you have matching destinations in either of those lists, they'll be excluded. Here's an example configuration using the `<excludedDestinations>` element.

Listing 10.7   Creating a list of excluded destinations

```
<networkConnectors>
  <networkConnector
    uri="static:(tcp://remote:61617)?useExponentialBackOff=false">
    <excludedDestinations>
      <queue physicalName="audit.queue-1"/>
      <queue physicalName="audit.queue-2"/>
      <queue physicalName="local.>"/>
      <topic physicalName="local.>"/>
    </excludedDestinations>
  </networkConnector>
</networkConnectors>
```

NETWORK PROPERTY: DYNAMICALLYINCLUDEDDESTINATIONS

You can ask the network to only pass messages to the remote broker for active message consumers that match the list of destinations for `dynamicallyIncludedDestinations`. The format is the same as the `excludedDestinations`. An empty list denotes that all messages will be passed to the remote broker, as long as they're not in the `excludedDestinations` list.

NETWORK PROPERTY: STATICALLYINCLUDEDDESTINATIONS

You can ask the network to only pass messages to the remote broker if they match the list of destinations for `staticallyIncludedDestinations`. The format is the same as the `excludedDestinations`; an example is provided in the following listing.

Listing 10.8   Setting options for included destinations

```
<networkConnectors>
  <networkConnector
    uri="static:(tcp://remote:61617)?useExponentialBackOff=false">
    <staticallyIncludedDestinations>
      <queue physicalName="management.queue-1"/>
      <queue physicalName="management.queue-2"/>
      <queue physicalName="global.>"/>
      <topic physicalName="global.>"/>
    </staticallyIncludedDestinations>
  </networkConnector>
</networkConnectors>
```

NETWORK PROPERTY: DECREASENETWORKCONSUMERPRIORITY

The `decreaseNetworkConsumerPriority` property influences the algorithm used to determine which message consumer for a queue should receive the next dispatched message. When enabled, it'll give a network consumer the lowest priority, meaning that messages from a local broker queue will only be sent to a remote broker if there are no local consumers or they're all busy. But the decrease in priority depends on the broker path. For example, if a consumer is two hops away from the broker it will be given the priority of –7, a consumer one hop away will be given the priority of –5, and a local consumer will be given priority 0. The `decreaseNetworkConsumerPriority` property is false by default.

NETWORK PROPERTY: NETWORKTTL

The `networkTTL` property denotes the maximum number of remote brokers a message can pass through before being discarded. This is useful for ensuring messages aren't forwarded needlessly, if you have a cyclic network of connected brokers. The default value for the `networkTTL` property is 1.

NETWORK PROPERTY: NAME

The default name for a network connector is *bridge*. It's a good idea to give this property a unique value when the broker is first configured, so it can be found easily from JMX.

There are cases when it makes sense to have more than one network connection between the same local and remote brokers. In this case, each connector requires a unique name. So why have more than one network connection between the two same brokers? It comes down to performance. A network connection uses a single transport connection, and if you're anticipating a heavy load across a network, it makes sense to have more than one transport connection. You do need to be careful that you don't get duplicate messages, so you have to set up the network connections with the appropriate filters. Using one for queues and one for topics can often improve throughput for general messaging use cases, as depicted in figure 10.7.

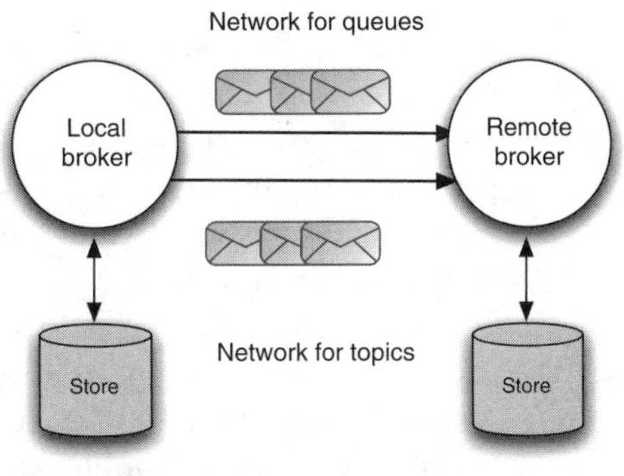

The corresponding configuration for figure 10.7 is shown next.

Figure 10.7   Using more than one network connection for message passing between ActiveMQ brokers

Listing 10.9   Setting options for included destinations

```
<networkConnectors>
  <networkConnector uri="static://(tcp://remotehost:61617)"
     name="queues_only"
     duplex="true"
   <excludedDestinations>
       <topic physicalName=">"/>
   </excludedDestinations>
  </networkConnector>
  <networkConnector uri="static://(tcp://remotehost:61617)"
```

```
        name="topics_only"
        duplex="true"
      <excludedDestinations>
          <queue physicalName=">"/>
      </excludedDestinations>
   </networkConnector>
</networkConnectors>
```

Having looked at how networks operate and how to configure them, we can now use this knowledge to help scale your ActiveMQ applications.

10.3 *Deploying ActiveMQ for large numbers of concurrent applications*

Scaling your applications that make use of ActiveMQ can take some time and require some diligence. In this section, we examine three techniques to help you with this task. We'll start with vertical scaling, where a single broker is used for thousands of connections and queues. Then we'll look at scaling to tens of thousands of connections by horizontally scaling your applications using networks. Finally we'll examine traffic partitioning, which will balance scaling and performance, but will add more complexity to your ActiveMQ application.

10.3.1 *Vertical scaling*

Vertical scaling is a technique used to increase the number of connections (and therefore load) that a single ActiveMQ broker can handle. By default, the ActiveMQ broker is designed to move messages as efficiently as possible to ensure low latency and good performance. But you can make some configuration decisions to ensure that the ActiveMQ broker can handle both a large number of concurrent connections and a large number of queues.

By default, ActiveMQ will use blocking I/O to handle transport connections. This results in a thread being used per connection. You can use nonblocking I/O on the ActiveMQ broker (and still use the default transport on the client) to reduce the number of threads used. Nonblocking I/O can be configured via the transport connector in the ActiveMQ configuration file. An example of this is shown next.

Listing 10.10 Configure the NIO transport connector

```
<broker>
  <transportConnectors>
    <transportConnector name="nio" uri="nio://localhost:61616"/>
  </<transportConnectors>
</broker>
```

In addition to using a thread per connection for blocking I/O, the ActiveMQ broker can use a thread for dispatching messages per client connection. You can tell ActiveMQ to use a thread pool instead by setting the system property named `org.apache.activemq.UseDedicatedTaskRunner` to false. Here's an example:

```
ACTIVEMQ_OPTS="-Dorg.apache.activemq.UseDedicatedTaskRunner=false"
```

Ensuring that the ActiveMQ broker has enough memory to handle lots of concurrent connections is a two-step process. First, you need to ensure that the JVM in which the ActiveMQ broker is started is configured with enough memory. This can be achieved using the -Xmx JVM option as shown:

```
ACTIVEMQ_OPTS="-Xmx1024M \
-Dorg.apache.activemq.UseDedicatedTaskRunner=false"
```

Second, be sure to configure an appropriate amount of the memory available to the JVM specifically for the ActiveMQ broker. This adjustment is made via the <system-Usage> element's limit attribute. A good rule of thumb is to begin at 512 MB as the minimum for an ActiveMQ broker with more than a few hundred active connections. If your testing proves that this isn't enough, bump it up from there. You can configure the memory limit in the ActiveMQ configuration file as shown in the following listing.

Listing 10.11 Setting the memory limit for the ActiveMQ broker

```
<systemUsage>
    <systemUsage>
        <memoryUsage>
            <memoryUsage limit="512 mb"/>
        </memoryUsage>
        <storeUsage>
            <storeUsage limit="10 gb" name="foo"/>
        </storeUsage>
        <tempUsage>
            <tempUsage limit="1 gb"/>
        </tempUsage>
    </systemUsage>
</systemUsage>
```

It's also advisable to reduce the CPU load per connection. If you're using the Open-Wire wire format, disable tight encoding, which can be CPU intense. Tight encoding can be disabled on a client-by-client basis using URI parameters. Here's an example:

```
String uri = "failover://(tcp://localhost:61616?"
  + wireFormat.tightEncodingEnabled=false)";
ConnectionFactory cf = new ActiveMQConnectionFactory(uri);
```

We've looked at some tuning aspects for scaling an ActiveMQ broker to handle thousands of connections. So now we can look at tuning the broker to handle thousands of queues.

The default queue configuration uses a separate thread for paging messages from the message store into the queue to be dispatched to interested message consumers. For a large number of queues, it's advisable to disable this by enabling the optimize-Dispatch property for all queues, as shown next.

Listing 10.12 Setting the `optimizeDispatch` property

```
<destinationPolicy>
      <policyMap>
        <policyEntries>
          <policyEntry queue=">" optimizedDispatch="true"
/>
        </policyEntries>
      </policyMap>
</destinationPolicy>
```

Note the use of the wildcard > character in listing 10.11, which denotes all queues recursively.

To ensure you can scale not only to thousands of connections, but also to tens of thousands of queues, use either a JDBC message store or the newer and much faster KahaDB message store. KahaDB is enabled by default in ActiveMQ.

So far we've looked at scaling connections, reducing thread usage, and selecting the right message store. An example configuration for ActiveMQ, tuned for scaling, is shown in the following listing.

Listing 10.13 Configuration for scaling

```
<broker xmlns="http://activemq.apache.org/schema/core"
  brokerName="amq-broker"
  dataDirectory="${activemq.base}/data">

  <persistenceAdapter>
    <kahaDB directory="${activemq.base}/data"
      journalMaxFileLength="32mb"/>
  </persistenceAdapter>

  <destinationPolicy>
    <policyMap>
      <policyEntries>
        <policyEntry queue="&gt;" optimizedDispatch="true"/>
      </policyEntries>
    </policyMap>
  </destinationPolicy>

  <systemUsage>
    <systemUsage>
      <memoryUsage>
        <memoryUsage limit="512 mb"/>
      </memoryUsage>
      <storeUsage>
        <storeUsage limit="10 gb" name="foo"/>
      </storeUsage>
      <tempUsage>
        <tempUsage limit="1 gb"/>
      </tempUsage>
    </systemUsage>
  </systemUsage>

  <transportConnectors>
```

```
    <transportConnector name="openwire" uri="nio://localhost:61616"/>
  </transportConnectors>
</broker>
```

Note the use of all the suggested items for tuning ActiveMQ. Such tuning isn't enabled in the default configuration file, so be sure to give yours some attention.

Having looked at how to scale an ActiveMQ broker, now it's time to look at using networks to increase horizontal scaling.

10.3.2 Horizontal scaling

In addition to scaling a single broker, you can use networks to increase the number of ActiveMQ brokers available for your applications. As networks automatically pass messages to connected brokers that have interested consumers, you can configure your clients to connect to a cluster of brokers, selecting one at random to connect to. This can be configured using a URI parameter as shown:

```
failover://(tcp://broker1:61616,tcp://broker2:61616)?randomize=true
```

In order to make sure that messages for queues or durable topic subscribers aren't orphaned on a broker, configure the networks to use dynamicOnly and a low network prefetchSize. Here's an example:

```
<networkConnector uri="static://(tcp://remotehost:61617)"
    name="bridge"
    dynamicOnly="true"
    prefetchSize="1"
</networkConnector>
```

Using networks for horizontal scaling does introduce more latency, because potentially messages have to pass through multiple brokers before being delivered to a consumer.

Another alternative deployment provides great scalability and performance, but requires more application planning. This hybrid solution, called *traffic partitioning*, combines vertical scaling of a broker with application-level splitting of destinations across different brokers.

10.3.3 Traffic partitioning

Client-side traffic partitioning is a hybrid of vertical and horizontal partitioning. Networks are typically not used, as the client application decides what traffic should go to which broker(s). The client application has to maintain multiple JMS connections, and decide which JMS connection should be used for which destinations.

The advantages of not directly using network connections is that you reduce the overhead of forwarding messages between brokers. You do need to balance that with the additional complexity that results in a typical application. A representation of using traffic partitioning can be seen in figure 10.8.

We've covered both vertical and horizontal scaling, as well as traffic partitioning. You should now have a good understanding of how to use ActiveMQ to provide connectivity for thousands of concurrent connections and tens of thousands of destinations.

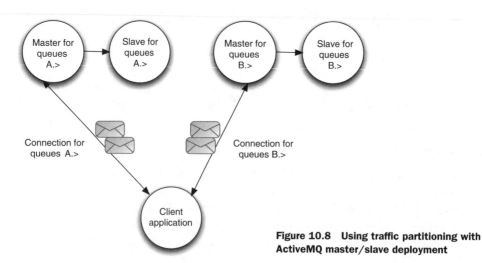

Figure 10.8   Using traffic partitioning with ActiveMQ master/slave deployment

10.4   *Summary*

In this chapter you've learned how to configure ActiveMQ brokers to provide high availability in production deployments, utilizing either a shared nothing or shared storage system. You've also learned options for failover for ActiveMQ clients and the performance trade-offs for having high availability configured for your applications.

We examined ActiveMQ for store and forward. This is used to provide global distribution of messages across wide area networks. We also demonstrated ActiveMQ configurations to filter out or filter in destinations that are required to be global for your application.

Finally we've seen how the configure ActiveMQ to scale for thousands of connections and tens of thousands of destinations.

Having read this chapter, you should now have a good understanding of how to deploy ActiveMQ to meet most deployment scenarios for any messaging application that you develop with ActiveMQ.

In the next chapter we'll look at advanced configuration of ActiveMQ to increase the flexibility of your applications that use ActiveMQ. We'll also examine some different ways to extend the functionality of ActiveMQ through the use of interceptors and Apache Camel.

11

ActiveMQ broker features in action

This chapter covers

- Using wildcards and composite destinations
- Utilizing advisory messages
- Understanding virtual topics and retroactive consumers
- Using ActiveMQ plug-ins
- An introduction to Apache Camel

In the previous chapter we looked at deploying ActiveMQ in enterprise environments: how to deploy ActiveMQ for high availability and for passing messages across geographically dispersed locations. In this chapter we'll look at some of the more advanced configuration options for the ActiveMQ message broker. We'll look at receiving messages from multiple destinations using wildcards, and sending messages to multiple destinations at the same time using composite destinations. We'll show how to actively listen for changes in the state of the ActiveMQ broker and for clients leaving and joining by using advisory messages. Other advanced features of the broker we'll look at include virtual topics, which let you broadcast messages over a topic, but have load balanced queues dispatch the messages. We'll also look at message redelivery and dead-letter queues, and how to extend the functionality of the ActiveMQ broker with interceptor plug-ins. Finally, we'll introduce Apache Camel, the popular integration framework, which can be embedded into an ActiveMQ broker to create a powerful integration engine and extend the flexibility and routing of ActiveMQ.

In the first section, we'll look at how to send and receive messages from more than one destination at a time, using composite destinations and wildcards.

11.1   Wildcards and composite destinations

In this section we'll look at two useful features of ActiveMQ: subscribing to multiple destinations using *wildcards*, and publishing to multiple destinations using *composite destinations*. ActiveMQ uses a special notation to denote a wildcard subscription; we'll describe that in the next section.

11.1.1   Consume from multiple destinations using wildcards

ActiveMQ supports the concept of destination hierarchies—where the name of a destination can be used to organize messages into hierarchies, an element in the name is delimited by a dot (.). Destination hierarchies apply to both topics and queues.

For example, if you had an application that subscribed to the latest results for sports on a Saturday afternoon, you could use the following naming convention for your topics:

<Sport>.<League>.<Team> -

For example, to subscribe to the latest result for a team called *Leeds* in an English football game, you'd subscribe to the topic: football.division1.leeds. Now Leeds plays both football and rugby, and for convenience, you'd want to see all results for Leeds for both football and rugby for the same `MessageConsumer`. This is where wildcards are useful.

Three special characters are reserved for destination names:

- .   A dot, used to separate elements in the destination name
- *   Used to match one element
- >   Matches one or all trailing elements

So to subscribe to the latest scores that all Leeds teams are playing in, you can subscribe to the topic named *.*.Leeds, as shown:

```
String brokerURI = ActiveMQConnectionFactory.DEFAULT_BROKER_URL;
ConnectionFactory connectionFactory =
  new ActiveMQConnectionFactory(brokerURI);
Connection connection = connectionFactory.createConnection();
connection.start();
Session session = connection.createSession(false, Session.AUTO_ACKNOWLEDGE);

Topic allLeeds = session.createTopic("*.*.Leeds");

MessageConsumer consumer = session.createConsumer(allLeeds);
Message result = consumer.receive();
```

If you wanted to find out the results of all the football games in Division 1, you'd subscribe to football.division1.*, and if you wanted to find out the latest scores for all rugby games, you could subscribe to rugby.>.

Wildcards and destination hierarchies are useful for adding flexibility to your applications, allowing for a message consumer to subscribe to more than one destination at a time. The ActiveMQ broker will scan any destination name for a match using wildcards, so generally the shorter the destination name, the better the performance.

But wildcards only work for consumers. If you publish a message to a topic named rugby.>, the message will only be sent to the topic named rugby.>, and not all topics that start with the name "rugby." There is a way for a message producer to send a message to multiple destinations: by using composite destinations, which we look at next.

11.1.2 *Sending a message to multiple destinations*

It can be useful to send the same message to different destinations at once. For example, when you need real-time analytics about your enterprise: an application used by a retail store might want to send a message to request more inventory. So a message is sent to a queue destination at the retail store's warehouse. But it may also want to broadcast that order to an in-store activity monitoring system. Usually you'd have to do this by sending the message twice and use two message producers—one for the queue and one for the topic. ActiveMQ supports a feature called *composite destinations* that allows you to send the same message to multiple destinations at once.

A composite destination uses a comma-separated name as the destination name. For example, if you created a queue with the name store.order.backoffice, store.order.warehouse, then the messages sent to that composite destination would actually be sent to the two queues from the same send operation, one queue named store.order.backoffice and one queue named store.order.warehouse.

Composite destinations can support a mixture of queues and topics at the same time. By default, you have to prepend the destination name with either queue:// or topic://. So for the store application scenario where you want to send an order message to both the order queue and also a topic, you'd set up your message producer as follows:

```
String brokerURI = ActiveMQConnectionFactory.DEFAULT_BROKER_URL;
ConnectionFactory connectionFactory = new ActiveMQConnectionFactory(brokerURI);
Connection connection = connectionFactory.createConnection();
connection.start();

Session session = connection.createSession(false, Session.AUTO_ACKNOWLEDGE);
Queue ordersDestination = session.createQueue("store.orders, topic://
    store.orders");
MessageProducer producer = session.createProducer(ordersDestination);
Message order = session.createObjectMessage();
producer.send(order);
```

Wildcards and composite destinations are powerful tools for building less-complicated and flexible applications with ActiveMQ.

Next we'll look at the management advisory messages that the ActiveMQ broker produces, and how you can subscribe to them to gain useful information on changes to your ActiveMQ system.

11.2 Advisory messages

Advisory messages are notification messages generated by the ActiveMQ broker as a result of changes to the broker. Typically, an advisory message will be generated every time a new administered object (connection, destination, consumer, producer) joins or leaves the broker, but advisory messages can be generated to warn about the ActiveMQ broker reaching system limits, too. Advisory messages are regular JMS messages that are generated on system-defined topics, which enables ActiveMQ applications to be notified asynchronously over JMS of changes in the ActiveMQ broker's state. They can be a good alternative to using JMX to find out about the running state of an ActiveMQ broker.

ActiveMQ uses advisory messages internally too, to notify connections about the availability of temporary destinations and notify networks about the availability of consumers, so you should take care if you want to disable them.

Every advisory message generated has a JMSType of Advisory and predefined JMS String properties, identifying the broker where the advisory was generated:

- originBrokerId—The ID of the broker that generated the advisory
- originBrokerName—The name of the broker that generated the advisory
- originBrokerURL—The first transport connector URL of the broker that generated the advisory

Advisory messages for changes in state to the administered objects usually use ActiveMQ-specific internal commands as the payload, but they do carry useful information. Let's look at how to listen for connections starting and stopping with ActiveMQ:

```
String brokerURI = ActiveMQConnectionFactory.DEFAULT_BROKER_URL;
ConnectionFactory connectionFactory =
  new ActiveMQConnectionFactory(brokerURI);
Connection connection = connectionFactory.createConnection();
connection.start();

Session session =
  connection.createSession(false, Session.AUTO_ACKNOWLEDGE);
Topic connectionAdvisory = AdvisorySupport.CONNECTION_ADVISORY_TOPIC;
MessageConsumer consumer = session.createConsumer(connectionAdvisory);

ActiveMQMessage message = (ActiveMQMessage) consumer.receive();

DataStructure data = (DataStructure) message.getDataStructure();
if (data.getDataStructureType() == ConnectionInfo.DATA_STRUCTURE_TYPE) {
    ConnectionInfo connectionInfo = (ConnectionInfo) data;
    System.out.println("Connection started: " + connectionInfo);
} else if (data.getDataStructureType() == RemoveInfo.DATA_STRUCTURE_TYPE) {
    RemoveInfo removeInfo = (RemoveInfo) data;
```

```
      System.out.println("Connection stopped: " + removeInfo.getObjectId());
} else {
   System.err.println("Unknown message " + data);
}
```

You can see from the example that we use a regular JMS construct to start listening to advisory topics. It's worth noting the use of the `AdvisorySupport` class, which contains the definition of all the advisory topic definitions. Things get harder when we start using ActiveMQ-specific command objects—although a `ConnectionInfo` is sent when a connection starts, a `RemoveInfo` is sent when a connection stops. The `RemoveInfo` does carry the `connectionId` (set as the `RemoveInfo`'s `objectId`)—so it's possible to correlate which connection has stopped.

Most advisory messages are specific to destinations. But the `AdvisorySupport` class does have some helper methods to determine which advisory topic to listen to. You can also use wildcards—so, for example, if you created an advisory topic for the queue named >, you'd get information for all queues.

Let's look at an example of listening for consumers coming and going for a queue named test.Queue:

Listing 11.1   Subscribing for consumer advisories

```
String brokerURI = ActiveMQConnectionFactory.DEFAULT_BROKER_URL;
ConnectionFactory connectionFactory =
  new ActiveMQConnectionFactory(brokerURI);
Connection connection = connectionFactory.createConnection();
connection.start();

//Lets first create a Consumer to listen too
Session session =
  connection.createSession(false, Session.AUTO_ACKNOWLEDGE);
//Lets first create a Consumer to listen too
Queue queue = session.createQueue("test.Queue");

MessageConsumer testConsumer = session.createConsumer(queue);

//so lets listen for the Consumer starting and stopping
Topic advisoryTopic  = AdvisorySupport.getConsumerAdvisoryTopic(queue);
MessageConsumer consumer = session.createConsumer(advisoryTopic);
consumer.setMessageListener(new MessageListener(){

public void onMessage(Message m) {
   try {
      System.out.println("Consumer Count = "
      + m.getStringProperty("consumerCount"));
      DataStructure data = (DataStructure) message.getDataStructure();
      if (data.getDataStructureType() ==
        ConsumerInfo.DATA_STRUCTURE_TYPE) {
       ConsumerInfo consumerInfo = (ConsumerInfo) data;
       System.out.println("Consumer started: " + consumerInfo);
      } else if (data.getDataStructureType() ==
               RemoveInfo.DATA_STRUCTURE_TYPE) {
       RemoveInfo removeInfo = (RemoveInfo) data;
       System.out.println("Consumer stopped: "
```

```
              + removeInfo.getObjectId());
        } else {
          System.err.println("Unknown message " + data);
        }
    } catch (JMSException e) {
      e.printStackTrace();
    }
});

testConsumer.close();
```

You'll notice in the example that we create a test consumer on the queue test.queue before we create the listener for consumer advisories on test.queue. This is to demonstrate that the ActiveMQ broker will also send advisory messages for consumers that already exist when you start to listen for them.

There are some advisories on destinations that aren't enabled by default; these are advisories on message delivery, slow consumers, fast producers, and so forth. To enable these advisories, you have to configure them on a destination policy in the ActiveMQ broker configuration file. For example, to configure an advisory message for slow consumers on all queues, you need to add the following to your configuration:

```
<destinationPolicy>
    <policyMap><policyEntries>
        <policyEntry queue=">" advisoryForSlowConsumers="true" />
    </policyEntries></policyMap>
</destinationPolicy>
```

You can use advisory messages to supplement your application behavior (for example, you could slow message production from your producers if you have slow consumers) or to supplement JMX monitoring of the ActiveMQ broker. Advisory messages are useful for getting dynamic information on changes to your ActiveMQ system.

Many different advisories are generated by the ActiveMQ broker to provide information about the running system. A dozen of the more useful advisory topics appear in the numbered list below, and their properties (matched by number) appear in table 11.1.

1 ActiveMQ.Advisory.Connection
2 ActiveMQ.Advisory.Producer.Queue
3 ActiveMQ.Advisory.Consumer.Queue
4 ActiveMQ.Advisory.Queue
5 ActiveMQ.Advisory.Expired.Queue
6 ActiveMQ.Advisory.SlowConsumer.Queue
7 ActiveMQ.Advisory.FastProducer.Queue
8 ActiveMQ.Advisory.MessageDelivered.Queue
9 ActiveMQ.Advisory.MessageConsumed.Queue
10 ActiveMQ.Advisory.FULL
11 ActiveMQ.Advisory.MasterBroker
12 ActiveMQ.Advisory.MessageDLQd.Queue

Table 11.1   Properties from the list of 12 ActiveMQ advisory topics

	Description	Properties	Data structure	Generated by default	Policy entry property
1	Generated when a connection start/stops	null	null	true	none
2	Producer start/ stop messages on a queue	String='producerCount'— number of producers	ProducerInfo	true	none
3	Consumer start/ stop messages on a Queue	String='consumerCount'— number of Consumers	ConsumerInfo	true	none
4	Queue created/ destroyed	null	null	true	none
5	Expired messages on a queue	String='orignalMessageId'— expired id	Message	true	none
6	Slow queue consumer	String='consumerId'— consumer ID	ConsumerInfo	false	advisoryForSlowConsumers
7	Fast queue producer	String='producerId'— producer ID	ProducerInfo	false	advisdoryForFastProducers
8	Message delivered to the broker	String='orignalMessageId'— delivered ID	Message	false	advisoryForDelivery
9	Message consumed by a client	String='orignalMessageId'— delivered ID	Message	false	advisoryForConsumed
10	A usage resource is at its limit	String='usageName'— name of usage resource	null	false	advisoryWhenFull
11	A broker is now the master in a master/slave configuration	null	null	true	none
12	Message sent to a dead letter queue	String='orignalMessageId'— delivered ID	Message	true	none

In the next section, we're going to change tack and look at an advanced feature called *virtual topics*, which can be used to supplement the way you consume messages, combining the features of both of topics and queues.

11.3 *Supercharge JMS topics by going virtual*

If you want to broadcast a message to multiple consumers, then you use a JMS topic. If you want a pool of consumers to receive messages from a destination, then you use a JMS queue. But there's no satisfactory way to send a message to a topic and then have multiple consumers receiving messages on that topic the way you can with queues.

The JMS spec requires that a durable subscriber to a topic use a unique JMS client ID and subscriber name. Also, only one thread (a single consumer) can be active at any time with that unique JMS client ID and subscriber name. This means that if that subscriber dies for some reason, there will be no failover to another consumer and there's no ability to load balance messages across competing consumers. But using JMS queue semantics allows the ability to fail over consumers, to load balance messages among competing consumers, and to use ActiveMQ message groups (see chapter 12), which allows sticky load balancing of messages to maintain message order. Furthermore, JMS queue depths can be monitored via JMX (see chapter 14). Using virtual topics works around these disadvantages while still retaining the benefits of JMS topics.

Virtual topics allow a publisher to send messages to a normal JMS topic while consumers receive messages from a normal JMS queue. So consumers subscribe to a queue to receive messages that were published to a topic. Figure 11.1 shows a diagram of how virtual topics are structured in ActiveMQ.

Some naming conventions are required to allow virtual topics to operate correctly. First, to identify that a topic is to be treated as a virtual topic, the topic name should always follow the pattern of *VirtualTopic.<topic name>*. So if you want to create a virtual topic for a topic whose name is *orders*, you need to create a destination with the name *VirtualTopic.orders*. This means that a publisher sends messages to a topic named *VirtualTopic.orders*. In order to consume from the queue that's backed by the virtual topic, consumers must subscribe to a queue whose name follows the pattern *Consumer.<consumer name>.VirtualTopic.<virtual topic name>*.

Suppose you want consumers to compete for messages on a queue, but you want that queue to be backed by a topic. You'd create a two queue receivers, each consuming from a queue named *Consumer.Foo.VirtualTopic.orders*. An example of this is shown next.

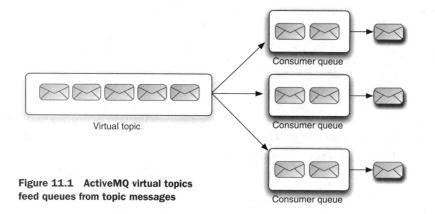

Figure 11.1   ActiveMQ virtual topics feed queues from topic messages

Listing 11.2 Using virtual topics

```
...
String brokerURI = ActiveMQConnectionFactory.DEFAULT_BROKER_URL;

ConnectionFactory connectionFactory =
  new ActiveMQConnectionFactory(brokerURI);
Connection consumerConnection = connectionFactory.createConnection();
consumerConnection.start();

String queueName = "Consumer.Foo.VirtualTopic.orders";

// Create the first consumer for Consumer.Foo.VirtualTopic.orders
Session sessionA =
  consumerConnection.createSession(false,Session.AUTO_ACKNOWLEDGE);
Queue fooQueueA = sessionA.createQueue(queueName);
MessageConsumer consumerA = sessionA.createConsumer(fooQueueA);
consumerA.setMessageListener(getMessageListener());

// Create the second consumer for Consumer.Foo.VirtualTopic.orders
Session sessionB =
  consumerConnection.createSession(false,Session.AUTO_ACKNOWLEDGE);
Queue fooQueueB = sessionB.createQueue(queueName);
MessageConsumer consumerB = sessionB.createConsumer(fooQueueB);
consumerB.setMessageListener(getMessageListener());

// Create the sender
String topicName = "VirtualTopic.orders";
Connection senderConnection = connectionFactory.createConnection();
senderConnection.start();
Session senderSession =
  senderConnection.createSession(false, Session.AUTO_ACKNOWLEDGE);
Topic ordersDestination = senderSession.createTopic(topicName);
MessageProducer producer =
  senderSession.createProducer(ordersDestination);
producer.setDeliveryMode(DeliveryMode.PERSISTENT);

// Send 2000 messages
for (int i = 0; i < 2000; ++i) {
  TextMessage message = createMessage(i);
  producer.send(message);
}
...
```

In listing 11.2, note that two consumers are subscribed to the same queue whose name follows the virtual topic naming pattern for the queue side. Also note that the producer is sending to a topic whose name follows the virtual topic naming pattern for the topic side. When the 2,000 messages are sent to the topic, each consumer will receive 1,000 messages from the queue.

Virtual topics are a convenient mechanism to combine the load balancing and failover aspects of queues, with the durability of topics. Not only does the consumer not need to worry about creating a unique JMS client ID and subscriber name, but the consumers are competing for messages in a load balanced manner using JMS queue semantics. If one of the consumers dies, the other consumer will continue to receive all the messages on the queue.

In the next section we'll look at using ActiveMQ to combine the longevity of durable subscribers, with the performance of normal topic subscribers.

11.4   *Retroactive consumers*

For applications that require messages to be sent and consumed as quickly as possible—for example, a real-time data feed—it's recommend that you send messages with persistence turned off.

There's a downside to consuming nonpersistent messages, in that you'll only be able to consume messages from the point when your message consumer starts. You can miss messages if your message consumer starts behind the message producer, or there's a network glitch and your message consumer needs to reconnect to the broker (or another one in a network).

In order to provide a limited method of retroactive consumption of messages without requiring message persistence, ActiveMQ has the ability to cache a configurable size or number of messages sent on a topic. There are two parts to this—your message consumers need to inform the ActiveMQ broker that it's interested in retroactive messages, and you need to configure the destination in the broker to say how many messages should be cached for consumption at a later point.

To mark a consumer as being retroactive, you need to set the retroactive flag for the message consumer. The easiest way to do that is to set the property on the topic name you use:

```
String brokerURI = ActiveMQConnectionFactory.DEFAULT_BROKER_URL;
ConnectionFactory connectionFactory =
  new ActiveMQConnectionFactory(brokerURI);
Connection connection = connectionFactory.createConnection();
connection.start();

Session session =
  connection.createSession(false, Session.AUTO_ACKNOWLEDGE);
Topic topic =
  session.createTopic("soccer.division1.leeds?consumer.retroactive=true");
MessageConsumer consumer = session.createConsumer(topic);
Message result = consumer.receive();
```

On the broker side, you can configure a number of recovery policies on a topic-by-topic basis. The default is called the `FixedSizedSubscriptionRecoveryPolicy`, which holds a number of messages in a topic, based on the calculated size the messages will take from the broker memory. The default size is 64 KB.

You can configure the subscription recovery policy on a named topic, or use wildcards to apply them to hierarchies. Here's a sample configuration snippet of how to change the default cache size for the `FixedSizedSubscriptionRecoveryPolicy` for all topics created in the ActiveMQ broker:

```
<destinationPolicy>
  <policyMap>
    <policyEntries>
      <policyEntry topic=">">
        <subscriptionRecoveryPolicy>
```

```
      <fixedSizedSubscriptionRecoveryPolicy maximumSize="8mb"/>
        </subscriptionRecoveryPolicy>
      </policyEntry>
    </policyEntries>
  </policyMap>
</destinationPolicy>
```

Retroactive message consumers are a convenient mechanism to improve the reliability of your applications without incurring the overhead of message persistence. We've seen how enable retroactive consumers and how to configure their broker-side counterpart, the SubscriptionRecoveryPolicy.

In the next section we're going to look at how ActiveMQ stores messages that can't be delivered to message consumers—dead-letter queues.

11.5 *Message redelivery and dead-letter queues*

When messages expire on the ActiveMQ broker (they exceed their time-to-live, if set) or can't be redelivered, they're moved to a dead-letter queue, so they can be consumed or browsed by an administrator at a later point.

Messages are normally redelivered to a client in the following scenarios:

- A client is using transactions and calls rollback() on the session.
- A client is using transactions and closes before calling commit.
- A client is using CLIENT_ACKNOWLEDGE on a session and calls recover() on that session.

A client application usually has a good reason to roll back a transacted session or call recover()—it may not be able to complete the processing of the message(s) because of its inability to negotiate with a third-party resource, for example. But sometimes an application may decide to not accept delivery of a message because the message is poorly formatted. For such a scenario, it doesn't make sense for the ActiveMQ broker to attempt redelivery forever.

A configurable POJO is associated with the ActiveMQ connection that you can tune to set different policies. You can configure the amount of time the ActiveMQ broker should wait before trying to resend the message, whether that time should increase after every failed attempt (use an exponential back-off and back-off multiplier), and the maximum number of redelivery attempts before the message(s) are moved to a dead-letter queue.

Here's an example of how to configure a client's redelivery policy:

```
RedeliveryPolicy policy = connection.getRedeliveryPolicy();
policy.setInitialRedeliveryDelay(500);
policy.setBackOffMultiplier(2);
policy.setUseExponentialBackOff(true);
policy.setMaximumRedeliveries(2);
```

By default, there's one dead-letter queue for all messages, called AcitveMQ.DLQ, which expired messages or messages that have exceeded their redelivery attempts get sent to. You can configure a dead-letter queue for a hierarchy, or an individual destination in the ActiveMQ broker configuration, like in the following example, where we set an `IndividualDeadLetterStrategy`:

```
<destinationPolicy>
  <policyMap>
    <policyEntries>
      <policyEntry queue=">">
        <deadLetterStrategy>
          <individualDeadLetterStrategy
            queuePrefix="DLQ."
            useQueueForQueueMessages="true"
            processExpired="false"
            processNonPersistent="false"/>
        </deadLetterStrategy>
      </policyEntry>
    </policyEntries>
  </policyMap>
</destinationPolicy>
```

Note that we configure this dead-letter strategy to ignore nonpersistent and expired messages, which can prevent overwhelming the ActiveMQ broker with messages, if you're using time-to-live on nonpersistent messages.

When a message is sent to a dead-letter queue, an advisory message is generated for it. You can listen for dead-letter queue advisory messages on the topic ActiveMQ.Advisory.MessageDLQd.*.

In the next section, we'll look at some of the interceptor plug-ins that are available to extend the behavior of the ActiveMQ broker.

11.6 *Extending functionality with interceptor plug-ins*

ActiveMQ provides the ability to supply custom code to supplement broker functionality. To do so requires a good understanding of the ActiveMQ broker internals, which is unfortunately outside the scope of this book. But some ActiveMQ broker interceptor plug-ins are provided with the ActiveMQ distribution; some we've already covered, such as the authentication plug-in, in chapter 6. There are some additional miscellaneous plug-ins, and for completeness, it's worth looking at those now.

We'll start with visualization, which uses two different plug-ins that generate graphical representations of connections and destinations.

11.6.1 *Visualization*

Visualization can be useful for identifying usage patterns for an ActiveMQ broker. For example, being able to see a diagram of all the connections and the destinations that they're consuming messages from can help identify rogue clients in production environments that have been erroneously consuming messages from the wrong queue. You can use two visualization plug-ins that generate a graph visualization file, which contains structural information for viewing structured data. You can use several tools to visualize the generated files, such as Graphviz (http://www.graphviz.org).

Two types of visualization plug-ins are available, one for connections (and associated consumers and producers) called *connectionDotFilePlugin,* and one for generating a destination hierarchy of all the queues and topics used in the ActiveMQ Broker, called *destinationDotFilePlugin.* When these plug-ins are enabled, they generate a *DOT file* on disk. A DOT file contains the structural information in a directed graph notation, suitable to be read by a graph visualization tool.

The connectionDotFilePlugin writes information about the client connections attached to the ActiveMQ broker to a DOT file on disk. By default the file is written into the current directory the ActiveMQ broker was started from and is called ActiveMQConnections.dot. Information about each client connection, including which destinations the client connection is sending messages to or receiving messages from, is also written to the DOT file. Every time there's a change to a client connection (for example, it starts or stops a message consumer), a new client connection starts, or an old one stops, the DOT file will be overwritten.

The connectionDotFilePlugin has only one property: the name of the file to write the state information into, as shown in table 11.2.

Table 11.2   Properties for the connection DOT plug-in

Property name	Default value	Description
file	ActiveMQConnections.dot	The path name to write state information in DOT format for connections to the ActiveMQ broker

The destinationDotFilePlugin is similar to the connectionDotFilePlugin. When this plug-in is enabled, it will write state information about the current destinations in use by the ActiveMQ broker to a DOT file that's by default called ActiveMQDestinations. dot. Whenever the state information of destinations changes within the broker, this DOT file will be updated. An example of the rendered DOT file for the destination-DotFilePlugin is shown in figure 11.2.

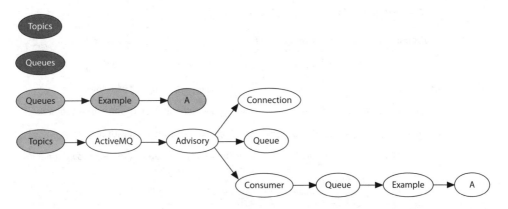

Figure 11.2   Active destinations for an ActiveMQ broker graphically generated by the destinationDotFilePlugin

The destinationDotFilePlugin has only one property: the name of file to write the state information into, as shown in table 11.3.

Table 11.3   **Properties for the destination DOT plug-in**

Property name	Default value	Description
file	ActiveMQDestinations.dot	The path name to write state information in DOT format for destinations to the ActiveMQ broker

All ActiveMQ broker plug-ins can be enabled within the configuration file for the broker. Here's an example of an ActiveMQ broker configuration file which has the connectionDotFilePlugin and destinationDotFilePlugin enabled.

Listing 11.3   Configuring visualization plug-ins for the ActiveMQ broker

```
<broker useJmx="false" persistent="true">
  <plugins>
    <connectionDotFilePlugin file="ActiveMQConnections.dot"/>
    <destinationDotFilePlugin file="ActiveMQDestinations.dot"/>
  </plugins>
</broker>
```

The next plug-in we'll look at was developed by one of ActiveMQ's many users to enhance the logging available for the ActiveMQ broker.

11.6.2   *Enhanced logging*

The logging interceptor (loggingInterceptor), if configured, allows you to log messages that are sent or acknowledged on an ActiveMQ broker, in addition to the normal logging done by ActiveMQ. This plug-in can be useful for tracing problems or auditing messages. A few properties for the logging interceptor can be configured, as shown in table 11.4.

Table 11.4   **Properties for the logging interceptor**

Property name	Default value	Description
logAll	false	Log all the events
logMessageEvents	false	Log events associated with messages
logConnectionEvents	true	Log events associated with connections
logConsumerEvents	false	Log events associated with producers
logProducerEvents	false	The maximum size of the message journal data files before a new one is used
logInternalEvents	false	Detailed information of workings of the broker

11.6.3 Central timestamp messages with the timestamp interceptor plug-in

The timestamp plug-in (timestampingBrokerPlugin), if configured, updates the time-stamp on messages as they arrive at the broker. This can be useful when there's a difference (however small) between the system clocks on a computer sending messages to an ActiveMQ broker and the computer the broker resides on. When messages are sent with the `timeToLive` property set, it's important that the system clocks between the sending machine and the broker are in sync; otherwise messages may get expired erroneously. A few properties for the timestamp plug-in can be configured, as shown in table 11.5.

Table 11.5   Properties for the message timestamp plug-in

Property name	Default value	Description
zeroExpirationOverride	0	When not zero, will override the expiration date for messages that currently don't have an expiration set
ttlCeiling	0	When not zero, will limit the expiration time
futureOnly	false	If true, won't update the timestamp of messages to past values

It's recommend that the timestampingBrokerPlugin be enabled on the ActiveMQ broker if you're using the `timeToLive` property on messages.

The next interceptor plug-in is used for generating messages about management statistics for the ActiveMQ broker.

11.6.4 Statistics

The statisticsBrokerPlugin will send MapMessages containing information about the statistics of the running of the ActiveMQ broker. There are two types of message: one for destinations and one that gives an overview of the broker itself.

To retrieve the statistics of the running broker with the statisticsBrokerPlugin enabled, send an empty message to the destination (queue or topic—it doesn't matter) called *ActiveMQ.Statistics.Broker*. The JMSReplyTo header names the destination where the statistics message is sent.

Similarly, to retrieve information about a destination, send an empty message to the name of the destination, prepended with *ActiveMQ.Statistics.Destination*. For example, to retrieve statistics for the destination Topic.Foo, send a message to the destination *ActiveMQ.Statistics.DestinationTopic.Foo*.

You enable an ActiveMQ broker plug-in by including it in the broker configuration file, as shown:

Listing 11.4 Configuring `plugins` for the broker

```
<broker useJmx="false" persistent="false">
  <plugins>
    <loggingBrokerPlugin logAll="true" logConnectionEvents="false"/>
    <timeStampingBrokerPlugin
      zeroExpirationOverride="1000"
      ttlCeiling="60000" futureOnly="true"/>
    <statisticsBrokerPlugin/>
  </plugins>
</broker>
```

Broker interceptors are a useful addition for extending the functionality of ActiveMQ. But you can provide more features and flexibility by embedding Apache Camel, the powerful integration framework, in the ActiveMQ broker. We'll look at Apache Camel integration next.

11.7 *Routing engine with Apache Camel framework*

Apache Camel is a simple-to-use integration framework that's easily embedded in containers and applications.

At the core of the Camel framework is a routing engine builder. It allows you to define your own routing rules, the sources from which to accept messages, and how to process and send them to other destinations. Camel defines an integration language that allows you to define routing rules, akin to business processes.

Although Apache Camel supports a large number of integration components, we'll demonstrate some relatively simple ways to extend the power of ActiveMQ by using Apache Camel for some simple routing.

Camel can use either a Java-based domain-specific language (DSL), or Scala DSL, or an XML-based DSL to define routes. We'll concentrate on the XML-based DSL, so we can extend an ActiveMQ broker functionality directly from an XML configuration file. Apache Camel uses simple English prepositions, such as *from* and *to*, to denote a route. It's easy to explain with an example. First we'll define a simple broker configuration file to include a Camel XML file with routing rules:

```
<beans>
  <broker brokerName="testBroker">
    <transportConnectors>
      <transportConnector uri="tcp://localhost:61616"/>
    </transportConnectors>
  </broker>
  <import resource="camel.xml"/>
</beans>
```

Note we call `import resource` *after* the broker definition to include a Camel XML configuration file. Apache Camel comes with both a generic JMS component and a more specific, optimized ActiveMQ component. Obviously we'll use the latter. The ActiveMQ component needs to be configured to communicate with the broker, and we'll use the vm:// transport to do this. Note we called the ActiveMQ broker *testBroker*, so this needs to be the name we use when we set up the vm:// transport in the Camel XML configuration file:

```
<bean id="activemq"
  class="org.apache.activemq.camel.component.ActiveMQComponent">
  <property name="connectionFactory">
    <bean class="org.apache.activemq.ActiveMQConnectionFactory">
      <property name="brokerURL"
        value="vm://testBroker?create=false&amp;waitForStart=1000"/>
      <property name="userName" value="DEFAULT_VALUE"/>
      <property name="password" value="DEFAULT_VALUE"/>
    </bean>
  </property>
</bean>
```

We can now define a route. A useful enhancement is to tap into messages broadcast on a topic, and place them in a queue for processing later:

```
<route>
  <from uri="activemq:topic:Test.Topic"/>
  <to uri="activemq:queue:Test.Queue"/>
</route>
```

This route will consume messages on the topic Test.Topic and route them to the queue Test.Queue. Simple, but useful stuff.

Let's demonstrate something more complex. The statistics broker plug-in (statisticsBrokerPlugin) will only publish a statistic message when requested. So it'd be useful to broadcast a message with statistical information periodically, and we can use Apache Camel to do that.

First, we need to ensure that the statisticsBrokerPlugin is enabled, as in the following example configuration:

```
<beans>
  <broker useJmx="false" persistent="false">
    <plugins>
      <statisticsBrokerPlugin/>
    </plugins>
  </broker>
  <import resource="camel.xml"/>
</beans>
```

Then, with Apache Camel, we'll do the following:

- Use the timer component to initiate the name of the route to poll.
- Communicate with the statistics plug-in using a request/reply pattern. In Apache Camel, a request/reply exchange is called *InOut*—we'll poll the queue named *Test.Queue*.
- Broadcast the result on a topic called *Statistics.Topic*.

The complete Apache Camel route is only three lines of code, as shown:

```
<route>
    <from uri="timer://foo?fixedRate=true&amp;period=1000"/>
    <inOut uri="activemq:queue:ActiveMQ.Statistics.DestinationTest.Queue"/>
    <to uri="activemq:topic:Statistics.Topic"/>
</route>
```

Apache Camel is an extremely flexible and feature-rich framework. We've only touched the surface of what you can achieve with it in conjunction with ActiveMQ. For more information, we encourage you to read *Camel in Action* (Claus Ibsen and Jonathan Anstey), available from Manning Publications.

11.8 *Summary*

In this chapter you've learned how to use wildcard and composite destinations, to improve the flexibility of your ActiveMQ applications to receive and send messages with multiple destinations. You now have an understanding of advisory messages generated by the ActiveMQ broker.

We've also covered the benefits of using virtual topics and retroactive consumers, and when to use them. We've also explained when dead-letter queues are used and how to configure them. Finally we covered how to use Apache Camel routes in ActiveMQ, for extending flexibility and functionality of the message broker.

In the next chapter, we'll examine advanced messaging features that can be used from the client side of ActiveMQ.

Advanced client options

Advanced client options

This chapter covers

- How to use exclusive consumers
- The power of message groups
- Understanding support for streams and blobs
- The failover transport
- Scheduling message delivery

In the last chapter we covered advanced ActiveMQ broker features. In this chapter we're going to look at some advanced features on the client side of ActiveMQ. We'll look at how to ensure that one message consumer will receive messages from a queue, regardless of how many message consumers have subscribed to it. This feature is called *exclusive consumer*, and can be used for ensuring that messages are always consumed in order, or as a distributed locking mechanism—for which we have an example. We'll look at message groups, where messages can be grouped together to be consumed by the same message consumer. ActiveMQ supports two different ways to send large payloads through ActiveMQ—using ActiveMQ streams and blob messages—and we'll look at both methods. As the client-side failover transport protocol is important for applications to survive network outages and broker failure, we'll look at its nuances in more detail. And, finally, we'll look at sending messages with a delay, and delay using scheduled messages.

One feature that you might be expecting in this chapter is different modes for client-side acknowledgement of messages. As we'll find out in the next chapter on ActiveMQ performance tuning, choosing the right mode for acknowledgement of messages is critical for good performance, so we'll cover acknowledgement modes and their consequences there.

12.1   *Exclusive consumers*

When messages are dispatched from an ActiveMQ broker, they'll always be in first in, first out order. But if you have more than one message consumer for a queue in your application(s), you can't guarantee that the order in which the messages were dispatched will be the same order in which your application will consume them. This is because you never have control over the scheduling of threads used to deliver the messages on the client side—even if all your message consumers are using the same connection. Ideally you'd only have one message consumer to ensure ordering of messages. But you may also need to support failover, to have another instance of your queue message consumer take over the processing of the queue messages if the first consumer fails. ActiveMQ can support having multiple message consumers on a queue, but having only one of them receive the messages from that queue. We'll discuss this concept in the following subsection.

12.1.1   *Selecting an exclusive message consumer*

For applications where message order is important, or you need to ensure that there will be only one message consumer for a queue, ActiveMQ offers a client-side option to have only one active message consumer process messages. The ActiveMQ message broker will select one consumer on the queue to process messages. The benefit of allowing the broker to make the choice is that if the consumer stops or fails, then another message consumer can be selected to be active, as depicted in figure 12.1.

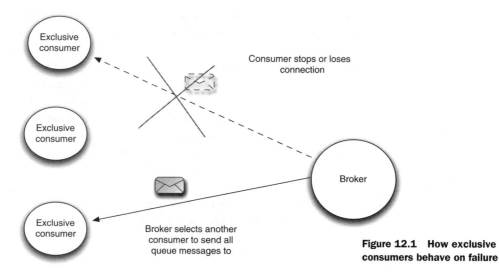

Figure 12.1   How exclusive consumers behave on failure

If you mix standard consumers and exclusive consumers on the same queue, the ActiveMQ message broker will still only deliver messages to one of the exclusive consumers. If all the exclusive consumers become inactive, and there's still a standard message consumer, then consumption of queue messages will return to the normal mode of delivery—the messages will be delivered in a round-robin fashion between all the remaining active standard message consumers.

You can create an exclusive consumer using a destination option on the client, like in the following code extract:

```
queue = new ActiveMQQueue("TEST.QUEUE?consumer.exclusive=true");
consumer = session.createConsumer(queue);
```

The ability to select a message consumer to be exclusive can be used for more than guaranteeing that messages are consumed by only one active message consumer. You can use the exclusive consumer pattern to create a distributed lock, as we'll demonstrate in the next section.

12.1.2 *Using exclusive consumers to provide a distributed lock*

Often you use messaging to broadcast data from an external resource, be that changes to records in a database, or comma-separated values appended to a file, or a raw real-time data feed. You might wish to build in redundancy, so if an instance of the application reading and broadcasting the changing data fails, another can take over. Often you can rely on locking a resource (row lock or file lock) to ensure that only one process will be accessing the data and broadcasting over a topic at a time. But when you don't want the overhead of using a database, or want to run processes across more than one machine (and can't use distributed locks), then you can use the exclusive consumer functionality to create a distributed lock. In figure 12.2 we show an application

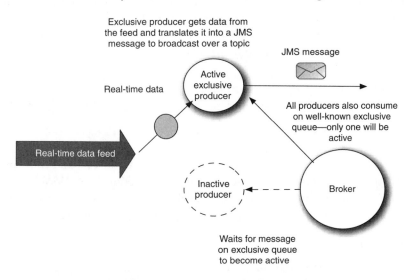

Figure 12.2 Using exclusive consumers as a distributed lock to create an exclusive producer application

where we want failover for a client reading data from a real-time feed. We only want one client to connect to the feed and distribute the events, but if it fails, we need another client available to take over.

In order to use exclusive consumers to create a distributed lock, we need our message producer to subscribe exclusively to a well-known queue. If the message producer receive a message from the queue, it becomes activated, and can then subscribe to the real-time feed and transform the real-time data into JMS messages. Here's a code snippet for the message producer to initiate a distributed lock:

```
public void start() throws JMSException {
    this.connection = this.factory.createConnection();
    this.connection.start();
    this.session =
      this.connection.createSession(false, Session.CLIENT_ACKNOWLEDGE);
    Destination destination = this.session.createQueue(this.queueName
      + "?consumer.exclusive=true");
    Message message = this.session.createMessage();
    MessageProducer producer = this.session.createProducer(destination);
    producer.send(message);
    MessageConsumer consumer = this.session.createConsumer(destination);
    consumer.setMessageListener(this);
}
```

In this example, we always send a message to the well-known queue, to start off consumption—this step could always be done externally by a management process. Note that we use `Session.CLIENT_ACKNOWLEDGE` mode to consume the message. Although we want to be notified that we're an exclusive consumer—and hence have the lock—we don't want to remove the message from the well-known queue. In this way, if we fail, another exclusive producer will be activated.

For this example, we'd implement the `MessageListener` to look like the following code snippet. If we're not already activated, we call a fictional method—`startProducing()`. If this were a real application, this method would start subscribing to a real-time feed and convert real-time data into JMS messages:

```
public void onMessage(Message message) {
    if (message != null  && this.active==false) {
        this.active=true;
        startProducing();
    }
}
```

We've shown that using an exclusive consumer allows us to ensure that only one message consumer will be active at a time. In the next section, we'll look at message groups, where the ActiveMQ broker can selectively choose a message consumer for all messages that have the same `JMSXGroupID` message header property set.

12.2 *Message groups*

We can refine the exclusive consumer concept further with message groups. Instead of all messages going to a single message consumer, messages can be grouped together for a single consumer, and a message producer can designate a group for a

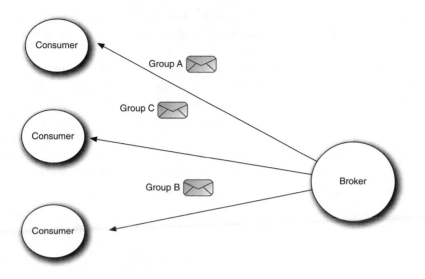

Figure 12.3 Message groups: messages with the same JMSXGroupID will be sent to the same consumer

message by setting the message header JMSXGroupID. The ActiveMQ broker will ensure that all messages with the same JMSXGroupID are sent to the same consumer, as shown in figure 12.3.

If the consumer designated by the ActiveMQ broker to receive messages for a given JMSXGroupID should close or become unavailable (a network outage, for example), then the ActiveMQ broker will select a different message consumer to dispatch the grouped messages to.

Using message groups is straightforward. The definition of a group is left up to a user and is done on the message producer—it just has to be unique for a particular queue. All the routing is done in the ActiveMQ message broker.

To create a group, you need to set a JMSXGroupID string property on the messages being sent by the message producer, as shown:

```
Session session =
  connection.createSession(false, Session.AUTO_ACKNOWLEDGE);
Queue queue = session.createQueue("group.queue");
MessageProducer producer = session.createProducer(queue);
Message message = session.createTextMessage("<foo>test</foo>");
message.setStringProperty("JMSXGroupID", "TEST_GROUP_A");
producer.send(message);
```

The previous example shows a message producer being created, and then setting a TextMessage to belong to the message group TEST_GROUP_A.

Message groups use normal message consumers, so no additional work is required to consume messages from a group. All the work is done by the message producer in defining the group messages belong to, and by the ActiveMQ broker in selecting a message consumer to send all the grouped messages to.

The ActiveMQ broker will add a sequence number to each message in a group, using the standard JMSXGroupSeq message header property. The sequence number will start from 1 for a new message group.

But from the perspective of the message consumer, you can't assume that the first message you receive for a new group will have the JMSXGroupSeq set to 1. If an existing message group consumer closes or dies, any messages being routed to its group will be assigned a new consumer. To help identify that a message consumer is receiving messages to a new group, or a group that it hasn't seen before, a Boolean property called JMSXGroupFirstForConsumer is set for the first message sent to the new message consumer. You can check whether a message is being sent to your consumer for the first time by seeing if this property has been set, as shown:

```
Session session = MessageConsumer consumer = session.createConsumer(queue);
Message message = consumer.receive();
String groupId = message.getStringProperty("JMSXGroupId");
if (message.getBooleanProperty("JMSXGroupFirstForConsumer")) {
  // do processing for new group
}
```

It's often the case that you start a number of message consumers to process messages at the same time. The ActiveMQ message broker will allocate all message groups evenly across all consumers, but if there are already messages waiting to be dispatched, the message groups will typically be allocated to the first consumer. To ensure an even distributed load, it's possible to give the message broker a hint to wait for more message consumers to start. To do this, you have to set up a destination policy in the ActiveMQ broker's XML configuration. Set the consumersBeforeDispatch-Starts property with the number of message consumers you expect your application to use, as the following example demonstrates:

```
 <destinationPolicy>
  <policyMap>
    <policyEntries>
      <policyEntry queue=">"
        consumersBeforeDispatchStarts="2"
        timeBeforeDispatchStarts="5000"/>
    </policyEntries>
  </policyMap>
</destinationPolicy>
```

The sample configuration tells the ActiveMQ broker that any queue (the name of the queue is >, which is a wildcard for any match) should wait for two consumers before dispatching. Additionally we've also set the timeBeforeDispatchStarts property to 5000ms to inform the ActiveMQ broker that if two message consumers aren't available within 5 seconds of getting the first message on the queue, it should use the first that becomes available.

Using message groups does add some minimal overhead to the ActiveMQ broker, in terms of storing routing information for each message group. It's possible to explicitly close a message group by sending a message to the ActiveMQ broker with the

JMSXGroupID set to the group you want to close and the JMSXGroupSeq property set to -1, like in the following example:

```
Session session =
  connection.createSession(false, Session.AUTO_ACKNOWLEDGE);
Queue queue = session.createQueue("group.queue");
MessageProducer producer = session.createProducer(queue);<foo />
Message message = session.createTextMessage("<foo>close</foo>");
message.setStringProperty("JMSXGroupID", "TEST_GROUP_A");
message.setIntProperty("JMSXGroupSeq", -1);
producer.send(message);
```

You can re-create a message group that has been closed by sending a new message to the group. But the group may be assigned to a different message consumer by the ActiveMQ broker.

Conceptually, message groups are like using message selectors. The difference is that message groups automatically handle the selection of message consumers, and they also handle the failover of message groups when a message consumer fails.

Having looked at exclusive consumers and message groups, in the next sections we're going to look at how to transport large messages using advanced client-side options with ActiveMQ, using either JMS streams or blob messages.

12.3 ActiveMQ streams

ActiveMQ streams are an advanced feature that allows you to use an ActiveMQ client as a Java IOStream. ActiveMQ will break an OutputStream into distinct chunks of data and send each chunk through ActiveMQ as a JMS message. A corresponding ActiveMQ JMS InputStream should be used on the consumer side to reassemble the data chunks.

If you use a queue as the destination for the stream, using more than one consumer on a queue (or an exclusive consumer) is fine because this feature uses message groups. This causes messages with the same group ID to be pinned to a single consumer. Using more than one producer in this scenario could cause problems with the message order.

The benefit of using JMS streams is that ActiveMQ will break a stream into manageable chunks and reassemble them for you at the consumer. So it's possible to transfer very large files using this functionality, as depicted in figure 12.4.

To demonstrate using streams, here's an example of reading a large file and writing it out over ActiveMQ:

```
//source of our large data
FileInputStream in = new FileInputStream("largetextfile.txt");

String brokerURI = ActiveMQConnectionFactory.DEFAULT_BROKER_URL;
ConnectionFactory connectionFactory =
  new ActiveMQConnectionFactory(brokerURI);
Connection connection = (ActiveMQConnection)
  connectionFactory.createConnection();
connection.start();
```

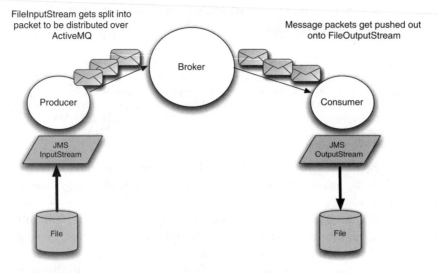

Figure 12.4   Using IOStreams to transfer a large file through ActiveMQ

```
Session session =
  connection.createSession(false, Session.AUTO_ACKNOWLEDGE);
Queue destination = session.createQueue(QUEUE_NAME);

OutputStream out = connection.createOutputStream(destination);

//now write the file on to ActiveMQ
byte[] buffer = new byte[1024];
while(true){
   int bytesRead = in.read(buffer);
   if (bytesRead==-1){
       break;
   }
    out.write(buffer,0,bytesRead);
}
//close the stream so the receiving side knows the steam is finished
out.close();
```

In the example, we create an ActiveMQConnection and create an OutputStream using a queue as the destination. We read the file using a FileInputStream, then write the FileInputStream onto the ActiveMQ OutputStream.

Note that we close the ActiveMQ OutputStream when we've completed reading the file. This is important so that the receiving side can determine whether the stream is finished. It's recommended that you use a new OutputStream for each file you send.

For completeness, here's the receiving end of an ActiveMQ stream:

```
//destination of our large data
FileOutputStream out = new FileOutputStream("copied.txt");

String brokerURI = ActiveMQConnectionFactory.DEFAULT_BROKER_URL;
ConnectionFactory connectionFactory =
  new ActiveMQConnectionFactory(brokerURI);
Connection connection = (ActiveMQConnection)
  connectionFactory.createConnection();
```

```
connection.start();
Session session =
  connection.createSession(false, Session.AUTO_ACKNOWLEDGE);

//we want to be an exclusive consumer
String exclusiveQueueName= QUEUE_NAME + "?consumer.exclusive=true";
Queue destination = session.createQueue(exclusiveQueueName);

InputStream in = connection.createInputStream(destination);

//now write the file from ActiveMQ
byte[] buffer = new byte[1024];
while(true){
    int bytesRead = in.read(buffer);
    if (bytesRead==-1){
        break;
    }
    out.write(buffer,0,bytesRead);
}
out.close();
```

In the example, we create an `ActiveMQConnection` and from that create an `Input-Stream` using a queue as a consumer. Note that we use an exclusive consumer by appending `"?consumer.exclusive=true"` to the name of the queue. We do this to ensure that only one consumer will be reading the stream at a time. We read the ActiveMQ `InputStream` and then write it to a `FileOutputStream` to reassemble the file on disk. Note that we expect the end of the file to be denoted by the end of the stream (or -1).

You can use streams with topics too—though if a consumer for a topic starts partway through the delivery of a stream, it won't receive any data that was sent before it was started.

ActiveMQ breaks the stream into manageable chunks of data and sends each chunk of data as a separate message. This means that you have to be careful when using them, because if the message consumer should fail partway through reading the `InputStream`, there's currently no way to replay the messages already consumed by the failed message consumer.

ActiveMQ streams are useful for transferring large payloads, though you'll need to think about how an application using ActiveMQ streams should handle failure scenarios. There's an alternative and more robust method of sending large payloads: using blob messages, which we cover in the next section.

12.4 Blob messages

ActiveMQ introduced the concept of *blob messages* so that users can take advantage of ActiveMQ message delivery semantics (transactions, load balancing, and smart routing) in conjunction with very large messages. A blob message doesn't contain the data being sent, but is a notification that a blob (binary large object) is available. The blob itself is transferred out of bounds, by either FTP or HTTP. In fact, an ActiveMQ `BlobMessage` only contains the URL to the data itself, with a helper method to grab an `InputStream` to the real data. Let's work through an example.

First we look at how to create a blob message. In this example we'll assume that a large file already exists on a shared website, so we have to create a blob message to notify any interested consumers that it exists, as shown:

```
import org.apache.activemq.BlobMessage;
...

String brokerURI = ActiveMQConnectionFactory.DEFAULT_BROKER_URL;
ConnectionFactory connectionFactory =
  new ActiveMQConnectionFactory(brokerURI);
Connection connection = connectionFactory.createConnection();
connection.start();
ActiveMQSession session = (ActiveMQSession)
  connection.createSession(false, Session.AUTO_ACKNOWLEDGE);
Queue destination = session.createQueue(QUEUE_NAME);
MessageProducer producer = session.createProducer(destination);
BlobMessage message =
session.createBlobMessage(new URL("http://example.com/bigfile.dat"));
producer.send(message);
```

In the example, we create a JMS connection, and from that an ActiveMQ session which has methods to support blob messages. We create a blob message from the URL of the file on our shared site (http://example.com) and send the blob message on a well-known queue (QUEUE_NAME).

Here's the corresponding message consumer for blob messages:

```
import org.apache.activemq.BlobMessage;
...

// destination of our Blob data
FileOutputStream out = new FileOutputStream("blob.dat");

String brokerURI = ActiveMQConnectionFactory.DEFAULT_BROKER_URL;
ConnectionFactory connectionFactory =
  new ActiveMQConnectionFactory(brokerURI);
Connection connection = (ActiveMQConnection)
  connectionFactory.createConnection();
connection.start();
Session session =
  connection.createSession(false, Session.AUTO_ACKNOWLEDGE);
Queue destination = session.createQueue(QUEUE_NAME);

MessageConsumer consumer = session.createConsumer(destination);
BlobMessage blobMessage = (BlobMessage) consumer.receive();

InputStream in = blobMessage.getInputStream();
// now write the file from ActiveMQ
byte[] buffer = new byte[1024];
while (true) {
    int bytesRead = in.read(buffer);
    if (bytesRead == -1) {
        break;
    }
    out.write(buffer, 0, bytesRead);
}
out.close();
```

In the example we create a message consumer on our well-known queue (QUEUE_NAME). We assume that all messages sent to this queue are of type `org.apache.activemq.BlobMessage`. A blob message has a helper method to get an `InputStream` to the remote URL that the message producer created the blob message with. We grab the `InputStream` and use it to read the remote file and write it to a local disk, called blob.dat.

Using blob messages is more robust than stream messages, as each one is an atomic unit of work. But they do rely on an external server being available for storage of the actual data—in this example a file.

12.5 Surviving network or broker failure with the failover protocol

We introduced the failover protocol in chapter 4, where we explained the basics behind allowing a client to fail over to another ActiveMQ broker in the case of failure. The failover protocol is the default protocol used by the Java client, so it's worth looking in more detail at some of its optional features and capabilities.

By default, you specify in the client URI one or more ActiveMQ brokers that could be used for the connection:

```
failover:(tcp://host1:61616,tcp://host2:61616,ssl://host2:61616)
```

By the way, specifying the failover transport URI like this is okay, too, although it can get a bit messy if there are any embedded query parameters.

ActiveMQ will connect to one of the brokers defined in the list, selecting one at random. With the failover protocol, the ActiveMQ client will instantiate a periodic keepalive protocol, so that it can detect whether the broker is no longer reachable (connection or broker lost). When it detects that the broker is no longer available, it will randomly select another broker from the list provided at startup. If only one broker URI is provided, the client will periodically check to see if the broker is available again. It's possible to listen for transport interrupts by setting a `TransportListener` on the ActiveMQ connection:

```
import org.apache.activemq.ActiveMQConnection;
import org.apache.activemq.ActiveMQConnectionFactory;
import org.apache.activemq.transport.DefaultTransportListener;

...

ActiveMQConnection connection = (ActiveMQConnection)
  connectionFactory.createConnection();
  connection.addTransportListener(new DefaultTransportListener() {
      public void onException(IOException arg0) {
          System.err.println("This is bad");
      }

      public void transportInterrupted() {
          System.out.println("Transport interrupted");
      }
```

```
        public void transportResumed() {
            System.out.println("Transport resumed");
        }
    });
```

```
connection.start();
```

When you supply the failover protocol with more than one transport URI to use, by default it will select one at random to use, to ensure load balancing of clients across brokers. When you want to have a guaranteed order of brokers that the client will connect to, you need to disable the random selection of brokers by disabling the randomize failover property:

```
failover:(tcp://master:61616,tcp://slave:61616)?randomize=false
```

If none of the ActiveMQ brokers specified by the failover URI are available, then by default the failover transport will wait before trying again. The failover protocol will wait an increasing amount of time between each successive failure to connect to an ActiveMQ broker—this is called an *exponential back-off*. The failover protocol by default has useExponentialBackOff enabled. The wait time between successive attempts to connect is called the initialReconnectDelay (initial value is 10ms) and the multiplier to increase the wait time is called the backOffMultiplier (default value is 2.0). You can also set the maximum time period for the failover protocol by using maxReconnectDelay (default is 30000ms). An example configuration is shown next:

```
failover:(tcp://master:61616,tcp://slave:61616)?\
backOffMultiplier=1.5,initialReconnectDelay=1000
```

One potential problem that you may run into using any transport protocol based on TCP is the ability to know when a peer (for ActiveMQ, this will be the broker) has died. This can happen for several reasons, like the failure of the ActiveMQ broker or loss of network. Also, if there's a firewall between the ActiveMQ client and broker, it may drop the connection if it's inactive for some time. It's possible to configure keepalive on the TCP connection, but this is operating system–specific and can require changes to kernel parameters—and doesn't work well in heterogeneous environments. For this reason, ActiveMQ uses a keepalive protocol on top of its transports, to keep firewalls open and also detect whether the broker is no longer reachable. The keepalive protocol periodically sends a lightweight command message to the broker, and expects a response. If it doesn't receive one within a given time period, ActiveMQ will assume that the transport is no longer valid. The failover transport listens for failed transports and will select another transport to use on such a failure. The parameter used by the keepalive protocol in ActiveMQ is maxInactivityDuration, which is an OpenWire property; the default is 30000 (milliseconds). You can specify a different timeout to be used with the failover transport, as shown:

```
failover:(tcp://host1:61616?wireFormat.maxInactivityDuration=1000,\
tcp://host2:61616?wireFormat.maxInactivityDuration=1000)
```

Note that you have to set this parameter (and any other OpenWire properties) on the transports used by the failover protocol, not the failover protocol itself.

By default, the delivery mode for sending messages from an ActiveMQ client is persistent (this is so ActiveMQ is compliant with the JMS specification). A message sent with a persistent delivery mode will be synchronous—send() will block until it gets a receipt from the broker that it has successfully received and stored the message. For applications where performance is important, using nonpersistent delivery can dramatically improve results (see chapter 13). When nonpersistent delivery is used, messages are sent asynchronously, which has the downside that you can potentially lose messages in flight if a transport fails. You can configure the failover transport to prevent this by enabling message caching with the trackMessages failover transport property. You can also control the maximum size of this message cache by use of the maxCacheSize failover property—the default is 128 KB (the memory allocation size allowed for the message cache). Here's an example configuration for enabling caching and setting the maximum cache size:

```
failover:(tcp://host1:61616,tcp://host2:61616)?\
trackMessages=true,maxCacheSize=256000
```

For high-performance applications, fast failover is important too. It takes a considerable amount of time to build up a new transport connection (in the order of tens to hundreds of milliseconds), so to enable fast failover, ActiveMQ can optionally allow the failover protocol to build a backup connection ready to go if the primary transport fails. The failover property to set to allow a backup connection is unsurprisingly called backup. You can have more than one backup enabled (the default is 1) by setting the failover property backupPoolSize. An example failover URI using backup is shown next:

```
failover:(tcp://host1:61616,tcp://host2:61616,\
tcp://host3:61616)?backup=true,backupPoolSize=2
```

So far we've looked at configuring the failover transport with a static list of URIs to the broker, but an ActiveMQ broker does know what brokers it's connected to, so it can optionally dynamically update clients with changes to the cluster as brokers come and go. To enable dynamic updates of brokers to an ActiveMQ client, we need to enable the property updateClusterClients on the TransportConnector used in the ActiveMQ broker configuration. Properties on the TransportConnector are used to control the updates; these are as shown in table 12.1.

Table 12.1 TransportConnector properties for updating clients of cluster changes

Property	Default value	Description
updateClusterClients	false	If true, pass information to connected clients about changes in the topology of the broker cluster.
rebalanceClusterClients	false	If true, connected clients will be asked to rebalance across a cluster of brokers when a new broker joins the network of brokers.

Table 12.1 `TransportConnector` properties for updating clients of cluster changes (*continued*)

Property	Default value	Description
`updateClusterClientsOnRemove`	false	If true, will update clients when a cluster is removed from the network. Having this as separate option enables clients to be updated when new brokers join, but not when brokers leave.
`updateClusterFilter`	null	Comma-separated list of regular expression filters used to match broker names of brokers to designate as being part of the failover cluster for the clients.

An interesting property is `rebalanceClusterClients` which, if enabled, ensures that the ActiveMQ clients will evenly distribute themselves across the cluster when a new broker joins.

An example configuration for an ActiveMQ broker on a machine named *tokyo* using these properties is shown next:

```
<broker>
  ...
  <transportConnectors>
    <transportConnector name="clustered"
      uri="tcp://0.0.0.0:61616"
      updateClusterClients="true"
      updateClusterFilter="*newyork*,*london*" />
  </<transportConnectors>
  ...
</broker>
```

This configuration will update any clients that are using the failover transport protocol with the locations of any brokers joining that have *newyork* or *london* in their broker names. With `updateClusterClients` enabled, you only need to configure the failover protocol with one broker in the cluster, for example:

```
failover:(tcp://tokyo:61616)
```

As the client will be updated automatically as new brokers join and leave the cluster, if the machine *tokyo* should fail, the client would automatically fail over to either *newyork* or *london*.

You may wish for your clients to automatically be distributed around all the machines in a cluster, so all the machines share the load of your messaging application. By enabling the property `rebalanceClusterClients` on the `TransportConnector`, as ActiveMQ brokers join and leave the cluster, this will automatically happen.

In this section we've taken a deeper look at some the functionality that can be used with the failover transport protocol. You should now have a better understanding of how to configure an ActiveMQ client to detect and survive a network outage or broker failure.

In the next section we're going to look at scheduling a message to be delivered by the ActiveMQ broker at some time in the future.

12.6   *Scheduling messages to be delivered by ActiveMQ in the future*

The ability to schedule a message to be delivered after a delay, or at regular intervals, is an extremely useful feature provided by ActiveMQ. One unique benefit is that messages that are scheduled to be delivered in the future are stored persistently, so that they can survive a hard failure of an ActiveMQ broker and be delivered on restart.

You specify that you want a message to be delivered at a later time by setting well-defined properties on the message. For convenience, the well-known property names are defined in the `org.apache.activemq.ScheduledMessage` interface. These properties are shown in table 12.2.

Table 12.2   `TransportConnector` properties for updating clients of cluster changes

Property	type	Description
AMQ_SCHEDULED_DELAY	false	The time in milliseconds that a message will wait before being scheduled to be delivered by the broker
AMQ_SCHEDULED_PERIOD	false	The time in milliseconds after the start time to wait before scheduling the message again
AMQ_SCHEDULED_REPEAT	false	The number of times to repeat scheduling a message for delivery
AMQ_SCHEDULED_CRON	String	Use a cron entry to set the schedule

To have a message wait for a period of time before its delivered, you only need to set the `AMQ_SCHEDULED_DELAY` property. Suppose you want to publish a message from your client, but have it actually delivered in 5 minutes time. You'd need to do something like the following in your client code:

```
MessageProducer producer = session.createProducer(destination);
TextMessage message = session.createTextMessage("test msg");
long delayTime = 5 * 60 * 1000;

message.setLongProperty(ScheduledMessage.AMQ_SCHEDULED_DELAY, delayTime);
producer.send(message);
```

ActiveMQ will store the message persistently in the broker, and when it's scheduled, it will deliver it to its destination. This is important, because although you've specified that you want the message to be delivered in 5 minutes time, if the destination is a queue, it will be posted to the end of the queue. So the actual delivery time will be dependent on how many messages already exist on the queue awaiting delivery.

You can also use a the `AMQ_SCHEDULED_PERIOD` and `AMQ_SCHEDULED_REPEAT` properties to have messages delivered at a fixed rate. The following example will send a message 100 times, every 30 seconds:

```
MessageProducer producer = session.createProducer(destination);
TextMessage message = session.createTextMessage("test msg");
```

```
long delay = 30 * 1000;
long period = 30 * 1000;
int repeat = 99;

message.setLongProperty(ScheduledMessage.AMQ_SCHEDULED_DELAY, delay);
message.setLongProperty(ScheduledMessage.AMQ_SCHEDULED_PERIOD, period);
message.setIntProperty(ScheduledMessage.AMQ_SCHEDULED_REPEAT,
  COUNT repeat);
producer.send(message);
```

Note that we specified the repeat as being 99, as the first message + 99 = 100. If you schedule a message to be sent once, the message ID will be the same as the one you published. If you schedule a repeat, or use the AMQ_SCHEDULED_CRON property to schedule your message, then ActiveMQ will create a unique message ID for the delivered message.

Cron is a well-known job scheduler on Unix systems, and it uses an expression string to denote when a job should be scheduled. ActiveMQ uses the same syntax, as described next:

```
.--------------- minute (0 - 59)
|  .------------- hour (0 - 23)
|  |  .---------- day of month (1 - 31)
|  |  |  .------- month (1 - 12) - 1 = January
|  |  |  |  .---- day of week (0 - 7) (Sunday=0 or 7
|  |  |  |  |
*  *  *  *  *
```

For example, if you want to schedule a message to be delivered at 2 a.m. on the twelfth day of every month, you'd need to do the following:

```
MessageProducer producer = session.createProducer(destination);
TextMessage message = session.createTextMessage("test msg");
message.setStringProperty(ScheduledMessage.AMQ_SCHEDULED_CRON,
  "0 2 12 * *");
producer.send(message);
```

You can combine scheduling with cron and a simple delay and repeat, but the cron entry will always take precedence. For example, instead of sending one message at 2 a.m. on the twelfth day of every month, you may want to schedule 10 messages to be delivered every 30 seconds:

```
long delay = 30 * 1000;
long period = 30 * 1000;
int repeat = 9;

MessageProducer producer = session.createProducer(destination);
TextMessage message = session.createTextMessage("test msg");

message.setStringProperty(ScheduledMessage.AMQ_SCHEDULED_CRON,
  "0 2 12 * *");
message.setLongProperty(ScheduledMessage.AMQ_SCHEDULED_DELAY, delay);
message.setLongProperty(ScheduledMessage.AMQ_SCHEDULED_PERIOD, period);
message.setIntProperty(ScheduledMessage.AMQ_SCHEDULED_REPEAT,
  COUNT repeat);

producer.send(message);
```

In this section we've looked at how to schedule messages for sometime in the future using ActiveMQ. You should now be able to send messages after a delay, send multiple instances of the same message at regular intervals, and use a cron entry to schedule message delivery.

12.7 Summary

In this chapter we learned about some of the advanced features that an ActiveMQ client can use above and beyond the JMS specification.

We learned about exclusive consumers, and walked through an example of using them as a distributed locking mechanism to ensure (paradoxically) that only one producer will be running for a distributed application. We've seen the power of using message groups to group messages together so that they're consumed by the same message consumer.

We also looked at two different ways of transporting large payloads with ActiveMQ: ActiveMQ streams and blob messages. You should also have a much better understanding of the options available when using the failover transport protocol, and how to schedule delivery of messagse in the future with ActiveMQ.

In the next chapter we'll look at performance tuning with ActiveMQ, and some of the trade-offs between reliability and performance.

Tuning ActiveMQ
for performance

This chapter covers

- Learn general tuning techniques
- How to optimize producers and consumers
- An example application that has been tuned

The performance of ActiveMQ is highly dependent on a number of different factors, including the broker network topology, the transport, the quality of service and speed of the underlying network, hardware, operating system, and the Java Virtual Machine.

But you can apply some performance techniques to ActiveMQ to improve performance regardless of its environment. Your application may not need guaranteed delivery, in which case reliable, nonpersistent messaging would yield much better performance. It may make sense to use embedded brokers to reduce the paths of serialization that your messages need to pass through. And, finally, a multitude of tuning parameters can be applied, each of which have benefits and caveats. In this chapter we'll walk through all the standard architectural tweaks, tuning tricks, and more so that you have the best information to tune your application to meet your goals for performance.

Before we get to the complex tuning tweaks, we'll walk through some general but simple messaging techniques using nonpersistent message delivery and batching messages together. Either one of these can reap large performance benefits—definitely the first thing to consider if performance is going to be critical.

As we walk through the different tuning options for ActiveMQ, we'll demonstrate them with example snippets of code, finally pulling all the tuning techniques together in an example data feed application.

13.1 *General techniques*

You can do two simple things to improve JMS messaging performance: use nonpersistent messaging, or if you really need guaranteed messaging, then use transactions to batch up large groups of messages. Usually nonpersistent message delivery isn't a consideration unless you don't care that a message will be lost (for example, in real-time data feeds, since the status will be sent repeatedly within such a short period of time), and batching messages in transactions won't always be applicable. But ActiveMQ incorporates failsafes for reliable delivery of nonpersistent messages so that only catastrophic failure would result in message loss. In this section we'll explain why nonpersistent message delivery and batching messages are faster, and why they could be applicable to use in your application if you don't need to absolutely guarantee that messages will never be lost.

13.1.1 *Persistent versus nonpersistent messages*

The JMS specification allows for two message delivery modes: persistent and nonpersistent delivery. The default delivery mode is persistent. When a producer sends a message to the broker that's marked as persistent, the message broker will always persist it to its message store before dispatching it to a consumer. This is to guard against catastrophic failure, or for later delivery to consumers who might not yet be active. If you're using nonpersistent delivery, then the JMS specification allows the messaging provider to make best efforts to deliver the message to currently active message consumers. ActiveMQ provides additional reliability here, which is covered later in this section. Nonpersistent messages are significantly faster than persistent messages—there are two reasons for this:

- Messages are sent asynchronously from the message producer, so the producer doesn't have to wait for a receipt from the broker. This is shown in figure13.1.
- Persisting messages to the message store (which typically involves writing to disk) is slow compared to messaging over a network.

The main reason for using persistence is to negate message loss in the case of a system outage. But as we saw in chapter 12, ActiveMQ can be configured to prevent this by configuring the failover transport to cache asynchronous messages to resend again on

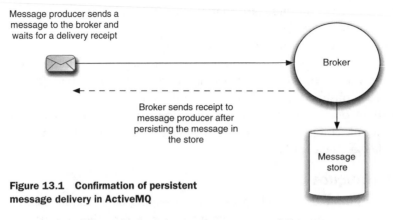

Figure 13.1   Confirmation of persistent message delivery in ActiveMQ

a transport failure (using the `trackMessages` failover transport property). ActiveMQ also prevents duplicate messages by using message auditing at both the client and the ActiveMQ broker. So for usage scenarios where only reliability is required (as opposed to guaranteed message delivery), a nonpersistent delivery mode can meet your needs.

As by default the message delivery mode is persistent, you have to explicitly set the delivery mode on the `MessageProducer` to send nonpersistent messages as can be seen in the following listing.

Listing 13.1   Persistent message delivery

```
MessageProducer producer = session.createProducer(topic);
producer.setDeliveryMode(DeliveryMode.NON_PERSISTENT);
```

We've seen why there's such a big performance difference between persistent and nonpersistent delivery of messages, and the steps that ActiveMQ takes to improve reliability of nonpersistent messages. The benefit of reliable message delivery allows nonpersistent messages to be used in many more cases than would be typical of a JMS provider.

Having covered nonpersistent messages, let's move on to the second generalized technique for improving performance of delivering messages in your application—batching messages together. The easiest way to batch messages is to use transaction boundaries, which are explained next.

13.1.2 *Transactions*

When you send messages using a transaction, only the *transaction boundary* (the `Session.commit()` method) results in synchronous communication with the message broker. So it's possible to batch up the production and/or the consumption of messages to improve performance of sending persistent messages. An example of this is shown next.

| Listing 13.2 | Transacted and nontransacted example |

```
public void sendTransacted() throws JMSException {
    ActiveMQConnectionFactory cf = new ActiveMQConnectionFactory();
    Connection connection = cf.createConnection();
    connection.start();

    Session session =
        connection.createSession(true, Session.SESSION_TRANSACTED);
    Topic topic = session.createTopic("Test.Transactions");
    MessageProducer producer = session.createProducer(topic);
    int count =0;
    for (int i =0; i < 1000; i++) {
        Message message = session.createTextMessage("message " + i);
        producer.send(message);

        if (i!=0 && i%10==0){
            session.commit();
        }
    }
}

public void sendNonTransacted() throws JMSException {

    ActiveMQConnectionFactory cf = new ActiveMQConnectionFactory();
    Connection connection = cf.createConnection();
    connection.start();

    //create a default session (no transactions)

    Session session =
        connection.createSession(false, Session.AUTO_ACKNOWELDGE);
    Topic topic = session.createTopic("Test.Transactions");
    MessageProducer producer = session.createProducer(topic);
    int count =0;
    for (int i =0; i < 1000; i++) {
        Message message = session.createTextMessage("message " + i);
        producer.send(message);
    }
}
```

So we've covered some of the easy pickings in terms of performance, use of nonpersistent messaging where possible, and now use of transaction boundaries for persistent messages if it makes sense for your application. We're now going to start (slowly) delving into some ActiveMQ specifics for techniques that can aid performance. The first is to use an embedded broker. Embedded brokers cut down on the amount of serialization and network traffic that ActiveMQ uses, as messages can be passed around in the same JVM.

13.1.3 *Embedding brokers*

It's often a requirement to co-locate applications with a broker, so that any service that's dependent on a message broker will only be available at the same time as the message broker, as shown in figure 13.2. Creating an embedded broker is straightforward, but one of the advantages of using the VM transport is that messages delivered

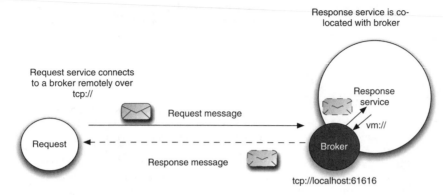

Figure 13.2   Embedding an ActiveMQ broker with a service

through a broker don't incur the cost of being serialized on the wire to be transported across the network, making it ideal for applications that need to service lots of responses quickly.

You can create an embedded broker with a transport connector to listen to TCP connections but still connect to it using the VM transport. By default, a broker always listens for transport connections on vm://<broker name>. The following listing is an example of setting up a service using an embedded broker to listen for requests on a queue named service.queue.

Listing 13.3   Creating a queue service

```
BrokerService broker = new BrokerService();
broker.setBrokerName("service");
broker.setPersistent(false);
broker.addConnector("tcp://localhost:61616");
broker.start();

ActiveMQConnectionFactory cf =
  new ActiveMQConnectionFactory("vm://service");
cf.setCopyMessageOnSend(false);
Connection connection = cf.createConnection();
connection.start();
Session session =
  connection.createSession(false, Session.AUTO_ACKNOWLEDGE);

final MessageProducer producer = session.createProducer(null);

Queue queue = session.createQueue("service.queue");
MessageConsumer consumer = session.createConsumer(queue);
consumer.setMessageListener(new MessageListener() {
    public void onMessage(Message msg) {
        try {
            TextMessage textMsg = (TextMessage)msg;
            String payload = "REPLY: " + textMsg.getText();
            Destination replyTo = msg.getJMSReplyTo();
            textMsg.clearBody();
            textMsg.setText(payload);
```

```
            producer.send(replyTo, textMsg);
        } catch (JMSException e) {
            e.printStackTrace();
        }
    }
}
});
```

You can test out this service with a `javax.jms.QueueRequestor` that connects to the service's embedded broker via the TCP transport connector, as shown in the following listing.

Listing 13.4 Connecting a `QueueRequestor`

```
ActiveMQConnectionFactory cf =
  new ActiveMQConnectionFactory("tcp://localhost:61616");
QueueConnection connection = cf.createQueueConnection();
connection.start();
QueueSession session =
  connection.createQueueSession(false, Session.AUTO_ACKNOWLEDGE);
Queue queue = session.createQueue("service.queue");
QueueRequestor requestor = new QueueRequestor(session,queue);
for(int i =0; i < 10; i++) {
    TextMessage msg = session.createTextMessage("test msg: " + i);
    TextMessage result = (TextMessage)requestor.request(msg);
    System.err.println("Result = " + result.getText());
}
```

As an aside, ActiveMQ by default will always copy the real message sent by a message producer to insulate the producer from changes to the message as it passes through the broker and is consumed by the consumer, all in the same Java Virtual Machine. If you intend to never reuse the sent message, you can reduce the overhead of this copy by setting the `copyMessageOnSend` property on the `ActiveMQConnectionFactory` to false, as shown next.

Listing 13.5 Using the `setCopyMessageOnSend` method

```
ActiveMQConnectionFactory cf = new ActiveMQConnectionFactory();
cf.setCopyMessageOnSend(false);
```

We've looked at some relatively easy-to-implement techniques to improve messaging performance. Using an embedded broker co-located with an application is a relatively trivial change to make. The performance gains and atomicity of the service co-located with its broker can be an attractive architectural change, too. Having gone through some of the easier "quick wins," we're going to start moving into some more difficult configuration areas. So the next section will touch on the OpenWire protocol and list some parameters you can tune to boost the performance of your messaging applications. These are dependent on both the hardware and the type of network you use.

13.1.4 Tuning the OpenWire protocol

It's worth covering some of the options available on the OpenWire protocol. The OpenWire protocol is the binary format used for transporting commands over a transport (such as TCP) to the broker. Commands include messages and message acknowledgements, as well as management and control of the broker. Table 13.1 shows some OpenWire wire format parameters that are relevant to performance.

Table 13.1   OpenWire tuning parameters

Parameter name	Default value	Description
tcpNoDelayEnabled	false	Provides a hint to the peer transport to enable/disable `tcpNoDelay`. If this is set, it may improve performance where you're sending lots of small messages across a relatively slow network.
cacheEnabled	true	Commonly repeated values (like `producerId` and `destination`) are cached, enabling short keys to be passed instead. This decreases message size, which can have a positive impact on performance where network performance is relatively poor. The cache lookup involved does add overhead to CPU load on both the clients and the broker machines, so take this into account.
cacheSize	1024	Maximum number of items kept in the cache. This shouldn't be bigger than Short.MAX_VALUE/2. The larger the cache, the better the performance where caching is enabled. But one cache will be used with every transport connection, so bear in mind the memory overhead on the broker, especially if it's loaded with a large number of clients.
tightEncodingEnabled	true	A CPU-intensive way to compact messages. We recommend disabling this if the broker starts to consume all the available CPU.

You can add these parameters to the URI used to connect to the broker in the following way. The following listing demonstrates disabling tight encoding, using the `tightEncodingEnabled` parameter.

Listing 13.6   Enabling tight encoding on the wire format

```
String uri =
    "failover://(tcp://localhost:61616?wireFormat.cacheEnabled=false&\
    wireFormat.tightEncodingEnabled=false)";
ActiveMQConnectionFactory cf = new ActiveMQConnectionFactory(url);
cf.setAlwaysSyncSend(true);
```

These parameters are dependent on the type of application, type of machine(s) used to run the clients and the broker, and type of network used. Unfortunately this isn't an exact science, so some experimentation is recommended.

As we've lightly introduced some of the tuning parameters available on the Open-Wire protocol, in the next section we'll look at some of the tuning parameters available on the TCP transport.

13.1.5 *Tuning the TCP transport*

The most commonly used transport for ActiveMQ is the TCP transport. Two parameters directly affect performance for this transport:

- `socketBufferSize`—The size of the buffers used to send and receive data over the TCP transport. Usually the bigger the better (though this is operating system dependent, so it's worth testing!). The default value is 65536, which is the size in bytes.
- `tcpNoDelay`—The default is false. Normally a TCP socket buffers up small pieces of data before being sent. When you enable this option, messages will be sent as soon as possible. Again, it's worth testing this out, as whether this boosts performance can be operating system dependent.

Here's an example transport URI where the `tcpNoDelay` property is enabled:

> **Listing 13.7   Using the `tcpNoDelay` setting to tune the TCP transport**

```
String url = "failover://(tcp://localhost:61616?tcpNoDelay=true)";
ActiveMQConnectionFactory cf = new ActiveMQConnectionFactory(url);
cf.setAlwaysSyncSend(true);
```

We've covered some general techniques to improve performance at the application level, and looked at tuning the wire protocol and the TCP transport. In the next two parts of this chapter, we'll look at tuning message producers and then message consumers. ActiveMQ is flexible in its configuration, and its producers can be configured to optimize their message exchanges with the broker, which can boost throughput considerably.

13.2   *Optimizing message producers*

The rate at which producers send messages to an ActiveMQ message broker before they're dispatched to consumers is a fundamental element of overall application performance. We'll now cover some tuning parameters that affect the throughput and latency of messages sent from a message producer to an ActiveMQ broker.

13.2.1 *Asynchronous send*

We've already covered the performance gains that can be achieved if you use nonpersistent delivery for messages. In ActiveMQ nonpersistent delivery is reliable, in that delivery of messages will survive network outages and system crashes (as long as the producer is active—it holds messages for redelivery in its failover transport cache). But you can also get the same performance gain for persistent messages by setting the `useAsyncSend` property on the message producer's connection factory, as shown next.

Listing 13.8   Enabling asynchronous sends

```
ActiveMQConnectionFactory cf = new ActiveMQConnectionFactory();
cf.setUseAsyncSend(true);
```

This will set a property that tells the MessageProducer not to expect a receipt for messages it sends to the ActiveMQ broker. This means that a producer will not wait until the message is on disk before sending another message.

If your application requires guaranteed delivery, it's recommend that you use the default delivery mode, persistent delivery, and preferably use transactions too.

The reasons for using asynchronous message delivery for gaining performance should be well understood, and setting a property on the ActiveMQ connection factory is a straightforward way of achieving that. Next we'll cover a commonly misunderstood feature in ActiveMQ: producer flow control. We see a lot of questions about producers slowing down or pausing, and understanding flow control will allow you to mitigate this situation in your applications.

13.2.2 *Producer flow control*

Producer flow control allows the message broker to slow the rate of messages that are passed through it when resources are running low. This typically happens when consumers are slower than the producers, and messages are using memory in the broker awaiting dispatch.

A producer will wait until it receives a notification from the broker that it has space for more messages, as shown in figure 13.3. Producer flow control is necessary to prevent a broker's usage limits for memory and temporary store space from being overrun, especially for wide area networks.

Producer flow control is enabled by default for persistent messages but must be explicitly enabled for asynchronous publishing (persistent messages, or for connections configured to always send asynchronously). You can enable flow control for asynchronous publishing by setting the producerWindowSize property on the connection factory.

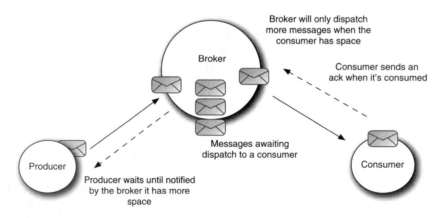

Figure 13.3 `MessageProducer` **feedback with producer flow control enabled**

Listing 13.9　Setting the producer window size

```
ActiveMQConnectionFactory cf = new ActiveMQConnectionFactory();
cf.setProducerWindowSize(1024000);
```

The `producerWindowSize` property is used to specify the number of bytes allowed in the producer's send buffer before it'll be forced to wait for a receipt from the broker that it's still within its usage limits. If this isn't enabled for an asynchronous publisher, the broker will still pause message flow, which defaults to blocking the message producer's transport. Blocking the transport will block all users of the connection, which can lead to deadlock if the message consumers are sharing the connection. Producer flow control allows blocking only the producer rather than the entire connection.

Although protecting the broker from running low on memory is a noble aim, it doesn't aid our cause for performance when everything slows down to the slowest consumer! So let's see what happens when you disable producer flow control, as shown in bold in the following code. You can do this in the broker configuration on a destination policy.

Listing 13.10　How to disable flow control

```
<destinationPolicy>
  <policyMap>
    <policyEntries>
      <policyEntry topic="FOO.>"
        producerFlowControl="false"
        memoryLimit="10mb" />
    </policyEntries>
  </policyMap>
</destinationPolicy>
```

With producer flow control disabled, messages for slow consumers will be off-lined to temporary storage by default, enabling the producers and the rest of the consumers to run at a much faster rate as outlined in figure 13.4. Additionally, the system usage memory limit determines the point at which messages are offloaded to disk by the pending message cursors. The system usage memory limit setting is applied across the broker. This limit needs to be lower than the destination memory limits so that they can kick in before producer flow control.

Disabling producer flow control enables messaging applications to run at a pace independent of the slowest consumer, though there's a slight performance hit in off-lining messages. In an ideal world, consumers would always be running as fast as the fastest producer, which neatly brings us to the next section on optimizing message consumers.

TUNING PRODUCER FLOW CONTROL

By default, when producer flow control is enabled and there's not enough space in the broker for more messages, the producer's send operation will block until space becomes available on the broker. There are two ways to tune this parameter so that it

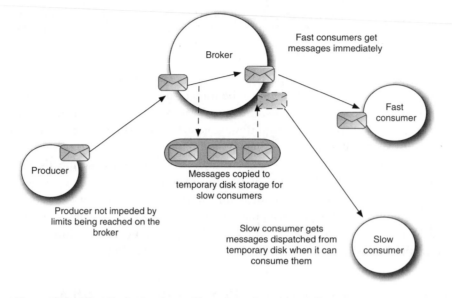

Figure 13.4   What the broker does with producer flow control disabled

doesn't block indefinitely and essentially hang the producer until space becomes available.

The first tuning option for producer flow control is named sendFailIfNoSpace:

```
<systemUsage>
 <systemUsage sendFailIfNoSpace="true">
   <memoryUsage>
     <memoryUsage limit="128 mb"/>
   </memoryUsage>
 </systemUsage>
</systemUsage>
```

The sendFailIfNoSpace property puts control back into the hands of the producer by throwing an exception on the client side when a send operation is attempted and space isn't available, instead of blocking the send operation indefinitely. This allows the producer to catch the exception, wait a bit, and attempt the send the operation again.

The second tuning option for producer flow control was made available in ActiveMQ 5.4.1. This property is named sendFailIfNoSpaceAfterTimeout:

```
<systemUsage>
 <systemUsage sendFailIfNoSpaceAfterTimeout="5000">
   <memoryUsage>
     <memoryUsage limit="128 mb"/>
   </memoryUsage>
 </systemUsage>
</systemUsage>
```

The sendFailIfNoSpaceAfterTimeout property provides a slightly different kind of control. This property causes the send operation to fail with an exception on the client side, but only after waiting the given amount of time for space to become available.

13.3 Optimizing message consumers

In order to maximize application performance, you have to look at all the participants—and as we have seen so far, consumers play a big part in the overall performance of ActiveMQ. Message consumers typically have to work twice as hard as message producers, because in addition to consuming messages, they have to acknowledge that the message has been consumed. We'll explain some of the biggest performance gains you can get with ActiveMQ by tuning the consumers.

Typically the ActiveMQ broker will deliver messages as quickly as possible to consumer connections. Once messages are delivered over the transport from the ActiveMQ broker, they're typically queued in the session associated with the consumer, where they wait to be delivered. In the next section we'll explain why and how the rate at which messages are pushed to consumers is controlled, and how to tune that rate for better throughput.

13.3.1 Prefetch limit

ActiveMQ uses a push-based model for delivery, delivering messages to consumers when they're received by the ActiveMQ broker. To ensure that a consumer won't exhaust its memory, there's a limit (prefetch limit) to how many messages will be delivered to a consumer before the broker waits for an acknowledgement that the messages have been consumed by the application. Internal to the consumer, messages are taken off the transport when they're delivered and placed into an internal queue associated with the consumer's session, as shown in figure 13.5.

A consumer connection will queue messages to be delivered internally. The size of these queues plus the number of in-flight messages (messages that have been dispatched to the consumer but haven't yet been acknowledged) is limited by the

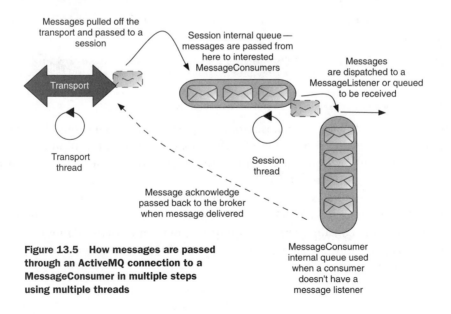

Figure 13.5 How messages are passed through an ActiveMQ connection to a MessageConsumer in multiple steps using multiple threads

prefetch limit for that consumer. In general, the larger the prefetch size, the faster the consumer will work.

But this isn't always ideal for queues, where you might want to ensure that messages are evenly distributed across all consumers on a queue. In this case with a large prefetch, a slow consumer could have pending messages waiting to be processed that could've been worked on by a faster consumer. In this case, a lower prefetch number would work better. If the prefetch is zero, the consumer will pull messages from the broker and no push will be involved.

There are different default prefetch sizes for different consumers:

- Queue consumer default prefetch size = 1000
- Queue browser consumer default prefetch size = 500
- Persistent topic consumer default prefetch size = 100
- Nonpersistent topic consumer default prefetch size = 32766

The prefetch size is the number of outstanding messages that your consumer will have waiting to be delivered, not the memory limit. You can set the prefetch size for your connection by configuring the `ActiveMQConnectionFactory` as shown next.

Listing 13.11   Configuring the prefetch policy on the `ActiveMQConnectionFactory`

```
ActiveMQConnectionFactory cf = new ActiveMQConnectionFactory();

Properties props = new Properties();
props.setProperty("prefetchPolicy.queuePrefetch", "1000");
props.setProperty("prefetchPolicy.queueBrowserPrefetch", "500");
props.setProperty("prefetchPolicy.durableTopicPrefetch", "100");
props.setProperty("prefetchPolicy.topicPrefetch", "32766");

cf.setProperties(props);
```

Or you can pass the prefetch size as a destination property when you create a destination:

Listing 13.12   Setting the prefetch size when creating a destination

```
Queue queue = new ActiveMQQueue("TEST.QUEUE?consumer.prefetchSize=10");
MessageConsumer consumer = session.createConsumer(queue);
```

Prefetch limits are an easy mechanism to boost performance, but should be used with caution. For queues, you should consider the impact on your application if you have a slow consumer, and for topics, factor how much memory your messages will consume on the client before they're delivered.

Controlling the rate at which messages are delivered to a consumer is only part of the story. Once the message reaches the consumer's connection, the method of message delivery to the consumer and the options chosen for acknowledging the delivery of that message back to the ActiveMQ broker have an impact on performance. We'll cover these in the next section.

13.3.2 *Delivery and acknowledgment of messages*

Something that should be apparent from figure 13.5 is that delivery of messages via a `javax.jms.MessageListener.onMessage()` will always be faster with ActiveMQ than calling `javax.jms.MessageConsumer.receive()`. If a `MessageListener` isn't set for a `MessageConsumer`, then its messages will be queued for that consumer, waiting for the `receive()` method to be called. Not only will maintaining the internal queue for the consumer be expensive, but so will the context switch by the application thread calling the `receive()` method.

As the ActiveMQ broker keeps a record of how many messages have been consumed to maintain its internal prefetch limits, a `MessageConsumer` has to send a message acknowledgment for every message it has consumed. When you use transactions, this happens at the `Session.commit()` method call, but is done individually for each message if you're using auto-acknowledgment.

Some optimizations are used for sending message acknowledgments back to the broker, which can drastically improve the performance when using the DUPS_OK_ACKNOWLEDGE session acknowledgment mode. In addition, you can set the `optimizeAcknowledge` property on the ActiveMQ `ConnectionFactory` to give a hint to the consumer to roll up message acknowledgments.

Listing 13.13 Setting the `optimizeAcknowledge` property

```
ActiveMQConnectionFactory cf = new ActiveMQConnectionFactory();
cf.setOptimizeAcknowledge(true);
```

When using `optimizeAcknowledge` or the DUPS_OK_ACKNOWLEDGE acknowledgment mode on a session, the message consumer can send one message acknowledgment to the ActiveMQ message broker containing a range of all the messages consumed. This reduces the amount of work the message consumer has to do, enabling it to consume messages at a much faster rate.

Table 13.2 below outlines the different options for acknowledging messages and how often they send back a message acknowledgment to the ActiveMQ message broker.

Table 13.2 ActiveMQ acknowledgment modes

Acknowledgment mode	Sends an acknowledgment	Description
Session.SESSION_TRANSACTED	Rolls up acknowledgments with `Session.commit()`.	Reliable way for message consumption and performs well, providing you consume more than one message in a commit.
Session.CLIENT_ACKNOWLEDGE	All messages up to when a message is acknowledged are consumed.	Can perform well, providing the application consumes a lot of messages before calling acknowledge.

Table 13.2   ActiveMQ acknowledgment modes (continued)

Acknowledgment mode	Sends an acknowledgment	Description
Session.AUTO_ACKNOWLEDGE	Automatically sends a message acknowledgment back to the ActiveMQ broker for every message consumed.	This can be slow but is often the default mechanism for message consumers.
Session.DUPS_OK_ACKNOWLEDGE	Allows the consumer to send one acknowledgment back to the ActiveMQ broker for a range of messages consumed.	An acknowledgment will be sent back when the prefetch limit has reached 50% full. The fastest standard way of consuming messages.
ActiveMQSession.INDIVIDUAL_ACKNOWLEDGE	Sends one acknowledgment for every message consumed.	Allows great control by enabling messages to be acknowledged individually but can be slow.
optimizeAcknowledge	Allows the consumer to send one acknowledgment back to the ActiveMQ broker for a range of messages consumed.	A hint that works in conjunction with Session.AUTO_ACKNOWLEDGE. An acknowledgment will be sent back when 65% of the prefetch buffer has been consumed. This is the fastest way to consume messages.

The downside to not acknowledging every message individually is that if the message consumer were to lose its connection with the ActiveMQ broker for any reason, then your messaging application could receive duplicate messages. But for applications that require fast throughput (such as real-time data feeds) and are less concerned about duplicates, using `optimizeAcknowledge` is the recommended approach.

The ActiveMQ message consumer incorporates duplicate message detection, which helps minimize the risk of receiving the same message more than once.

13.3.3 *Asynchronous dispatch*

Every session maintains an internal queue of messages to be dispatched to interested message consumers (as can be seen from figure 13.5). The usage of an internal queue together with an associated thread to do the dispatching to message consumers can add considerable overhead to the consumption of messages.

You can disable a property called `alwaysSessionAsync` on the ActiveMQ `ConnectionFactory` to turn this off. This allows messages to be passed directly from the transport to the message consumer. This property can be disabled as shown in the following code.

Listing 13.14   Disabling the `alwaysSessionAsync` property

```
ActiveMQConnectionFactory cf = new ActiveMQConnectionFactory();
cf.setAlwaysSessionAsync(false);
```

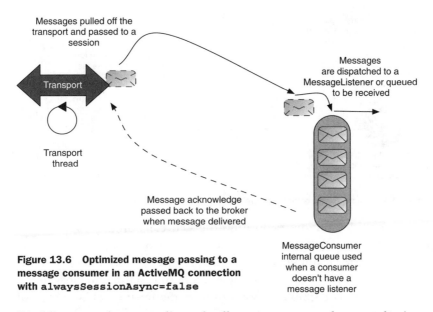

Messages pulled off the transport and passed to a session

Transport

Transport thread

Messages are dispatched to a MessageListener or queued to be received

Message acknowledge passed back to the broker when message delivered

MessageConsumer internal queue used when a consumer doesn't have a message listener

Figure 13.6   Optimized message passing to a message consumer in an ActiveMQ connection with `alwaysSessionAsync=false`

Disabling asynchronous dispatch allows messages to be pass the internal queueing and dispatching done by the session, as shown in figure 13.6.

So far we've looked at some general techniques you can use to improve performance, such as using reliable messaging instead of guaranteed and co-locating an ActiveMQ broker with a service. We've covered different tuning parameters for transports, producers, and consumers.

Because using examples is the best way to demonstrate something, in the next section we'll demonstrate how to improve performance with an example application of a real-time data feed.

13.4   Tuning in action

Let's demonstrate pulling some of these performance-tuning options together with an example application. We'll simulate a real-time data feed, where the producer is co-located with an embedded broker and a consumer listens for messages remotely. This is shown in figure 13.7.

We'll demonstrate using an embedded broker to reduce the overhead of publishing the data to the ActiveMQ broker. We'll show some additional tuning on the message producer to reduce message copying. The embedded broker itself will be configured with flow control disabled and memory limits set to allow for fast streaming of messages through the broker.

Finally the message consumer will be configured for straight-through message delivery, coupled with a high prefetch limit and optimized message acknowledgment.

First we set up the broker to be embedded, with the memory limit set to a reasonable amount (64 MB), memory limits set on each destination, and flow control disabled. The policies for the destinations in the broker are set up using the default `PolicyEntry`, as seen in the following code listing. A `PolicyEntry` holds configuration

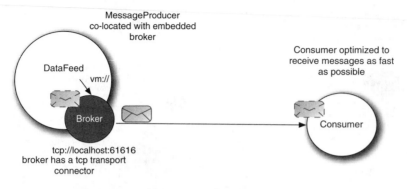

Figure 13.7   The sample tuned data feed application

information for a destination used within the ActiveMQ broker. You can have a separate policy for each destination, create a policy to only apply to destinations that match a wildcard (for example, naming a `PolicyEntry` foo.> will only apply to destinations starting with *foo*). For our example, we're only setting memory limits and disabling flow control. For simplicity, we'll only configure the default entry, which will apply to all destinations.

Listing 13.15   Creating the embedded broker

```
import org.apache.activemq.broker.BrokerService;
import org.apache.activemq.broker.region.policy.PolicyEntry;
import org.apache.activemq.broker.region.policy.PolicyMap;
 ...

BrokerService broker = new BrokerService();
broker.setBrokerName("fast");
broker.getSystemUsage().getMemoryUsage().setLimit(64*1024*1024);

PolicyEntry policy = new PolicyEntry();

policy.setMemoryLimit(4 * 1024 *1024);
policy.setProducerFlowControl(false);

PolicyMap pMap = new PolicyMap();

pMap.setDefaultEntry(policy);

broker.setDestinationPolicy(pMap);
broker.addConnector("tcp://localhost:61616");
broker.start();
```

This broker is uniquely named *fast* so that the co-located data feed producer can bind to it using the VM transport.

Apart from using an embedded broker, the producer is straightforward, except that it's configured to send nonpersistent messages and not use message copy. The example producer is configured as shown next.

Listing 13.16   Creating the producer

```
ActiveMQConnectionFactory cf = new ActiveMQConnectionFactory("vm://fast");

cf.setCopyMessageOnSend(false);

Connection connection = cf.createConnection();
connection.start();

Session session = connection.createSession(false, Session.AUTO_ACKNOWLEDGE);
Topic topic = session.createTopic("test.topic");
final MessageProducer producer = session.createProducer(topic);

producer.setDeliveryMode(DeliveryMode.NON_PERSISTENT);
for (int i =0; i < 1000000;i++) {
        TextMessage message = session.createTextMessage("Test:"+i);
        producer.send(message);
}
```

The consumer is configured for straight-through processing (having disabled asynchronous session dispatch) and using a `javax.jms.MessageListener`. The consumer is set to use `optimizeAcknowledge` to gain the maximum amount of consumption. This can be seen in the following code.

Listing 13.17   Creating the consumer

```
ActiveMQConnectionFactory cf =
  new ActiveMQConnectionFactory("failover://(tcp://localhost:61616)");

cf.setAlwaysSessionAsync(false);
cf.setOptimizeAcknowledge(true);

Connection connection = cf.createConnection();
connection.start();

Session session = connection.createSession(false, Session.AUTO_ACKNOWLEDGE);

Topic topic = session.createTopic("test.topic?consumer.prefetchSize=32766");

MessageConsumer consumer = session.createConsumer(topic);

final AtomicInteger count = new AtomicInteger();

consumer.setMessageListener(new MessageListener() {
  public void onMessage(Message message) {
      TextMessage textMessage = (TextMessage)message;
      try {
              if (count.incrementAndGet()%10000==0)
                  System.err.println("Got = " + textMessage.getText());
      } catch (JMSException e) {
          e.printStackTrace();
      }
  }
});
```

In this section we've pulled together an example for distributing real-time data using ActiveMQ. We created a demo producer and configured it to pass messages straight through to an embedded broker. We created the embedded broker, and disabled flow control. Finally, we configured a message consumer to receive messages as quickly as possible.

We recommend trying to change some of the configuration parameters we've set (such as the `optimizeAcknowledge` property) to see what impact that has on performance.

13.5   *Summary*

In general, message performance can be improved by asking ActiveMQ to do less. Consider the overhead of persisting messages and the cost of transporting both messages and client acknowledgments over the wire. If possible, use reliable messaging or batching of messages in transactions to reduce the overhead of passing a receipt from the broker to the producer that it has received a message. You can reduce the amount of work the ActiveMQ broker does by setting suitable memory limits (more is better) and deciding whether producer flow control is suitable for your application. The message consumer has to work twice as hard as the message producer, so optimizing delivery with a `MessageListener` and using straight-through message processing together with an acknowledgment mode or transactions that allow acknowledgments to be batched can reduce this load.

In this chapter you learned about some general principles for improving performance with any JMS-based application. We also dove into some of the internals of ActiveMQ and how changes to the configuration can increase performance. We learned when and when not to use those options, and their side effects. We also brought the different aspects of performance tuning together in an example real-time data feed application.

You should now have a better understanding of where the performance bottlenecks may occur when using ActiveMQ, and when and why to alleviate them. We've shown how to tune your message producers and message consumers, as well as the configuration parameters and their impact on your application architecture. You should be able to make the right architectural decisions for your application to help performance, and have a good understanding of the downsides in terms of guaranteeing delivery and how ActiveMQ can be used to mitigate them.

In the next and final chapter of this section, we'll look at how to administer and monitor ActiveMQ brokers using JMX, the ActiveMQ web console, and much more.

Administering and
monitoring ActiveMQ

The final topic left to be covered is management and monitoring of ActiveMQ broker instances. As with any other infrastructure software, it's important for developers and administrators to be able to monitor broker metrics during runtime and notice any suspicious behavior that could possibly impact messaging clients. Also, you might want to interact with your broker in other ways. For example, you might want to change broker configuration properties or send test messages from administration consoles. ActiveMQ implements some features beyond the standard JMS API that allow for administration and monitoring both programmatically and by using well-known administration tools.

We'll start this chapter with the explanation of the *Java Management Extension API* (JMX), the standard API for managing Java applications. Next, we'll explain the concept of *advisory messages*, which allow you to receive important notifications from the broker in a more messaging-like manner.

In later sections we'll focus on administrator tools for interacting with brokers. We'll explore some of the tools embedded in the ActiveMQ distribution such as the *command agent* and the *web console* as well as some of the external tools such as *JConsole*.

Finally, we'll explain how to adjust the ActiveMQ logging mechanism to suit your needs and demonstrate how to use it to track down potential problems. We'll also show you how to change the ActiveMQ logging preferences during runtime.

Now, let's get started with explaining how to use the JMX API with ActiveMQ. In the following section you'll learn how to configure JMX in ActiveMQ, and how you can write Java applications to gather various ActiveMQ statistics. It's an important topic because many tools we'll cover later use JMX to access the broker, so this is a lengthy section.

14.1   The JMX API and ActiveMQ

Nearly every story on management and monitoring in the Java world begins with *Java Management Extensions* (JMX). The JMX API allows you to implement *management interfaces* for your Java applications by exposing functionality to be managed. These interfaces consist of *management beans*, usually called *MBeans*, which expose resources of your application to external management applications. For this purpose, ActiveMQ exposes its management API through JMX, and it can be used to manage and monitor the broker during runtime. Some of these management and monitoring tasks may include

- Obtaining broker statistics, such as number of consumers (total or per destination)
- Adding new connectors or removing existing ones
- Changing some of the broker configuration properties

These tasks and many more can be achieved using JMX in ActiveMQ. Because JMX is the standard API for Java application management, most monitoring tools support the ability to execute JMX queries. This makes it incredibly easy to integrate the monitoring of a Java application into an existing tool that supports JMX.

In this section we'll learn how JMX is used with ActiveMQ. We'll start by explaining the difference between local and remote access to the broker's management API, and how to expose ActiveMQ JMX MBeans. While doing this, we'll cover various configuration options used to adapt JMX to your needs. Next, we'll see an example of a Java application that uses the JMX API to gather various broker statistics. Finally, we'll explain some more advanced JMX configuration topics, such as remote access and security.

14.1.1   Local vs. remote JMX access

The JVM provides what's known as the *JMX agent*. The JMX agent is comprised of the MBean server, some agent services, and some protocol adapters and connectors. The JMX agent is used to expose the ActiveMQ MBeans. In order to control various aspects of the JMX agent, a set of properties is provided. Through the use of these properties, various features in the JMX agent can be enabled and disabled. For more information, see the document titled "Monitoring and Management for the Java Platform" (http://mng.bz/0Dzg).

Here's a snippet from the ActiveMQ startup script for Linux/Unix concerning the JMX capabilities:

```
if [ -z "$SUNJMX" ] ; then
  #SUNJMX="-Dcom.sun.management.jmxremote.port=1099 \
-Dcom.sun.management.jmxremote.authenticate=false \
-Dcom.sun.management.jmxremote.ssl=false"
  SUNJMX="-Dcom.sun.management.jmxremote"
fi
```

Here's the same snippet from the ActiveMQ startup script for Windows concerning the SUNJMX variable:

```
if "%SUNJMX%" == "" set SUNJMX=-Dcom.sun.management.jmxremote
REM set SUNJMX=-Dcom.sun.management.jmxremote.port=1099 \
-Dcom.sun.management.jmxremote.authenticate=false \
-Dcom.sun.management.jmxremote.ssl=false
```

Note that each snippet demonstrates the use of a variable named SUNJMX. This variable is specific to the ActiveMQ startup scripts, and is used to hold the JMX properties that are recognized by the JVM. Each snippet shows that the only JMX property that's enabled by default is the com.sun.management.jmxremote property. Don't let the name of this property fool you, as it enables the JMX agent for *local access* only. This can be easily tested by starting up JConsole and seeing ActiveMQ in the list of locally accessible objects as shown in figure 14.1.

Figure 14.1 Accessing ActiveMQ locally from JConsole

Upon selecting the ActiveMQ run.jar and clicking the Connect button, the main screen will appear in JConsole, as shown in figure 14.2.

Note in figure 14.2 that the ActiveMQ JMX domain (listed as org.apache.activemq) is near the cursor. Using the default configuration and startup script in

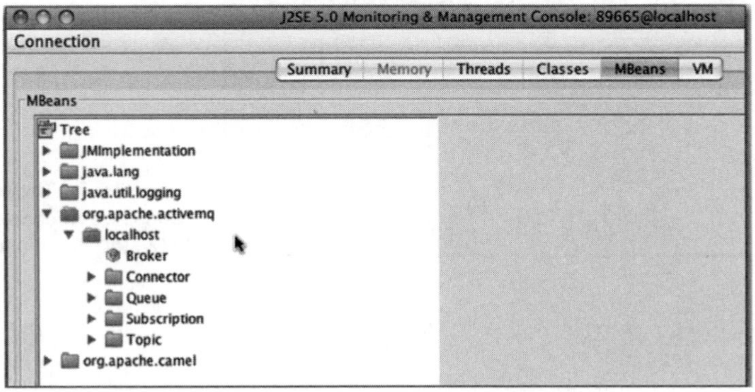

Figure 14.2 The main JConsole screen with the ActiveMQ domain included

ActiveMQ, this is what will appear in JConsole, indicating that the JMX agent is enabled for *local* access. But attempts to access ActiveMQ *remotely* (from a remote host) via JConsole will fail, as the JMX agent hasn't been exposed on a specific port number using the com.sun.management.jmxremote.port property. More on this later.

Here's a snippet from the default broker configuration with the useJmx attribute explicitly enabled (shown in bold):

```
<broker xmlns="http://activemq.org/config/1.0" useJmx="true"
  brokerName="localhost"
  dataDirectory="${activemq.base}/data">
...

</broker>
```

By simply changing the useJmx attribute from true to false, the ActiveMQ domain will no longer be available for access:

```
<broker xmlns="http://activemq.org/config/1.0" useJmx="false"

  brokerName="localhost"
  dataDirectory="${activemq.base}/data">
...

</broker>
```

Upon making this small configuration change, you'll be able to access the JMX agent via the ActiveMQ run.jar, but the ActiveMQ domain won't be available (see figure 14.3). This is because the JMX agent for the JVM and the domain for ActiveMQ are distinct. The JMX agent in the JVM is controlled by the com.sun.management.jmxremote property, whereas the ActiveMQ domain is controlled by the useJmx attribute in the broker configuration file.

14.1.2   *Exposing the JMX MBeans for ActiveMQ*

By default, the MBeans for ActiveMQ are enabled to be exposed for ease of use. In order to fully utilize the MBeans, there are additional properties in the broker configuration file to enable additional functionality. Listing 14.1 shows in bold what needs to be changed in the broker configuration to enable JMX support.

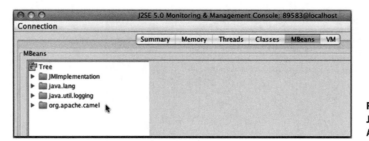

Figure 14.3   The main JConsole screen without the ActiveMQ domain included

Listing 14.1 ActiveMQ JMX configuration

```
<broker xmlns="http://activemq.org/config/1.0" useJmx="true"

  brokerName="localhost"
  dataDirectory="${activemq.base}/data">

  <managementContext>
    <managementContext connectorPort="2011" jmxDomainName="my-broker" />
  </managementContext>

  <transportConnectors>
    <transportConnector name="openwire" uri="tcp://localhost:61616" />
  </transportConnectors>
</broker>
```

Two important items in the preceding configuration file are related to the JMX configuration. The first is the useJmx attribute of the <broker> element that enables/disables JMX support. The value of this attribute is true by default so the broker uses JMX by default, but it's included in this example configuration for demonstration purposes.

By default, ActiveMQ starts a connector which enables remote management on port 1099 and exposes MBeans using the org.apache.activemq domain name. These default values are sufficient for most use cases, but if you need to customize the JMX context further, you can do so using the <managementContext> element. In our example we changed the port to 2011 and the domain name to my-broker. See the properties for the management context in table 14.1.

Now we can start the broker with the following command:

```
$ ${ACTIVEMQ_HOME}/bin/activemq console \
xbean:${EXAMPLES}src/main/resources/org/apache/activemq/book/ch14/ \
activemq-jmx.xml
```

Table 14.1 ManagementContext **properties**

Property name	Default value	Description
useMBeanServer	true	If true, try to locate and use the existing JVM's MBeanServer
jmxDomainName	org.apache.activemq	The JMX domain name
createMBeanServer	true	If true and if no MBeanServer can be located, create a new MBeanServer
createConnector	true	If true then create a JMX connector to the MBeanServer for remote management
connectorPort	1099	The port number to be used by the JMX connector
rmiServerPort	0	The port number to be used by the RMI server
connectorPath	/jmxrmi	The path to be used by the JMX connector

Among the usual log messages shown during the broker startup, you may notice the following line:

```
INFO  ManagementContext  - JMX consoles can connect to
service:jmx:rmi:///jndi/rmi://localhost:2011/jmxrmi
```

This is the JMX URL we can use to connect to the broker using a utility such as JConsole, as discussed later in the chapter. As you can see from the output, the port number for accessing the broker via JMX has been changed from 1099 to 2011.

Now that JMX support has been enabled in ActiveMQ, you can begin utilizing the JMX API to interact with the broker.

14.1.3 Exploring broker properties using the JMX API

Using the JMX API, statistics can be obtained from a broker at runtime. The example shown in the following listing connects to the broker via JMX and prints out some of the basic statistics such as total number of messages, consumers, and queues. Next it iterates through all available queues and prints their current size and number of consumers subscribed to them.

Listing 14.2   ActiveMQ broker statistics

```
public class Stats {

 public static void main(String[] args) throws Exception {

  JMXServiceURL url = new JMXServiceURL(
    "service:jmx:rmi:///jndi/rmi://localhost:2011/jmxrmi");
  JMXConnector connector = JMXConnectorFactory.connect(url, null);
  connector.connect();
  MBeanServerConnection connection =
    connector.getMBeanServerConnection();             ◁— Creates connection
                                                         to MBean server

  ObjectName name = new ObjectName(
    "my-broker:BrokerName=localhost,Type=Broker");
  BrokerViewMBean mbean =                                  Queries for
    (BrokerViewMBean) MBeanServerInvocationHandler         broker MBean
      .newProxyInstance(connection, name, BrokerViewMBean.class, true);  ◁—

  System.out.println("Statistics for broker " + mbean.getBrokerId()
    + " - " + mbean.getBrokerName());
  System.out.println("\n----------------\n");
  System.out.println("Total message count: " +
     mbean.getTotalMessageCount() + "\n");
  System.out.println("Total number of consumers: " +
     mbean.getTotalConsumerCount());
  System.out.println("Total number of Queues: " +        Grabs some
     mbean.getQueues().length);                        ◁— broker statistics

  for (ObjectName queueName : mbean.getQueues()) {
   QueueViewMBean queueMbean =
     (QueueViewMBean) MBeanServerInvocationHandler
       .newProxyInstance(connection, queueName, QueueViewMBean.class,
        true);
   System.out.println("\n----------------\n");
```

```
    System.out.println("Statistics for queue " + queueMbean.getName());
    System.out.println("Size: " + queueMbean.getQueueSize());
    System.out.println("Number of consumers: " +
        queueMbean.getConsumerCount());
  }
 }

}
```

◁─┐ **Grabs some queue statistics**

The preceding example is using the standard JMX API to access and use broker and request information. For starters, we have to create an appropriate connection to the broker's MBean server. Note that we've used the URL previously printed in the ActiveMQ startup log. Next, we'll use the connection to obtain the MBean representing the broker. The MBean is referenced by its name, which in this case has the following form:

`<jmx domain name>:BrokerName=<name of the broker>,Type=Broker`

The JMX object name for the ActiveMQ MBean using the default broker configuration is as follows:

`org.apache.activemq:BrokerName=localhost,Type=Broker`

But recall back in listing 14.1 that the JMX domain name was changed from `local-host` to `my-broker`. Therefore the JMX object name for the changed broker configuration looks like the following:

`my-broker:BrokerName=localhost,Type=Broker`

With this object name to fetch the broker MBean, now the methods on the MBean can be used to acquire the broker statistics as shown in listing 14.2. In this example, we print the total number of messages (`getTotalMessageCount()`), the total consumer count (`getTotalConsumerCount()`), and the total number of queues (`getQueues().length()`).

The `getQueues()` method returns the object names for all the queue MBeans. These names have a format similar to the broker MBean object name. For example, one of the queues we're using in the jobs queue is named JOBS.suspend and it has the following MBean object name:

`my-broker:BrokerName=localhost,`**`Type=Queue,Destination=JOBS.suspend`**

The only difference between this queue's object name and the broker's object name is in the portion marked in bold. This portion of the object name states that this MBean represents a type of `Queue` and has an attribute named `Destination` with the value `JOBS.suspend`.

Now it's time to examine the job queue example to see how to capture broker runtime statistics using the example from listing 14.2. But first the consumer must be slowed down a bit to be sure that some messages exist in the system before the statistics are gathered. For this purpose the following broker URL is used:

```
private static String brokerURL =
        "tcp://localhost:61616?jms.prefetchPolicy.all=1";
```

Note the parameter on the URI for the broker (the bold portion). This parameter ensures that only one message is dispatched to the consumer at a time.

Additionally, the consumer can be slowed down by adding a one-second sleep to the thread for every message that flows through the `Listener.onMessage()` method. Here's an example of this:

```
public void onMessage(Message message) {
  try {
    //do something here
    System.out.println(job + " id:" + ((ObjectMessage)message).getObject());
    Thread.sleep(1000);
  } catch (Exception e) {
    e.printStackTrace();
  }
}
```

The consumer (and listener) modified in this manner have been placed into package `org.apache.activemq.book.ch14.jmx`, and we'll use them in the rest of this section.

Now the producer can be started just like it was started in chapter 3:

```
mvn exec:java -Dexec.mainClass=org.apache.activemq.book.ch3.jobs.Publisher
```

And the modified consumer can be run as well:

```
mvn exec:java -Dexec.mainClass=org.apache.activemq.book.ch14.jmx.Consumer
```

Finally, run the JMX statistics class using the following command:

```
mvn -e exec:java -Dexec.mainClass=org.apache.activemq.book.ch14.jmx.Stats
```

The `org.apache.activemq.book.ch14.jmx.Stats` class output is shown next:

```
Statistics for broker ID:dejanb-52630-1231518649948-0:0 - localhost

-----------------

Total message count: 670

Total number of consumers: 2
Total number of Queues: 2

-----------------

Statistics for queue JOBS.suspend
Size: 208
Number of consumers: 1

-----------------

Statistics for queue JOBS.delete
Size: 444
Number of consumers: 1
```

Note that the statistics from the `Stats` class are output to the terminal. There are many more statistics on the MBeans from ActiveMQ. The example shown here is meant only to be an introduction.

As you can see, it's easy to access ActiveMQ using the JMX API. This will allow you to monitor the broker status, which is useful in both development and production environments. But what if you want to restrict access to the JMX capabilities?

14.1.4 Advanced JMX configuration

In some situations, advanced configuration of the JMX agent is necessary. This includes remote access, restricting access to a specific host, and restricting access to particular users via authentication. Most of these tasks are fairly easy to achieve through the use of the JMX agent properties and by slightly modifying the ActiveMQ startup script.

Again, remember the snippet from the ActiveMQ startup script for Linux/Unix concerning the JMX capabilities:

```
if [ -z "$SUNJMX" ] ; then
  #SUNJMX="-Dcom.sun.management.jmxremote.port=1099 \
-Dcom.sun.management.jmxremote.authenticate=false \
-Dcom.sun.management.jmxremote.ssl=false"
  SUNJMX="-Dcom.sun.management.jmxremote"
fi
```

Recall also the same snippet from the ActiveMQ startup script for Windows concerning the SUNJMX variable:

```
if "%SUNJMX%" == "" set SUNJMX=-Dcom.sun.management.jmxremote
REM set SUNJMX=-Dcom.sun.management.jmxremote.port=1099 \
-Dcom.sun.management.jmxremote.authenticate=false \
-Dcom.sun.management.jmxremote.ssl=false
```

Note the portions that are commented out. These three additional properties will be covered in this section, as well as a fourth related property.

ENABLING REMOTE JMX ACCESS

Sometimes it's necessary to allow access to the JMX agent from a remote host. Enabling remote access to the JMX agent is easy. The default ActiveMQ startup scripts include a configuration for remote access to the JMX agent using the com.sun.management.jmxremote.port property, but it's commented out. By adding this property to the uncommented portion of the SUNJMX variable, remote access will be enabled on the specified port number.

Here's a snippet from the ActiveMQ startup script for Linux/Unix with the com.sun.management.jmxremote.port property enabled:

```
if [ -z "$SUNJMX" ] ; then
  SUNJMX="-Dcom.sun.management.jmxremote.port=1234 \
-Dcom.sun.management.jmxremote.authenticate=false \
-Dcom.sun.management.jmxremote.ssl=false"
fi
```

Here's the same snippet from the ActiveMQ startup script for Windows with the com.sun.management.jmxremote.port property enabled:

```
if "%SUNJMX%" == "" set SUNJMX=-Dcom.sun.management.jmxremote.port=1234 \
-Dcom.sun.management.jmxremote.authenticate=false \
-Dcom.sun.management.jmxremote.ssl=false
```

Note that the `com.sun.management.jmxremote.port` property is now enabled and port number 1234 has been specified. Also, two additional JMX properties related to JMX security have been enabled as well. Specifically the `com.sun.management.jmxremote.authentication` property and the `com.sun. management.jmxremote.ssl` property have both been set to false. These two properties are included and set to false to disable security because otherwise they're both true by default for remote monitoring. The JMX agent in the JVM where ActiveMQ is started will be available for access via port number 1234. After enabling remote access, you can test this using JConsole's Remote tab as shown in figure 14.4.

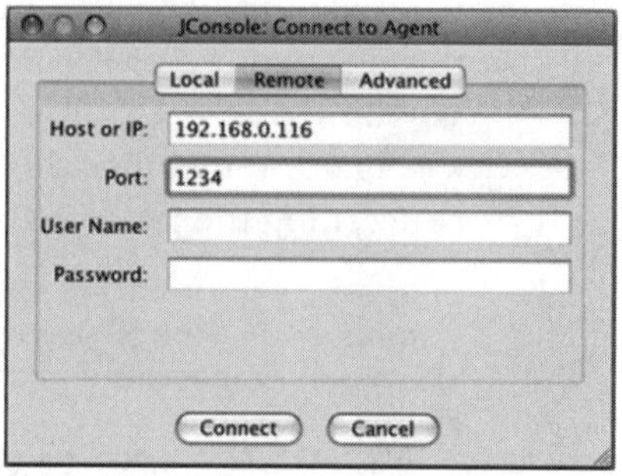

Upon successfully connecting to the remote ActiveMQ instance, you'll be able to remotely manage and monitor ActiveMQ.

Figure 14.4   Accessing the JMX agent remotely on port 1234

NOTE   In order for the JMX remote access to work successfully, the /etc/hosts file must be in order. Specifically, the /etc/hosts file must contain more than just the entry for the localhost on 127.0.0.1. The /etc/hosts file must also contain an entry for the real IP address and the hostname for a proper configuration. Here's an example of a proper configuration:

```
127.0.0.1        localhost
192.168.0.23     urchin.bsnyder.org   urchin
```

Note the portion of the /etc/hosts file that contains an entry for the localhost and an entry for the proper hostname and IP address.

14.1.5 *Restricting JMX access to a specific host*

Sometimes you need to restrict the use of JMX to a specific host in a multi-homed environment, such as the host on which ActiveMQ is running. The fourth related property mentioned earlier will provide this type of restriction via the Java SE, not by ActiveMQ itself. The `java.rmi.server.hostname` property is used to provide just such a restriction. As defined in the Java SE documents on the section about RMI properties (http://mng.bz/65hS):

> *The value of this property represents the host name string that should be associated with remote stubs for locally created remote objects, in order to allow clients to invoke methods on the remote object. In 1.1.7 and later, the default value of this property is the IP address of the local host, in "dotted-quad" format.*

This property must be added to the SUNJMX variable in the ActiveMQ startup script. Here's an example of adding this property to the ActiveMQ startup script for Linux/ Unix:

```
if [ -z "$SUNJMX" ] ; then
  SUNJMX="-Dcom.sun.management.jmxremote \
-Djava.rmi.server.hostname=192.168.0.23"
fi
```

And here's an example of adding this property to the ActiveMQ startup script for Windows:

```
if "%SUNJMX%" == "" set SUNJMX=-Dcom.sun.management.jmxremote \
-Djava.rmi.server.hostname=192.168.0.23
```

This slight change to use the `java.rmi.server.hostname` property simply notes the name of the host to which the access should be restricted. After making this change, the ActiveMQ MBeans can only be accessed from this host.

14.1.6 *Configuring JMX password authentication*

Password authentication for the JMX agent is controlled by an access file and a password file. The access file is used to define roles and assign permissions to those roles. The password file is used to map roles to passwords. The JDK provides examples of each of these files, so the best way to begin is to take a look at these files. The files are located in the $JAVA_HOME/jre/lib/management/ directory and are named jmxremote.access and jmxremote.password.template. Each of these files is intended to provide a starting point for you to define your own values.

Here are the contents of the default jmxremote.access file:

```
monitorRole readonly
controlRole readwrite
```

Note that `monitorRole` is the role name and `readonly` is the access level. *The role name needs to correspond to a role name in the password file.*

The contents of the default jmxremote.password.template file is empty but provides the following suggestion:

```
monitorRole QED
controlRole R&D
```

Note that `monitorRole` is the role name and `QED` is the password. *This role name corresponds to the role name in the jmxremote.access file.* The idea with the jmxremote. password.template file is that it should be used as a template—you should make a copy of the file to use as your password file and make changes specific to your needs.

To make a copy of the jmxremote.password.template file for Mac OS X, use the following command:

```
$ cp /System/Library/Java/JavaVirtualMachines/1.6.0.jdk/Contents/Home/lib/ \
management/jmxremote.password.template \
/System/Library/Java/JavaVirtualMachines/1.6.0.jdk/Contents/Home/lib/ \
management/jmxremote.password
```

To make a copy of the jmxremote.password.template file for Linux/Unix, use the following command:

```
$ cp $JAVA_HOME/jre/lib/management/jmxremote.password.template \
$JAVA_HOME/jre/lib/management/jmxremote.password
```

To make a copy of the jmxremote.password.template file for Windows, use the following command:

```
> copy %JAVA_HOME%\jre\lib\management\jmxremote.password.template \
%JAVA_HOME%\jre\lib\management\jmxremote.password
```

Edit the new jmxremote.password file so that the contents match the following:

```
myRole foo
yourRole bar
```

Note that two new roles have been defined with their own passwords.

Now edit the jmx.access file to include the two new roles so that the contents match the following:

```
myRole readwrite
yourRole readonly
```

Note how the roles in the jmxremote.access and jmxremote.password files correspond to one another.

The last requirement is to enable password authentication on the JMX agent. To do so, remove the `com.sun.management.jmxremote.authenticate` property from the SUNJMX variable in the ActiveMQ startup script. Here's an example of removing this property from the ActiveMQ startup script for Linux/Unix:

```
if [ -z "$SUNJMX" ] ; then
  SUNJMX="-Dcom.sun.management.jmxremote \
-Dcom.sun.management.jmxremote.port=1099
-Dcom.sun.management.jmxremote.ssl=false"
fi
```

And here's an example of removing this property from the ActiveMQ startup script for Windows:

```
if "%SUNJMX%" == "" set SUNJMX=-Dcom.sun.management.jmxremote \
-Dcom.sun.management.jmxremote.port=1099 \
-Dcom.sun.management.jmxremote.ssl=false
```

After removing the `com.sun.management.jmxremote.authenticate` property, the last thing to do is make sure that the user running the JVM has access to the jmxremote.password file.

> **NOTE** After copying the jmxremote.password.template file, chances are that you'll need to change the permissions on that file to disallow read access. If read access is allowed on the jmxremote.password file, the following error will potentially rear its head when starting up ActiveMQ:
>
> ```
> $ ./bin/activemq console
> Error: Password file read access must be restricted:
> /System/Library/Java/JavaVirtualMachines/1.6.0.jdk/Contents/Home/lib/ \
> management/jmxremote.password
> ```

The only thing left to do is start up ActiveMQ and make sure that there are no errors:

```
$ ./bin/activemq console
INFO: Using default configuration
(you can configure options in one of these file:
/etc/default/activemq /Users/bsnyder/.activemqrc)

INFO: Invoke the following command to create a configuration file
./bin/activemq setup [ /etc/default/activemq |
/Users/bsnyder/.activemqrc ]

INFO: Using java
'/System/Library/Frameworks/JavaVM.framework/Home/bin/java'
INFO: Starting in foreground, this is just for debugging purposes
(stop process by pressing CTRL+C)
Java Runtime: Apple Inc. 1.6.0_22
/System/Library/Java/JavaVirtualMachines/1.6.0.jdk/Contents/Home
  Heap sizes: current=258880k  free=253105k  max=258880k
    JVM args: -Xms256M -Xmx256M
     -Dorg.apache.activemq.UseDedicatedTaskRunner=true
-Djava.util.logging.config.file=logging.properties
-Dcom.sun.management.jmxremote
-Dactivemq.classpath=/Users/bsnyder/amq/apache-activemq-5.4.1/conf;
-Dactivemq.home=/Users/bsnyder/amq/apache-activemq-5.4.1
-Dactivemq.base=/Users/bsnyder/amq/apache-activemq-5.4.1
ACTIVEMQ_HOME: /Users/bsnyder/amq/apache-activemq-5.4.1
ACTIVEMQ_BASE: /Users/bsnyder/amq/apache-activemq-5.4.1
Loading message broker from: xbean:activemq.xml
 WARN | destroyApplicationContextOnStop parameter is deprecated,
please use shutdown hooks instead
 INFO | PListStore:/Users/bsnyder/amq/apache-activemq-5.4.1/data/
localhost/tmp_storage started
 INFO | Using Persistence Adapter: KahaDBPersistenceAdapter
[/Users/bsnyder/amq/apache-activemq-5.4.1/data/kahadb]
 INFO | ActiveMQ 5.4.1 JMS Message Broker (localhost) is starting
 INFO | For help or more information please see:
http://activemq.apache.org/
 INFO | Scheduler using directory:
/Users/bsnyder/amq/apache-activemq-5.4.1/data/localhost/scheduler
 INFO | JobSchedulerStore:/Users/bsnyder/amq/apache-activemq-5.4.1/data/
localhost/scheduler started
 INFO | Listening for connections at: tcp://mongoose.local:61616
 INFO | Connector openwire Started
 INFO | ActiveMQ JMS Message Broker
(localhost, ID:mongoose.local-50084-1292777410913-0:0) started
 INFO | Logging to org.slf4j.impl.JCLLoggerAdapter
(org.eclipse.jetty.util.log) via org.eclipse.jetty.util.log.Slf4jLog
 INFO | jetty-7.0.1.v20091125
 INFO | ActiveMQ WebConsole initialized.
 INFO | Initializing Spring FrameworkServlet 'dispatcher'
 INFO | ActiveMQ Console at http://0.0.0.0:8161/admin
 INFO | Initializing Spring root WebApplicationContext
 INFO | Connector vm://localhost Started
 INFO | Camel Console at http://0.0.0.0:8161/camel
 INFO | ActiveMQ Web Demos at http://0.0.0.0:8161/demo
 INFO | RESTful file access application at http://0.0.0.0:8161/fileserver
 INFO | Started SelectChannelConnector@0.0.0.0:8161
```

Now start up JConsole on a remote machine and attempt to use JConsole to remotely connect to ActiveMQ. Figure 14.5 shows what will happen when attempting to remotely log in to the JMX agent using a role name and password that don't exist in the jmxremote.access/jmxremote. password file pair. To successfully make a remote connection to the JMX agent, you must use the correct role name and password as shown in figure 14.6.

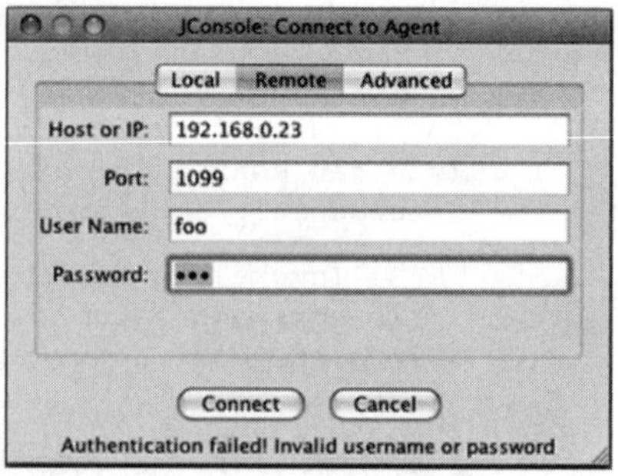

Figure 14.5 Attempting to remotely connect to the JMX agent with the wrong role name and password

Hopefully these advanced JMX configurations will help you with your ActiveMQ configurations and your ability to properly configure access.

Beyond the JMX features for monitoring and managing ActiveMQ, there are additional means of monitoring the inner workings of ActiveMQ via what are known as advisory messages.

14.2 *Monitoring ActiveMQ with advisory messages*

The JMX API is a well-known mechanism often used to manage and monitor a wide range of Java applications. But since you're already building a JMS application using ActiveMQ, shouldn't it be natural to receive messages regarding important broker events using the same JMS API? Fortunately, ActiveMQ provides what are

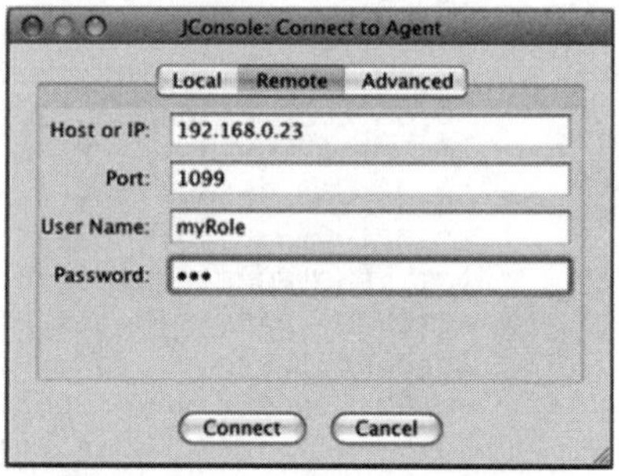

Figure 14.6 Making a successful remote connection to the JMX agent requires the correct role name and password.

known as *advisory messages* to represent administrative commands that can be used to notify messaging clients about important broker events.

14.2.1 *Configuring advisory support*

Advisory messages are delivered to topics whose names use the prefix `ActiveMQ.` `Advisory`. For example, if you're interested in knowing when connections to the broker are started and stopped, you can see this activity by subscribing to the `ActiveMQ.Advisory.Connection` topic. A variety of advisory topics are available depending on what broker events interest you. Basic events such as starting and stopping consumers, producers, and connections trigger advisory messages by default. But for more complex events, such as sending messages to a destination without a consumer, advisory messages must be explicitly enabled as shown next.

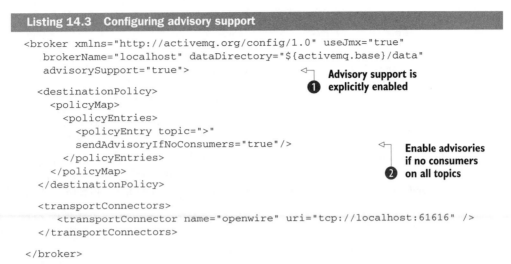

Listing 14.3 Configuring advisory support

```
<broker xmlns="http://activemq.org/config/1.0" useJmx="true"
    brokerName="localhost" dataDirectory="${activemq.base}/data"
    advisorySupport="true">                          Advisory support is
                                                  ❶ explicitly enabled

    <destinationPolicy>
      <policyMap>
        <policyEntries>
          <policyEntry topic=">"
          sendAdvisoryIfNoConsumers="true"/>       Enable advisories
        </policyEntries>                            if no consumers
      </policyMap>                               ❷ on all topics
    </destinationPolicy>

    <transportConnectors>
      <transportConnector name="openwire" uri="tcp://localhost:61616" />
    </transportConnectors>

</broker>
```

Advisory support can be enabled using the advisorySupport attribute of the <broker> element ❶. Please note that advisory support is enabled by default, so technically there's no need to set the advisorySupport attribute unless you want to be explicit about the configuration. The second and more important item is the use of a *destination policy* to enable more complex advisories for your destinations ❷. In the example, the configuration instructs the broker to send advisory messages if the destination has no consumers subscribed to it. One advisory message will be sent for every message that's sent to the destination.

To demonstrate this functionality, start the broker using the example configuration from above (named activemq-advisory.xml) via the following command:

```
$ ./bin/activemq \
xbean:src/main/resources/org/apache/activemq/book/ch14/activemq-advisory.xml
```

14.2.2 *Using advisory messages*

To demonstrate this functionality, we need to create a simple class that uses the advisory messages. This Java class will use the advisory messages to print log messages to standard output (stdout) whenever a consumer subscribes/unsubscribes, or a message is sent to a topic that has no consumers subscribed to it. This example can be run along with the stock portfolio example to make use of the advisory messages (and therefore, certain broker events).

To complete this demonstration, we must modify the stock portfolio producer. ActiveMQ will send an advisory message when a message is sent to a topic with no consumers, but only when those messages are nonpersistent. Because of this, we need to modify the producer to send nonpersistent messages to the broker by setting the delivery mode to nonpersistent. Using the publisher from chapter 3, the following listing shows this simple modification (marked as bold):

Listing 14.4   Forcing an advisory message

```
public Publisher(String brokerURL) throws JMSException {
    factory = new ActiveMQConnectionFactory(brokerURL);
    connection = factory.createConnection();
    connection.start();
    session = connection.createSession(false, Session.AUTO_ACKNOWLEDGE);
    producer = session.createProducer(null);
    producer.setDeliveryMode(DeliveryMode.NON_PERSISTENT);
}
```

The consumer modified in this manner has been placed into package org.apache.
activemq.book.ch14.advisory and we'll use it in the rest of this section.

Now let's take a look at our advisory messages example application shown next.

Listing 14.5   Advisory example

```
public class Advisory {

    protected static String brokerURL = "tcp://localhost:61616";
    protected static transient ConnectionFactory factory;
    protected transient Connection connection;
    protected transient Session session;

    public Advisory() throws Exception {
      factory = new ActiveMQConnectionFactory(brokerURL);
      connection = factory.createConnection();
      connection.start();                                          Create the
      session =                                                    JMS session
        connection.createSession(false, Session.AUTO_ACKNOWLEDGE);
    }

    public static void main(String[] args) throws Exception {
      Advisory advisory = new Advisory();
      Session session = advisory.getSession();
      for (String stock : args) {

        ActiveMQDestination destination =
          (ActiveMQDestination)session.createTopic("STOCKS." + stock);

        Destination consumerTopic =                 Obtains consumer advisory topic
          AdvisorySupport.getConsumerAdvisoryTopic(destination);
        System.out.println("Subscribing to advisory " + consumerTopic);
        MessageConsumer consumerAdvisory =
          session.createConsumer(consumerTopic);
        consumerAdvisory.setMessageListener(new ConsumerAdvisoryListener());

        Destination noConsumerTopic =               Obtains no consumer advisory topic
          AdvisorySupport.
            getNoTopicConsumersAdvisoryTopic(destination);
        System.out.println("Subscribing to advisory " + noConsumerTopic);
        MessageConsumer noConsumerAdvisory =
          session.createConsumer(noConsumerTopic);
          noConsumerAdvisory.setMessageListener(
          new NoConsumerAdvisoryListener());

      }
    }
}
```

```
public Session getSession() {
 return session;
 }

}
```

Listing 14.5 provides a demonstration using standard JMS messaging. In the main method, all topics of interest are traversed and consumers are created for the appropriate advisory topics. Note the use of the `AdvisorySupport` class, which you can use as a helper class for obtaining an appropriate advisory destination. In this example, subscriptions were created for the *consumer* and the *no topic consumer* advisory topics. For the topic named `topic://STOCKS.CSCO`, a subscription is created to the advisory topics named `topic://ActiveMQ.Advisory.Consumer.Topic.STOCKS.CSCO` and `topic://ActiveMQ.Advisory.NoConsumer.Topic.STOCKS.CSCO`.

> **NOTE** Wildcards can be used when subscribing to advisory topics. For example, subscribe to `topic://ActiveMQ.Advisory.Consumer.Topic.>` in order to receive advisory messages when a consumer subscribes and unsubscribes to all topics in the namespace recursively.

Now let's take a look at the consumer listeners and how they process advisory messages. First we'll explore the listener that handles consumer start and stop events, shown next.

Listing 14.6 Consumer advisory listener

```
public class ConsumerAdvisoryListener implements MessageListener {

 public void onMessage(Message message) {
  ActiveMQMessage msg = (ActiveMQMessage) message;
  DataStructure ds = msg.getDataStructure();
  if (ds != null) {
   switch (ds.getDataStructureType()) {          Consumer created
   case CommandTypes.CONSUMER_INFO:             new subscription
    ConsumerInfo consumerInfo = (ConsumerInfo) ds;
    System.out.println("Consumer '" + consumerInfo.getConsumerId()
      + "' subscribed to '" + consumerInfo.getDestination()
      + "'");
    break;                                       Consumer
   case CommandTypes.REMOVE_INFO:                unsubscribed
    RemoveInfo removeInfo = (RemoveInfo) ds;
    ConsumerId consumerId = ((ConsumerId) removeInfo.getObjectId());
    System.out.println("Consumer '" + consumerId + "' unsubscribed");
    break;
   default:
    System.out.println("Unknown data structure type");
   }
  } else {
   System.out.println("No data structure provided");
  }
 }
}
```

Every advisory is basically a regular instance of an `ActiveMQMessage` object. In order to get more information from the advisory messages, the appropriate data structure must be used. In this particular case, the message data structure denotes whether the consumer is subscribed or unsubscribed. If we receive a message with the `Consumer-Info` as data structure, it means that it's a new consumer subscription and all the important consumer information is held in the `ConsumerInfo` object. If the data structure is an instance of `RemoveInfo`, it means that this is a consumer that just unsubscribed from the destination. The call to `removeInfo.getObjectId()` method will identify which consumer it was.

In addition to the data structure, some advisory messages may contain additional properties that can be used to obtain important information that couldn't be included in the data structure. The complete reference of available advisory channels, along with appropriate data structures and properties you can expect on each of them, can be found at the Advisory Message page on the ActiveMQ website (http://mng.bz/j749).

Next is an example of a consumer that handles messages sent to a topic with no consumers.

Listing 14.7   No consumer advisory listener

```
public class NoConsumerAdvisoryListener implements MessageListener {
 public void onMessage(Message message) {
  try {
   System.out.println("Message "
       + ((ActiveMQMapMessage)message).getContentMap()
       + " not consumed by any consumer");
  } catch (Exception e) {
   e.printStackTrace();
  }
 }

}
```

In this example, the advisory message is the actual message sent to the destination. So the only action to take is to print the message to standard output (stdout).

RUNNING THE EXAMPLE

To run the example from the command line, use the following command:

```
$ mvn -e exec:java \
-Dexec.mainClass=org.apache.activemq.book.ch14.jmx.Advisory \
-Dexec.args="tcp://localhost:61616 CSCO ORCL"

...

Subscribing to advisory
topic://ActiveMQ.Advisory.Consumer.Topic.STOCKS.tcp://localhost:61616
Subscribing to advisory
topic://ActiveMQ.Advisory.NoConsumer.Topic.STOCKS.tcp://localhost:61616
Subscribing to advisory
topic://ActiveMQ.Advisory.Consumer.Topic.STOCKS.CSCO
```

```
Subscribing to advisory
topic://ActiveMQ.Advisory.NoConsumer.Topic.STOCKS.CSCO
Subscribing to advisory
topic://ActiveMQ.Advisory.Consumer.Topic.STOCKS.ORCL
Subscribing to advisory
topic://ActiveMQ.Advisory.NoConsumer.Topic.STOCKS.ORCL

...
```

Note that the example application has subscribed to the appropriate advisory topics, as expected.

In a separate terminal, run the stock portfolio consumer using the following command:

```
$ mvn -e exec:java -Dexec.mainClass=org.apache.activemq.book.ch3.Consumer \
-Dexec.args="tcp://localhost:61616 CSCO ORCL"
```

Upon running this command, the Advisory application will print the following output to the terminal:

```
Consumer 'ID:dejan-bosanacs-macbook-pro.local-64609-1233592052313-0:0:1:1'
subscribed to 'topic://STOCKS.CSCO'
Consumer 'ID:dejan-bosanacs-macbook-pro.local-64609-1233592052313-0:0:1:2'
subscribed to 'topic://STOCKS.ORCL'
```

This means that two advisory messages were received, one for each of the two consumers that subscribed.

Now we can start the stock portfolio publisher that was modified earlier to send nonpersistent messages. This application can be started in another terminal using the following command:

```
$ mvn -e exec:java \
-Dexec.mainClass=org.apache.activemq.book.ch14.advisory.Publisher
-Dexec.args="tcp://localhost:61616 CSCO ORCL"
```

Note that the messages are being sent and received as expected. But if the stock portfolio consumer is stopped, the Advisory application output will print messages similar to the following:

```
...
Consumer 'ID:dejan-bosanacs-macbook-pro.local-64609-1233592052313-0:0:1:2'
unsubscribed
Consumer 'ID:dejan-bosanacs-macbook-pro.local-64609-1233592052313-0:0:1:1'
unsubscribed
Message {up=false, stock=ORCL, offer=11.817656439151577,
price=11.805850588563015}
not consumed by any consumer
Message {up=false, stock=ORCL, offer=11.706856077241527,
price=11.695160916325204}
not consumed by any consumer
Message {up=false, stock=ORCL, offer=11.638181080673165,
price=11.62655452614702}
not consumed by any consumer
Message {up=true, stock=CSCO, offer=36.51689387339347,
```

```
price=36.480413459933544}
not consumed by any consumer
Message {up=false, stock=ORCL, offer=11.524555643871604,
price=11.513042601270335}
not consumed by any consumer
Message {up=true, stock=CSCO, offer=36.583094870955556,
price=36.54654832263293}
not consumed by any consumer
Message {up=false, stock=ORCL, offer=11.515997849703322,
price=11.504493356346975}
not consumed by any consumer
Message {up=true, stock=ORCL, offer=11.552511335860867,
price=11.540970365495372}
not consumed by any consumer
...
```

The first two messages indicate that the two consumers unsubscribed. The rest of the messages sent to the stock topics aren't being consumed by any consumer, and that's why they're delivered to the Advisory application.

14.2.3 Conclusion

Although it took some time to dissect this simple example, it's a good demonstration of how advisory messages can be used to act on broker events asynchronously, just as is standard procedure in message-oriented applications.

So far we've shown how the ActiveMQ APIs can be used to create applications to monitor and manage broker instances. Luckily, you won't have to do that often, as many tools are provided for this purpose already. The following section takes a look at some of these tools.

14.3   Tools for ActiveMQ administration

A wide range of tools exist for monitoring and administering ActiveMQ. Which ones you'll be using depends primarily on the environment you're using, your setup, and also on your preferences. We'll start this section with an explanation of command-line tools. Next we'll see how we can use the JMS API to issue commands to ActiveMQ using the *command agent* (and how you can use it to access your broker using chat clients). The general-purpose management console for Java platform named *JConsole* and how it can be used with ActiveMQ is our next topic. Finally, we'll cover the ActiveMQ *web console*, integrated with ActiveMQ, which provides you with a nice user interface for inspecting ActiveMQ resources. Most of these tools use the JMX API to communicate with the broker, so be sure to enable JMX support as explained earlier in the chapter. So let's see what more can we do from the command line besides starting a broker.

14.3.1 Command-line tools

You already know how to use the bin/activemq script to start the broker. In addition to this script, the bin/activemq-admin script can be used to monitor the broker state from the command line. The activemq-admin script provides the following functionality:

- Start and stop the broker
- List available brokers
- Query the broker for certain state information
- Browse broker destinations

In the following sections, we'll explore this functionality and the commands used to expose it through the use of examples. For the complete reference and explanation of all available command options, please refer to the Command-Line Tools page on the ActiveMQ website (http://mng.bz/lj9a).

STARTING AND STOPPING THE BROKER

The standard method for starting ActiveMQ is to use the following command on the command line:

```
$ cd apache-activemq-5.4.1
$ ./bin/activemq
```

In addition, the following command using the bin/activemq script can also be used:

```
$ ./bin/activemq-admin start
```

Using the same script, ActiveMQ can also be stopped using the following command:

```
$ ./bin/activemq-admin stop
```

The bin/activemq script is a nice alternative for stopping the broker. It'll attempt to use the JMX API to do this, so be sure to enable JMX support if you plan to use this script. Please note that the bin/activemq script connects to the default ActiveMQ JMX URL to send commands, so if you made some modifications to the JMX URL (as we did for the earlier JMX examples) or the JMX domain, be sure to provide the correct JMX URL and domain to the script using the appropriate parameters. For example, to stop the previously defined broker that starts the JMX connector on port 2011 and uses the my-broker domain, the following command should be used:

```
$ ./bin/activemq-admin stop \
--jmxurl service:jmx:rmi:///jndi/rmi://localhost:2011/jmxrmi \
--jmxdomain my-broker
```

This command will connect to ActiveMQ via JMX to send a command to the broker telling it to stop.

Now it's time to see how to get information from ActiveMQ using the command line.

LISTING AVAILABLE BROKERS

In some situations, multiple brokers may be running in the same JMX context. Using the bin/activemq script you can use the `list` command to list all the available brokers as shown next.

Listing 14.8   The activemq-admin list command

```
$ ./bin/activemq-admin list
Java Runtime: Apple Inc. 1.5.0_16
/System/Library/Frameworks/JavaVM.framework/Versions/1.5.0/Home
  Heap sizes: current=1984k  free=1709k  max=65088k
    JVM args: -Dactivemq.classpath=/tmp/apache-activemq-5.4.1/conf;
-Dactivemq.home=/tmp/apache-activemq-5.4.1
-Dactivemq.base=/tmp/apache-activemq-5.4.1
ACTIVEMQ_HOME: /tmp/apache-activemq-5.4.1
ACTIVEMQ_BASE: /tmp/apache-activemq-5.4.1
Connecting to pid: 99591
BrokerName = localhost
```

As you can see in listing 14.8, we have only one broker in the given context and its name is localhost.

QUERYING THE BROKER

Starting, stopping, and listing all available brokers are useful features, but what you'll probably want to do more often is query various broker parameters. Let's take a look at demonstrating the query command being used to grab information about destinations.

Listing 14.9   The activemq-admin query command

```
$ ./bin/activemq-admin query -QQueue=*
Java Runtime: Apple Inc. 1.5.0_16
/System/Library/Frameworks/JavaVM.framework/Versions/1.5.0/Home
  Heap sizes: current=1984k  free=1709k  max=65088k
    JVM args: -Dactivemq.classpath=/tmp/apache-activemq-5.4.1/conf;
-Dactivemq.home=/tmp/apache-activemq-5.4.1
-Dactivemq.base=/tmp/apache-activemq-5.4.1
ACTIVEMQ_HOME: /tmp/apache-activemq-5.4.1
ACTIVEMQ_BASE: /tmp/apache-activemq-5.4.1
Connecting to pid: 99591
DequeueCount = 0
Name = TEST.FOO
MinEnqueueTime = 0
CursorMemoryUsage = 0
MaxAuditDepth = 2048
Destination = TEST.FOO
AverageEnqueueTime = 0.0
InFlightCount = 0
MemoryLimit = 1048576
Type = Queue
EnqueueCount = 0
MaxEnqueueTime = 0
MemoryUsagePortion = 0.0
ProducerCount = 0
UseCache = true
MaxProducersToAudit = 32
CursorFull = false
BrokerName = localhost
```

```
ConsumerCount = 0
ProducerFlowControl = true
Subscriptions = []
QueueSize = 0
MaxPageSize = 200
CursorPercentUsage = 0
MemoryPercentUsage = 0
DispatchCount = 0
ExpiredCount = 0

DequeueCount = 0
Name = example.A
MinEnqueueTime = 0
CursorMemoryUsage = 0
MaxAuditDepth = 2048
Destination = example.A
AverageEnqueueTime = 0.0
InFlightCount = 0
MemoryLimit = 1048576
Type = Queue
EnqueueCount = 0
MaxEnqueueTime = 0
MemoryUsagePortion = 0.0
ProducerCount = 0
UseCache = true
MaxProducersToAudit = 32
CursorFull = false
BrokerName = localhost
ConsumerCount = 1
ProducerFlowControl = true
Subscriptions = [org.apache.activemq:BrokerName=localhost,
Type=Subscription,persistentMode=Non-Durable,
destinationType=Queue,destinationName=example.A,
clientId=ID_mongoose.local-59784-1255450207356-3_0,
consumerId=ID_mongoose.local-59784-1255450207356-2_0_1_1]
QueueSize = 0
MaxPageSize = 200
CursorPercentUsage = 0
MemoryPercentUsage = 0
DispatchCount = 0
ExpiredCount = 0
```

In listing 14.9, the bin/activemq-admin script was used with the query command and a query of -QQueue=*. This query will print all the state information about all the queues in the broker instance. In the case of a broker using a default configuration, the only queue that exists is one named example.A (from the Camel configuration example in the conf/activemq.xml file) and these are its properties.

The command-line tools reference page contains the full description of all available query options. If you call the query command without any additional parameters, it'll print all available broker properties, which can you can use to get a quick snapshot of a broker's state.

BROWSING DESTINATIONS

Browsing destinations in the broker is another fundamental administrative task. This functionality is also exposed in the bin/activemq-admin script. The following is an example of browsing one of the queues we're using in our job queue example.

> **Listing 14.10 The `activemq-admin browse` command**

```
${ACTIVEMQ_HOME}/bin/activemq-admin browse \
--amqurl tcp://localhost:61616 JOBS.delete
ACTIVEMQ_HOME: /workspace/apache-activemq-5.2.0
ACTIVEMQ_BASE: /workspace/apache-activemq-5.2.0
JMS_HEADER_FIELD:JMSDestination = JOBS.delete
JMS_HEADER_FIELD:JMSDeliveryMode = persistent
JMS_HEADER_FIELD:JMSMessageID =
ID:dejan-bosanacs-macbook-pro.local-64257-1234789436483-0:0:1:1:2
JMS_BODY_FIELD:JMSObjectClass = java.lang.Integer
JMS_BODY_FIELD:JMSObjectString = 1000001
JMS_HEADER_FIELD:JMSExpiration = 0
JMS_HEADER_FIELD:JMSPriority = 4
JMS_HEADER_FIELD:JMSRedelivered = false
JMS_HEADER_FIELD:JMSTimestamp = 1234789436702

JMS_HEADER_FIELD:JMSDestination = JOBS.delete
JMS_HEADER_FIELD:JMSDeliveryMode = persistent
JMS_HEADER_FIELD:JMSMessageID =
ID:dejan-bosanacs-macbook-pro.local-64257-1234789436483-0:0:1:1:3
JMS_BODY_FIELD:JMSObjectClass = java.lang.Integer
JMS_BODY_FIELD:JMSObjectString = 1000002
JMS_HEADER_FIELD:JMSExpiration = 0
JMS_HEADER_FIELD:JMSPriority = 4
JMS_HEADER_FIELD:JMSRedelivered = false
JMS_HEADER_FIELD:JMSTimestamp = 1234789436706

JMS_HEADER_FIELD:JMSDestination = JOBS.delete
JMS_HEADER_FIELD:JMSDeliveryMode = persistent
JMS_HEADER_FIELD:JMSMessageID =
ID:dejan-bosanacs-macbook-pro.local-64257-1234789436483-0:0:1:1:4
JMS_BODY_FIELD:JMSObjectClass = java.lang.Integer
JMS_BODY_FIELD:JMSObjectString = 1000003
JMS_HEADER_FIELD:JMSExpiration = 0
JMS_HEADER_FIELD:JMSPriority = 4
JMS_HEADER_FIELD:JMSRedelivered = false
JMS_HEADER_FIELD:JMSTimestamp = 1234789436708
...
```

The browse command is different from the previous commands, as it doesn't use JMX, but browses queues using the QueueBrowser from the JMS API. For that reason, you need to provide it with the broker URL using the -amqurl switch. The final parameter provided to this command is the name of the queue to be browsed.

As you can see, a fair number of monitoring and administration operations can be achieved from the command line. This functionality can help you to easily check the broker's state and can be helpful for diagnosing possible problems. But this isn't the end of the administrative tools for ActiveMQ. There are still a few more advanced administrative tools; they're explained in following sections.

14.3.2 *Command agent*

Sometimes issuing administration commands to the broker from the command line isn't easily achievable, mostly in situations when you don't have shell access to the machines hosting your brokers. In these situations you'll want to administer your broker using some of the existing administrative channels. The *command agent* allows you to issue administration commands to the broker using plain old JMS messages. When the command agent is enabled, it'll listen to the `ActiveMQ.Agent` topic for messages. All commands such as `help`, `list` and `query` submitted in form of JMS text messages will be processed by the agent and the result will be posted to the same topic.

In this section we'll demonstrate how to configure and use the command agent with the ActiveMQ broker. We'll also go one step further and introduce the XMPP transport connector, and see how you can use practically any instant messaging client to communicate with the command agent.

Let's begin by looking at the following configuration example.

Listing 14.11   Command agent configuration

```
...
  <broker xmlns="http://activemq.apache.org/schema/core"
    brokerName="localhost"
    dataDirectory="${activemq.base}/data">

    <transportConnectors>
      <transportConnector name="openwire" uri="tcp://localhost:61616"/>
      <transportConnector name="xmpp" uri="xmpp://localhost:61222"/>
    </transportConnectors>

  </broker>

  <commandAgent xmlns="http://activemq.apache.org/schema/core"
    brokerUrl="vm://localhost"/>
...
```

Two details are important in this configuration fragment. First we've started the XMPP transport connector on port 61222 to expose the broker to clients via *XMPP* (the *Extensible Messaging and Presence Protocol*). This was achieved by using the appropriate URI scheme, like we do for all supported protocols. XMPP is an open XML-based protocol mainly used for instant messaging and developed by the Jabber project (http://jabber.org/). Since it's open and widespread, a lot of chat clients already support this protocol, and you can use these clients to communicate with ActiveMQ.

For the purposes of this book, we chose to use the Adium (http://www.adiumx.com/) instant messaging client. This client runs on Mac OS X and speaks many different protocols, including XMPP. Any XMPP client can be used here. The first step is always to provide the XMPP client with the details to connect to ActiveMQ, such as server host, port, username, and password, as shown in figure 14.7. Of course, you should connect to your broker on port 61222 since that's where the XMPP transport connector is running, and you can use any user and password.

After successfully connecting to the broker, you have to join the appropriate chat room, which basically means that you'll subscribe to the topic with the same name. In this example we'll subscribe to the ActiveMQ.Agent topic, so we can use the command agent.

Typing a message in the chat room sends a message to the topic, so you can type your commands directly into the messaging client. An example of the response for the help command is shown in figure 14.8.

More complex commands are supported as well. Figure 14.9 shows how you can query the topic named TEST.FOO using the query -QTopic=TEST.FOO command.

Figure 14.7   Connecting to the broker's agent topic using XMPP (chat) client

The example shown in this section introduced the use of XMPP protocol. This allows you to use instant messaging applications to interact with the ActiveMQ command agent to administer the broker via standard JMS messages. Now let's return to some classic administration tools such as JConsole.

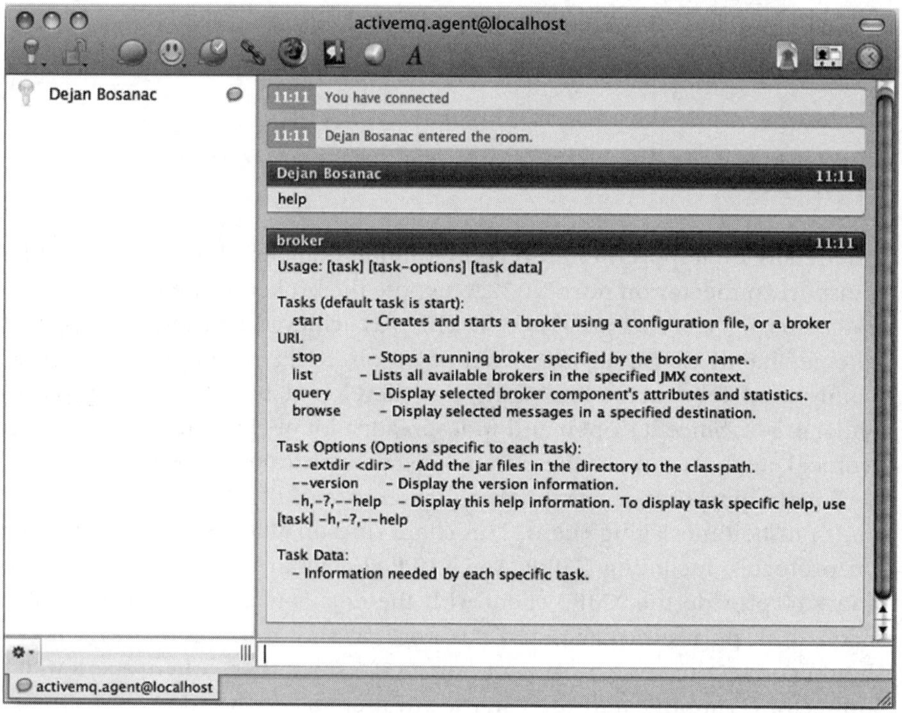

Figure 14.8   The result of executing help in XMPP client using the command agent

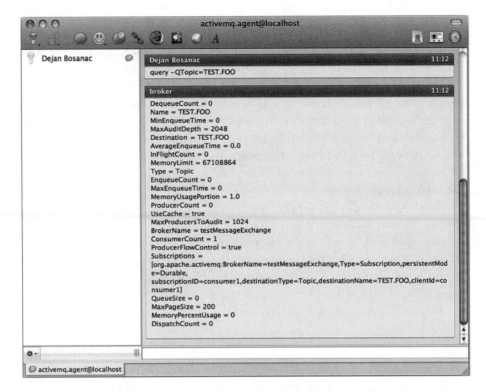

Figure 14.9 The result of executing query in XMPP client using command agent

14.3.3 JConsole

As we said earlier, the JMX API is the standardized API used by developers to manage and monitor Java applications. But the API isn't so useful without a client tool. That's why the Java SE comes with a tool named *JConsole*, the Java monitoring and management console. JConsole is a client application that allows you to browse and call methods of exposed MBeans. Because ActiveMQ requires the Java SE to run, JConsole should be available, and is handy for quickly viewing broker state. In this section, we'll cover some of its basic operations with ActiveMQ.

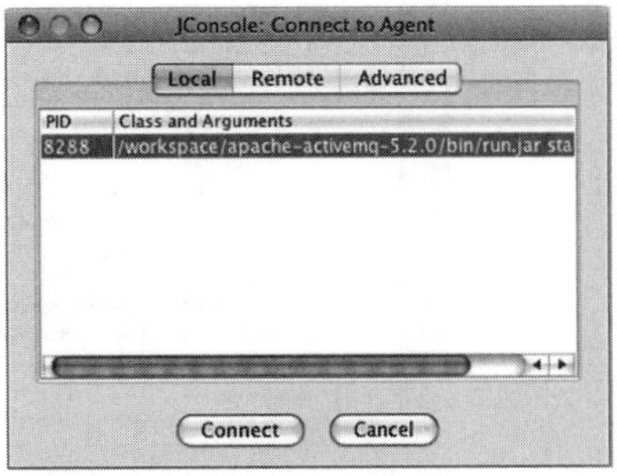

The first thing you should do after starting JConsole (using the `jconsole` command on the command line) is choose or locate the application you want to monitor (see figure 14.10).

In this figure, we see a local Java process running. This is the case when ActiveMQ and JConsole are started on the same machine. To monitor ActiveMQ on a remote machine, be sure to start a JMX connector from the ActiveMQ configuration

Figure 14.10   Connecting to ActiveMQ using JConsole

file (via the `createConnector` attribute from the `<managementContext>` element). Then you can enter host and port information (such as `localhost` and `1099` in case of a local broker) in the Remote tab, or the full URL (such as `service:jmx:rmi:///` `jndi/rmi://localhost:1099/jmxrmi`) in the Advanced tab.

Upon successfully connecting to the local ActiveMQ broker, figure 14.11 demonstrates some of what you are able to see. This figure shows that the ActiveMQ broker exposes information about all of its important objects (connectors, destinations, subscriptions, and so on) via JMX. In this particular example, all the attributes for `queue://example.A` can be easily viewed. Such information as queue size and number of producers and consumers can be a valuable debugging aid for your applications or the broker itself.

Besides peaking at the broker state, you can also use JConsole (and the JMX API) to execute MBean methods. If you go to the Operations tab for the destination named `queue://example.A`, you'll see all available operations for that particular queue as shown in figure 14.12. This figure shows that the `sendTextMessage` button allows you to send a simple message to the queue. This can be a simple test tool to produce messages without writing any code.

Now let's look at another similar tool that's distributed with ActiveMQ.

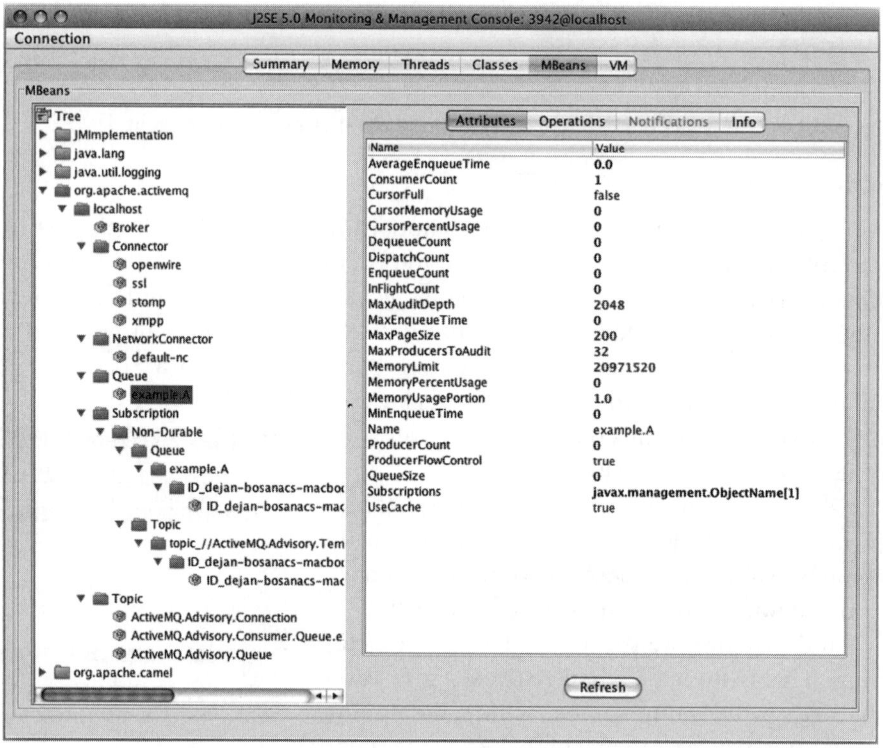

Figure 14.11   Viewing queue properties using JConsole

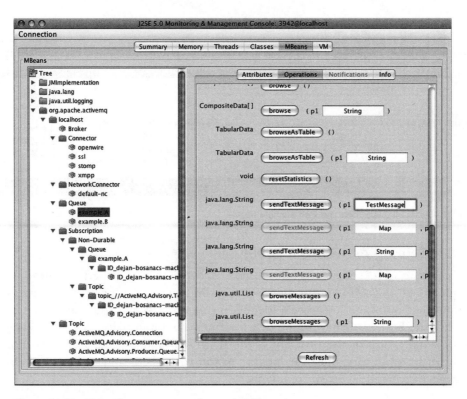

Figure 14.12 Executing queue operations using JConsole

14.3.4 *Web console*

In chapter 9, we saw how an internal web server is used to expose ActiveMQ resources via REST and Ajax APIs. The same web server is used to host the *web console*, which provides basic management functions via a web browser. Upon starting ActiveMQ using the default configuration, you can visit http://localhost:8161/admin/ to view the web console.

The web console is far more modest in capabilities compared to JConsole, but it allows you to do some of the most basic management tasks using an user interface adapted to ActiveMQ management. Figure 14.13 shows a screenshot of the web console viewing a list of queues with some basic information.

For every destination, you can also execute certain management operations. For example, you can browse, purge, and delete queues, or send, copy, and move messages to various destinations. Figure 14.14 shows the page that displays basic message properties.

The ActiveMQ web console provides some additional pages for viewing destinations and sending messages. As stated earlier, this functionality is fairly basic and is meant to be used for development environments, not production environments.

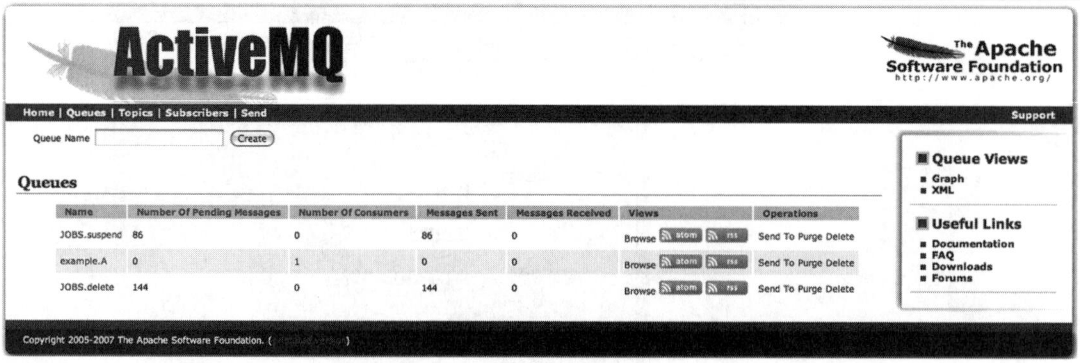

Figure 14.13   Show all queues via the web console page

14.4   *Configuring ActiveMQ logging*

So far we've seen how you can monitor ActiveMQ either programmatically or using tools such as JConsole. But there's one more way you can peek at the broker status, and that's through its internal logging mechanism. When you experience problems with the broker's behavior, the first and most common place to begin looking for a potential cause of the problem is the data/activemq.log file. In this section you'll learn how you can adjust the logging to suit your needs and how it can help you in detecting potential broker problems.

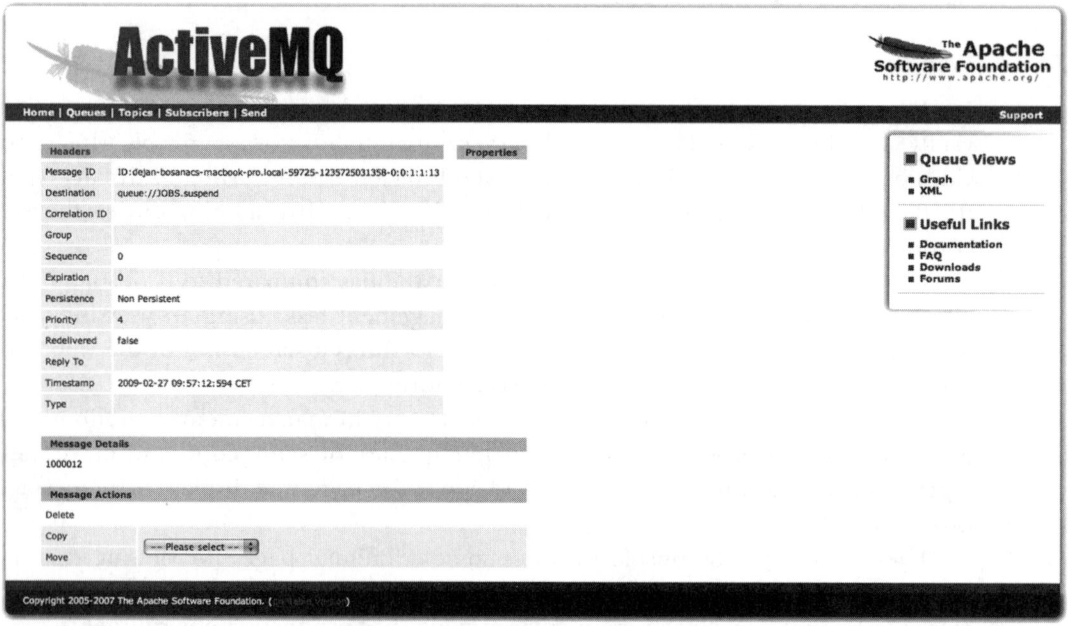

Figure 14.14   View a message via the web console page

In this section we'll see how we can adapt ActiveMQ logging for brokers and clients. We'll also introduce a logging interceptor that can be used to track messages between brokers and clients. Let's start with the broker-related logging discussion.

14.4.1 *Broker logging*

ActiveMQ uses the *Apache Commons Logging* API (http://mng.bz/xdQM) for its internal logging purposes. So if you embed ActiveMQ in your Java application, it'll fit whatever logging mechanisms you already use. The standalone binary distribution of ActiveMQ uses *Apache Log4J* (http://mng.bz/940F) library as its logging facility.

The ActiveMQ logging configuration can be found in the conf/log4j.properties file. By default, it defines two log appenders: one that prints to standard output, and another that prints to the data/activemq.log file. The following listing shows the standard Log4J logger configuration.

> **Listing 14.12   Default logger configuration**

```
log4j.rootLogger=INFO, stdout, out
log4j.logger.org.apache.activemq.spring=WARN
log4j.logger.org.springframework=WARN
log4j.logger.org.apache.xbean.spring=WARN
```

As you can see in listing 14.12, by default ActiveMQ will only print messages with a log level of INFO or above, which should be enough for you to monitor its usual behavior. In case you detect a problem with your application and want to enable more detailed debugging, you should change the level for the root logger to DEBUG. Just be aware that the DEBUG logging level will output considerably more logging information, so you'll probably want to narrow debug messages to a particular Java package. To do this, you should leave the root logger at the INFO level and add a line that enables debug logging for the desired class or package. For example, to enable trace-level logging for the TCP transport, add the following configuration to the conf/log4j.properties file:

```
log4j.logger.org.apache.activemq.transport.tcp=TRACE
```

After making this change in the conf/log4j.properties file and restarting ActiveMQ, you'll begin to see the following log output:

```
TRACE TcpTransport
- TCP consumer thread for tcp:///127.0.0.1:49383 starting
DEBUG TcpTransport
- Stopping transport tcp:///127.0.0.1:49383
TRACE TcpTransport
- TCP consumer thread for tcp:///127.0.0.1:49392 starting
DEBUG TcpTransport
- Stopping transport tcp:///127.0.0.1:49392
```

In addition to starting/stopping ActiveMQ after changing the logging configuration, one common question is how to change the logging configuration at runtime. This is a reasonable request, since you may not want to stop ActiveMQ to change the logging

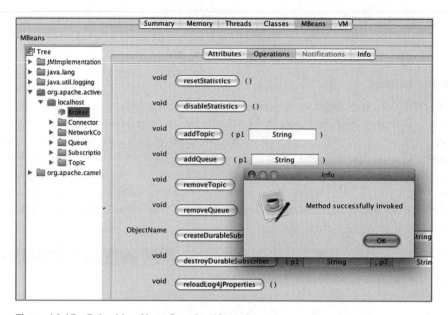

Figure 14.15   Reload Log4J config using JConsole

configuration. Luckily, you can use the JMX capabilities in ActiveMQ along with JConsole to achieve this. Just make the necessary changes to the conf/log4j.properties file and save them. Then open JConsole and select the `Broker` MBean as shown in figure 14.15.

Locate the button `reloadLog4jProperties` on the `Broker` MBean's Operations tab. Click the button named `reloadLog4jProperties` and the conf/log4j.properties file will be reloaded and your changes will be applied.

In addition to logging from the broker side, logging is also available on the client side.

14.4.2 *Client logging*

Logging on the broker side is definitely necessary, but how do you debug problems on the client side in your Java applications? The ActiveMQ Java client APIs use the same logging approach as the broker, so you can use the same style of Log4J configuration file in your client application as well. In this section we'll show you a few tips on how you can customize client-side logging and see more information about what's going on inside the client-to-broker communication.

For starters, a Log4J configuration file must be made available to the client-side application. The following listing shows an example Log4J configuration file that will be used in this section.

Listing 14.13   Client logging

```
log4j.rootLogger=INFO, out, stdout

log4j.logger.org.apache.activemq.spring=WARN
log4j.logger.org.springframework=WARN
```

```
log4j.logger.org.apache.xbean.spring=WARN
```

log4j.logger.org.apache.activemq.transport.failover.FailoverTransport=DEBUG
log4j.logger.org.apache.activemq.transport.TransportLogger=DEBUG

As you can see, the standard INFO level is being used for the root logger. Additional configuration has been added (marked in bold) to monitor the failover transport and TCP communication.

Now, let's run our stock portfolio publisher example, but with some additional properties that will allow us to use logging settings previously defined.

```
$ mvn exec:java \
-Dlog4j.configuration=file:\
src/main/resources/org/apache/activemq/book/ch14/log4j.properties \
-Dexec.mainClass=org.apache.activemq.book.ch14.advisory.Publisher \
-Dexec.args="failover:(tcp://localhost:61616?trace=true) CSCO ORCL"
```

The log4j.configuration system property is used to specify the location of the Log4J configuration file. Also note that the trace parameter has been set to true via the transport connection URI. Along with setting the TransportLogger level to DEBUG, this will allow all the commands exchanged between the client and the broker to be easily viewed.

Let's say an application is started while the broker is down. What will be seen in the log output are messages like the following:

```
2009-03-19 15:47:56,699 [ublisher.main()] DEBUG FailoverTransport
- Reconnect was triggered but transport is not started yet.
Wait for start to connect the transport.
2009-03-19 15:47:56,829 [ublisher.main()] DEBUG FailoverTransport
- Started.
2009-03-19 15:47:56,829 [ublisher.main()] DEBUG FailoverTransport
- Waking up reconnect task
2009-03-19 15:47:56,830 [ActiveMQ Task  ] DEBUG FailoverTransport
- Attempting connect to: tcp://localhost:61616?trace=true
2009-03-19 15:47:56,903 [ActiveMQ Task  ] DEBUG FailoverTransport
- Connect fail to: tcp://localhost:61616?trace=true, reason:
java.net.ConnectException: Connection refused
2009-03-19 15:47:56,903 [ActiveMQ Task  ] DEBUG FailoverTransport
- Waiting 10 ms before attempting connection.
2009-03-19 15:47:56,913 [ActiveMQ Task  ] DEBUG FailoverTransport
- Attempting connect to: tcp://localhost:61616?trace=true
2009-03-19 15:47:56,914 [ActiveMQ Task  ] DEBUG FailoverTransport
- Connect fail to: tcp://localhost:61616?trace=true, reason:
java.net.ConnectException: Connection refused
2009-03-19 15:47:56,915 [ActiveMQ Task  ] DEBUG FailoverTransport
- Waiting 20 ms before attempting connection.
2009-03-19 15:47:56,935 [ActiveMQ Task  ] DEBUG FailoverTransport
- Attempting connect to: tcp://localhost:61616?trace=true
2009-03-19 15:47:56,937 [ActiveMQ Task  ] DEBUG FailoverTransport
- Connect fail to: tcp://localhost:61616?trace=true, reason:
java.net.ConnectException: Connection refused
2009-03-19 15:47:56,938 [ActiveMQ Task  ] DEBUG FailoverTransport
- Waiting 40 ms before attempting connection.
```

With debug level logging enabled, the failover transport provides a detailed log of its attempts to establish a connection with the broker. This can be extremely helpful in situations where you experience connection problems from a client application.

Once a connection with the broker is established, the TCP transport will start tracing all commands exchanged with the broker to the log. An example of such traces is shown next:

```
2009-03-19 15:48:02,038 [ActiveMQ Task  ] DEBUG FailoverTransport
- Waiting 5120 ms before attempting connection.
2009-03-19 15:48:07,158 [ActiveMQ Task  ] DEBUG FailoverTransport
- Attempting connect to: tcp://localhost:61616?trace=true
2009-03-19 15:48:07,162 [ActiveMQ Task  ] DEBUG Connection:11
- SENDING: WireFormatInfo {...}
2009-03-19 15:48:07,183 [127.0.0.1:61616] DEBUG Connection:11
- RECEIVED: WireFormatInfo { ... }
2009-03-19 15:48:07,186 [ActiveMQ Task  ] DEBUG Connection:11
- SENDING: ConnectionControl { ... }
2009-03-19 15:48:07,186 [ActiveMQ Task  ] DEBUG FailoverTransport
- Connection established
2009-03-19 15:48:07,187 [ActiveMQ Task  ] INFO  FailoverTransport
- Successfully connected to tcp://localhost:61616?trace=true
2009-03-19 15:48:07,187 [127.0.0.1:61616] DEBUG Connection:11
- RECEIVED: BrokerInfo { ... }
2009-03-19 15:48:07,189 [ublisher.main()] DEBUG Connection:11
- SENDING: ConnectionInfo { ... }
2009-03-19 15:48:07,190 [127.0.0.1:61616] DEBUG Connection:11
- RECEIVED: Response {commandId = 0, responseRequired = false,
correlationId = 1}
2009-03-19 15:48:07,203 [ublisher.main()] DEBUG Connection:11
- SENDING: ConsumerInfo { ... }
2009-03-19 15:48:07,206 [127.0.0.1:61616] DEBUG Connection:11
- RECEIVED: Response { ... }
2009-03-19 15:48:07,232 [ublisher.main()] DEBUG Connection:11
- SENDING: SessionInfo { ... }
2009-03-19 15:48:07,239 [ublisher.main()] DEBUG Connection:11
- SENDING: ProducerInfo { ... }
Sending: {offer=51.726420585933745, price=51.67474584009366,
up=false, stock=CSCO}
on destination: topic://STOCKS.CSCO
2009-03-19 15:48:07,266 [ublisher.main()] DEBUG Connection:11
- SENDING: ActiveMQMapMessage { ... }
2009-03-19 15:48:07,294 [127.0.0.1:61616] DEBUG Connection:11
- RECEIVED: Response { ... }
Sending: {offer=94.03931872048393, price=93.94537334713681,
up=false, stock=ORCL}
on destination: topic://STOCKS.ORCL
```

For the purpose of readability, some details of specific commands have been left out except for one log message, which is marked bold. These traces provide a full peek into the client-broker communication, which can help to narrow application connection problems further.

This simple example shows that with a few minor configuration changes, many more logging details can be viewed. But beyond standard Log4J-style logging, ActiveMQ also provides a special logger for internal broker events.

14.4.3 *Internal broker event logging*

The previous sections demonstrated how the broker side and the client side can be monitored through the use of standard Log4J logging. Similar functionality is available on the broker side for internal broker operations using a *logging interceptor* (aka *logging plug-in*). ActiveMQ plug-ins were introduced in chapter 6 where you saw how they can be used to authenticate client applications and authorize access to broker resources. The logging interceptor is a simple broker plug-in that uses the broker's internal event mechanism to log internal broker events. The types of events that are logged can be controlled via the configuration of the logging plug-in using the properties shown in table 14.2.

The logging plug-in is useful for seeing more information about the broker's internal events. This can be useful for debugging purposes during development as well as for informational purposes during production deployment. It provides more finite logging for particular event types and allows you to see more information about what the broker's doing.

To install this plug-in, add the `<loggingBrokerPlugin/>` element to the list of your plug-ins in the conf/activemq.xml configuration file. Here's an example of this:

```
...
    <plugins>
      <loggingBrokerPlugin/>
    </plugins>
...
```

After restarting the broker, you'll see output indicating that the logging plug-in has been activated. After table 14.2 we see an example of such output during the broker startup.

Table 14.2 Logging plug-in properties

Property name	Default value	Description
logAll	false	Log all events
logMessageEvents	false	Log only events related to producing, consuming, and dispatching messages
logConnectionEvents	true	Log only events related to connections and sessions
logTransactionEvents	false	Log only events related to transaction handling
logConsumerEvents	false	Log only events related to message consumption
logProducerEvents	false	Log only events related to message production
logInternalEvents	false	Log only events related to internal broker operations such as failover, querying internal objects, and so on

```
...
Loading message broker from: xbean:activemq.xml
 INFO | Created LoggingBrokerPlugin: LoggingBrokerPlugin(logAll=false,
logConnectionEvents=true, logConsumerEvents=false,
logProducerEvents=false, logMessageEvents=false,
logTransactionEvents=false, logInternalEvents=false)
...
```

Note that the logging plug-in is using the default configuration. Send some messages to the broker, and you'll see the following output from the broker:

```
...
INFO | Adding Connection :
org.apache.activemq.broker.ConnectionContext@1c45ce17
INFO | Adding Session : SessionInfo {commandId = 3, responseRequired =
false, sessionId = ID:mongoose.local-58504-1278340965484-0:0:1}
INFO | Removing Session : SessionInfo {commandId = 0, responseRequired =
false, sessionId = ID:mongoose.local-58504-1278340965484-0:0:-1}
INFO | Removing Session : SessionInfo {commandId = 3, responseRequired =
false, sessionId = ID:mongoose.local-58504-1278340965484-0:0:1}
INFO | Removing Connection : ConnectionInfo {commandId = 1,
responseRequired = true, connectionId =
ID:mongoose.local-58504-1278340965484-0:0,
clientId = ID:mongoose.local-58504-1278340965484-1:0, userName = null,
password = *****, brokerPath = null, brokerMasterConnector = false,
manageable = true, clientMaster = true}
...
```

Note that the output indicates that a connection and session were added to the broker (a connection and a session were created), and a connection and session were removed from the broker (a connection and session were destroyed). These are events that are logged from a producer connecting to the broker, sending some messages, and disconnecting from the broker. If you want to see more detailed information, then you need to enable the appropriate logging properties as listed in table 14.2.

Coupled with the other logging techniques, the logging interceptor can help you to gain a much better perspective of the internal broker activities while building message-oriented systems.

14.5   Summary

After we learned how to configure the broker and write applications using it, this last chapter showed us how we can administer and monitor ActiveMQ instances in production. We saw how we can do it programmatically and also covered some of the tools most often used for this purpose.

With this discussion, we've come to the end of the topics planned for this book. We hope you enjoyed reading it, and that it helps bring your ActiveMQ and messaging knowledge to the next level. This should by no means be the end of your journey into ActiveMQ, since it's a project that is being continuously developed and improved.

index

<title>INDEX</title>

OSGI in Action
Creating Modular Applications in Java
by Richard S. Hall, Karl Pauls, Stuart
  McCulloch, and David Savage

ISBN: 978-1-933988-91-7
375 pages
$49.99
March 2011

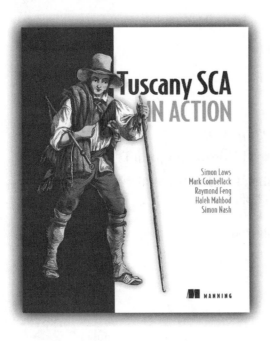

Tuscany SCA in Action
by Simon Laws, Mark Combellack,
  Raymond Feng, Haleh Mahbod,
  Simon Nash

ISBN: 978-1-933988-89-4
472 pages
$59.99
February 2011

For ordering information go to www.manning.com

RELATED MANNING TITLES

Camel in Action
by Claus Ibsen and Jonathan Anstey

　ISBN: 978-1-935182-36-8
　552 pages
　$49.99
　December 2010

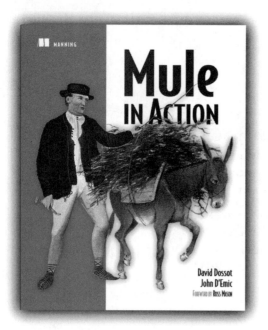

Mule in Action
by David Dossot and John D'Emic

　ISBN: 978-1-933988-96-2
　432 pages
　$44.99
　July 2009

For ordering information go to www.manning.com

Open Source SOA
by Jeff Davis

ISBN: 978-1-933988-54-2
448 pages
$49.99
May 2009

Open-Source ESBs in Action
Example Implementations in Mule
and ServiceMix

by Tijs Rademakers and Jos Dirksen

ISBN: 978-1-933988-21-4
528 pages
$44.99
September 2008

For ordering information go to www.manning.com

RELATED MANNING TITLES

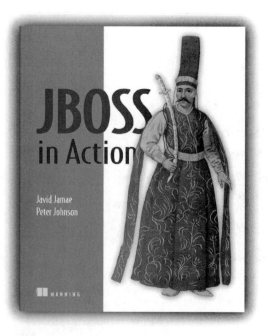

JBoss in Action
Configuring the JBoss Application Server
by Javid Jamae and Peter Johnson

    ISBN: 978-1-933988-02-3
    496 pages
    $49.99
    January 2009

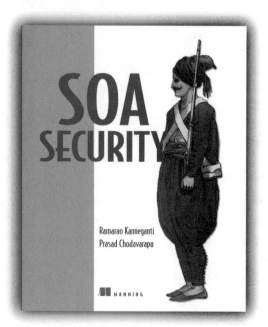

SOA Security
by Ramarao Kanneganti and
   Prasad A. Chodavarapu

    ISBN: 978-1-932394-68-9
    512 pages
    $59.99
    December 2007

For ordering information go to www.manning.com